Inexpressible Privacy

Inexpressible Privacy

The Interior Life of Antebellum American Literature

MILETTE SHAMIR

PENN

University of Pennsylvania Press

Philadelphia

10   9   8   7   6   5   4   3   2   1

Published by
University of Pennsylvania Press
Philadelphia, Pennsylvania 19104-4112

Library of Congress Cataloging-in-Publication Data

Shamir, Milette.
  Inexpressible privacy : the interior life of antebellum American literature / Milette
Shamir.
    p. cm.
  Includes bibliographical references and index.
  ISBN-10: 0-8122-3906-7 (cloth : alk. paper)
  ISBN-13: 978-0-8122-3906-5
  1. American prose literature—19th century—History and criticism.   2. Narration
(Rhetoric)—History—19th century.   3. Architecture, Domestic, in literature.
4. Personal space in literature.   5. Dwellings in literature.   6. Privacy in literature.
I. Title.
PS368.S43 2006
818'.409353—dc22   2005042342

To Aram and Eli

Contents

When I detect a beauty in any of the recesses of nature, I am reminded, by the serene and retired spirit in which it requires to be contemplated, of the inexpressible privacy of a life,—how silent and unambitious it is.

—Henry David Thoreau, *"Natural History of Massachusetts"*

Introduction

This book began with a moment of naïve but genuine perplexity. When I first arrived in the United States to pursue my research, I was struck by what then seemed an inexplicable paradox. On the one hand, never had I felt so engulfed by privacy. The white, middle-class American socialscape—with its isolated, suburban homes and anonymous public spaces, with its codes of politeness and respect for what is none of anyone else's business—seemed very far removed from the crowded, meddlesome, Mediterranean setting I had left behind. On the other hand, never had I witnessed such compulsion to *expose*. This was the heyday of confessional talk shows on television, of political scandal in the public arena, and of identity politics in academia, and I was amazed by how smoothly private stories seemed to translate into public currency and marketable commodity in the United States.

As I began to read the vast literature on privacy, this sense of paradox only intensified. Privacy, I learned, was both what ensured democracy and what stood in the way of its just fulfillment; it was the American's most fundamental right, yet philosophically and legally untenable as a right. Privacy was elegized ad nauseam as a disappearing value, one trampled by the combined assaults of intrusive bureaucracy, mass capitalism, and postmodern epistemologies; at the same time, daily infringements on it were greeted with striking indifference. And, what is more, these conflicting views could not be mapped neatly onto the political scene. They did not instantiate basic ideological differences between, say, conservative and liberal positions, or liberal and radical positions, but, rather, were deployed on an ad hoc basis, weaving their way in and out of arguments across the political spectrum, sometimes coexisting within the same discourse.

Privacy, Jonathan Franzen writes, is "the Cheshire cat of values: not much substance, but a very winning smile."[1] But it may well be that what plagues the concept of privacy is not substantial lack but *excess*. As I began to research the origins of the modern meanings of privacy, I found an emergent discourse burdened with disparate and antithetical values and modalities of selfhood. Liberalism's seemingly stable and coherent definition of privacy, I discovered, in fact conceals inherent ambivalences, between self-expression and reticence, between domestic life and psychic life, between materiality and inalienability, between normative identity and its unassimilable residues. This conceptual overflow, I argue in this book, has determined the shape of interior life for the middle class, from the spaces of its homes to the stories that it tells.

Inexpressible Privacy traces the lineage of the modern American "cult of privacy" (as one historian once described it)[2] back to the middle decades of the nineteenth century, roughly between 1830 and 1870. These decades witnessed, in tandem with the emergent structures of industrial capitalism and the formation of the middle class, a complete overhaul of the meaning of privacy.[3] As liberalism completed its rise as the dominant ideology of white, middle-class America, privacy shed the last vestiges of its connotations under republican ideology: as the state of being deprived and disconnected, reduced to sameness, and lacking in full humanity. In the course of the eighteenth century, liberalism as a political philosophy reversed the republican hierarchy of public over private, elevating the private to a position of primacy and endowing privacy with its present meaning as a moral good, a natural right, and a constitutive condition of personhood. From the 1830s, an array of prescriptive discourses implemented liberal thought by sealing, regulating, and sanctifying private spaces, both domestic and subjective.[4]

Architecture designed the ideal middle-class home with familial and individual privacy as its foremost principle. Common law began to insist on a "right to privacy" that supplemented and exceeded the older paradigm of property rights. Conduct manuals prescribed new codes of polite behavior meant to erect barriers around the home and the self. Such discourses combined to overlay what Henri Lefebvre, in his now-classic *The Production of Space*, calls "perceived" space—the spatial organization "secreted" by relations of production and reproduction—with "conceived" space—a symbolic map of protective private zones idealized and enforced by hegemonic social and political institutions.[5]

But this symbolic map does not tell a complete story. In inscribing a thick, unambiguous line that separates, privileges, and shelters the private, such discourses rendered invisible the mesh of fantasies, anxieties, and conflicts produced by this very inscription, what Lefebvre terms the experiencing of space "as *lived*."[6] It is in the realm of fiction that traces of the cult of privacy's imaginary can be found. When antebellum fiction took up the middle-class private domain as its primary topos, it propelled into narrative motion the fixed (perceived and conceived) space of privacy, thus elevating to the surface the ideological, social, and psychic conflicts inherent in the process of its enclosure and exposing its fractured and permeable quality. As Michel de Certeau has argued, architecture and other prescriptive disciplines design a "place" (*lieu*), where "the law of the 'proper' rules" and where elements are organized in an orderly fashion, "distributed in relationships of coexistence." But stories turn place into space (*espace*); they disturb the proper management of place and "and make it function in a polyvalent unity of conflictual programs or contractual proximities."[7] *Inexpressible Privacy* focuses on this dialectic between prescriptive place and fictive space. It examines how the plots, themes, and genre properties of antebellum fiction developed in relation to the symbolic organization and enclosure of the private home. But it further suggests that an analysis of the zone of privacy through literary narrative can reveal the complex web of privileges and dispossessions, of spatial allocations and competing significations that fractured, and continue to fracture, this ideally harmonious place.

The Architectured Self

The decades that frame my analysis mark a crucial period in the history of American architecture. Until the 1830s, architecture was left in the hands of a few visiting European architects and local gentlemen amateurs. They designed mostly public buildings and upper-class mansions, leaving the construction of more modest homes in the hands of technical-minded carpenters and masons. But during that decade, American architecture began to claim the status of a profession. Design artists such as Alexander Jackson Davis and Itiel Town separated themselves from art academies and began the process of defining their vocation and creating a demand for their services.[8] They did so primarily between the covers of dozens of pattern books for the design of private homes, books aimed at the growing pool of middle-class homeowners and that, often with phenomenal success, flooded the market by the 1840s. The success of pattern-book writers like William Ranlett, Gervase Wheeler, and, most dramatically, Andrew Jackson Downing depended on addressing or, more accurately, *arousing* the middle-class man's desire for privacy.[9]

What these architects newly offered their public is made apparent by the house design that they sought to revise. In the first three decades of the nineteenth century, American architecture made extensive use of the so-called Greek style, a principle of design prescribing square, open spaces ornamented by capitals, pediments, pilasters, and porticoes. The Greek style inspired the design of private houses and public buildings alike and thus rendered private space virtually indistinguishable from public space. As the *North American Review* complained retrospectively, the Greek style was "the Procrustes bed, on which the relentless measure of all our public and private wants and uses is taken. . . . Thus, market-house, cottage, bank, town-hall, law-school, church, brewery, and theater . . . are all the same."[10]

Visitors to America, including Alexis de Tocqueville, were struck by this phenomenon, and Charles Dickens was impressed with the way these structures "could be so looked through and through, that the idea of any inhabitant being able to hide himself from the public gaze, or have any secrets from the public eye, was not entertainable for a moment."[11] Dickens's is an appropriate remark, for the conceptual code that underlay this architectural style still followed the declining republican ideal in subsuming private interests under public welfare. As Benjamin Latrobe, the celebrated federal architect, put it, in America, as in Greece, "every citizen felt himself an important, and thought himself an essential, part of his republic."[12] This political ideal, both captured and enabled by the Greek style, stressed the participation of the individual in public life and assumed the private homogeneity of the citizenry.

But by the 1830s, the Greek style of design, like the ideological principles at its foundations, was beginning to face stiff competition. When liberalism rose as the dominant ideology of the emergent middle class, the weight shifted from the common good to individual pursuit of happiness and from private homogeneity to private difference, protected by a political code of public noninterference. This shift lay at the base of the professionalization of architecture: Davis and Downing, David Henry Arnot, James Jackson Jarves, and virtually every other architect interested in domestic design embarked on their careers by mounting an attack on the Greek style. While it was well suited for public buildings, they proposed, the private sphere required an altogether different design. The alternative they offered was what came to be known en masse as the "Picturesque" style, dominated by Gothic domestic architecture.[13]

As Robert Harbison writes, "shutting oneself up in a Gothic cottage [was] a different thing from musing in a pavilion."[14] The Gothic house introduced a radical change in the conception of private space: the prominent templelike door disappeared and was replaced by an emphasis on tall, narrow, pointed windows, as if to replace open access and visibility with a cautious gaze. Displaying sharp angles, vaults, broken lines, and irregular corridors, Gothic architecture strove to break the traditional square spaces in all directions and thus to fracture the rigidity, boredom, and uniformity of the Greek house. It promised to create interest, variety, and surprise and, since the exterior no longer reflected internal space, to defy public knowledge of the private interior. What the Gothic house was designed to capture was the increasing privatization of middle-class family life, the removal of the sphere of intimate relations from public scrutiny. It elevated the parlor—the room of familial and social intimacies governed by the figure of the domestic woman—to a symbol of the middle-class mode of living.

But, with even greater insistence, the Gothic house was designed to capture the isolated, subjective interiority of the middle-class *man*. A house, said Downing, "ought to be significant of the whole private life of man—his intelligence, his feelings, and his enjoyments." It should correspond to the "habits, education, tastes, and manners—in short, the life of the proprietor," and it should, "above all things, manifest individuality."[15] The Gothic house was intended as a massive reification of man's private existence, displayed before, but also protected from, society. Accordingly, alongside the parlor, architects called for the installation of a study, an enclave for the solitary mental pursuits of the house's owner, a masculine sanctum sanctorum barred from the entrance of all others. To deepen the moat between private and social spaces, architects called on men to move away to the rural but commutable suburbs, "to isolate the human mind, as it were, from the vastness of aggregate life."[16] The suburban house, destined to become the hallmark of the American middle class by the end of the century, was thus conceived as the object of the middle-class man's desires, the marker of his status and dominion, the expression of his private fantasies, the American dream, then, in more senses than one.

What the pattern book left unexplored, however, was the tensions inherent in its prescriptions. How could the new house design evince the unique, intractable individuality of its owner at the same time that it conformed to the rigid models dictated by the pattern book? How could it reconcile, in other words, private freedom with social normativity, what John Stuart Mill called the "social tyranny" of prevailing fashions and norms, which threaten to penetrate "deeply into the details of life, enslaving the soul itself"?[17] How could the suburban house both address the desire for spiritual withdrawal, the isolation of "the human mind, as it were, from the vastness of aggregate life," *and* display so loudly and elaborately materialism, acquired wealth, and social status? And how could it function as the realm of the middle-class man's inviolable, separatist personhood *and* betoken the feminine, domestic values of intimate self-display and affective exchange? What would keep this ideally harmonious home from becoming fractured, divided between disparate values and interests, betrayed from within? Such questions, while repressed in architectural discourse, repeatedly surfaced in works of fiction.

Consider the example of Edgar Allan Poe's "The Masque of the Red Death" (1842). Poe, as a critic once wrote, "was bathed in the air of his time, and he was a man of a time when people were living 'Gothically' all about him."[18] The frequent appearances of Gothic architecture in

Poe's tales, that is, do not simply evince the American author's participation in the European tradition of Gothic literature (an idea that Poe himself refuted with indignation in the preface to *Tales of the Grotesque and the Arabesque*) but speak to the material and ideological transformations of his own time. Poe's highly individualized, phantasmagorical constructs, in other words, can be read in direct relation to the liberal American citizen's dream of "architecturing" the private self. "The Masque of the Red Death" is a tale structured around a spatial blueprint: its entire middle section moves through the interior of the Gothic castle that Prince Prospero has built for himself and his entourage to escape from the plague ravaging his dominion. Prince Prospero may be a version of those prosperous middle-class merchants who, as the tale was composed, were erecting Gothic mansions in the suburbs of Boston, New York, Richmond, and Philadelphia. His fracturedly designed and bizarrely decorated castle, planned according to his "own eccentric yet august taste,"[19] resembles nothing so much as the homes of these privileged men, say, that of Mr. William Paulding in Tarrytown, New York, described by one antebellum observer as "an immense edifice of white or gray marble, resembling a baronial castle, or rather a Gothic monastery, with towers, turrets, and trellises; minarets, mosaics, and mouse-holes; archways, armories and airholes; peaked windows and pinnacled roofs, and many other fantasies . . . the whole constituting *an edifice of gigantic size, with no room in it.*"[20] The prince's abandonment of the plague-ridden masses, leaving the "external world [to] take care of itself" (p. 485), would thus speak to the liberal citizen's desire to withdraw from the public sphere, to forgo public participation in favor of a mode of authority grounded in the private sphere. Poe captures this desire through the description of the interior of the castle; he tells us to expect a public "long and straight vista" where, as in the Greek-style house, "the view of the whole extent is scarcely impeded" (p. 486), but instead we discover a meandering sequence of broken spaces that defy full visibility and culminate in the prince's scarlet-windowed chamber of privacy, a royal version of the middle-class man's study.

As for the border that the prince erects around this dream home, Poe describes "a strong and lofty wall . . . [with] gates of iron. . . . The courtiers, having entered, brought furnaces and massy hammers and welded the bolts. They resolved to leave means neither of ingress or egress to the sudden impulses of despair or of frenzy from within" (p. 485). What is puzzling about this wall is that it seems to be intended as much for blocking the inside from pouring out as for keeping the pestilence from entering. This wall constitutes a kind of a second layer of skin for the prince, to counter the symptoms of the "Red Death," namely, bodily "dissolution," a "profuse bleeding at the pores," the literal gutting of the interior. If the castle is an extension of the prince's body (at the midst of which is the "deep blood," heartlike, chamber of privacy), then the plague raging in the exterior world, defined by the "scarlet stain" it displays on the skin of its victims, is a metaphor for invasion and coerced exposure of interiority, for that "social tyranny" that deprives the private heart of life (in Mill's terms). This external threat is exacerbated by the presence of the "lodgers" in Prince Prospero's castle. As much as the prince may imagine he has complete control over them (he literally "shapes" them according to his fancies), nothing assures him that in their "impulses of despair or of frenzy" they will not unbolt the gates and join forces with the sickly masses outside. The fortified, architectured self thus proves to be a fragile construct, endangered by society without and by the domestic other within, doomed to have its innermost depths infected and destroyed.

Furthermore, as Louis Renza's reading suggests, if "Red Death" is a turning inside out, a coerced exposure of interiority, could it be linked to the deluge of fictional works that promulgated stories of private life to the antebellum mass readership?[21] Prince Prospero's chambers, after all, are trespassed into twice in this tale, ultimately, by the masked figure of the Red Death, but previously, by the omniscient narrator, who leads the reader through the interior, even into its most hallowed chamber. This parallel emerges with greater force at the tale's close, for who lives to tell a story that ends with the total dominion of death? In a sense, only Red Death himself (or "read death," in Renza's pun): the disembodied presence behind the mask that mimics the disembodied voice of the narrator. Thus, the act of narration itself finally emerges as the powerful and pernicious invader of privacy, the trigger for the dissolution of boundaries and for the seeping of the interior out to the "masses."

Such a reading regards Poe's tale as thematizing contemporaneous material and symbolic transformations as well as registering the anxieties generated by these transformations. "The Masque of the Red Death" evokes the possibility that with the architecturing of a zone for subjective privacy comes a depletion of this zone; that, like Mr. Paulding's Tarrytown mansion, the architectured self may turn out to be "an edifice of gigantic size, with no room in it."

Moreover, Poe seems to be presciently aware of the role that literary narratives may play in this depletion. Michel Foucault has proposed that, when liberal society pronounced certain spaces immune from public observation, the result was not silence but excessive speech: rather than remove those spaces from scrutiny, the act immediately generated a proliferation of disciplinary discourses that regulated their putatively private contents.[22] Taking their cue from Foucault, a number of powerful studies have established that nineteenth-century fiction is precisely where some of the most intensive work of regulating the "private" subject is performed. Not only is the home exposed in fiction as the realm of intimate discipline, carried out by the domestic woman, but by emplotting private life in narrative convention, fiction disciplines the very spaces it insists are both sheltered and free. "Whenever the novel censures policing power," writes D. A. Miller, "it has already reinvented it, in *the very practice of novelistic representation.*"[23]

In this book, I will stress both the usefulness and the limitations of the Foucauldian approach. Paying close attention to both gender and genre, I will claim that *some* forms of antebellum fiction, especially those that, like the sentimental novel, are associated with "parlor" femininity and its regime of intimate discipline, do indeed lend themselves to a Foucauldian critique by translating the contents of the private into normalizing, pedagogical narratives. What such works embrace is precisely a mode of power founded on the exposure of privacy, a mode that can be deployed to counter the privileges accorded to the white, middle-class, liberal individual but denied to women, slaves, and the unpropertied class. But other forms of writing, I will demonstrate, those associated with the writing of men (and with the liberal ethos captured by the space of the study), can be defined precisely by their refusal to narrate, expose, and thus police the architectured self. In response to the anxiety we find in Poe that narrative may kill, the writing of Nathaniel Hawthorne, Herman Melville, and Frederick Douglass constructs zones of inexpressible, intractable interiority that may not evince the presence of an extradiscursive subjectivity that *precedes* the text but that do *create* such a subjectivity as their textual effect. As Renza argues in relation to Poe's fiction, such narrational acts "look for, want, perversely seek to produce the unreadable text, or, to be more precise, a radically private position in writing it."[24] The terrain of antebellum fiction, I will claim, is divided between the desire to express the self and the desire to find reprieve from self-expression, between the social imperative to invade the architectured self and the wish to carve out a chamber of "radical privacy" within it.

Privacy and the Letters of the Law

I intend my second example to move us toward this hypothesis even as it takes us from the domain of architecture to the domain of law. The right to privacy (as I discuss more fully in Chapter 4) came into being in the middle decades of the nineteenth century in common-law courts. More specifically, it emerged out of a series of cases involving the unauthorized publication of letters. When a person writes about private affairs in a letter, these courts were asked, who has control over the fate of this letter? Is it the person who has the letter in his or her possession? Is it the person who authored it? Or is it the person whose affairs are inscribed in it? The deliberation between the first two options was relatively simple, as both involved the legal paradigm that has dominated American law from its inception: the right of property. Within this paradigm, judges needed simply to weigh the right to material property (the actual paper and ink of the letter) against the right to intellectual property (which resides in the writer). But the third option stretched the limits of the property paradigm to its breaking point, since the people whose stories were told in the letter could not make any viable claim to ownership, and yet it became evident to the courts that they needed to be offered some form of protection as well. Their claim to privacy, furthermore, revised the very language used by the law. Judges needed to devise a way to talk about the private contents of the letters without themselves being charged with the exposure they were asked to prevent. It is out of this scenario that the right to privacy was invented, a right that from its inception was dressed in the language of innuendo and intimation. The right to privacy thus produced a private zone at once tethered to narrative (to personal stories that became valuable, contested commodities) and needing protection from narrative (i.e., put at risk at the moment in which they were written down).

Given this context, it is perhaps not surprising that one of the first persons to speak explicitly about a legal right to privacy in America was a postal worker. In 1855, J. Holbrook, special agent to the U.S. Postal Service, published anecdotes drawn from his professional experience in a book entitled *Ten Years among the Mailbags*. Holbrook opened his book with the grandiose declaration that "a mail bag is an epitome of human life."[25] It is not public affairs, Holbrook explained, but the private stories that are recorded and circulated in letters—stories about the joys of birth, the agony of death in the family, the intricate progress of courtship—that are the true essence of human life.

Holbrook could make such an assertion only to a society that had already undergone the shift from republican to liberal ideals. Under the republican model (as Hannah Arendt has argued), the private sphere was perceived as so narrowly referential, so rooted in basic human *sameness*, that it produced few stories worth telling. But with the rise of bourgeois liberalism, private stories gained extraordinary clout. As Jürgen Habermas has productively shown, when an emergent bourgeoisie began to privilege and seal off a zone of privacy in the home and the heart, personal letters became the most important genre of writing. "In the age of sentimentality," Habermas writes, "letters were containers for the 'outpourings of the heart'" and "the psychological interest increased in the dual relation to both one's self and the other: self-observation entered a union partly curious, partly sympathetic with the emotional stirrings of the other I." Thus, "subjectivity, as the innermost core of the private, *was always already oriented to an audience*."[26] When Holbrook imagined the mailbag as "an epitome of human life," he captured precisely this notion of a valuable private experience that is at the same time always performative, constructed for intimate exchange with an other. Holbrook describes the postal system as the modern alternative to the republican public forum, the "secret channel" that "flows among the privacies of domestic circles" to transmit and exchange precious private stories (p. xvii).

As such, Holbrook continues, the mail must be protected by law. "The laws of the land," he writes, "are intended not only to preserve the person and material property of every citizen sacred from intrusion, but to secure the privacy of his thoughts, so far as he sees fit to withhold them from others. Silence is as great a privilege as speech, and it is as important that every one should be able to maintain it whenever he pleases, as that he should be at liberty to utter his thoughts without restraint" (p. xviii). It is precisely at this point, however, that Holbrook's minor text becomes interesting, for, if the essence of private life indeed lies in its epistolary emplotment, as Habermas argues, what does *silence* have to do with it? What Holbrook intuits as the right to privacy is both the right to produce and to selectively trade personal stories *and* the right to shun the always other-geared inscription of the self. An individual has a right to "secure the privacy of his thoughts, so far as he sees fit to *withhold* them from others," he suggests, to be silent rather than to speak in protective intimacy. The letter that epitomizes interior life in that sense is the *dead* letter (to which Holbrook devotes a whole chapter), the letter that clutters those secret channels flowing within and between spheres of intimacy, that is to be publicly archived but never opened, and whose contents (assuming any) are forever barred from any form of appropriation, be it commercially or emotionally motivated.

It is precisely this ambivalence between the stories and the silences that pervade private space that surfaces in the case of a much better known former postal worker. Two years before Holbrook's book appeared, Herman Melville published "Bartleby, the Scrivener," his fictional meditation on the right to privacy. A story set not in a secluded Gothic mansion but in a law office in the midst of New York's busy commercial zone, "Bartleby" is nonetheless about private space. As Gillian Brown points out, the narrator whose office this is describes it in terms of a home, a "snug retreat" where nothing is "ever suffered" to invade his privacy.[27] The office is like a home also because its workers are like a family; their tastes, moods, secret follies, and private ambitions are all open to the narrator's view, read on their faces or inspected in the contents of their "private" drawers. When Bartleby walks into this scene of intimate policing, he immediately produces a division within it. This is true in a literal sense, since the narrator places Bartleby behind a high folding screen that isolates him from the sight of the others, but it is also true in a more profound sense, for what Bartleby will come to stand for is the refusal to turn private contents into a tradable story. This is the main demand imposed on him; for while the narrator is willing to put up with Bartleby's refusal to work, the one condition that he poses for letting Bartleby stay in his retreat is that he tell "*any thing* about [him]self," answer "openly and unreservedly" questions "touching his history, &c."—precisely, of course, what Bartleby, "offended at being mobbed in his privacy," prefers not to do.[28] Defined not by a coherent, other-oriented narrative but by his "dead-wall reveries," Bartleby comes to stand for what psychoanalyst D. W. Winnicott calls "the incommunicado element," that silent internal zone that is beyond articulation, perpetually unavailable to intimate exchange. If the "snug" office, then, is a version of the bourgeois interior, Bartleby's presence splits that interior between intimacy and solitude, narrative and silence; "and thus in a manner," as the narrator puts it, "privacy and society were conjoined" (p. 642).

Melville's story thus helps us rethink Habermas's analogy between liberal interiority and the personal letter, both "always already oriented to an audience." If Bartleby *is* a kind of a letter ("billeted upon me," as the narrator says), he is, of course, a dead letter, one that Melville will archive but refuse to open in public. Here we might point out that the setting of the story is not really a home but a law office. Like the lawyers in antebellum common-law courts who were confronted with claims to privacy, the narrator arms himself with the tool of property rights: he justifies his intrusive attempts to know Bartleby's story by arguing that his "desk is mine, and its contents too, so I will make bold to look within" (p. 652). But what he will come to validate—alas, too late—is the supraordinate right to privacy. In telling a story that refuses to be told, he will present the public sphere with the possibility of speaking about the private without violating it.

No less important is the way that this refusal to tear the self open does not signify for Melville the disavowal of intimacy, but its redefinition. The sentimental novel, against which conventions Melville habitually defined his writing, sought to externalize and narrativize the private into a form of affective currency that circulated within and between homes. Had the narrator's desire to write "the complete life of Bartleby" been fulfilled, he would have produced precisely such a narrative, "at which good natured gentlemen might smile, and sentimental souls might weep" (p. 635). Melville, like other writers in the American romantic tradition, dismisses the sentimental mode of sympathy predicated on self-revelation and proposes instead a masculine ("fraternal" [p. 652]) mode of intimacy based on the concealment of the self. "There was something about Bartleby," says the narrator (capturing the feeling of most readers since), "that not only strangely disarmed me, but in a wonderful manner touched and disconcerted me" (p. 644). The story imagines a "bond of common humanity" forged precisely on the denial of the confessional mode and the power hierarchy it implies (p. 652), an idealized, noninvasive form of intimacy posed over and against the intimate revelations of the sentimental text.

By showing us how, in Adam Phillips's words, "there cannot be private language" but there can be a sense, "conveyed in language, of a person's irreducible privacy,"[29] Melville helps us move beyond the Foucauldian approach to nineteenth-century fiction. As Debra Morris points out, recent years have indeed witnessed a revision in poststructuralist thought precisely around the notion of a silent intractability within the liberal individual. "More and more frequently," she writes, "self-described 'postmodernist' theorists invoke this individual, and cite her private and exquisitely particularizing experience, as a springboard for a new type of politics, a new form of political belonging."[30] One might think, for example, of Judith Butler's conjoining of Foucauldian and psychoanalytical perspectives in *The Psychic Life of Power* to revise her own earlier arguments about the thoroughly performative quality of the self, proposing instead a subjective model that includes "inassimilable remainders" produced by the process of subjectification. Or one might think of Foucault's later work, where an ethics of self, the "process in which the individual delimits that part of himself that will form the object of his moral practice," is proposed against the tyrannical discursive technologies that in Foucault's earlier work seem fully to saturate the subject. Indeed, in his late years, Foucault became interested precisely in "developing silence as a cultural ethos," one that not only countered the modern "obligation of speaking" but that also formed the basis for "friendship, emotional admiration, even love."[31] In such acts of self-revision, the liberal interior begins to emerge not as the unified, sheltered object of its own symbolic nor as the fully discursive or performative site of the poststructuralist critique, but as a space meaningfully and, perhaps, promisingly divided between performance and its backstage: discourse and silence.

Privacy, Property, Intimacy

We also have available a different vocabulary to describe the liberal conception of privacy as inherently fractured. As Seyla Benhabib has pointed out, privacy "as invoked by the modern tradition of political thought [has] included at least three distinct dimensions." First, it was understood as "the sphere of moral and religious conscience," the shelter of irreducible differences in opinions, faiths, tastes, or world views, differences that were seen as "rationally 'irresolvable'" in the public sphere. Second, it pertained to economic privileges and liberties; privacy, in that sense, was invoked as protection from public interference in the realm of commodity exchange. Third, privacy referred to the intimate domain, a domain "meeting the daily needs of life, of sexuality, and reproduction" and defined in opposition both to the public sphere and to the marketplace.[32]

Political critiques of liberalism, however, have often allowed one of these three dimensions to overshadow the rest. The Marxist critique of privacy, for example, privileges private property as the operative term. For Raymond Williams, privacy is simply an abstraction meant to conceal and justify private property, a "record of legitimation" of bourgeois economic privileges. From this perspective, privacy is reduced to a relation of property. This is true not only in the sense of what Philip Harper terms "proprietary privacy" (the privilege of withdrawal from social policing granted only to the white, heterosexual property owner and denied to his constitutive others—women, slaves, the urban underclass, or those who fall outside the heterosexual norm) but also in the more radical sense that one's relation to one's self is perceived as commodified. Taking their cue from C. B. Macpherson's influential *The Political Theory of Possessive Individualism*, a number of scholars have pointed to the irony that at the core of liberalism's fantasy of autonomous, "sacred" self lies the notion of *self* property, a notion that renders even the core of that self alienable.[33]

Meanwhile, much of feminist scholarship has tended to privilege the third, domestic, dimension of privacy, so that, as Jeff Weintraub puts it, "the formulation 'domestic/public' is often used almost interchangeably with 'private/public'" as well as with "female/male."[34] A dominant strain in feminist thought critiques the way liberalism pushed the sphere of intimate relations behind a "veil of ignorance" and—as this sphere was perceived as at once the sphere of women and of women's subjugation— thereby both excluded women from the universal, abstract, supposedly egalitarian public sphere and left unexamined and untreated the hierarchal, oppressive aspect of domestic life. As redress, feminism in the 1970s and the 1980s proposed a politics of presence, one that translates hidden, private experience into a coherent social identity and pushes this identity into the limelight.

By shifting the perspective from the oft-theorized border between the public and the private to the internal boundaries that traverse the private sphere, *Inexpressible Privacy* aims to highlight and sharpen the conflicts between these three dimensions of privacy instead of blurring them. For instance, I stress the way in which the first (subjective) and the second (proprietary) meanings of privacy were seen as at once mutually supportive *and* drastically irreconcilable, the way liberal selfhood is constructed both on the premise of private property and through the denial of property (recall that in Locke's *Second Treatise* only a portion of the self is described in terms of self-possession; another portion is understood as inalienable and "belonging" to a force greater than the self). In critiquing "proprietary privacy," I will argue, we put ourselves in danger of losing sight of that nontradable, publicly nonnegotiable dimension of subjective difference that even those social groups most oppressed by liberal hegemony were (and are) unwilling to forgo completely.

I also highlight the conflict between the first (subjective) and the third (domestic) dimensions of privacy. In too easily equating the private sphere with femininity, I argue, some feminist approaches gloss over the gendered differences within that sphere (always the sphere of men as well as of women) and over the competing desires and priorities that attended its formation. In the texts I examine, femininity is associated with the violation of the first dimension of privacy in the name of the third (thus, bourgeois women are associated at once with privacy *and* with the threat to privacy), while masculinity is defined both through subjective difference and through the universal abstractions of the public sphere (thus, bourgeois men can at once enjoy public power *and* the privilege of protection from the power of the public). The success of the politics of presence, I suggest, lies in its personalization of the abstract, liberal public sphere; but its limitation may lie in its failure to claim for women and other minoritized subjects the right to (and the power achieved by) an interiority that supersedes social identity.

In focusing on these internal frictions, I attempt to rethink some of the most deeply entrenched critical tenets of antebellum fiction. First, I modify the still too prevalent notion, promoted by 1970s and 1980s criticism, that antebellum fiction can be neatly partitioned into two gendered traditions, romantic and domestic, "Renaissance" and "other Renaissance," where the latter, grounded in feminine, intimate familialism, subverts the values of the oppressive masculine world represented by the former. This model began to undergo revision in the 1990s, when new scholarship proposed to view the literary traditions of male and female writers as jointly performing the ideological work of the white, liberal middle class.[35] My study revises both the older and the newer paradigms even as it remains indebted to them. Like the former, it highlights gender difference as important to literary taxonomy, yet, by analyzing the function of gender difference *within* the domestic sphere and its literature, it amends the lingering assumptions about the "femininity" of the home. Like the latter, it examines the imbrication of domesticity and individualism, yet it also underscores the points of friction produced by this far-from-easy alliance.

Second, I also join critical efforts to rethink the construction of manhood in antebellum literature. Traditional American studies found in antebellum literature a drama of liberated, unbounded masculinity played against the backdrop of the frontier, the wilderness, or the vastness of the ocean. This critical metanarrative (pejoratively dubbed "the melodrama of beset manhood" by feminist critics) underscored the motif of man's (and the male writer's) liberating escape from the private sphere, the sphere of sentiment, embodiment, and trivial particularity, and into "open air," the realm of abstraction, objectivity, and the universal. Echoing classic liberalism, this metanarrative assumed an identity between public universality and white masculinity, thereby not only excluding fiction by women and other marked subjects from the canon but also reducing the texts it did canonize to fit its central escape drama and flattening some of their most salient dimensions in the process. This interpretation of American literature could not account for the imagining of masculinity as closely linked to enclosed, interior, private spaces—a link that we repeatedly find in the works of Hawthorne, Thoreau, Poe, and Melville—or for the fact that these writers' works often revolve around anxieties of intrusion, penetration, and borderlessness rather than express a will to break open or flee. *Inexpressible Privacy* recasts the analysis of antebellum manhood in the context of the middle-class interior to show that both male hero and male writer often find freedom in retreating behind a "veil of ignorance." Their liberation lies not in escaping *from* but in escaping *into* the privacy of the home, albeit what the terms "privacy" and "home" mean in masculine romances is very different from what they mean in the annals of domestic womanhood.

The book aims, third, to complicate readings of fiction by women and other subalterns. Such readings frequently point out that the disembedded and disembodied public voice favored by liberalism, the privilege of abstraction afforded first and foremost to white, propertied men, meant that other voices, belonging to "overembodied" and excluded subjects, were privatized and silenced. Thus, the literature of subalterns is often read as a valorous attempt to make public their unheard voice, to force into the public sphere the private stories and identities on whose repression the liberal public sphere was constituted. *Inexpressible Privacy* supplements such readings by pointing to a companion impetus in subaltern fiction: the desire to find shelter from visibility and social identity, to carve out a niche of empowered privacy for the disenfranchised subject. This niche, to borrow the words of Geoffrey Sanborn, "is what prods us to identify ourselves with something and troubles all identifications"; it is seemingly a resistance to politics but arguably its prerequisite.[36] While subaltern literature often regards privacy as the ruse of white masculine power and while it capitalizes politically on the exposure of the private in public (thus foreshadowing late twentieth-century identity politics), it simultaneously seeks to extend the right to privacy to those to whom it has been historically denied, realizing that the claim to full humanity involves the privilege to disappear from, not just to appear in, public.

Chapter 1 reads domestic fiction alongside blueprints of Victorian architecture. I show how both domestic novelists and domestic architects managed the contradictions inherent in the emergent middle-class social matrix by splitting and gendering the spaces of the home, pitting the parlor—the wifely realm of intimacy, sociability, and display—against the study—the husband's enclave of reticence, retirement, and isolation. While this plan's marriage of oppositions, performed to create a harmonious symmetry in the domestic interior, appeared to be an equalizing one, it was not, in fact; the values of masculine privatism were ultimately understood to override those associated with feminine domesticity. Thus, what initially seemed like a loss of patriarchal power in favor of a more balanced form of marriage turned out to be a recasting of this power in covert, interiorized terms.

I then argue in Chapter 2 that the psychic structure developed in some classic psychoanalytical texts extends from the logic of the divided interior. I examine two psychoanalytic theories that draw from domestic architecture their metaphors for the human mind to show that, while these models converge in imagining the mind as split into a zone of sociability and a zone of solitariness, they diverge in their valuation of this division. For Freud, the realm of absolute privacy connotes deprivation, absence, and horror; but for Winnicott, a more liberal thinker, it connotes well-being and plenitude. With the opposition between Freud and Winnicott in mind, I proceed to read three short stories, by Hawthorne, Melville, and Stowe, stories that share the project of linking subjective space with domestic space and staging a conflict between a liberal theology of privacy and a counterethics of the exposure of interior life.

Chapter 3 transports the analysis of the divided plot from the psychic to the national scene. It begins with a close analysis of the "house-divided" metaphor, a metaphor that gained momentum in the political arena during the decades leading to the Civil War. I show how this rhetoric, which drew on the material and symbolic division of the bourgeois private sphere, was deployed by politicians to promise domestic unity by relegating slavery to a space behind the pall of privacy, beyond the reach of public discussion and intervention. This ubiquitous logic of concealment and containment was countered by the abolitionists' strategy of exposure, a strategy perfected in such narratives as Stowe's *Uncle Tom's Cabin*, which casts the figures of the slave and the bourgeois white woman as domestic informants, thereby both warning white property owners of an internal threat to their proprietary privacy and forcing into the public sphere the embodied presence of women and blacks. This strategy backfired, however, in failing to undo the problematic link between race, gender, and interiority. It assumed that race and gender were elements closest to one's subjective core and that this core could be translated smoothly into a coherent narrative of identity. I read Frederick Douglass's response to *Uncle Tom's Cabin*, "The Heroic Slave," as an attempt to liberate subjectivity from this politics of exposure.

Chapter 4 juxtaposes the aesthetics of the Hawthornian romance with the development in legal discourse of the right to privacy. It shows that the mid-nineteenth-century invention of that right involved not only the recognition of privacy as a viable legal category, distinct from and even inhospitable to property rights, but also an expansion of the legal boundaries of the private to encompass both thought and action, both the mind and the home. The middle-class's right to privacy appeared more democratic and universal than the right of property, to be enjoyed by all alike, regardless of financial status. But the right to privacy, I argue, did have class distinctions built into it. The intrusion against which the middle-class home shut its doors was not only that of the government but also of what Hawthorne habitually calls "the multitudes," revealing privacy to be a class privilege shaped by anxiety about intrusion from the top and the bottom of the social spectrum. In linking the literary with the legal, furthermore, Chapter 4 offers a revision of current Foucauldian readings of the novel by suggesting that romance, with its distinctive ambiguity and imaginative latitude, branches away from the novel precisely over the question of the author's right to police private space.

Chapters 5 and 6 turn to the writing of Henry David Thoreau, perhaps the most elaborate theorist of the link between manhood and privacy. In Chapter 5 I argue that *Walden* joins a variety of antebellum texts in suturing "natural" or "true" masculine identity to private space, a space designed to resist the threats of permeability from within (domestic womanhood) and from outside (homosociability). The home, in this discourse, is not perceived as "entirely the domain of wives," a space from which "men were increasingly exiled . . . unable to return without fear of feminization," as historians nowadays sometimes describe it,[37] but, on the contrary, as a space that signaled the achievement and protection of manly independence. Thoreau can, in that sense, be read as the philosopher of the great migration of the middle class to the suburb, a spatiosocial transformation that has the liberal myth of private manhood as its underlying rationale.

Whereas Chapter 5 emphasizes Thoreau's withdrawal from the social, Chapter 6 examines his means of participating in it. I argue that, against the Victorian "feminization" of intimacy and sentiment, the romantic writer developed an alternative logic of intimacy, one that repudiated its conventional definition as the exchange of concrete, commodified stories about the private self. Thoreau theorizes a mode of fraternal intimacy based on abstraction rather than embodiment, on concealment rather than revelation, on distance rather than physical proximity, on silence rather than speech, a mode of "depersonalizing intimacy" that is not merely schematized but also performed in his texts in the relationship between (male) writer and (male) reader. I propose to resist reading Thoreau's abstract relations and spare personal revelations simply as affective foreclosures and to see that, given liberalism's construction of the masculine self, such relations might satisfy a desire for equal (and potentially politicized) fraternal identification and offer a valid critique of antebellum as well as contemporary theories that too quickly laud self-exposure as a basis for a just public sphere.

A word, finally, about national exceptionalism. I own up to a certain artificiality in my decision to delimit my discussion of nineteenth-century liberalism's construction of privacy to the United States. The middle-class American house design, for instance, was heavily influenced by European architecture, and the legal right to privacy found its origins in British common law and developed coextensively in England. Indeed, throughout this book I draw from non-American sources, be it in alluding to the models of British architects such as Robert Kerr or in using Freud and Winnicott's theories. I do wish to claim, however, the special case of American privacy. On the one hand, in the United States national identity itself was early on tethered to privacy. "It is from the fact that we are an in-door people that much of our peculiarity and our advantage comes," wrote John F. W. Ware in 1864; "make this whole nation an out-of-doors people, teach them to find their amusement, their happiness, away from home, in gardens, in cafes, in the streets, and it would be as difficult to maintain our Republic as it has been to establish one in Paris and Rome."[38] On the other hand, claims to privacy have always been more politically and emotionally fraught in the United States, whether because of its particular history (Puritan, republican) or because it lacks established, shared traditions and manners capable of rendering the boundary between public and private appear natural, self-evident, and uncontestable. Privacy, in that sense, may indeed be "the Oz of America," as Lauren Berlant has put it, the place where Americans like to imagine there is no trouble, but where trouble really only begins.[39]

Chapter 1

Divided Plots: Gender Symmetry and the Architecture of Domestic Space

To a woman, the house is life militant; to a man, it is life in repose. . . .
Woman, by the very necessities of her existence, must have a different idea
of home than what man has.
—Appleton's Journal

Bona fide architects know
that doors are not emphatic enough, and interpose,
as a march between two realms, so alien, so disjunct,
the no-man's-land of a stair.
—W. H. Auden[1]

In 1846, Sarah J. Hale, an influential writer and the editor of antebellum America's most popular women's magazine, *Godey's Lady's Book*, published a novel entitled *Boarding Out: A Tale of Domestic Life*. The novel was meant to teach readers the lessons of wifely compliance and marital harmony. Its plot traces the deterioration of a typical middle-class family as a result of the wife's obstinate decision, influenced by the advice of an intimate confidante, to sell their suburban home and move to a boardinghouse in the city. Life in a boardinghouse, she is convinced, not only will reduce her household chores but also will open up the family's life to social opportunities and improve its status. Her loving but desolate husband, in an attempt to dissuade her through a kind of shock therapy, holds an auction in their parlor, where strangers gather to barter for the family's prized possessions. The doors to his own study, significantly, remain locked and his books are spared the fate of the piano and parlor ornaments. Although devastated by the spectacle, the wife nonetheless holds firm in her decision to relocate, and so the couple moves to an apartment in the city, where they participate in vivacious urban social life, but at the heavy price of domestic privacy.

The new life-style soon proves to be fatal: it leads to bankruptcy and to the death of their child. Tearful and repentant, the wife agrees to move back to a private house in the suburbs, where, away from both society's and the reader's prying eyes, we are assured, domestic harmony will be restored (as surely as will the family's possessions).

To a reader familiar with descriptions of domestic fiction and its motivating ideology, what historians have called "the cult of domesticity," this novel may seem somewhat strange. We assume that the domestic novel is structured on the marriage plot, a plot that promises peace and harmony at the moment when the heroine, after many a trial and tribulation, is finally brought into her lover's domain in marriage. *Boarding Out*, by contrast, displays a domestic interior plagued by contradictory values and aspirations long after the sealing of the marital bond. We assume that the cult of domesticity perceived the ideal middle-class home to be a paradisiacal haven, protected by the figure of the morally sound, angelic woman. But in *Boarding Out* the home is imagined as a space torn asunder by conflict, opened up to intrusion by the wife, and finally restored to privacy by the husband. It is precisely its dramatization of a deep split in the domestic interior, however, that makes Hale's novel utterly conventional, for the set of oppositions that it constructs is one that appears again and again on the pages of magazines and novels in the decades before the Civil War, and not only in stories, like Hale's, produced for a female audience but also in those geared specifically to the growing pool of middle-class male readers. The home is repeatedly portrayed in these divided-plot stories as a battle arena where opposite sets of values, codified by gender and mapped onto architectural space, compete. In Hale's novel these oppositions are so clearly registered that they can be distilled into graphic form:

Husband	Wife
Hermetic enclosure	Permeability
Isolation	Sociability and intimacy
Economic functionalism	Lavish consumption
The suburb	The city
Study	Parlor

Each side of this list represents a part of a distinctly middle-class social matrix, a matrix that encompassed both the modern city and the suburb, that prescribed both an ethos of economic restraint and of conspicuous consumption, that upheld the ideal of both solitude and intimacy. Hale's novel represents an attempt to cohere these ambivalences into a smooth, unified narrative: by carefully dividing the plot into gendered desires and dispositions, Hale acknowledges the existence of both sets of competing values and promises the possibility of their ultimate, happy cohabitation within the private sphere. Not unlike in contemporary marital-advice literature (where, say, men are from Mars and women are from Venus), the stability of the home in *Boarding Out* is achieved by working through a process of acute division and sharpening of gender differences, not through their erasure.

Hale's book came out during the same year in which *Godey's Lady's Book* inaugurated, as a monthly feature, the publication of architectural designs for private homes. Between 1846 and 1898, when the magazine finally folded, it published over 450 immensely popular blueprints for the exterior and interior of model homes. As early as 1849, the magazine's editors boasted that one town should be called "Godeyville," "so numerous have the cottages been put up there from our plans," and in 1868, magazine owner Louis Antoine Godey estimated that more than four thousand homes had been built using *Godey's* plates.[2] *Godey's*, along with the dozens of popular antebellum architectural pattern books written by such influential designers as Calvert Vaux, Gervase Wheeler, and (first and foremost) Andrew Jackson Downing (books from which the magazine drew most of its designs), announced a veritable revolution in domestic architecture, the arrival of a new interior-space plan destined to become the ideal and token of a middle-class status and mode of living. Much like the plot of *Boarding Out*, this new way of organizing interior space deployed gender difference as one of its main structural principles by splitting the home into "feminine" and "masculine" domains and often underscored the separation of the study—the husband's place of retirement and intellectual pursuits—from the parlor, the wifely realm of intimacy, sociability, and display. Fiction writers, those whom, like Hale, we associate with the domestic tradition, as well as those whom we regard as this tradition's rivals (the fact that *Godey's* contributors included Poe, Longfellow, Emerson, and Hawthorne is frequently overlooked), published their work alongside these new architectural designs and often entered into dialogue with their spatial prescriptions. Their stories propelled the fixed blueprints into narrative motion, helped investigate the notion of the home as a divided realm, and employed the splitting and gendering of the domestic interior as metaphor for themes ranging from subjective interiority to national cohesion.

The present chapter focuses on changes in the domestic interior as prescribed by antebellum architects and their link to transformations in gender definitions and marital structure that attended the rise of the middle class. My emphasis here will be on what Henri Lefebvre categorizes as "perceived" space—the space "secreted" by relations of production and reproduction—and on "conceived" space—the space idealized by its official designers, architects among them. I also begin to trace the tensions produced by these spatial arrangements in their middle-class users, men and women, tensions captured most saliently in fiction. These fall within what Lefebvre terms "lived" space, the realm of fantasies, metaphors, and symbols produced by the subjective experiencing of fixed (perceived and conceived) spatial arrangements.[3] This link between subjectivity and domestic space will be taken up more elaborately in Chapter 2.

When historians traditionally listed "domesticity, privacy, comfort, the concept of the home and of the family" as the "principal achievements of the Bourgeois Age,"[4] they tended to disregard the gendered undertones and internal tensions concealed in this list and hence perpetuated a view, itself a remnant of the nineteenth century, whereby the bourgeois interior was seen as a univalent, harmonious, and stable unit of meaning. But terms like "domesticity" and "privacy" are not, of course, gender neutral, nor should they be assumed to have simply worked in unison to form the middle-class vision of the private sphere; rather, they represent different sets of desires and priorities that did not always coexist harmoniously within the domestic interior.[5]

We might begin, then, by evoking two frames of reference regularly employed to describe the embourgeoisement of the nineteenth-century private sphere, each forceful in its own right, but each, as we shall see, not smoothly reconcilable with the other. The first is what historians often describe as the separation of the spheres and the rise of the cult of domesticity; the emergent view of the world as naturally divided into two utterly separate but neatly complementary spheres: the public sphere of politics and commerce, under the responsibility of men; and the more highly esteemed private sphere of subjective emotions and familial nurture, under the care of women. The annals of the cult of domesticity tend to use the terms "female," "private," and "domestic" interchangeably: privacy is the state of being within the family and close circle of associates, and the private person is she who is embedded in, defined by, and valued through intimate, affective relations.[6]

The second frame of reference is the rise of liberal individualism: the cultivation of an atomistic, autonomous selfhood whose possessions and political rights protect from the intrusion of society. If the cult of domesticity's private person is the bourgeois woman, the liberal individual is, first and foremost, white, propertied, and male. Like the cult of domesticity, liberal individualism assumed the existence of unseverable links between the self and the home: the home was perceived as the self's site of origin and determining influence, and also as its primary metaphor; indeed, the individual was imagined *as* a house, bounded by walls that concealed his interior, defined his zone of rights, and protected him from the invasion of others: "chacun chez soi, chacun pour soi," in Tocqueville's famous summation. But unlike the cult of domesticity, liberal individualism based this metaphor on the notion of ownership, not intimacy: the private individual owned the self as he owned his house, in fact, he owned the self *because* he was a property owner, and he required protection from any threat to this (self) ownership, including that posed by the people closest to him, such as his own family. Privacy is thus defined within this frame of reference as the state of being let alone, and in contrast to domesticity.[7]

These two frames of reference are, of course, imbricated. Both impose a clear divide between the public and the private spheres and worship the home as a sanctuary from a dangerous and intrusive public world. Both, moreover, regard the distance or barrier between the spheres as a necessary condition for selfhood, whether to ensure the autonomy of the liberal individual or the purity of the domestic woman. But in the 1970s and the 1980s, when feminist scholars first began their intense and productive interrogation of the domestic sphere, this imbrication tended to be overlooked. Often adopting the separate-spheres ideology as its premise as well as its object of inquiry, equating too quickly, that is, the private sphere with womanhood and individualism with the exterior world of politics and the marketplace, such scholarship charted a map on which liberal and domestic ideologies were shown to occupy different, oppositional, even mutually antagonistic spheres, a map on which domesticity, with its values of intimacy, nurturance, and empathy, was shown to oppose and even amend the harsh, unethical realities of the exterior masculine world. In literary terms, this scholarship argued for the existence of two canons: the traditional, romantic canon of the male "American Renaissance" writers, which captures the essence of liberal individualism; and the recovered, "other Renaissance," canon of female domestic fiction, which subverts that essence.[8]

In the 1990s, however, feminist scholarship thoroughly revised this separate-spheres model. Gillian Brown, Amy Kaplan, and Lori Merish (to name only a few) began to view antebellum domesticity and liberal individualism as mutually implicated, as working in tandem to produce hegemonic bourgeois ideology. With titles like "Domestic Individualism," "Manifest Domesticity," and "Sentimental Materialism," which collapsed the separation of the spheres, these studies exposed the cult of domesticity's complicity in the world of self-geared politics, racist practices, imperial expansion, and volatile capitalism. The literary traditions of male and female writers were now shown to jointly perform the ideological work of the white, upper-class, liberal United States. Where the separate-spheres scholarship located a rigid boundary between domesticity and liberal individualism, this hegemony model found overlaps and continuities; where the former emphasized difference, symmetry, and opposition, the latter located unity of interests, homology, and a (politically suspect) form of harmony between the spheres, actions, and writings of privileged men and women.[9]

My own project of entering the divided interior of the bourgeois private sphere draws from and revises both these approaches. It retains the separate-spheres focus on difference, yet refuses the automatic equation of the home with womanhood. Instead, I shift the focus from the boundary between the masculine public and the feminine private to the gendered division *within* the home. I am indebted to the more current readings' insights into the interdependency of domesticity and liberalism, yet my approach questions the tendency to gloss over the frictions embedded in this alliance and the way the two frames of reference that endow the bourgeois home with meaning clash. I concur with the current tendency to read romantic and domestic literature as sharing the same conceptual space, yet I stress these genres' competition for that space. I revise, that is, the view of the middle-class, white home as univalent and instead view it, in Joan Wallach Scott's words, as "the constant subject of great differences of opinion," as accommodating disparate and antithetical values, categories of selfhood, and modes of representation.[10] I intend to show how the middle-class private sphere, far from the fixed, stable space that nineteenth-century architects of domesticity often described it to be, was in fact an overflowing conceptual space, burdened with conflicting and even paradoxical definitions of the private, with visions of liberal and domestic interiority, with ideals of solitariness and social and familial intimacy.

In *The Structural Transformation of the Public Sphere*, Jürgen Habermas indeed analyzes the rise of the bourgeois family in terms of an internal division. From the late eighteenth century, he argues, "the line between private and public sphere extended right through the home. The privatized individuals stepped out of the intimacy of their living rooms into the public sphere of the salon, but the one was strictly complementary to the other." This divided interior, he argues, captures a major friction within the bourgeois conception of interiority. As a property owner who experienced a degree of economic freedom in the marketplace, the bourgeois man came to believe in the existence of his autonomous interiority and to associate this newly conceived psychological emancipation with the space of the home. But his belief in his own interior freedom depended precisely on the denial of its economic basis, on the liberation of that inner realm from any powers outside itself, and, first and foremost, from market forces. Hence the function of the home as the shelter for interiority continually collided with its other, more material, functions: the reproduction of capital; the maintaining of class status;

and the inculcation of social norms. Those functions exposed the home's relation to the social and economic spheres, and hence threatened to undermine the bourgeois subject's view of the home as "let alone" by the social and economic spheres.[11]

I argue that domestic architecture sought to manage this tension by carefully segregating the domestic interior, allocating symmetrical territories to the home's socioeconomic function and to its function as a pure shelter for interiority, and gendering these territories feminine and masculine, respectively. But in order for the home to preserve its ideal unity and harmony despite this division, domestic architecture also sought to override it by affirming, over the home's divided spaces, the ultimate control of the husband—the home's legal owner and master—and of the ideology of privacy for which he stood.

Hale's *Boarding Out* demonstrates this logic with precision. As we have seen, the novel first sorts out oppositional desires under gendered rubrics and then collapses this symmetry in favor of those values associated with the husband. Although there is a difference between the domestic-division plot and the marriage plot, what Hale's novel shares with the latter, we now note, is the positioning of privacy as its ultimate telos. The marriage plot may be said to be motivated by a single desire for privacy: it strives toward that moment when, living happily ever after, the conjugal couple will be let alone, that utopian moment when, freed from the internal social obstacles of the novel's imagined universe, the couple will be removed simultaneously from the scrutiny of the public world and that of the reader. In that sense, the marriage plot reenacts through narrative what some historians claim is the greatest motivating force in middle-class formation: the desire for "limited access and greater control over the observability of behavior."[12] *Boarding Out* similarly advances toward that moment of disappearance from observability, but it does so with a specific gender bend: the condition of invisibility and privacy toward which this novel strives is imagined as masculine, endangered by the close friendships, materialistic desires, and social agendas of women, who wrongly equate privacy with social intimacy and status. And while the novel constructs a symmetry between the husband's and the wife's visions of the private sphere, it is the masculine vision that finally subsumes the feminine. Only the triumph of masculine privacy, the reader is told, will ultimately ensure the existence of a feminine sphere of motherly love and sisterly friendship and the promotion of social status.

In thus posing privacy as its vanishing point, the plot of Hale's novel attempts to gloss over at least two double binds inherent in the divided interior and its problematic cohabitation of domesticity and liberal individualism. First, it conceals the contradictory move by which women are imagined as at once the embodiment of the private sphere and a threat to its privacy. The virtues attributed to the True Woman—the ability to nurture intimacy and to display propriety—virtues on which the sanctity and status of the home rely, are precisely those that are imagined to endanger privacy and propel a process by which, in the words of one antebellum writer, "the domestic circle is broken, the privacy of the house is invaded, and the house degenerates into a boarding house."[13] The wife in *Boarding Out*, that is, represents the way the middle class both architectured a space for women's agency and seriously delimited this space by imagining women as the home's internal hazard, the enemy within who endangered the principle of privacy.

Echoing novels like Hale's, middle-class magazines were fond of reporting the horrors of a distinctly feminine view of the private sphere: "Privacy? Oh, no, indeed, you needn't worry about that—we're just like one family—everyone knows about everyone else" (as *Harper's* "quoted" one boardinghouse landlady).[14] Mutual knowledge, enabled by a feminine commitment to familial collectivity and conspicuous consumption, was the obverse side of the cultural token that fixed the value of women's "natural" proclivity toward love, intimacy, and material objects. Indeed, this tense duality surfaces again and again in women's writing, writing that is torn between the need to display domestic propriety and the desire to be granted individual privacy, or to be exonerated from self-display.

No less taxing was the double bind produced in the divided interior in relation to middle-class manhood. As we shall see, the segregated interior that allocated symmetrical spaces for men and women enabled the replacement of an older, more rigidly patriarchal domestic model—in which the father was the undisputed master of his household—with the more democratic model of the affectionate, consensual marriage. The subsumption of gender symmetry under the overriding principle of domestic "harmony," like the ultimate triumph of the husband in *Boarding Out*, points to the way patriarchy subtly sought to reassert itself over the presumed equilibrium of the new domestic order. But this patriarchal reclamation was problematic. Men were now encouraged to view the home as a solitary retreat, a place of reprieve for the individual, a niche hidden away from the stringent demands of law, politics, and public performance. In the words of one Victorian architect, John Ruskin, the home was to be its owner's "place of peace; the shelter, not only from all injury, but from all terror, doubt and division."[15] Thus, on the one hand, men were encouraged to view their position in the home in terms of escape from the turmoil of the exterior world, even in terms of passivity; on the other hand, they were expected to assert control over the very space in which they treasured the privileges of solitude and inaction.

Put in a different vocabulary, they were expected to exert the law of the father precisely over a realm that they were instructed to view as altogether outside the realm of the law. Little wonder, then, that the divided plot is haunted by anxieties about invasion and loss of masculine control, anxieties that often transform into self-pity or even violence. I shall pick up both these double binds later in this chapter as well as in the next, but first I shall describe the history of the domestic interior in the (mostly northeastern) United States and the process of its spatial and conceptual division.

Dividing Interior Space

To begin to understand that spatial and conceptual division, we might look at the layout of domestic interiors prior to the antebellum period. The majority of colonial and early-republic Americans, with slight regional variations, lived in simple frame houses of a similar design (Fig. 1). The main floor, where most daily activities took place, including domestic production, household chores, amusement, and entertaining guests, constituted either a single large room or a hall and a parlor. In either case, its focal point was a large fireplace whose chimney supported an additional gallery or half-floor above, where family members, lodgers, and other household adjuncts slept. This interior plan was imported from England by seventeenth-century settlers and remained basically intact all through the colonial period and into the nineteenth century. Its simple divisions, horizontal and vertical, were to be found in country cottages as well as in urban row houses, in lodgings for farmers as well as in the houses of artisans.[16]

Three main features distinguish this interior plan from that which appeared in the first half of the nineteenth century to cater to the needs and desires of the emergent middle class. First, both the single-cell and the hall-and-parlor design created only crude partitions of space on the basis of function, and the uses of space were surprisingly fluid. While, in a sense, the upstairs was more "private" than the "public" downstairs, beds were regularly found downstairs as well, and, in fact, the married couple's bed, arguably the most private of spaces in modern perception, was often located in the parlor. And while there was some distinction between labor and leisure in the hall-and-parlor design (activities like candlemaking, cooking, and handicrafts took place in the hall, and more-social activities occurred in the parlor), the boundary between them was often blurred, and each room was in fact a multipurpose room, as the vagueness and proliferation of names for each attest. The hall was also called the "great room," "outer room," "dwelling room," and "fire room," and the parlor, the "chamber" or "inner room." The production activities that pervaded the hall-and-parlor design's spaces

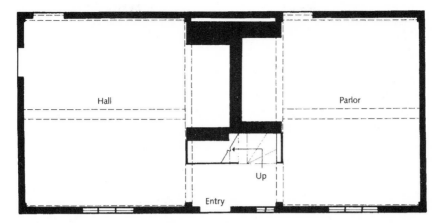

Figure 1. The colonial hall-and-parlor floor plan, featuring a central chimney. Reproduced from Clark, *The American Family Home.* Copyright 1986 by the University of North Carolina Press.

signaled its overriding commitment to an ethos of work, while the sparse ornamentation bespoke the attendant ethos of frugality and anti-luxury. Overall, then, the seventeenth- and eighteenth-century interior was largely a production-oriented, functional, and communal space that made few accommodations for individual privacy and shaped open, visible spaces shared by the nuclear family and its adjuncts.[17]

Second, with the exception of a very thin upper crust of wealthy merchants, prominent clergy, political leaders, and other members of the social elite, virtually the entire population lived in either single-cell or hall-and-parlor houses. Other than an uncertain and relatively insignificant break between single- and double-celled houses, this interior plan seems to have denoted no particular position on the social scale and to have carried with it no meaning in terms of class hierarchy.[18] On the contrary: the homogeneous house plan of the seventeenth and eighteenth centuries testified to America's democracy and equality. In America, J. Hector St. John de Crevecoeur affirmed, a traveler "views not the hostile castle and the haughty mansion, contrasted with the clay-built hut and miserable cabin"; instead, "[a] pleasing uniformity of decent competence appears throughout our habitation."[19]

Third, this design was particularly well suited to the form of patriarchy that characterized colonial America. Its multifunctional spaces captured and enabled the position of the father as the undisputed head of the family. As John Demos's now-classic study of the colonial family shows, in this "little commonwealth" the woman's ideal attitude was that of "revered subjection," and she was legally and socially subsumed under the personhood of her husband.[20] In a domestic interior that enmeshed activities and disallowed spaces of individual privacy, the power of the head of the household was both visible and direct. A central chimney, for instance, meant that no hallway separated the rooms of the house and therefore that no rooms were barred from entrance and no spaces left invisible. (As we shall see in the next chapter, this large, phallic chimney indeed became a prevalent symbol of residual patriarchal control.) This plan allowed the father to "make life difficult for his family by consistent surveillance, and although perhaps not so aggressively patriarchal as his ancestors, he did maintain a firm hand on the family."[21]

In contrast, the interior plan that began to emerge at the end of the eighteenth century, and that was to become the hallmark of the middle class by the mid-nineteenth, mirrored and enabled a new familial model, one based (in its ideal if not necessarily in practice) on the equality of marital partners rather than on the mastery of the husband. Initially borrowing its design from similar developments in European and, particularly, British domestic architecture, this interior plan (so many versions of which were featured on *Godey's* pages) was characterized by increased consideration for privacy and by the allocation of specialized spaces to each member of the household. It emphasized a break between the main and upper floors through the enlargement, elaboration, and relocation of the staircase, the marker of a boundary between a wholly private upstairs and a more-open downstairs. The upstairs was now regularly subdivided into four or more sleeping chambers, allowing for greater privacy for both parents and children, while the main floor was emptied of beds and other bedroom accessories and, as production was gradually extracted from the private sphere, also of work tools. The ideal main floor now habitually featured a symmetrical layout of a parlor (referred to as a "drawing room" or "salon" in more pretentious plans) and a study (or "library"), accompanied by a kitchen in the back or in the cellar and often an adjacent dining room as well (Fig. 2; in this particular plan, architect A. J. Downing retained a bedroom downstairs to accommodate "invalids, or persons advanced in years"). Rooms were newly designed to accommodate a precise function, and their separation into different realms was reinforced by the disappearance of the central chimney and the installation of a middle hallway, thereby solving, as influential British architect Robert Kerr explained in 1864, "the wretched inconvenience caused by 'thoroughfare rooms' which made *domesticity* and *retirement* unobtainable."[22]

Kerr's use of the terms "domesticity" and "retirement," terms that had distinctly gendered undertones for mid-century Victorians, alludes to the symbiotic relationship between this domestic design and evolving gender ideals. The goal of Victorian domestic architecture, in Mark Girouard's words, was to "protect the womanliness of women and encourage the manliness of men," a goal achieved by meticulously dividing

DESIGN II.

A Cottage in the English or Rural Gothic Style.

Fig. 9.

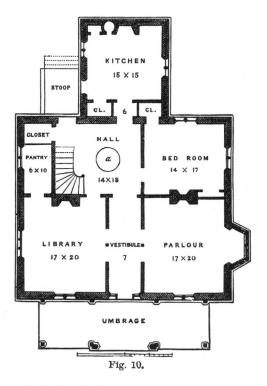

Fig. 10.

Figure 2. A. J. Downing's plan for "a cottage in the English or rural Gothic style." From *Cottage Residences*.

the spaces of the house between masculine and feminine domains.[23] This notion of gendered spaces was adopted initially from the design of the aristocratic British country mansion, a design that conceived parlors, breakfast rooms, and boudoirs as the lady's realm, and studies, libraries, dining rooms, and billiard rooms as the gentleman's domain. In the middle-class interior plan, gender segregation was distilled into one essential division: the parlor was regarded as a feminine space of "domesticity" and the study as a masculine preserve of "retirement."

This did not mean, however, that the rules regulating this allocation were similar in each case. While the study was purely a man's preserve, in the sense that women and children typically hesitated and sought permission before entering it, the lady's parlor was intended as a gathering place for men and women in pursuit of familial intimacy or social pleasures. The parlor, in fact, was itself a partitioned space, regularly subdivided into "male" and "female" sides. Even the furniture was gendered, as it were: the refined parlor featured, for example, a "gentleman's parlor chair" opposite a "lady's parlor chair." What the divided blueprint of Kerr and others offered their middle-class audience was an illusion of perfect symmetry and harmony produced by an emphasis on gender distinction and separation.[24]

This gendered division soon became a necessary attribute of privileged families and the goal of those aspiring to belong to their rank. Richard L. Bushman, in his study of the process of "refinement" that formed the American middle class, argues that the partitioned interior design created a definitive boundary between middling and upper ranks, on the one hand, and a lower rank, on the other: "The great divide in American society as refinement diffused into the middling ranks," he writes, "lay not between the small and great parlor houses, but between houses with parlors and those with none."[25] This basic division notwithstanding, antebellum architects did draw a distinction between more-genteel, upper-middle-class families, where the husband's "gentlemanly" status demanded a special room for his intellectual pursuits, and lower-middle-class families, for whom a separate study was not deemed a necessity.[26]

Thus, whereas until the beginning of the nineteenth century domestic architecture captured the fundamental equality of the majority of the population, it now signaled the division of America into distinct ranks, and particularly the advent of a large, white, middle class, itself internally hierarchized. Popular pattern books like A. J. Downing's *The Architecture of Country Houses*, in effect, helped shape class consciousness by arguing that an architect must learn to distinguish "the wants and the means, the domestic life and the enjoyments, the intelligence and the tastes" of the "working man" from those of the "gentleman," and on the basis of these qualitatively different outlooks plan entirely different homes. For less-affluent farmers or small-town workers, pattern books drafted a specific plan to fit their "simple and plain manner" and to create an "interior . . . so arranged, in short, as to enable the inmates wholly to 'do their own work' . . . without any loss of convenience, or the necessity of taking any unnecessary steps." The laborer's house, Downing explained, designed, as it were, to maximize production, "should show an absence of all pretensions. . . . It should rely on its own honest, straightforward simplicity, and should rather aim to be frank, and genuine, and open hearted like its owner, than to wear the borrowed ornaments of any class of different habits or tastes."[27] Accordingly, the laborer's cottage featured neither parlor nor study, but a large, unornamented, communal "living room" reminiscent of the colonial hall (Fig. 3). This design also perpetuated the residual colonial blend of private and social spaces by inserting a bedroom downstairs and prescribed that "above all, the chimneys should be larger and more generous-looking, to betoken the warmhearted hospitality" of the home, establishing, in effect, that the "frank," "open-hearted" laborer required no individual privacy and hence no hallway or spatial enclosures, and that his wife did not merit a domain of sociability, intimacy, or display of status.[28]

Plans for urban tenements pushed this logic even further (Fig. 4). Here no provisions were made to allow even for familial (let alone individual) privacy, as two or more families were cramped onto each floor. A row of bedrooms, interconnected in a railway fashion, allowed for almost no personal space, and the living rooms and kitchens at both ends were shared by as many tenants as the agent could pack onto each floor. While recent scholarship argues that the Victorian urban working class did manage to safeguard domestic privacy despite this cramped architectural layout (thereby offering an instance of Lefebvre's assertion that "lived in" or "practiced" space can subvert spaces as hegemonically perceived and conceived), the design of the urban tenement nonetheless captured the circular logic by which the upper classes at once denied the "laboring masses" a right to privacy, deeming it unsuited to their very "nature," and described this class's mode of living as "barbaric" precisely because of the absence of gendered partitioning.[29]

Interior plans thus provide one example of what Nancy Cott has argued was a primary characteristic of middle-class hegemony: the use of gender to sustain class categories. A dichotomized gender ideology, Cott maintains, secured "social classification for a population who refused to admit ascribed statuses, for the most part, but required determinants of social order."[30] By displaying itself via the splitting of the interior into masculine and feminine domains, the upper middle class at once distinguished itself from the lower ranks and made its plan appear universal and "proper," based as it was on "natural" gender differences.

Did the emergent middle class first create sharp dichotomies between

DESIGN I
A LABORER'S COTTAGE

Fig. 5

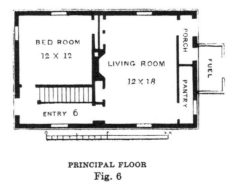

PRINCIPAL FLOOR
Fig. 6

Figure 3. A. J. Downing's plan for "a laborer's cottage." From *The Architecture of Country Houses.*

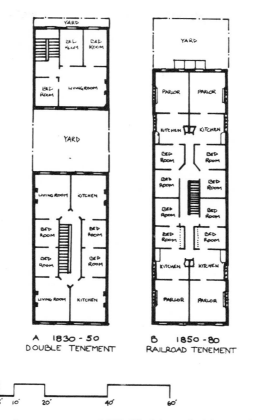

Figure 4. Plans for urban tenements, 1830–80. Adapted with permission from Wright, *Building the Dream*. Copyright by Pantheon Books (1981).

production and consumption, masculinity and femininity, and then design spatial separations to reflect these dichotomies? Or did the new organization of domestic spaces in fact generate and help naturalize the social and gender determinants on which this class based its collective identity? Lefebvre claims that both causal chains between space and social formation are correct. To be sure, social relations are evident in space, he argues, but this does not mean that space is their passive container. Rather, space serves within a hegemony that makes use of it. Space and social formations are in a dialectical relationship, many sociologists since Lefebvre have argued, that is marked by "cumulative interdependencies" or "simultaneities." Spatial organization depicts social classification but simultaneously reflects back on its users and shapes, orders, and coheres their social determinants. This cooperation of the social and spatial, the way space "speaks" for hegemony, means that the divided middle-class interior, reflecting a sharpening system of binaries and differentiation, in turn generated a way of thinking about each gender *through* the space with which it was most closely identified.[31]

The Parlor: Spectacles of Intimacy

While domestic architects generally insisted on the involvement of the architect in all stages of design, one area, they conceded, was more properly left to the arbitration of the house's mistress. Architect Calvert Vaux wrote in 1857:

A best parlor ought to express, in its proportions, colors and arrangement of furniture, an agreeable, hearty social welcome. The lady who studied her room when her guests had departed, after a lengthened and agreeable visit, so as to learn how the furniture had accommodated itself, as it were, to suit the social convenience of her friends, and who then modified her previous ideas accordingly, had the true artistic eye for beauty of arrangement, and certainly deserved to have a pleasant circle of acquaintances. There are but few strictly architectural features in a drawing-room that call for illustration. Good proportions can be supplied; but the lady of the house is the most important architect here.[32]

According to Vaux, the parlor, under the supervision of the house's mistress, was not a fixed space: in arranging it, she should continually trace the hidden spatial pattern created by its visitors to maximize its "hearty social welcome." To use Edward T. Hall's terminology, the antebellum parlor was conceived as a *sociopetal* space, functioning to draw people together and to maximize mutual observability and relations in order to boost the social pleasures and aspirations of the middle-class family.[33]

Shaped to accommodate a "pleasant circle of acquaintances," the parlor was neither public nor, strictly speaking, private space. Rather, as historians such as Karen Halttunen and John F. Kasson argue, it delineated a kind of third, social, space between public life and private life, literally positioned between the street and the deeper recesses of the home (Fig. 5).[34] Vaux prescribed in *Harper's Weekly* that the parlor or drawing room must "command a view of the street," since "American ladies, who are in the habit of spending the greater part of their time in their own apartments, think it far more lively and cheerful to look out on a busy thoroughfare than on a monotonous quadrangle."[35] It was no less important, however, that "the street" should look in at the "American lady." Positioned in front, the parlor served as a front, as an "elaborate social statement" or "a family's major act of self representation."[36]

The parlor thus provided a particularly good example of Erving Goffman's immensely influential theory of social interaction. Over four

Fig. 36

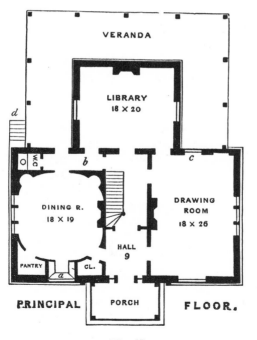

Fig. 37.

Figure 5. Downing's "cottage villa" with frontal drawing and dining rooms and rear library. From *Victorian Cottage Residences*.

decades ago, Goffman argued that communication between human beings was best described as a performance: we act in relation to others, he
argued, and we do so to achieve control. Goffman analyzed the way we
"perform" a socially desirable self by constructing "fronts," both "personal" (including clothes, posture, enunciation, gestures, and so forth)
and of "setting" (rooms, furniture, decor, and other props).[37] In the antebellum period, when class boundaries were still exceedingly precarious,
it was necessary for middle-class subjects to perform their refinement as
often and as convincingly as possible, and the parlor provided one of the
most important settings for this performance. As one observer expressed
it in 1846, the parlor was "a stage upon which parts are performed before
a public, that applauds or hisses, according to the merits of actor."[38]

As Vaux's words indicate, both the design of this stage and the orches-
tration of the performance were properly placed in the hands of
women, and while both men and women "belonged" in the parlor, its
values were associated first and foremost with femininity. The cult of domesticity assigned to women the task of safeguarding class boundaries
("yours it is to determine whether the beautiful order of society . . . shall
continue as it has been," as one writer charged his female readers, or
whether "society shall break up and become a chaos of disjointed and
unsightly elements"),[39] and it was from the parlor that they were to
spread refined, class-specific behavioral codes, not only through their
genteel decorum but also through the elegance of the stage itself. In architectural and domestic tracts, the parlor was described as a repository
for consumer objects that attested to the family's financial success and
refined taste. Books and magazine articles encouraged the mistress of
the house to spend money on furnishings, carpets, artwork, and other
parlor artifacts that had little functional value beyond sheer conspicuity.
(In one typical *Godey's* sketch, the "middling-class" parlor accommodates a sofa and six rarely used mahogany and haircloth chairs, there
simply to "reflect credit" on the family's "standing.")[40]

While women were encouraged to design the parlor, however, it
would be no less true to say that the parlor helped design antebellum
womanhood. As Goffman argued (decades before Judith Butler made a
similar argument about the performativity of gender), "a correctly
staged and performed scene leads the audience to impute a self to a
performed character, but this imputation—this self—is a *product* of a
scene that comes off, and is not a *cause* of it."[41] The parlor as "front,"
that is, did not merely reflect but *implanted* the True Woman's inner disposition for refined taste and genteel behavior. This dialectic between
personhood and space, the way parlor and person merged in the performance of bourgeois womanhood, was captured in the blend of fashion and interior decoration; the skirted furniture and lush draperies

mimicked women's skirts and gowns, for example, and dress fabrics often repeated the design of wallpapers.[42]

The parlor woman's function as marker of status was inseparable from her more-immediate, affective familial role. The "female character," as one writer noted, relied on the "cheerful performance of social *and* family duties," and the parlor was designed to accommodate both.[43] In her architectural writing, Edith Wharton, upholding in 1898 the "architectural principles . . . of the past," explained that "in houses of average size, where there are but two living rooms—the master's library, or 'den,' and the lady's drawing-room,—it is obvious that the latter ought to be used as *salon de famille,* or meeting place for the whole family."[44] In the well-regulated middle-class home, the parlor functioned not only for entertaining guests but also as a gathering place for family members in the evenings, where, drawn together by the magnetic force of the wife and mother's affections, they were to enjoy each other's company and pursue collective activities like Bible reading, games, or conversation. Indeed, the woman's social role was merely an extension of her function as the family's emotional adhesive, of what was perceived as her essential capacity for such emotions as empathy, affection, and compassion. When architects like Vaux insisted on the sociopetence of the parlor, they, in fact, articulated the common belief in an almost mystical feminine capacity for drawing the outside world into the sentimental family circle.[45]

But in this apparently smooth continuity between the familial and the social lay a potential snag: given sentimental ideology's insistence on the strict separation between the material and the spiritual, between the exterior, market-oriented world and the interior heart(h), how could the parlor function at once as an extroverted display of materiality and as an introverted niche of sentiment, at once as a space for spectacle and for intimacy? Put differently, how could domestic ideology reconcile the spirituality and ethereality of the domestic angel with her predilection for consumer objects? Lori Merish's analysis of what she terms "sentimental materialism" persuasively works through this incongruity. In her reading, the antebellum parlor's material refinement and its emotional refinement—the consumer objects and the sentimental conduct it housed—were not perceived by the antebellum middle class as clashing but as mutually constitutive. The parlor's ornaments, that is, attested not only to financial success and status but also to a proper emotional and spiritual disposition. Consumer goods were grasped as objects of affection, and as the medium of emotional exchange, but no less as external evidence of women's innate affective propriety. Thus the parlor woman was, in fact, the first avatar of what Michael Warner calls the modern "mass subject"—the subject whose "inner" identity is imagined to be embodied in, predicated on, or fully expressed by consumer goods, practices, and styles.[46]

But the merger of materialism and sentimentalism in the ideal parlor-woman was also a source for collective anxiety. Consider, for example, the endless stream of sketches, anecdotes, and jokes that explored the scenario of the hard-working husband, his clothes bespeckled, barred from entering the best parlor by an overly fastidious and socially ambitious wife. This was an image of both the parlor and womanhood gone awry, distorting the delicate balance between material objects and familial affections by placing the former squarely before the latter. An article in *Harper's Monthly*, for example, condemned the "otherwise sensible and prudent housewives," who "in order to have a mansion sufficiently lofty to rise to the standard of fashionable height, and rooms spacious and resplendent enough to hold the swelling importance and catch the fastidious eye of the modish, . . . restrict themselves and their families to the narrowest quarters and the shortest commons."[47] *Atlantic Magazine* similarly bemoaned the fate of the husband whose wife "would like to have his children sleep three in a bed, and live in the kitchen, in order that the best rooms should always be swept and garnished for company."[48]

Perhaps even more disturbing, however, was the opposite scenario: that woman's "natural" inclination toward love and intimacy would not be withheld, but too lavishly practiced, that, instead of treating family as strangers, she would treat strangers as family, thereby rendering the home's walls permeable. If the family's social status depended on the feminine front it erected in the parlor, then the very traits that defined that front as genteel—display of objects, sociopetence, and sentimentality—could potentially also tear down that front and expose that which the family needed to keep backstage to maintain its standing, such as domestic disputes, financial difficulties, or disobedient servants and children. If the wife, as in *Boarding Out*, were to overextend her affection, she would threaten to render the house's inner workings visible. The very essence of the parlor—the sentiments that "dwell in woman's heart"—posed a continuous threat to the inviolability of the home and to its control over its own observability. Thus, the elaborate emotional connection between women, the celebrated world of female bonds and rituals of love, were both encouraged as a sign of True Womanhood and continuously checked and regulated by parlor etiquette. For instance, according to etiquette manuals, intimate friendship between women introduced into the house a "class of tattlers . . . who visit their friends and take note of all the habits and customs of the family, the conversations at table, the government of children, treatment of servants, family expenditures, employments and dress of the mistress," all "told in detail at the next visiting place."[49] To fill every crack in the genteel front, parlor etiquette discouraged too-close an inspection of the parlor's objects, engaging in too-intimate a conversation on domestic matters, or even prolonging a social call beyond a short period of time. "Discourage the first indications of undue intimacy, by making your own visits rather few, and rather far between," advised Eliza Leslie, primary authority on bourgeois women's behavior; "a young lady of good sense, and proper self-respect will never be too lavish in her society."[50] The right to familial privacy, according to these manuals, superseded the bonds of intimate friendship, and women were warned to avoid, above all, "seeing the skeleton in your friend's closet," regardless of how inviting the luxuriously ornamented closet might appear to be.[51]

The design of middle-class womanhood in relation to the sociopetal space of the parlor created yet another form of tension. As liberal individualism began to define personhood in terms of inviolability and solitariness, the bourgeois woman, defined in opposition to these terms, was thereby deprived of full personhood. Since the parlor was, by definition, a permeable, performative space that brought men and women together, the parlor woman literally had no room of her own at the precise moment when having such a room became a prerequisite for personal liberty. Charlotte Perkins Gilman wrote toward the end of the nineteenth century: "such privacy as we have at home is family privacy, an aggregate privacy, and this does not insure—indeed, it prevents—individual privacy . . . the home is the one place on earth where no one of the component individuals can have any privacy . . . at present any tendency to withdraw and live one's own life on any plane of separate interest or industry is naturally resented, or at least regretted, by the other members of the family. This affects women more than men."[52]

Goffman's analysis of the fronts we erect in social interaction points to the importance of "backstage" areas, where "the performer can relax . . . can drop his front, forgo speaking his lines, and step out of character."[53] What the records of domesticity often reveal, however, are the psychological pressures brewing within middle-class women, who did not have at their disposal such backstage areas, ironically, at the very moment when they were figured as icons of privacy. Eliza Leslie gave a momentary outlet to such pressures in an 1841 novella, first serialized in *Godey's Lady's Book*, entitled "Mr. and Mrs. Woodbridge." The novella tells of a young, urban, middle-class couple in the process of moving to their first home. Like *Boarding Out*, it blames the predictably beautiful-but-foolish wife and her meddling confidantes, the aptly named Mrs. Pinchington and Mrs. Squanderfield (standing for the wifely "two besetting sins" of parsimony in affective investment and undue extravagance in consumption), for the destruction of matrimonial "harmony." Mrs. Woodbridge objects to her sensible husband's plan for the interior of their new home and insists that the little room he reserved for his library be turned into a sitting and dining room, thereby "saving" the "Saxony carpets, and silk curtains, and silk-covered lounges, and large glasses, and chandeliers, and beautiful mantel-lamps" of the parlor. After a lengthy dispute, it becomes apparent that what the wife really wants is not the preservation of property but, quite simply, privacy: "To put an end to this foolery," she proclaims, "I tell you once and for all, Harvey Woodbridge, that I must and will have this very apartment for an eating-room, or a dining-room, or a sitting-room, or whatever you please to call it—to take our meals in *without danger of being caught at them,* and to stay in when I am not drest and *do not wish to be seen.*"[54] Leslie, forever the strict pedagogue of True Womanhood, is clearly condemning this desire for relief from surveillance (needless to say, this novella, like *Boarding Out,* ends with the triumph of the husband and his library over the wife and her parlor). A proper woman has nothing to hide. But, at the same time, Leslie does identify this desire in the middle-class woman and she does give it a voice.

Others voiced this desire in their letters and diaries. Harriet Beecher Stowe, in a letter written during her absence from home, describes both a pressing need for relief from the performance of feminine identity and a muted concern that this need negates that very identity; she rejoices in her "state of retirement in this place, in which [she has] enjoyed what [she has] long been hoping to enjoy—a season of tranquil vegetation," but adds, "I have forgotten almost the faces of my children—all the details of home and almost that I am a married woman."[55] Civil War diarist Mary Boykin Miller Chesnut quotes in her diary an acquaintance who described married life as "an institution worse than the Spanish Inquisition, worse than Torquemada," because one's family members "set upon you, fall foul of you, watch and harass you from morn till dewy eve. They have a perfect right to your life, night and day . . . no locks or bolts or bars can keep them out," and added bitterly, "Private life, indeed!"[56] An article in *The Lady's Repository* observes that in the typical family the son has "his room . . . his sanctum, and mothers or sisters hesitate to break in upon [his] privacy." The author goes on to wonder "where is the corresponding privacy in most girls' lives? If they do retire to their rooms with books or pen they are not supposed to be particularly engaged, and nobody shrinks from interrupting their employment."[57]

Moreover, the mere availability of a space for retiring did not necessarily secure the middle-class woman's privacy in its profounder sense. Those women who were lucky enough to have such a sanctuary soon learned that they were expected to use it for the perfecting of their performed identity, not as a means of escape from it. One wrote in her diary:

"a retired chamber is one of the choicest blessings I enjoy . . . here may I review my feelings, mourn over my numerous imperfections . . . veiled from the world."[58] Such women could claim private space only on condition that nothing about that space threatened social codes; a version of Foucault's panopticon, private space was where social surveillance was to be internalized, not shunned. Consider a sketch by Fanny Fern (Sarah Willis Parton), popular author of domestic fiction, entitled "Mother's Room." The sketch enters the private space of the generic middle-class mother ("our" mother) and slowly pans across the room to reveal its every detail. It inspects the "ample cushioned chair, with its all-embracing arm"; pauses on the "cozy sofa upon which childish feet were never forbidden to climb"; examines "the closet," which hides nothing more than healing potions and toys; and, finally, reaches the "wrinkled face, beautiful with its halo of goodness" of the avatar of blessed maternity herself. The sketch captures the peculiar blend of material objects and feminine affection that we have discussed: the cushioned chair is anthropomorphized into a mother, and the mother appears as yet another cozy piece of furniture in the room. But even more disturbingly, it creates the illusion of privacy even as it depletes the concept of privacy of its most important meaning. It invades private space only to reveal that this private space would never warrant invasion because it is never really private: it conceals nothing, welcomes all, and exists in precisely the same form in every proper household. Like the domestic woman itself, the room is accorded the status of interiority provided that, a priori, nothing about that interiority truly demands concealment or resists exposure. As a private space, then, "Mother's Room" is a dead space. Not surprisingly, it is ventured into and exposed by Fern only "when she who sanctified it is herself among the sanctified." The presence of an actual living woman within this shrine would have complicated its perfectly transparent conventionality. Only at her death, when the messy details of her life can no longer disrupt the stillness of her room, can this interior be presented to the reader's approval and nostalgia without threatening a social architecture that associates femininity with impeccable propriety. Just as, under the cult of domesticity, the ideal woman is always already an angel, so is her private space always already a shrine.[59]

Feminist critics have marveled for many years about Victorian women's success in producing literature, despite the grueling conventionality and deadening lack of privacy that characterized their domestic existence. But a stronger argument has been offered as well: that some modes of writing, associated primarily with women, were not simply hampered by but also took their shape from the characteristics of the domestic spaces in which they were produced. Indeed, Joan D. Hedrick has coined the term "parlor literature" to describe the domestic writing of some antebellum authors. While parlor literature was written by men as well as women (just as the parlor's spaces were shared by both), it is a mode of writing that by the 1850s and the 1860s had come to be tightly associated with femininity. Like the parlor itself, Hedrick explains, parlor literature was inherently social and intimate in tone. Connected in its origins to letter writing, it emphasized the revelation and exchange of personal information to resemble intimate conversation. Since it was designed to be read aloud, collectively, for entertainment, amusement, and instruction, it captured the parlor's peculiar blending of intimacy and spectacle.[60] Lori Merish similarly argues that the domestic novel, like the epistolary novel, its originating genre, typically embeds the self in relations of exchange, where private information becomes a form of currency, thus capturing the parlor's ethos of "sentimental materialism"—the erasure of boundaries between persons and objects. The domestic novel's realism, Merish adds, its detailed descriptions of settings and objects, likewise reflects this ethos, the notion that consumer objects are "endowed with psychological or characterological import."[61]

Habermas argues that, just as the "living room and salon were under the same roof; and just as the privacy of the one was oriented toward the public nature of the other, and as the subjectivity of the privatized individual was related from the very start to publicity, so both were conjoined in literature that had become 'fiction.' "[62] The rise of fiction out of letters, diaries, and other, more private, modes of expression, he claims, signals the way in which the private individual, from his inception, performed his interiority in front of an audience, and did so in writing.

But Habermas's argument tends to disregard gender. At least in the antebellum northern United States, the public/private division within the home, as well as the public/private division in the conception of the self, was clearly and insistently gendered. Just as the parlor was associated with femininity, so was the mode of writing that performed interiority in front of an audience most meaningfully linked to women's domestic writing. The domestic novel, I mean to say, recasts Goffman's theatrical metaphors in narrative terms. We have discussed parlor femininity as implanted by performance and grounded in materiality, as existing as a front and in front of an external other, as not allowed to occupy backstage areas of invisibility and relief from inspection, or, at most, as occupying "dead" private space. As I will discuss more fully in the next chapters, the domestic novel both grasped and promoted this formation by designing characters whose interiority was fully conspicuous, objectified, and exchangeable, and by promoting a mode of writing that harbored few or no backstage areas "behind" the narrative façade, no regions of unlit thoughts, implied feelings, elisions in meaning, or narrative silences. This is in marked contrast to the mode of writing developed concurrently by writers who defined themselves in competition with the domestic tradition and in relation to another, more private, region of the domestic interior.

The Study: Making and Unmaking the Self

Across the hall, the study stood as a kind of mirror image of the parlor, in both a complementary and an oppositional relationship to it. While the parlor delineated a space of sociability, intimacy, and display, the governing principles of the study were privacy, seclusion, and restraint. Looking back at Renaissance domestic architecture, Mark Wigley argues that, as "privacy *within* the house developed beyond the privacy of the house, . . . [t]he first truly private space was the man's study . . . which no one else enters, an intellectual space beyond that of sexuality." As the space of "immaterial knowledge," antithetical to woman's spaces of "material masks," Wigley points out, the first study was "the true center of the house" and marked "the internal limit to the woman's authority." Originally, this masculine enclave helped consolidate man's power over the household because it functioned as a storage space for the family secrets—financial or genealogical records, for example—now barred from the inspection of anyone but the paterfamilias. These secrets, Wigley explains, were "not just stored in this space. They [were] literally produced there. The private space is the space of private writing. It makes available the new literary form of the memoir which began as a record and consolidation of the family but increasingly became a celebration of the private individual."[63]

This genealogy of the study allows us to trace a shift that accompanied its appearance as a fixture in the middle-class home: increasingly sealed off from the interference of women, children, and servants, it no longer symbolized simply patriarchal control but also withdrawal from the family into a private, sealed-off, interiorized selfhood. The study was indeed the birthplace of the liberal individual, and his most cherished sanctum. But, as I will explain below, the study functioned not only as the site of his self-fashioning, as Wigley would have it, but also as an opportunity for self-*forgetting*. As Emerson explains, it was "a matter of vital importance to all book reading & book writing men, to be at night the autocrat of a chamber be it ever so small—6 feet by 6—wherein to dream, write, & declaim alone."[64] Writing and reverie: the weaving and unweaving of narratives of the self.

Just as the parlor did not merely reflect but helped implant the attributes of True Womanhood, so, too, did the design of the study help naturalize rather than merely express the traits of the gentleman. Downing explained to his readers that "there is no portion of the house" that "to a man fond of . . . good books, is more peculiarly the sanctum or own room than the library."[65] If the parlor was a sort of busy museum, in which the family's various valuables were cheerfully displayed, the study, according to architects, was to "be quiet, and comparatively grave in color. Some shade of fawn or neutral tint for the walls, the furniture of dark oak, or wood like the book-cases, and the carpet selected so as to accord with the severe and quiet tone of the walls and furniture."[66] If the parlor spoke loudly of social status, the study was designed for reservedness, for hiding rather than displaying, for severity rather than mirth. The study's ornamentation, architects prescribed, was to follow the Victorian "muscular" style, a style that, in its classical or Gothic variations, conveyed through austerity the gentlemanly ethos of denial of sensual pleasures, of restraint, and stern intellectualism.[67] If the parlor was sociopetal, the study was *sociofugal,* "as the *matériel* from whence it dispenses enjoyment is within itself," as Downing put it.[68] While the parlor was installed to serve as the house's front, the study was often pushed to the rear of the main floor (*Atlantic* even advised men to locate the study in the attic), "thus having always *perfect seclusion,* with a cool and shady retreat," as architect Gervase Wheeler advised his readers.[69] In Leslie's "Mr. and Mrs. Woodbridge," the space claimed by the husband for his library is "a narrow room in the back-building" with "short windows, a low ceiling," and "in every respect very plainly finished."[70] To strengthen its conception as the realm of personal autonomy, privacy, and solitude, architects often opened a separate doorway to the outside from the study. A gentleman of "professional occupation or literary taste" could come and go as he pleased, without having his movements monitored by the other members of the household.[71]

So designed, the study captured the bifurcated existence of the middle-class man. The economic processes that attended the rise of the middle class—the extraction of the modes of production from the private sphere coupled with the ostensible withdrawal of middle-class women's labor from the marketplace—meant that, if bourgeois women's lives were largely restricted to the limited spaces of the private sphere (at least in prescriptive terms), men's lives were now emphatically divided between work and leisure, their subjectivity, between public and private modalities. We have seen that for bourgeois women private space *was* the performance stage; for men, however, private space promised an escape from the performativity of their public, social, and even familial roles. The description of the home as a "retreat" was thus meaningful first and foremost for men. Walter Benjamin writes that, "for the private person, living space becomes, for the first time, antithetical to the place of work. The former is constituted by the interior; the office is its complement. The private person who squares his accounts with reality in his office demands that the interior be maintained in his illusions. This need is all the more pressing since he has no intention of extending his commercial considerations into social ones. In shaping his private environment he represses both."[72] For Benjamin, the nineteenth-century domestic interior allowed men to cultivate illusions of a separate interiority by repressing the forces of production and the social world. As we have seen, Habermas argues that the bourgeois individual's notion of a separate interiority depended on the social and economic realms but also on the disavowal of its dependence on these realms. To the extent that those realms were perceived as performative, and hence artificial, so was the home, and the study especially, designed to provide a retreat from them and into a fantasy land of authentic selfhood. In that space, the professional man could still be, in Emerson's words, an "autocrat"; he could indulge in concealed aspects of his being and imagine himself rid of social masks and the need to perform endlessly. As *Godey's Lady's Book* explained to its readers in 1841, in the private interior "a man shrinks to his natural dimensions, and throws aside the ornaments or disguises which he feels, in privacy, to be useless incumbrances, and to lose all effect when they become familiar."[73]

We have, of course, become suspicious of the notion, so definitive of liberal individualism, that in the privacy of the home "man shrinks to his natural dimensions," that he somehow becomes free to indulge in his true self, unconstrained by social demands. Michel Foucault's early work on discipline has long instructed us to question the possibility of such backstage spaces of relief from surveillance, social policing, and the need to perform. For example, Francis Barker (like Wigley) follows Foucault in theorizing the connection between the creation of masculine spaces within the home, the rise of the genre of the memoir, and the invention of bourgeois subjectivity, to argue that all three newly formed private spaces (study, memoir, self) are in fact not marked by autonomy but by public restriction, specifically, by the disavowal of sexuality and the body.[74] That the study can be read as a site of performance and repression rather than of liberation and authenticity is indeed evident in its design. In some sense, the study's décor was no less theatrical or display oriented than the parlor's: its heavy shelves, gilded book-covers, and ornamented desks bespoke of class status as loudly as did the parlor's various knickknacks, and its grave tones, neutral tints, and "quiet severity" were meant to evince the rigorous self-discipline and denial of sensuality of its gentleman inmate. Its very description as an intellectual space of masculine *restraint*, where certain activities, but not others, take place, where certain books are read but others are excluded, where certain thoughts are written but others remain unsaid, all work against the spiritual and intellectual autonomy that Victorian architects and writers frequently associated with that space. Indeed, this is where Goffman's binary opposition of "front" and "backstage" regions seems untenable. Given Goffman's intuition that we perform even when we are alone, that social performance has an audience not only in an external other but also in the self (as we have seen in the case of women's "dead" private spaces), is there a sense in which the solitary study as backstage is conceptually different from the parlor as the front? If Foucault is correct that the modern subject is constituted by self-discipline, is there any force to the liberal distinction between private and social/public spaces?

As I discussed more fully in the Introduction, however, to entirely collapse this distinction is to risk excluding some important considerations. In particular, it is to overlook the possibility, raised by some current theories that revise Foucauldian orthodoxy, that liberal, self-policed subjectivity nonetheless accommodates residues left over by the inscription of power. While such theories do not accept that there is a "natural" or "true" self that *precedes* the processes of social discipline and performance, they do describe residues of the self continuously left over by these processes. Judith Butler's work combining Foucauldian and Freudian frameworks suggests that the process of subjectification is never complete; it always leaves behind some inassimilable remainder, the psychic stuff that is left over in the process of molding the self into its normative shape.[75] I propose that we read the middle-class, masculine private space as designed both for the processes of disciplined subjectification and for the accommodation of this psychic debris. While it would be wrong to deny Barker's argument that the ethos of restraint, silence, and immateriality that formed the study as a distinct space signals the repression of the body and its illicit pleasures, this disembodiment can also be viewed, as Benjamin's remarks suggest, as a form of pleasure in itself: the pleasure of *escaping* embodiment, of *withholding* articulation, of *refraining* from performance. While, as Wigley argues, the study is the site of self-fashioning through reading and writing, it is also the site of *dis*integration, of relief from the demand to discipline the self. It is the place where one can passively sink into daydream and reverie, the inner zones that do not necessarily conform to or support one's performed persona, where one can escape from the active orientation of one's life. From Emerson to Gaston Bachelard (whose motto was "the house shelters day-dreaming, the house protects the dreamer, the house allows one to dream in peace"),[76] the study is conceived as a space designed for indulging aspects of one's being that are beyond the limits of discipline, performance, and the linear narratives of self-fashioning.

Given the study's function of sheltering the residues of the process of subjectification, it is little wonder that the voices that described the home to men emphasized a few key terms such as "privacy," "solitude," and "inviolability," rather than "sociability," "intimacy," or "sentiment," the key terms in women's literature. John Ware, a prominent mid-century writer, explained that the main principle regarding the home that "should be thought of is *seclusion*. The home ought not to be open to the casual eye, or the secrets of it liable to the prying or the propinquity of neighbors. It ought to stand apart, neither subject to overlooking or overhearing. . . . The house should be within an enclosure sacred to it." Ware reinforced this point with etymology: "it is a curious fact that the word *home*, in its derivations, signifies to enclose. A home is an enclosure, a secret, separate place,—a place shut in from, guarded against, the whole world outside." To the house, he explained, "privacy is absolutely essential"; the presence of an outsider "breaks up much of the peculiar life of home, interrupts its free and steady flow." In short, he wrote, "not as a matter of pride or mere feeling, but as a matter of principle, I would not occupy a house where I was not or could not be alone."[77]

John Ruskin, who had more influence on American architecture, perhaps, than any American architect, advocated the building of homes precisely on these conceptual foundations. Domestic architecture should convey, he wrote (in a passage I cite earlier), the idea of the home as "the place of peace; the shelter, not only from all injury, but from all terror, doubt and division. . . . so far as the anxieties of the outer life penetrate into it, and the inconsistently-minded, unloved, or hostile society of the outer world is allowed by either husband or wife to cross the threshold it ceases to be a home."[78] Ware's and Ruskin's unswerving insistence on the seclusion, enclosure, and secrecy of the home, coupled with their wariness of any penetration or intrusion, capture what was now a distinctly masculine vision of the home as man's fragile fortress against the assaults of an exterior, coercive world.

Ware's seemingly uncomplicated proclamation that he "would not occupy a house where [he] was not or could not be alone" hints that the home was understood to harbor internal threats as well. The desire to be let alone in one's home, that is, profoundly clashed with the home's function as the sphere of love, intimacy, and familial bonds. Recall, for instance, Emerson's famous resolve to "shun father and mother and wife and brother when my genius calls me."[79] In fact, as Robin Evans argues, the architectural blueprint that designated spatial pockets of privacy in the home had by the same move created "a territorial envelope in which we . . . shroud our bodies against the assaults of intimacy." Within a segregated spatial plan, the self becomes "not just at risk in the presence of others, but actually disfigured by them." Privacy, according

to Evans, is the source of a modern sense of intimacy as a form of violence: if the self is metaphorized as an enclosed shelter, then any crossing of its boundaries becomes a form of attack or transgression, a threat
of exposure.[80]

The study, then, and the defensive conception of the home of which
it was the purest expression, helped crystallize the ideal of an inviolable
but perpetually vulnerable masculinity, an ideal that also regarded intimacy as the weakening of its boundaries and the potential exposure of
backstage aspects that threatened its very integrity and consistency. If, as
Jennifer Nedelsky suggests, the notion of the self as an impermeable,
bounded space was central to white, upper-class American masculinity
from the republic's early decades and was strengthened by such over-
wrought maxims as "A man's home is his castle," this notion had "fear,
anger, and resentment built into it," since any gesture of intimacy, sociability, or collectivity could be construed as a potential violation, a threat
to one's control and autonomy.[81]

All this allows us to connect the study not with the domestic novel, the
genre we have previously relegated to the parlor, and not only, as Wigley
and Barker suggest, with the memoir or diary (traditionally the genres
of self-discipline and self-fashioning) but also with antebellum romance.
Looking at a later period in American literature, Sarah Luria makes a
similar point. She suggests that Henry James's and Edith Wharton's well-
known love for the private spaces of reading and writing should be
linked to their "restrained" mode of literary composition and to their famous disdain for the (parlor) culture of conspicuous consumption and
its attendant literary aesthetics.[82] But this link applies with greater force
to writers of the American Renaissance. I mentioned in the previous section that the shape of the domestic novel can be traced to the sociopetence and conspicuity of the parlor, its realistic, confessional form to a
view of the self as fully externalized and made ready for intimate exchange. American romance, with its constitutive features—ambiguity,
elusive symbolism, and multiplicity of meanings—relates instead to what
I will discuss in the next chapters as a non-narrative form of privacy, that
way of imagining the self as harboring an incommunicable, fundamen-
tally impenetrable, residue.

The explicit link between non-narrative privacy, the study, and romance was made in several places in the traditional antebellum canon,
most frequently in Hawthorne's prefaces to his tales and romances.
Compare, for example, his preface to *Mosses from an Old Manse* with
Fern's "Mother's Room." Like that of Fern's sketch, the purpose of
Hawthorne's preface is to walk the reader into private space; indeed, its
subtitle promises that in it "the author makes the reader acquainted
with his abode."[83] But whereas for Fern the center of the abode is the

room of the mother, for Hawthorne its most important space is "in the rear of the house, the most delightful little nook of a study that ever offered its snug seclusion to a scholar" (p. 1124). And whereas Fern's domestic space is filled with concrete, itemized objects that capture and promote its emotional and spiritual effects, Hawthorne's study is sparsely decorated and barely described. As in Ware's and Ruskin's prescriptions for the ideal house, the Old Manse "had not quite the aspect of belonging to the material world," and its most important features were "remote[ness]," "dim[ness]," "retirement," "seclusion," and "privacy" (p. 1123); "all the artifice and conventionalism of life was but an impalpable thinness upon its surface," Hawthorne explains, and "the depth below was none the worse for it" (p. 1142). Not surprisingly, then, the whole preface is a prolonged exercise in deferral. After promising at the outset to "acquaint the reader" with the depths of the house, that is, with his study, Hawthorne makes detour after detour to avoid letting us into its hallowed precincts. He walks us out to the neighboring river and to the surrounding meadow, through the orchard and the garden, all the while apologizing for his "digressions," for the reader's "despair of finding his way back into the Old Manse" (p. 1133). After thirty pages of such digressions, we realize that we will never gain access to Hawthorne's interior space: "Has the reader gone wandering, hand in hand with me, through the inner passages of my being, and have we groped together into all its chambers, and examined their treasures or their rubbish?" Hawthorne confirms, "Not so. We have been standing on the green sward, but just within the cavern's mouth, where the common sunshine is free to penetrate, and where every footstep is therefore free to come. I have appealed to no sentiment or sensibilities, save such as are diffused among us all. So far as I am a man of really individual attributes, I veil my face" (p. 1143). To have introduced the reader into the study would have been to enter Hawthorne's innermost spaces, where the scraps (both "treasure" and "rubbish") of his identity are buried. It would have been, moreover, to push its contents to the narrative surface, to force it to the "cavern's mouth," and thus to conventionalize it, just as Fern's description of "Mother's Room" empties out the interiority of its occupant. The preface thus ends where it begins: with an invitation for the reader to enter Hawthorne's study, but only by reading the tales that follow; we now understand that this invitation is, in fact, the liberal individual's polite "Do not enter" sign.

The annals of the antebellum romance feature again and again the metaphor that links enclaves of privacy within the home to privileged masculine subjectivity as well as anxiety about the fragility of a subjectivity so construed, an anxiety directed first and foremost against the domestic woman. Whether by imagining scenes of violence against the domestic woman or by pretending she does not exist, writers in the romantic tradition dramatize the conflict between the ideal of privacy, associated with masculine interiority, and the ideal of intimacy, associated with women's domestic presence. From Poe's "Ligeia," in which the eponymous heroine embodies the entrance of intimacy and sexuality into the narrator's study and is transformed in his murderous fantasies into a haunting ghost, to Hawthorne's "The Birth Mark," in which a wife is killed after crossing the internal boundary into her husband's sanctum sanctorum, masculine space signifies irreducible individuality and solitude, private reverie and caprice, and the plot dramatizes the catastrophic results of this space's invasion by women, who stand for the opposite principles of intimacy, sexuality, and materiality. (In the comparatively peaceful preface to *Mosses*, nothing indicates that Hawthorne shared the Old Manse with his wife, Sophia.)[84]

Moreover, what these stories arguably share as their background is the reconfiguration of the husband's role within an emergent, more democratic marital model. No longer the patriarch that his forefathers were, the liberal individual desires to shun the intimacies of wife and family in his pursuit of privacy but thereby also relinquishes the former masculine prerogative of centralizing and regulating every aspect of domestic life. The "autocrat of the study," that is, replaces the monarch of the "little commonwealth." While the study bespoke the masculine prerogative of privacy, it also signified a decided *loss* of masculine power. Mrs. Woodbridge, to return to a previous example, responds to her husband's desire to plan the home's interior by condemning "the man that meddles with house affairs, and undertakes to advise his wife about her domestic concerns; instead of sticking to his store or his office . . . as all men ought."[85] But if the husband now abandoned his former domestic responsibilities, if the domestic interior became truly divided into symmetrical spaces and into equal (if opposing) dominions, what was to keep the home together? How was the domestic sphere to maintain its cohesion, order, and idealized harmony if it was so conspicuously split between interests and outlooks? Such questions entered not only the works of domestic writers but also right into the aesthetic vocabulary of domestic architecture.

Asymmetrical Symmetries

I have argued thus far that antebellum domestic architecture, alongside other discourses such as literature, captured the way in which the contradictions inherent in the emergent middle-class system of values were carefully managed by the segregation and gendering of conflicting desires and competing subjective economies. But this marriage of oppositions

within the middle-class interior, I have also suggested, was only seemingly equal. As we have seen, in pedagogical novels the values of liberal
individualism—privacy, restraint, relief from observability—ultimately
overrode those associated with domesticity—consumption, conspicuity,
intimate self-revelation. Parlor femininity was at once construed as a crucial and equal component of the middle class interior and as a threat to
its supraordinate emphasis on privacy. What initially appeared as a loss
of patriarchal power in favor of a more balanced marital structure, that
is, turned out to be a recasting of this power under different terms,
thereby providing a version of what Carole Pateman calls "liberal patri-
archalism."[86] To close this chapter, I wish to look more closely at one of
the most popular domestic architecture books in the antebellum United
States, Downing's *The Architecture of Country Houses*, in order to trace the
same problematic logic within the language of domestic architecture,
where an anxiety about insurgent domestic femininity was often both
implied and contained in the language of spatial aesthetics.

Recall Lefebvre's suggestion that architects, like other official practitioners of space, operate in the domain of "representations of space,"
or space as "conceived." What they work with is a set of abstract spatial
ideals that may *seem* removed from social relations but in fact "also play a
part in social and political practice."[87] The seemingly abstract aesthetic
ideals prescribed by antebellum domestic architects, that is, can be interpreted as addressing the tense multivalence of the middle-class interior. What pattern books sometimes provided, through the language of
spatial aesthetics, was moral justification for masculine dominance. In
The Architecture of Country Houses, Downing lists the various aesthetic
ideals that ensure the success of any house design. He first prescribes
"proportion," or "that nice relation of all the parts to each other and to
the whole, which gives to that whole the stamp of the best, most suitable,
and perfect form." He then highlights "symmetry," or the "balance of
opposite parts necessary to form an agreeable whole." "In architecture,"
he explains, symmetry "is the arrangement on each side of a centre, of
two parts that balance each other, and that do not make a whole without
this centre." Next, Downing calls for "Harmony," or "an agreement
made in the midst of the variety of forms, sounds, or colors, by some
one feeling which pervades the whole, and brings all the varied parts
into an agreeable relation with each other . . . under the influence of its
magical power for unison." Finally, he insists on "Unity," which is "the
predominance of one single feeling, one soul, one mind in every portion, so that, whether of the simplest or the most complicated form, the
same spirit is recognised throughout the whole."[88] Seemingly diverse,
these four principles in fact reiterate a single idea. What they all have in
common is the *management of difference*: in each instance, Downing strives

for the subsumptions of multiplicity—"parts," "opposite parts," "variety," and so on—under singularity—the "magical power" of the "agreeable whole," the "centre," or "unity," or, in more anthropomorphic terms, the "one single feeling, one soul, one mind" of the house. When we consider that for domestic architects such as Downing the "feeling," "soul," or "mind" that the house conveys are always those of its *owner*, this subsumption of multiplicity can be read as an allegory of the desire to contain a diversity of wills under the husband's or father's singular will.

Elsewhere, Downing's language conveys a more palpable concern with the home's potentially dangerous internal divisions. In his discussion of structure versus ornamentation in the house's design, he warns his readers to use the latter with discretion; ornamentation can get out of hand, he explains, ceasing to be bound by the dictates of the house's structure: "If this connexion does not appear the whole is vicious . . . if the first form does not seem in accordance with its accessories; and if, in short, it is perceived that two wills, without harmonizing together, have operated in the execution of the work" (p. 378), the house is an aesthetic failure. Once again, Downing's rhetoric seeps outside the bounds of aesthetics and into the moral and social domains. Considering that ornamentation was considered the "feminine" aspect of the house and the province of the house's mistress, what lies under Downing's words is the notion that the "harmony" of the home depends on the subordination of her desires to those of the house's "backbone," her husband. The moralist streak in Downing's aesthetics is most evident in the excessive language he employs to describe what happens when the principles of "harmony" are not followed. In such cases, the results are disastrous; indeed, they "shock a tasteful and consistent mind": the house in its "tasteless diversity and discord" becomes not merely "odd" or "grotesque" but veritably "wearisome and perplexing," "confus[ing]," even "painful and destructive" (pp. 16–18).

But how are such dangers to be avoided? Downing follows a long tradition in offering two aesthetic models: the Picturesque and the Beautiful. The Picturesque, he explains, is a style that is "manifested with something of rudeness, violence, or difficulty." Picturesque domestic architecture conveys a "force of expression" that "grows out of strong character in the inhabitant" (by which, once again, Downing means the proprietor) and that imposes itself on all other elements of the structure. The Beautiful, by contrast, gently conveys both "the perfect balance between a beautiful idea and the material form in which it is conveyed to the eye" and "an embodiment in which the idea triumphs over the material and brings it into perfect subjection—we might almost say, of repose." The Beautiful, in other words, captures the problematic logic of the divided plot in its full extent: it both produces an equilibrium between (masculine) intellect and (feminine) materiality and strives toward the "perfect subjection" of the latter to the former under the regime of privacy, or "repose." What Downing's discussion implicitly offers, then, is two models of domestic management: the one, reminiscent of traditional patriarchy, asserts itself despotically on all other components of the household; the second, linkable with the rise of the democratic household, promotes a gentle imposition of power under the guise of equality. While the former has certain advantages, Downing concludes, the latter is clearly to be favored in the design of private homes, just as "the beauty and symmetry of Washington is more satisfactory than the greater power and lesser balance of Napoleon" (pp. 28–29).

Downing's aesthetic criteria, then, conceal a theory of power; they weave a moral plot similar to that of prescriptive novels such as Hale's or Leslie's, a plot that promotes gender symmetry only to have the Washingtonian head of the household override it in the name of privacy. Indeed, the connection between domestic architecture and popular literature is one that architects themselves recognized: "we may safely carry out this illustration," writes Downing, "and say that the temples and cathedrals are the orations and epic poems, the dwelling-houses the familiar epistles or conversations of the particular style."[89] This connection was also recognized by major antebellum writers like Nathaniel Hawthorne, Herman Melville, and Harriet Beecher Stowe, who wrote fiction that explicitly thematized the division of the domestic interior and explored its psychological manifestations. In future decades, this connection was elaborated on in the realm of psychoanalysis, which occasionally used the metaphors of domestic space to develop theories of the psyche as inherently divided yet somehow whole. If in this chapter we have focused mostly on domestic space as "conceived" by architecture, in the next we will turn to space as "lived," as linked, that is, to subjective interiority by both literature and psychoanalysis.

Chapter 2

Dream Houses: Divided Interiority in Three Antebellum Short Stories

He thought this particular story was his private business. Analytic treatment does not, of course, recognize any such right of asylum.

—*Sigmund Freud*

It is joy to be hidden but disaster not to be found.

—*D. W. Winnicott* [1]

In his autobiographical *Memories, Dreams, Reflections*, Carl Gustav Jung relates that in 1909, during a trip to America on which he accompanied Sigmund Freud, he subjected to his mentor's analysis a particularly lucid dream. "I was in a house I did not know," the dream went, "which had two stories. This was 'my house.' I found myself in the upper story, where there was a kind of salon furnished with fine old pieces in rococo style. On the walls hung a number of precious old paintings. I wondered that this should be my house, and thought, 'Not bad.' But then it occurred to me that I did not know what the lower floor looked like." [2] He then recalls descending through a series of rooms and cellars that boast an increasingly antiquated decor, finally reaching an underground cave. Jung writes, "It was plain to me that the house represented a kind of image of the psyche," where "consciousness was represented by the salon" and each subsequent floor represented "successive layers of consciousness" (pp. 160–61).

But as plain as this seemed to Jung, Freud's interpretation was different. Freud was intrigued by the dream; he, too, after all, regarded domestic architecture as an archsymbol of the psyche, explaining at one time that in dreams "the one typical—that is regular—representation of the human figure as a whole is that of a *house*." [3] But he was convinced that in this particular instance Jung's dream expressed a latent death wish represented by the subterranean cave. He tried to force this interpretation on his younger colleague, to the point where the latter felt he needed to betray himself to appease his elder. It did not help that Freud, fearing to "risk [his] authority," had previously refused to submit his own dreams to Jung's analysis (p. 158). This incident marked the beginning of a rift between the two psychoanalysts, as Jung began openly to object to some of Freud's views, particularly his view of the unconscious as "maliciously" withholding meaning from consciousness. Jung believed instead that it was the unconscious that had to ward off the assaults of consciousness and its "tricks" (pp. 161–62).

When the dream of the house recurred, long after his trip with Freud, Jung used it to elaborate on his own understanding of the psyche's structure. In this more recent dream, the house's vertical layering was replaced by a horizontal divide. This time he saw that

> beside my house stood another, that is to say, another wing or annex, which was strange to me. . . . I discovered there a wonderful library, dating largely from the sixteenth and seventeenth centuries. Large fat folio volumes bound in pigskin stood along the walls. Among them were a number of books embellished with copper engravings of a strange character, and illustrations containing curious symbols such as I had never seen before. . . . The unknown wing of the house was a part of my personality, an aspect of myself; it represented something that belonged to me but of which I was not yet conscious. . . . Some fifteen years later I had assembled a library very like the one in the dream. (P. 202)

The composite house of Jung's dreams is thus divided between a main edifice, featuring an elegant salon, and an annex that contains a mysterious library, a division that comes to evince for Jung the fundamental division of the psyche. The salon of the first dream symbolizes the self's surface, its "rococo" embellishments, the mostly conscious, accessible aspect of the self that Jung elsewhere calls the "persona" and links with social masks and performativity. Jung does not instantaneously "recognize himself" in this room and "wonder[s] that this should be [his] house," but he is pleased with the plush richness of its display. The library, by contrast, with its store of cryptic texts and undecipherable knowledge, represents the unconscious, the hidden aspect of the self to the exploration of which Jung would devote his career.

Jung's dream house thus offers a clear example of how the domestic blueprint that attended the rise of the bourgeoisie (in continental Europe, much as in England and the United States) entered the discourse of psychology and shaped the way it imagined psychic interiority. Even without venturing into Jung's famous theories about the androgyny of the self, it is clear that the divided psyche that he depicts is patterned on the gendering of the interior that we explored in detail in Chapter 1. That actual salons were the bourgeois woman's realm of sociability, materiality, and conspicuity led Jung to link this space with the performative, normative, potentially deceptive aspect of the self. That domestic libraries typically constituted a masculine preserve of privacy and relief from social discipline led to their association with the invisible, uncharted unconscious. It is also clear that Jung thereby reaffirmed a certain hierarchy: the most profound psychic truths, after all, will be found in the masculine (and only seemingly supplementary) "annex" of solitude, concealed knowledge, and mysterious meanings.

When Jung eventually set out, near lake Zurich, to build Bollingen, his dream house actualized in stone, he first designed a round main house intended for familial and social intimacies, which revolved around what he described as a "maternal hearth." He then added a narrower towering annex as his private retreat, a locked space where, as he put it, "I could exist for myself alone" and that nobody else was allowed to enter. On his wife's death, he reported feeling an inner obligation to "become what I myself am"; he "could no longer hide . . . behind the 'maternal' and 'spiritual' " structures and added an upper story that bridged both parts of the house and that "represent[ed] myself or my ego-personality." When Jung's house was completed, after years of building and adding, planning and replanning, he finally felt that "all parts fitted together and that a meaningful form had resulted: a symbol for psychic wholeness" (pp. 223–25). The sharply divided and explicitly gendered architecture of the earlier Bollingen was, in the final version, combined into a "harmonious" whole, its "feminine" part subsumed within the structure so as to disarm challenges to the autonomous, mature masculine ego.

What Gaston Bachelard would call Jung's *maison onirique* thus offers a particularly clear instance of the way psychoanalysis developed its structures in reference to domestic architecture, or, as Bachelard puts it, the way "the house image would appear to have become the topography of our intimate being." In his now-classic *The Poetics of Space*, Bachelard argues that domestic architecture does not merely provide a symbol for psychic interiority but also actively shapes this interiority and allows us access into it. "Our soul is an abode," he writes, "and by remembering 'houses' and 'rooms,' we learn to 'abide' within ourselves. . . . the house images move in both directions: they are in us as much as we are in them." For Bachelard, domestic space leaves such an indelible mark on our psychic constitution, it is such a direct and frequent participant in our narratives of interiority, that to explore the inner self we must undergo "topoanalysis" as well as psychoanalysis, to penetrate our earliest relations with our physical homes. The best place from which to launch such an exploration, he suggests, is literature: it is in the realm of poetics that the symbiosis between the home and the soul is most forcefully and poignantly forged.[4]

In this chapter I will follow Bachelard's lead in linking domestic space, psychic interiority, and literary texts. But unlike Bachelard, who

treats the domestic interior as if it transcends the specificities of historical time and social configurations, I will attempt to show that the psychic
structure developed by psychoanalysis extends from what I call the "divided plots" of the Victorian middle class. As the example of Jung already suggests, the house that bestows shape on our inner being is itself
shaped by social determinants such as class and gender. In the first part
of the chapter, I will examine two psychoanalytic theories that imagine a
divided psyche along the lines of the divided private sphere of the middle class. While these two models converge in imagining (as Jung did)
the psyche as split into realms of privacy and sociability, they contrast in
their valuation of this division. For Freud (at least, the Freud of "Resistance and Repression" and "The 'Uncanny' "), the realm of privacy connotes deprivation, absence, and horror. For Winnicott, a more traditional
liberal thinker, it connotes well-being and plenitude. For both theorists,
the split interior also raises questions of power and privilege. Jung's anecdote of his altercation with Freud suggested that to imagine a part of
the self as sealed off is also to claim power by withholding it from others
(Freud's refusal to submit his dreams to Jung's analysis) as well as to risk
the painful indignation of its invasion by the other, an invasion that is always a distortion (Jung's mortification about Freud's misreading of his
dream).

With that in mind, I will return, in the second part of the chapter, to
the antebellum northeastern United States, to read three short stories
by Hawthorne, Melville, and Stowe. My reading of "Wakefield," "I and
My Chimney," and "The Ravages of a Carpet" will link the psychic architecture elaborated on by psychoanalysis to its earlier versions in mid-
nineteenth-century fiction. These three stories share a common project:
to propel into narrative motion the fixed spaces of the newly divided
bourgeois private sphere and to bring to the forefront the gendered
tensions inherent in the middle-class formation of interiority, those sour
spots of friction hidden by the hegemonic, normalizing vocabulary of
domestic "harmony." More specifically, by focusing on the plot of marital disputes over domestic territory, all three writers comment on liberal
individualism's privileging of a sealed, masculine space within the home
and, more crucially, within the mind and the text, and on the conflicts
produced by this masculine privilege in familial and intimate life. All
three texts stage a conflict, in later decades theorized in the writing
of Freud and Winnicott, between a (masculine) ethos of privacy and a
(feminine) counterethos of exposure. All three, moreover, tell their
story from the perspective of the husband who fights for the protection
of his privacy and power against a female insurgency.

But they do so from widely divergent perspectives and using widely divergent narrative codes: Hawthorne and Melville work through these
conflicts using the style of romance; Stowe uses the style of domestic

fiction. Romanticism and sentimentalism, I will show, are exposed in these stories to be neither mutually exclusive nor ideologically akin, but overlapping within and competing over the same conceptual—psychic and domestic—space. While Hawthorne and Melville join the husbands/narrators of their stories in claiming that the ethos of privacy overrides all other aspects of personal life and use the aesthetic tools of romance to convey this, Stowe uses the conventions of domestic fiction to undermine that ethos and to imagine, in the spirit of the parlor woman, a different kind of interiority, one defined by intimate revelation rather than concealment. Stowe mimics the voice of Hawthorne's and Melville's husbands/narrators, but in mimicking that masculine voice she also seeks to reform, even feminize, it.

In analyzing the two competing models of interiority that emerge from these texts, my point would not be to read antebellum fiction *through* psychoanalysis but to use the vocabulary of psychoanalysis to suggest that in mid-nineteenth-century fiction lies the foundation for that psychic architecture that still dominates thinking about our mental makeup. As Joel Pfister so powerfully argues in *The Production of Personal Life*, in the writing of Hawthorne and his contemporaries we may find "the emergence of psychological codes . . . that are beginning to construct middle-class readers' assumptions about interiority," and our attention should turn "to examining the role that [antebellum] fiction played in the production of the 'psychological' and to specifying the cultural conditions for its emergence."[5] My argument will go farther in this direction to suggest not only that writers like Hawthorne, Melville, and Stowe paved the way for the contemporary understanding of interiority but also that this understanding is often played out, but not sufficiently historicized, in current literary criticism. That is, we read antebellum fiction through the lens of the liberal divided interior, often without considering that this divided interior was produced by the very fiction that is our object of analysis.

Freud: Privacy as Deprivation

Even as he recounted the story of his disillusionment with Freud, Jung was careful to credit his former mentor with expounding on what he called psychoanalysis's most fundamental insight: "that psychic life has two poles" (p. 169). Freud, like Jung, sometimes chose to imagine this polarity in architectural terms. One particularly elaborate example appears in "Resistance and Repression" when Freud urges us to

compare the system of the unconscious to a large entrance hall, in which the mental impulses jostle one another like separate individuals. Adjoining this entrance hall there is a second, narrower, room—a kind of drawing-room—in which consciousness, too, resides. But on the threshold between these two rooms a watchman performs his function: he examines the different mental impulses, acts as a censor, and will not admit them into the drawing-room if they displease him. . . . If they have already pushed their way forward to the threshold and have been turned back by the watchman, then they are inadmissible to consciousness; we speak of them as repressed. But even the impulses which the watchman has allowed to cross the threshold are not on that account necessarily conscious as well; they can only become so if they succeed in catching the eye of consciousness. . . . We are therefore justified in calling this second room the system of the preconscious. . . . it is the same watchman whom we get to know as resistance when we try to lift the repression by means of the analytic treatment.[6]

Freud's interior blueprint, like Jung's, is split. In his version, too, the drawing room represents consciousness or, more accurately, "preconsciousness," since it includes both mental impulses that "succeed in catching the eye," thus entering fully into consciousness, and those that manage to enter that "space" but fail to get noticed. Freud imagines the preconscious, then, as a kind of a parody of the bourgeois parlor, where gregarious individuals gather to strive for conspicuity and distinction. But Freud's blueprint is also markedly different from Jung's. It does not allocate an inner space of repose to the unconscious, a solitary "annex" where the mysterious truths of one's deepest being are silently archived. Freud imagines the unconscious, instead, as a crowded and loud entrance hall, peopled with rowdy mental impulses that attempt to bypass the "watchman" of repression and to crash the party in the respectable drawing room. This metaphor helps us understand the claim that psychoanalysis "tells the story from the standpoint of consciousness" (in Roy Schafer's words).[7] Here it is preconsciousness that occupies the inner, privileged space of one's psychic topography, whereas the unconscious (that Freudian unconscious that Jung will describe, and dispute, as "malicious") is imagined as potentially *uncanny*, at once internal and alien, at once invasive and elusive of our conscious stabs at coherence, visibility, and meaning.

Indeed, Freud's more famous (if less explicit) analogy between domestic and psychic interiority appears in "The 'Uncanny' " (1919). What initially grabs his attention in this essay is precisely the link between the vocabulary of innerness and the vocabulary of domesticity. As one may recall, Freud launches his investigation of the uncanny (*unheimlich*) by burrowing in dictionaries for the meaning of its opposite, the "homelike" (*heimlich*). He finds that the word contains "two sets of ideas, which, without being contradictory, are yet very different."[8] The two denotative clusters of *heimlich*, as it turns out, reflect precisely what we have been describing as the split interiority of bourgeois domesticity. Like the middle-class home divided between realms of intimacy and realms of solitude, *heimlich* carries the meanings of "familial," "intimate, friendly comfortable," "familiar, friendly, intimate," "amicable," "unreserved," as well as the meaning of "[that which is] concealed, kept from sight, so that others do not get to know of or about it, withheld from others" (pp. 220–25). It is this duality enfolded within the vocabulary of domesticity—between what is familial and what is solitary, what is shared and what is withheld—that Freud then imposes on his description of psychic interiority. The psyche as home is grasped as divided between familiarity and visibility (the "drawing room" of [pre]consciousness), on the one hand, and estrangement, concealment, and reticence (the "entrance hall" of the unconscious), on the other. Thus, the *unheimlich*, that special brand of anxiety that interests Freud here, linguistically the opposite of *heimlich*, is really a principle endemic to its internal division: the uncanny is the recurring success of mental impulses, repressed in the process of maturation, in passing through the door that separates the entrance hall from the drawing room, in slipping by the watchman, as it were, and in entering, uninvited, the realm of familiarity, visibility, and consciousness.

Freud's oft-celebrated deconstruction of binaries here, the way the second meaning of *heimlich* ("concealed, kept from sight") merges with *unheimlich*, its seeming negation ("uncanny" in English etymology means "beyond knowledge"),[9] nevertheless neglects to highlight a significant residue of this merger. By infusing the states of concealment, invisibility, and reservedness with the feeling of horror (albeit an attractive and fascinating form of horror), Freud obscures the fact that those states have positive as well as insidious connotations. This requires a deliberate oversight by Freud, since the dictionaries he consults do indeed cite some of these positive connotations. One dictionary, for instance, associates in its examples the second meaning of *heimlich* with the sacred ("a holy, *heimlich* effect") and with liberty ("freedom is the whispered watchword of *heimlich* conspirators") (p. 224). When Freud merges the concealed with what we repress in the maturational process (and hence with anxiety and fear), he ignores a potential aura of positivity around the states of invisibility, solitude, and reticence. These states represent for Freud, first and foremost, danger, risk, since they are the most conducive for the "trespass" of the uncanny. As Adam Phillips puts it, for Freud, solitude means "the absence of the visible and absence of an object; and the risk, as in dreams, that innermost thoughts will come to light." In the Freudian account, the fear of solitude begins in early childhood, when it is produced by the keenly felt absence of the mother and by visitations of dangerous thoughts. The constitution of the child as a separate being thus entails a sense of lack, a failure of the holding environment, and an uncanny feeling of being radically other to oneself (two notions that Lacan will later underscore).[10] By adulthood, solitude comes to signify not only deprivation but also the risk of passively succumbing to this unfamiliar otherness, of relinquishing one's delusion of self-control, of letting one's guard (or watchman) down. Phillips points out that, "in [Freud's] work, as opposed to his life, there is as it were, a *repression* of solitude, of its theoretical elaboration."[11] Nowhere is this repression as evident, I would argue, as in the closing paragraph of "The 'Uncanny,' " where Freud asserts that, "concerning the factors of silence, solitude and darkness, we can only say that they are actually elements in the production of the infantile anxiety from which the majority of human beings have never become quite free" (p. 252). He blatantly refrains from elaborating on this assertion, thus leaving his masterly essay without a sense of closure. What he thereby evades is a fuller exploration of the states of privacy, an exploration that could uncover valences beyond anxiety, risk, or deprivation.

Freud's disavowal of privacy, evident in the absence of spaces of repose in his architecture of the psyche and in the evasion of privacy's potential positivity in "The 'Uncanny,' " is inseparable from the commitment (of some Freudian thinkers, if certainly not all) to the process of narrating the self. Schafer describes this telos, possibly the main objective of Freudian analysis, as the joint goal of the analyst and the analysand to increase the "coherence and significance" of the analysand's life story.[12] It is responsible for one of the stormiest dramas of Freudian thought, "present in every clinical encounter," namely, "the conflict between knowing what a life is and the sense that a life contains within it something that makes such knowing impossible."[13] On the one hand, such Freudian psychoanalysis will seek to cure by weaving a conscious, coherent, causal narrative out of the odd filaments of one's life. On the other hand, the unconscious will always be present as a force that threatens to sabotage this narrative, to undo its cohesion.

Freud elaborates on this drama in "Resistance and Repression" as he lays out his therapeutic methodology. In psychoanalysis, he explains, the analyst encourages the patient to bring forth whatever thoughts, feelings, or associations that come to mind at the moment of analysis, and to try to avoid, as much as possible, self-censorship. The patient must make visible, in particular, those thoughts and feelings that seem too "*disagreeable*," "*indiscreet*," "*unimportant*," or "*irrelevant*" (p. 287; emphasis in original); precisely those mental fragments, that is, that seem *not* to fit into the patient's own articulation, those elements that, to return to Goffman's metaphor, the patient wants to keep "backstage" because they interfere with the smooth operation of his or her "fronts." Freud explains that patients will forever try to resist the exposure of such fragments by reserving for themselves certain regions of the self by barring, through silence, the analyst's access to them. The patient typically "defend[s] himself with the argument that he thought this particular story was his private business," Freud explains, hastening to add that psychoanalytical treatment "does not, *of course*, recognize any such right to asylum" (p. 288; emphasis added). Since much Freudian analysis is committed to articulation, since its method is the exposure of the concealed splinters of interiority (even as it recognizes the ultimate impossibility of this project), the analyst can never allow the patient to claim a "right to asylum" as a way to hide these splinters. That which the patient thinks he or she can cherish as "private" represents the undefeatable enemy of consciousness and narrativity, whether an enemy in the form of an evasive fugitive or that of a trespassing saboteur.

Winnicott: Privacy as Plenitude

While for Freud the states of privacy—solitude, invisibility, and silence— are rife with anxiety because, from our early childhood, they are linked with deprivation (of the mother) and danger (of the return of the repressed), for Winnicott these states trigger a sense of plenitude and protection. Winnicott begins "The Capacity to Be Alone" (1958) by pointing out that classic psychoanalysis traditionally ignored the positive aspects of "aloneness" and its important role in emotional maturation. This positivity is rooted in a paradox, Winnicott explains: our adult capacity to be alone, a sign of our emotional well-being, has its basis in childhood, when, far from always signifying a lack, being alone often meant being in the reliable presence of the protective mother (or mother substitute or mother symbol). The child's initial capacity to be on his or her own grows in tandem with awareness of the mother's continued existence in the protective environment, despite her possible physical absence. This later develops into the more sophisticated adult capacity to be alone, when the protective environment had already been thoroughly introjected.

But why does Winnicott place such importance on this capacity in the first place? "It is only when alone (that is to say, in the presence of someone)," he explains, "that the infant can discover his own personal life. The pathological alternative is a *false life* built on reactions to external stimuli. When alone in the sense that I am using the term, and only when alone, the infant is able to do the equivalent of what in an adult would be called relaxing. *The infant is able to become unintegrated, to flounder, to be in a state in which there is no orientation*, to be able to exist for a time without being either a reactor to an external impingement or an active person with a direction of interest or movement."[14] Like Freud, Winnicott understands the state of solitude in terms of passivity, of relinquishing control, of momentarily forgoing the impulse to exist in response to external demands and to follow the linear orientation of one's life. But whereas for Freud solitude therefore becomes a terrifying risk, a door left ajar for the uncanny, Winnicott regards this risk as a reward. Since, in health, solitude implies, paradoxically, the continued presence of the protective object, it is a state in which we feel we can *afford* temporarily to "unintegrate," to lose ourselves and renounce, in passivity, the tight control of coherence (recall, for example, Harriet Beecher Stowe's desire for "a season of tranquil vegetation" that would offer her relief from the performance of domestic womanhood). Solitude thus makes available precisely that "asylum" the "right" to which Freud denies his patients. Or, as Phillips asks, what is Winnicott's belief in the continual, benign presence of the protective object if not the denial of the uncanny?[15]

In Winnicott's version of the divided psyche, silence joins solitude in demarcating for us that mental asylum we so desperately need. He claims in "Communicating and Not Communicating" (1963) that the value of communication should not be taken for granted. Whereas theorists typically underscore the importance of articulation and self-revelation, our right to "speak our minds," Winnicott instead stakes a claim "to the right *not* to communicate."[16] This right is asserted over and against what Winnicott describes as the potential *voraciousness* of communication. One of our most frightening fantasies, he explains, is not the fantasy of being consumed by the other but the fantasy of simply being found by the other, of being forced to enunciate that within the self which suffers no enunciation. Thus, while it is true that one part of us forever expresses the need to communicate itself externally, communication "easily becomes linked with some degree of false or compliant object-relating" (p. 184). Self-narration is always an externally geared performance (as Goffman might say) and hence is linked with the cultivation of what Winnicott calls a "false self," which lacks realness. Meanwhile, another part of us resists this need to communicate (perform, please, comply). Like children playing hide and seek, we both desire to be found and, with equal force, desire *not* to be found. It is this second desire that Winnicott associates with the "true self" and with "feeling real." "*Each individual is an isolate, permanently non-communicating, permanently unknown, in fact unfound,*" he explains in an often-cited passage:

At the centre of each person is an incommunicado element, and this is sacred and most worthy of preservation. I would say that the traumatic experiences that lead to the organization of primitive defences belong to the threat to the isolate core, the threat of its being found, altered, communicated with. . . . Rape, and being eaten by cannibals, these are mere bagatelles as compared with the violation of the self 's core, the alternation of the self 's central elements by communication seeping through the defences. For me this would be the sin against the self. We can understand the hatred people have of psycho-analysis which has penetrated a long way into the human personality, and which provides a threat to the human individual in his need to be secretly isolated. (p. 187; emphasis in original)

This belief in a "sacred" noncommunicable core the violation of which is a "sin," what Phillips calls Winnicott's "negative theology of the self," is where his divergence from Freudian orthodoxy becomes most apparent.

For Winnicott, traditional psychoanalysis can be experienced by patients as more rapacious than even cannibalism or rape. The problem with the Freudian insistence on exposure, the denial of the right to an internal asylum (of the right, that is, not to communicate) is, first and foremost, that it interferes with the core self's constitutive desire not to be found. But a further problem is that, in presuming to find that core, psychoanalysis in fact *creates* it. One of Winnicott's first postulates in "Communicating and Not Communicating" is that, from infancy, one "creates what is in fact lying around waiting to be found" (p. 181). When the analyst "finds" his patient's "core," Winnicott implies, he is in fact "creating" this core, an act of creation that is false and dangerous to an equal degree. (As we have seen, for Winnicott all communicating tends to slip into the spurious; here the further danger is that of an external authority's exploitation of self-communication.) We might think back, for example, to Jung's mortification over Freud's (mis)interpretation of his house dream and the added indignation over Freud's imperious refusal to submit his own dreams to analysis. It is such mental cannibalism that Winnicott's form of analysis is designed to avoid. In his therapeutic model, the silence of the patient is not, as for Freud, evidence of resistance but of *achievement*, a token of the patient's mature and healthy capacity to be both alone and incommunicative. The analyst's obligation is "to express the limit of his understanding" (p. 189) and not to insist on intrusive "discovery" and a coherent story: "there is room for the ideal of unrelated thought sequences which the analyst will do well to accept as such, not assuming the existence of a significant thread," Winnicott writes elsewhere; in fact, "free association that reveals a coherent theme is already affected by anxiety, and the cohesion of ideas is a defense organization."[17] It is narrative itself, rather than the refusal to narrate, that evinces for Winnicott the patient's anxious resistance.

This suspicion of full disclosure and narrative cohesion is a distinctive quality of what Phillips calls the "British school of 'not-knowing,'" which includes, besides Winnicott, Masud Khan and Marion Milner. Khan's work on perversion, for example, defines the pervert not, as we would expect, as she or he who embraces the utterly strange but as someone who *denies* its existence, who denies, that is, the very notion of unknowability. Khan's pervert is someone who always knows in advance what she or he wants to find out. Classic psychoanalysis, in this reading, has a perverse quality to it. A case in point for Khan is the classic view of dreams as "the royal road to the unconscious," as open secrets or texts readily available to the skilled analyst's interpretation. In reading the dream, one might say, the Freudian analyst may end up creating what he or she knew in advance would be found. For Khan, by contrast, the dream (or what he calls the "dream experience") is not a readable text but a synecdoche of the incommunicable, permanently unfound core of the self, and thus cannot be and, ethically speaking, *should* not be rendered fully interpretable. The dream experience signifies that which is utterly strange, beyond the analyst's realm of knowledge or interpretive skills. As Phillips writes, "clearly, there cannot be private language; but there can be a sense, Khan implies, conveyed in language, of a person's irreducible privacy."[18]

My point thus far has not been simply to reduce Freud and Winnicott to irreconcilable polarities. I wished to emphasize, rather, the extent to which both (and psychoanalysis more generally) share a genealogy in that pervasive, mainstream structure of thought that, at least from the early decades of the nineteenth century, insisted on a binary division between solitude and sociability, reticence and conspicuity, as one of its most definitive features. The work performed by psychoanalysts from Freud on was meant to elaborate the interiorization of this division, its inscription as a psychic scission, mapping out, often with the aid of metaphors of domestic space, what R. D. Laing (who was influenced by Goffman as well as by Freud and Winnicott) was eventually to call the "divided self."[19] We have seen how this division, related to but not subsumed under the unconscious/conscious binary, runs through both Freud's and Winnicott's psychic topographies. But we have also seen that their topographies are markedly different from one another, a difference that is more normative than descriptive. Winnicott writes from the "private" side of this divide; he is closely allied with the tradition of liberal individualism, whose rhetoric of the "true," "sacred," and "inviolable" self he adopts. Freud, at least the Freud who emerges from our analysis here, speaks from the opposite side, as it were, from that contiguous "drawing room" position that, as I argue in Chapter 1, is both inherent in the bourgeois interior and constitutes its internal critique, a position that threatens to "perversely" violate the sanctity of the private self for the sake of disclosure and visibility.

Before returning to antebellum fiction, I wish to suggest that this normative difference can also be linked to different ethics of reading. It does not seem coincidental, for example, that Winnicott's most famous work appeared in the decade when New Criticism set the tone in literary studies. New Criticism, with its emphasis on ambiguity and paradox (Winnicott's favorite trope), assumed precisely that "sense, conveyed in language, of a person's irreducible privacy" promoted by Winnicott and his disciples. New Criticism not only implicitly argued for the writer's right to be "left alone" by the reader, since it ruled out historical context and authorial intention as relevant to interpretation, but also explicitly inscribed limits on the critic's knowledge, in the spirit of Winnicottian analysis, by underscoring the ambiguous, undecipherable essence of what New Criticism appropriately called the "silent object," the literary text. On the other hand, we now seem to be just over the cusp of an opposite critical wave. The present dominance of Foucauldian epistemologies, that is to say, while often pitted against the Freudian analytic tradition, in fact shares with that tradition a central objective—the critique of that liberal "negative theology" that insists on the sacredness of private selfhood.

D. A. Miller's influential essay on "open secrets" is exemplary in this regard. When we encounter a "secret" in a novel, Miller maintains, we should not be reading it as evidence of the author's irreducible privacy or of the consecrated inviolability of "true selves" as such. Rather, secrets are a mechanism by which socially determined subjects can pretend that they are partially inaccessible to the very forces/discourses that shape their subjectivity in its entirety: "Secrecy would thus be the subjective practice in which the oppositions of private/public, inside/outside, subject/object are established, and the sanctity of their first term kept inviolate."[20] Thus, while every secret is an "open secret," in the sense that what it pretends to conceal is really determined and predictable, we persist in declaring it unknown in order to disavow ("in a mechanism reminiscent of Freudian disavowal") the nonexistence of that cached part of the self that Miller calls the "hoard" of liberal ideology. In this version of the game of hide and seek, the secret subject needs constantly to resist: (a) the fact that she or he is in actuality entirely visible, and (2) the fact that no one is looking for her or him anyway. This model of subjectivity is typified inside the novel by its characters, whose secrets are always open to readers and outside the novel by readers themselves; readers take pleasure in the pretense that *their* secrets, unlike those of the novel's characters, are closed, that they do indeed harbor a unique, inaccessible self. But this pleasure comes at the same time as the very act of reading the novel contributes to the vacuity of any such pretense, since the novel itself is a primary instrument of invasive social discipline. Miller's mode of interpretation is thus "perverse" in Khan's sense of the term: his concept of open secrets is the denial of unknowability as part of the experience of reading fiction.

But in what sense are secrets *always* already open? From a radical

Foucauldian perspective, since subjects are constituted in their totality by social discipline, they can "hoard" nothing truly remarkable, unique, or counterhegemonic. When we open the imaginary box of secret subjectivity, all we are bound to find are the smooth inner workings of social discipline. Note, however, that Miller's critique of liberal subjectivity introduces a terminological substitution within our discussion: he uses of the term "secrecy," that is, where we used "privacy." The two are not coterminous. "Secrecy" assumes the existence of something uncommunicated but *potentially communicable,* a counternarrative or identity that chafes against the social discourses that define the subject. "Privacy," in the liberal-Winnicottian use, relies on no such assumption. For Winnicott, we recall, any act of self-narration, being intersubjective, is already "compliant"; in that sense, Winnicott would probably concur with Miller's notion of open secrets: there cannot be a counternarrative of the self, an alternative, coherent identity that escapes the ruses of power or the banalities of appeasement. But his point is that the subject's private core is outside narrativity, outside intersubjective exchange, and hence cannot be described as "secret" or ever really be "open."

Preempting an objection to his argument along these lines, Miller claims that this presumed ineffability of the self's private "core" in liberalism simply makes no sense: "just as we can say of this hoard in a capitalist economy that it is worth nothing as soon as it has been removed from circulation and exchange, so we might wonder what value can be put upon an innerness that is never recognized in intersubjectivity. . . . if the secret subjective content is so well concealed, how do we know it is there?"[21] Miller's argument thus relies on the very terms that he critiques: just as in capitalism nothing can have an existence that is not reified and externalized and thereby rendered valuable as currency, so will the critic posit that nothing can exist, can be of interpretive value, that is not objectified, or openly present in the text.

By this I do not mean that Miller is wrong. On the contrary, his mode of reading is precisely right when it comes to the genre of the domestic novel, which, as I began to suggest in Chapter 1, is indeed premised on the paradigm of the two-dimensional, reified, exchangeable self. But the critic's reluctance to recognize the textual presence of a permanently "closed" aspect of the self becomes more problematic when practiced on texts that are based on a different paradigm, those in which "privacy" is a more operable term than "secrecy." This problem crops up at moments in Eve Sedgwick's immensely influential *Epistemology of the Closet.* Acknowledging, at the outset, her critical debt to Miller's work on open secrets, Sedgwick zooms in on the homosexual closet as *the* open secret par excellence, the subjective space whose contents are simultaneously grasped as ineffable ("the love that dares not speak its name") and as utterly transparent ("we know what *that* means"). Sedgwick traces the presence of this open secret in several texts, among them *Billy Budd* by Herman Melville and "The Beast in the Jungle" by Henry James, two works that have traditionally been read by liberal critics as thematizing the elusiveness of the private self. Her strong argument (what she would call a "universalist" claim) is that the very ideology of privacy that underwrites these texts as well as their reception is "structured—indeed fractured—by the [late nineteenth-century] endemic crisis of homo/heterosexual definition."[22] Their celebrated indeterminacy, in other words, cannot be severed from a historically specific, inherently muddled, contemporaneous discourse on (homo)sexuality. But her second, more problematic, argument (a "minoritizing" claim) *resolves* rather than historicizes the indeterminacy of these texts by "disclosing" the latent homosexual desire of two of their main characters, Marcher and Claggart. Here her reading ceases to critique the incoherence surrounding the liberal concept of privacy and reveals, instead, a specific, quite coherent, *secret* desire. As Christopher Lane has pointed out, "at such moments—and despite its theoretical sophistication—*Epistemology of the Closet* comes close to the gay literary criticism of the 1970s and 1980s that troped on latency and disclosure" and that tended to reduce all silences to veiled forms of homosexual meaning.[23] Sedgwick approaches the kind of ahistorical criticism, Lane argues, that plugged the same homosexual secret into moments of textual uncertainty in texts across genres, continents, and eras. The critical act of substituting the secret for the private only to declare that secret "open," that is to say, can sever the text from—rather than restore—its historical context.

Conversely, I would argue, to read privacy into the text need not imply either a blind acceptance of the liberal "negative theology of the self," or, as was the case with New Criticism, an escape from historical texture. In the following reading of short stories by Hawthorne, Melville, and Stowe I suggest that some textual styles developed in relation to a historically specific, liberalist, and distinctly gendered architecture of private selfhood and thus demand to be read not as open secrets but in the manner that Khan reads dreams: as synecdoche of one's permanently sealed privacy.

Lying Fallow in London

Consider Hawthorne's 1835 short story "Wakefield." Jorge Luis Borges, who professed to admire "Wakefield" beyond any other work by Hawthorne, once wrote that with this story "we have already entered the world of Herman Melville, of Kafka," in which "the protagonist's profound *triviality* . . . contrasts with the magnitude of his perdition."[24]

Wakefield's profound triviality, however, contrasts first and foremost with the utter particularity of his deed. A middle-class, middle-aged London man who one day "took lodgings in the next street to his own house," where, "unheard of by his wife or friends," he "dwelt upwards of twenty years," Wakefield is introduced in the first paragraphs through an array of contradictory terms. On the one hand, he is "calm," "most constant," "habitual," of "a mind never feverish with riotous thoughts, nor perplexed with originality," a "man of habit"; on the other, his action is the "strangest delinquency," "as remarkable a freak as may be found in the whole list of human oddities," "without the shadow of a reason," "always exciting wonder," "unexampled," of "purest originality."[25]

But this ambivalence in Wakefield's description is not an indication of an unmentionable secret that he harbors; Wakefield is not a precursor of the "secret-life" protagonist, a Dr. Jekyll or a Dorian Gray who conceals a closeted identity behind his respectful, gentlemanly veneer. He is more prolifically discussed as heralding such characters as Melville's Bartleby or Albert Camus's Stranger, Meursault, conventional, humdrum men whose "freakish" acts point not to a secret counteridentity but to an inaccessible element within their divided mental architecture, an element incommunicable to anyone, least of all to themselves.

As with Bartleby or Meursault, moreover, the utter singularity of Wakefield's act paradoxically endows it with a universal appeal. "The incident, though of the purest originality, unexampled, and probably never to be repeated," Hawthorne writes, "is one, I think, which appeals to the general sympathies of mankind. We know, each for himself, that none of us would perpetrate such a folly, yet feel as if some other might" (p. 290). By "mankind," I think, Hawthorne means precisely that: his presentation of the story as a gendered, marital drama (Melville referred to the story as the tale of the "London *Husband*")[26] and his displaced identification with its truant hero, which he assumes also in his readers ("each for himself"), suggest that the "general" sympathy the story appeals to is one that belongs properly to *men*. (*New England Magazine*, where the tale was first published, was indeed geared toward a genteel male readership.)[27]

"Wakefield," I argue, imagines the creation of a definitively masculine realm of intractable privacy within the antebellum private sphere and within the self staged, appropriately enough, through the spatial splitting of the interior, "a change about the familiar edifice," in Hawthorne's words (p. 294). The story charts, in effect, a grotesque version of the divided-interior blueprint that we discussed at length in Chapter 1. Wakefield's relocating into a separate apartment and into a condition of privacy may be viewed not as an escape from the domestic sphere but as its enhancement: it results in a hybrid household, comprising separate masculine and feminine spaces, sharply divided by the London street, it-self a kind of extreme version of a central hallway, the "almost impassa-ble gulf" separating Wakefield's world from that of his wife (p. 295). Echoing the gendering of domestic space in his generation, Hawthorne registers in the tale a symmetrical layout whereby femininity is linked with intimacy, social compliance, and sociopetence, and masculinity with isolation, invisibility, and sociofugality. Midway through Wakefield's exile, for example, during a chance street meeting with his wife, Wake-field looks "apprehensively about"; she bears a "placid mien"; the hus-band, his eyes directed "inward," is "unwilling to display his full front to the world"; his wife, "a prayer book in her hand," is the vision of social respectability and integration. Their opposite trajectories having briefly crisscrossed, he "hurries to his lodgings, bolts the door, and throws him-self upon the bed"; she proceeds in the opposite direction, into the peo-pled church (p. 296). Like the marriages in the pedagogical novel of Sarah Hale or Eliza Leslie, the Wakefield marriage is literally a marriage of opposites.[28]

Hawthorne imagines Mrs. Wakefield as a conventional domestic woman, an "exemplary wife" who dominates the "little sphere of crea-tures and circumstances" of the parlor (p. 293), the only room in the Wakefield household ever mentioned in the tale (at the end, she ap-pears as the lively spirit of the parlor, her "grotesque shadow" dancing on its walls [p. 297]). To inhabit Mrs. Wakefield's parlor is to have a "place in her chaste bosom" (p. 292), to be subsumed into her propriety, senti-ments, and web of intimate relations. It is within this domestic regime, as Mrs. Wakefield's husband, that Wakefield's conventional and wholly predictable nature (what Winnicott would call his "compliant object-relating") thrives: "his matrimonial affections, never violent, were sobered into a calm, habitual sentiment; of all husbands, he was likely to be the most constant, because a certain sluggishness would keep his heart at rest. . . . Had his acquaintances been asked, who was the man in London the surest to perform nothing today which should be remembered on the morrow, they would have thought of Wakefield" (p. 291). Wakefield, too, is an "exemplary" spouse—he is constant, calm, habitual—but in his case, it is his proper performance of the marital role that drains him of vitality. In the parlor, he is a "dead citizen" (to borrow Lauren Berlant's term), epitomizing the kind of hackneyed identity produced in the zone of bourgeois domesticity, an identity that, like a dead meta-phor, is "not live, or in play; but dead, frozen, fixed, or at rest."[29]

All the while, however, Wakefield possesses another quality, an un-canny, subjective surplus described variably as "a quiet selfishness," "a peculiar sort of vanity," "a disposition to a craft," and a "little strange-ness" (p. 291). Wakefield's wife recognizes this uncanny element in her husband but, like the Freudian watchman who guards the drawing room of consciousness, she dismisses it. For her, they are "harmless," "petty," open secrets, "hardly worth revealing" (p. 291). As it turns out, this dismissal is crucially mistaken; Wakefield's "little strangeness" is the only cause that Hawthorne provides to account for his departure from Mrs. Wakefield's domain. When Wakefield removes himself to an apartment on the next street, he thereby carves out a niche for this "indefinable" excess (p. 293). His purpose, to the extent that he has one, is not rebelliously to embrace some identity alternative to his domesticated masculinity, but to enclose for himself a space *beyond* identity and coherence altogether, a backstage of solitude, silence, and invisibility, where in the next twenty years he will be able, to return to Winnicott's words, "to become unintegrated, to flounder, to be in a state in which there is no orientation" rather than be "an active person with a direction of interest or movement." The way Hawthorne puts it, Wakefield indulges in "long and lazy musing, that tended to no purpose, or had not vigor to attain it, [nor be] so energetic as to seize hold of words" (p. 291). Hawthorne is describing what Khan will call many years later "lying fallow," the nonverbal, receptive, disintegrative state of quietude we all occasionally require for well-being.[30] By creating this enclave of "vague" ineffability (p. 293)—"with the consciousness of a purpose, indeed, but without being able to define it sufficiently for his own contemplation" (p. 293)—Wakefield is not precisely abandoning domesticity. Rather, he has found a way to create within marriage a space of interior privacy by installing himself as an absent presence in his home, like an adult version of Winnicott's child, alone in the invisible proximity of its mother, or like Khan's subject, who requires a "wife . . . sitting around unobtrusively" to guarantee the success of the state of "lying fallow."[31] Wakefield was "always beside his wife and at his hearth," Hawthorne writes: "It was Wakefield's unprecedented fate to retain his original share of human sympathies, and to be still involved in human interests, while he had lost his reciprocal influence on them" (p. 297). What Wakefield will discover are the pleasures and deprivations endemic to this state of privacy.

Wakefield's act helps Hawthorne isolate a historical moment in which "a great moral change has been effected," in which the middle-class man has become "another man" as a result of a "new system being now established" (p. 294). At a time in which middle-class, northern, urban men increasingly began to leave their homes daily for work, thereby, indeed, withdrawing into a state of absent presence within the domestic sphere, Wakefield—introduced by Hawthorne as utterly strange and yet strangely typical—simply takes this logic to a violent extreme (violent not least because it almost leads to his wife's death). Hawthorne is fascinated by the psychological implications of this change, less so for the wife (as a parlor woman, she is represented as having no hidden interiority for the narrative to delve into) and more so for Wakefield himself; "our business is with the husband," Hawthorne writes (p. 292).

The retreat into privacy, we first learn, produces in Wakefield an almost pathological fear of being found, of being forced back into the realm of visibility, a fear that is predictably but disturbingly channeled toward his wife. In Wakefield's imagination, there is scarcely a difference between the dangerously deindividuating urban street (where he may at any moment "lose his individuality, and melt into the great mass of London life" [p. 292]) and his wife's domestic realm. The two form a united front against him. "There were footsteps," he fantasizes, "that seemed to tread behind his own, distinct from the multitudinous tramp around him; and, anon, he heard a voice shouting afar, and fancied that it called his name. Doubtless, a dozen busybodies had been watching him, and told his wife the whole affair" (p. 292). On his first day away from her, Wakefield catches a "far and momentary glimpse of his wife, passing athwart the front window, with her face turned towards the head of the street" (p. 294). Wakefield now inspects his worried wife from his newly acquired asylum as she, in turn, stands in her observation post, literally positioned between the interior and the street, thereby creating a spatial continuum of surveillance of parlor and city. The association tightens in the later street meeting: as Mrs. Wakefield throws a quizzical but unrecognizing look in his direction ten years after their separation, Wakefield feels not only her glance but also "that busy and selfish London stands to gaze after him" (pp. 295–96). This is an image of the parlor woman distilled into her essence as society's watchman, even while it is she who has long been the victim of her husband's stalking.[32]

But no less horrific for Wakefield than the prospect of being discovered is the prospect of not being looked for at all. "Poor Wakefield!" writes Hawthorne. "Little knowest thou thine own insignificance in this great world! No mortal eye but mine has traced thee" (p. 292). The tale, that is, captures not only the feeling of vigilance but also the sense of deprivation triggered by the desire for privacy. Watching his home from a distance, Wakefield is obsessed with "how the little sphere of creatures and circumstances, in which he was a central object, will be affected by his removal." "Will not," he asks himself, "the whole household—the decent Mrs. Wakefield, the smart maid-servant, and the dirty little footboy—raise a hue-and-cry, through London streets, in pursuit of their fugitive lord and master?" (p. 294). The answer, surprising because it is new, is no. As many men of Hawthorne's generation were bound to feel, men who had relinquished the position of the domestic patriarch occupied by their fathers in favor of an exterior world of work and an introjected "right to be left alone," Wakefield is forced into the displeasing

realization that to claim the privilege of privacy is also to "lose reciprocal influence" over the domestic sphere and to risk feeling abandoned
by it.[33]

But if that is the case, if "Wakefield" is partially about the abdication of
domestic power for the obscure pleasures of privacy, what is to be made
of Wakefield's reentry into the parlor at the end? This is a difficult question, because the tale seems to evade a literary frame of reference that
would clarify its ending. Borges writes that, while with "Wakefield" we
enter the world of Kafka, "if Kafka had written that story, Wakefield
would never have returned to his home";[34] his distinctly modernist form
of "perdition" would have been to remain a perpetual stranger in an
enigmatic and indecipherable universe, or, put in our terms, to lose any
remaining links to the coherent, if normalized, identity bestowed by the
domestic sphere. Nor, we should note, is Wakefield's return the happy
ending that belongs to the sentimental tradition. While in the initial
outlining of the story Hawthorne promises a sentimental ending
whereby Wakefield, happily ever after, "became a loving spouse till death"
(p. 290), when Hawthorne's tale finally catches up with that promise, the
narrator suggests that the return home might instead constitute Wakefield's death: "Would you go to the sole home that is left you? Then
step into your grave!" (p. 298). Wakefield's return does not ensure the
restoration of domestic harmony; it signals his ultimate demise.

Because "Wakefield" was written in a moment when the very boundaries of privacy were newly drawn, our efforts to fix its interpretation
within a stable literary frame are inevitably frustrated. Just as Wakefield
is divided between normalcy and strangeness, and just as his "household" is divided into feminine and masculine zones, so does the narrational voice seem at odds with itself, oscillating between sentimental and
protomodernist visions. This division is most clearly manifest in the way
Hawthorne repeatedly tropes on death in this story. Early on, it is Wakefield's self-banishment from his wife's parlor, his exit from the realm of
domestic visibility, that is interpreted as a form of death. For his circle of
acquaintances, to leave the home is to cease to exist: "his death was reck-
oned certain, his estate settled, his name dismissed from memory"
(p. 290). For his wife, too, Wakefield's departure signifies death, and she
"imagines him in a coffin" or "dreams of him in Heaven" (p. 292). The
narrator seems to concur with this sentiment: "get thee home to good
Mrs. Wakefield," he urges: "Remove not thyself, even for a little week,
from thy place in her chaste bosom" (p. 292). Soon, however, we sense
that Wakefield's self-removal is a means of survival. As Mrs. Wakefield
contemplates her husband's "crafty smile," the embodied sign of his "little strangeness," she "sometimes doubts whether she is a widow" (p. 292).
After Wakefield's first night alone, when he momentarily considers

reentering his wife's realm, the narrator warns him, "Wakefield! whither are you going?" (p. 293). The "change about the familiar edifice," effected in "the magic of a single night," also triggers a shift in narrational position: "Fool!" he tells the homebound Wakefield, "it is another world" (p. 295). If, in the beginning, separation amounted to death, now the narrator compares a return home to "Doom's day" (p. 297).

And yet Hawthorne concludes with a sentimental moral that preaches the lethal dangers of "stepping outside" and warns against the "fearful risk of losing [one's] place forever" (p. 298). The narrator's final description of Wakefield's reentrance into the parlor is thus profoundly ambivalent: is it a triumph over his former resistance to domestication, a taming of the uncanny? The fact that the tale ends precisely at that moment, thus removing Wakefield forever from visibility and coherence, suggests otherwise. Or is his return a form of self-annihilation, a succumbing to the deadening fixities of narrative, to bourgeois dead citizenship? It is as if, were it not for the need to create closure, Hawthorne would have wanted nothing more for his protagonist than to leave him in the same state of "lying fallow" that has been his for the last twenty years.

This diegetic ambivalence is further evident in the way Hawthorne initially introduces the story. In what would become a characteristic of his later romances, Hawthorne both insists that the tale is grounded in truth (based on a newspaper story) and emphatically points out its fictionality ("If the reader choose, let him do his own meditation; or if he prefer to ramble with me through the twenty years of Wakefield's vagary, I bid him welcome" [p. 290]). Thus Hawthorne at once implies that the role of fiction is to make visible and coherent the freakish particulars of a person's private existence (he pretends that the narrator's omniscient eye actually "traced" Wakefield's retreat into privacy) and that fiction should register the impossibility of doing precisely that. Since, as Hawthorne astutely points out, to interpret the story buried in the newspaper is always to imaginatively invent it, the author, like the reader, must set explicit limits on claims to know that story, especially since it thematizes precisely the desire to remove oneself from normalizing inspection. Hawthorne's explicit refusal to violate the mystery of Wakefield, to pretend that he holds the key to his secret, or even that such a ("perhaps nonexistent" [p. 291]) secret is there, validates the notion of a privacy beyond narrative convention. It is the anonymous Londoner's ironic fate that in order to surpass conventionality, to "perform [something] today that should be remembered on the morrow," he must remain shut up in the invisibility of his cozy little apartment, never to be exposed by writer or public. And in that he resembles nobody so much as the young Hawthorne himself, who, during the period he wrote

"Wakefield," established a life of seclusion and social passivity in the small attic of his family's house in Salem, where, in the protective but often invisible presence of his mother and sisters, he had, as he put it, "not lived, but only dreamed about living."[35] Hawthorne, habitually described by both his contemporaries and modern biographers as "reserved" and "reticent," never completely stepped out of this attic, figuratively speaking. Even in his later years, when he bought the Wayside, the first and only home that he actually owned, he simulated that space by constructing for himself, not unlike Jung with Bollingen, a towering annex with a private study "wherein to dream, write, & declaim alone" (to recall Emerson's words).[36] This "change about the familiar edifice" completely altered the façade of the Wayside by swallowing up the massive central chimney of its original colonial design and, as Hawthorne put it, "transform[ing] a simple and small old farm-house into the absurdest anomaly you ever saw" (Fig. 6).[37]

Around this time, as he looked back on his youth, he spoke of his Salem period in terms of waiting "patiently for the world to know me" and feeling "as if I were already in the grave, with only life enough to be chilled and benumbed." "But oftener," he admitted, "I was happy—at least, as happy as I then knew how to be, or was aware of the possibility of being."[38] Torn between a desire to be known to the world and a desire to withdraw from it, and experiencing the state of privacy both as a form of death and as a form of psychic fulfillment, the young Hawthorne, like his "London husband," prefigured Winnicott's insight that "it is joy to be hidden but disaster not to be found."

Of Chimneys and the Negative Theology of Self

Hawthorne's "absurdly anomalous" tower of privacy at the Wayside captured through architectural space the reconfiguration of masculinity in the private sphere, a process that had so anxiously resonated already in "Wakefield." This reconfiguration is also the subject of Melville's "I and My Chimney" (1856). But an influence on Melville's tale may be traced more directly to Hawthorne's 1841 sketch "Fire-Worship."[39] Here Hawthorne laments the "great revolution in social and domestic life" symbolized by the replacement of the open fireplace—the hallmark of the colonial central-chimney house design—with the stove found in spatially segregated antebellum dwellings.[40] Writing from the vantage point of his now fireless but stoved study, Hawthorne draws an extended analogy between the central fireplace and old-style patriarchy as embodied by his predecessor in the Old Manse's study, "the good man, a contemporary of the Revolution," to whom he is "an unworthy successor" (p. 843). Both the central fireplace and the old-fashioned patriarch,

Figure 6. The Wayside after Hawthorne's alterations in the early 1860s. Reproduced with permission of U.S. Department of the Interior, National Park Service, Harpers Ferry Center; artist, Steven N. Patricia.

Hawthorne laments, are fast disappearing from the world, an enormity to which he will "never be reconciled" (p. 841). The presence of the open fire connoted the patriarch's complete involvement in the life of each family member and the gentle management of "all needful offices for the household in which he was domesticated" (p. 842). "Nor did it lessen the charm of [the fire's] soft, familiar courtesy and helpfulness," Hawthorne adds, that, "were opportunity offered him, [he] would run riot through the peaceful house, wrap its inmates in his terrible embrace, and leave nothing of them save their white bones. This possibility of mad destruction only made his domestic kindness the more beautiful and touching" (p. 843). Such benevolent despotism is what Hawthorne imagines to be missing from his present home position, a position metaphorized, in turn, as the stove, with its Wakefieldian "barren and tedious eccentricities" (p. 846). Whereas the "grey patriarch" gathered his family, friends, and parishioners in his study, Hawthorne's room is as cold and sullen as the wintry outdoor landscape. A paternal influence, exercised through a combination of sentiment and potential violence, no longer exists in the modern house. Instead, there is "nothing to attract . . . children to one center," nothing to melt "humanity into one cordial heart of hearts"; "domestic life—if it may still be termed domestic—will seek its separate corners, and never gather itself into groups" (p. 847). The interior has been fractured and domestic authority, sociability, and familial intimacy irretrievably removed from the husband's domain, a fact that here seems to override any pleasure in the "eccentricities" of privacy.

Melville expresses his admiration for the sketch in "Hawthorne and His Mosses" (he is especially taken by the passage about the potential destructiveness of the domestic fire). In "I and My Chimney," he creates a narrator who, like Hawthorne's, seems to cling to a patriarchal past when man was the center of an indivisible interior. It is as though the "grey-headed old smoker" is Melville's version of what would have happened to Hawthorne's "grey patriarch" had he lived into the middle of the century. The narrator declares himself "quite behind the age," a "rearguard" to his own culture, and his "behindhandedness" is manifested primarily in his battle to preserve his overbearing chimney and the old-fashioned interior plan that its presence prescribes.[41] In terms more explicit than in "Wakefield," "I and My Chimney" dramatizes the social and psychological consequences of the sundering of the bourgeois private sphere, consequences that critics agree amount to, in Anthony Vidler's analysis, "a fear . . . of a loss of manhood" or, in Michael Rogin's, an anxiety over masculine retreat from "claims to large social power," newly the domain of women.[42] But this anxiety, I will once again argue, is a by-product of other gains: the acquisition, with the entrance of liberal individualism into the home, of a masculine space of retreat, physical and psychic, and the invention of a literary style that captures it.

Melville's tale was first published in *Putnam's*, a magazine that, more explicitly than *New England Magazine*, catered to the concerns of the growing ranks of upper-middle-class men.[43] It featured articles that, for instance, argued against women's rights from a masculine perspective, articles that were buttressed by companion articles such as "A Word for Men's Rights," a stringent defense of masculine power against the perceived threats of feminine insurgency. Indeed, the anxieties registered in "I and My Chimney" were a favored literary theme of *Putnam's* editors. A sketch entitled "Household Skeletons: A Meditation," for instance, recounts various fictitious examples of domestic disputes, all caused by "the vagaries of wives," and all shown to destroy a man's enjoyment of his own domicile. *Putnam's*, finally, carefully followed contemporaneous reforms in domestic architecture both in a long series of articles on New York's changing architectural landscape and in shorter reviews of architectural pattern books. It spoke approvingly, for instance, of an interior plan that located the parlor and the study on separate floors, a new urban architectural style that allowed middle-class homeowners to achieve elegance despite their need to economize in space by substituting height for expensive horizontal plots (an architectural trend that Melville comments on explicitly in "I and My Chimney"). In sum, if ladies' magazines like *Godey's* were the undisputed podium of the cult of domesticity, *Putnam's* may be said to have participated in the shaping of a masculine, liberal vision of the middle-class home and of the shifting role of men within it.[44]

This context for Melville's "thoroughly magazinish" tale (in one editor's praise) suggests that, while twentieth-century critics mostly chose to interpret the tale either allegorically (e.g., the chimney standing for federalism threatened by impending secession) or biographically (e.g., as addressing Melville's own *dementia domesticus*), contemporaneous readers probably read it more literally, bringing into its interpretation a persistent concern with the changing structure of the private sphere and the implications of those changes.[45] *Putnam's* readers were surely aware, for instance, of the mid-century fashion for renovating simply designed farmhouses into trendy gentlemen's country seats.[46] This trend—captured in "I and My Chimney" through the joint effort of the wife, the daughters, the architect Mr. Scribe, and the anonymous "architectural reformer" (who appears briefly at the end) to demolish the old-fashioned chimney and redesign the interior—was part of a larger historical process: the substitution of the Jeffersonian farmer ideal with a new mind-set that favored elegance and refinement, the displacement, in other words, of the rural by the suburban, the patrician by the bourgeois, the patriarchal family by the more democratic household.

There is nothing arbitrary, that is to say, about Melville's choice of the chimney to symbolize traditional patriarchal power (critics often note the proliferation of similes that equate the chimney with historical patriarchs from Caesar and Henry VIII to the pope). Nor is it simply its phallic shape that suggests this connection.[47] The central chimney is the most salient feature of a spatial design that enabled traditional patriarchy. Its sheer size declares its power for all to see, the narrator explains, "but it is within doors that the pre-eminence of my chimney is most manifest" (p. 1298). Unlike in modern houses, which, with their proliferation of flues, are "weak," and "treacherously hollow" (p. 1299), the presence of the chimney connotes domestic "harmony" because it draws the family and its friends into one center: "my family and guests are warming themselves of a cold winter's night, just before retiring, then though at the time they may not be thinking so, all their faces mutually look toward each other, yea, all their feet point to one centre" (p. 1305). Moreover, the presence of the chimney means that there is no dividing hallway, and the rooms are "dovetailed into each other" (p. 1323), a layout that allows for the smug superiority of the narrator over his puzzled guests, who cannot find their way about the house without his guidance. In one instance, the narrator gloats, this labyrinthine house plan helped eliminate an undesirable suitor of his daughter, who embarrassed himself by entering the pantry instead of exiting the door. Melville is extremely detailed about the way in which the chimney stands for the father's position as the "backbone" of the domicile, depicting, as it does, a domestic space characterized by paternal centrality, knowledge, and visual control, all of which are associated with the traditional patriarchal family (see Chapter 1; unsurprisingly, the narrator favors the Picturesque style, which we have seen architects like A. J. Downing associate with residual, imperious masculinity, with Napoleon rather than Washington.)

Like Hawthorne's in "Wakefield," Melville's dramatization of the changes in the private sphere relies on the staging of a gender symmetry and opposition. "If the doctrine be true, that in wedlock contraries attract," bemoans the narrator, "by how cogent a fatality must I have been drawn to my wife!" (p. 1308). The character of the wife (and her clones, their two daughters) is imagined through a newly formed ideal of parlor femininity, perceived as the consummate challenge to the traditional marital structure. Whereas the first sentence of the tale stresses that the narrator and his chimney are "old settlers" of the countryside (p. 1298), the wife, Judith Slater shows, is "of course, the human embodiment of the town house spirit; her narrow progressivism which insists on an egotistic, unchecked soaring is most vehemently expressed in her open rebellion against the chimney."[48] She embodies, that is, the rising bourgeois spirit of status display and social refinement, appropriately channeled into her obsession with dividing the interior of the house via the "projected grand entrance-hall of hers, which was to be knocked clean through the chimney . . . running her entries and partitions" (p. 1307). In her architecturally progressive view, the chimney is "the bully of the house" rather than its benevolent backbone, and her efforts to deconstruct it are linked to the fact that she "is desirous that, domestically, [the narrator] should abdicate; that, renouncing further rule, like the venerable Charles V., [he] should retire into some sort of monastery." The narrator thus finds himself "insensibly stripped by degrees of one masculine prerogative after another" (p. 1310). The female conspiracy to tear down the chimney and divide the interior with a central hallway is inseparable from the enclosure of the husband in his own "monastery," distanced and barred from the domestic throne.

The irony of "I and My Chimney," and the source of much of its humor, is that, despite the narrator's avid identification with the chimney, he has clearly already been stripped of his "masculine prerogatives." There is a clear gap between him and the object that he reveres and chooses as his symbol. The chimney, the narrator tells us, has "the centre of the house to itself, leaving but the odd holes and corners to me," and he has already been pushed to the "rear room" (p. 1299). From the very beginning, the chimney stands for a past ideal, for a form of masculine power already lost, since the husband has already withdrawn into his "odd" niche of solitude. Despite his conservative disposition, the narrator is as much the new man as his wife is the new woman, and what the couple battles over is not the restoration of traditional patriarchal power but the preservation of an emergent masculine prerogative: the right to be let alone. "I have not a single scheme or expectation on earth, save in unequal resistance of the undue encroachment of hers," he proclaims (p. 1308). What the husband is eager to protect is a space for—to return to Khan's terms—"lying fallow"; like Wakefield, he is a "dozy old dreamer" (p. 1308) who loves nothing more than to lose himself in reverie. The drama climaxes when the wife recruits the architect Mr. Scribe to write her husband a letter in which he is warned "that there is architectural cause to conjecture that somewhere concealed in our chimney is a reserved space, hermetically closed, in short, a secret chamber, or rather closet" and is asked "whether it is Christian-like knowingly to reside in a house, hidden in which is a secret closet" (pp. 1317–18).

Like Wakefield, who associates his wife's eyes with the "eyes" of the city, Melville's narrator is confronted with the united front of parlor women and a public ethos of exposure that threatens to violate masculine privacy (the wife's eyesight, the narrator tells us earlier, is as sharp as her tongue). This ethos misrepresents privacy as secrecy, and secrecy as immoral; it holds that every closet hides a skeleton and that every skeleton should be publicly displayed. It is only apt that the wife's favored reading material is newspaper stories of brutal behavior of husbands toward their wives, and that she insists that there is a "statute placing the keeping in private houses of secret closets on the same unlawful footing with the keeping of gunpowder" (p. 1320). The "progressiveness" that the tale associates with women is linked with both journalistic exposés that uncover domestic tyranny and a reformist legal philosophy according to which, as J. S. Mill expresses it, "the domestic life of domestic tyrants is one of the things which it is the most imperative on the law to interfere with."[49]

The surmised "hermetically closed" space is the sole legacy bequeathed to the narrator by his ancestor Captain Dacres and, if it exists, may contain a buried treasure or evidence of transgressions that the captain hid from the village's gossips all through his life. What the narrator wants to preserve in protecting the chimney is not his Revolution-era ancestor's potent and adventuresome masculinity but the one domestic prerogative that he embodies posthumously: to slumber "in a privacy as unmolested as if the billows of the Indian Ocean, instead of the billows of inland verdure, rolled over him" (p. 1318). In "I and My Chimney," we might say with Winnicott that "being eaten by cannibals" is a "mere bagatelle . . . as compared with the violation of the self's core."

The last third of the tale makes it clear that the domestic interior it so painstakingly depicts is first and foremost a reification of the narrator's psyche, and with that realization the story's "bantering tone all at once becomes earnest and solemn," as critics have long noticed.[50] Equating the wife with Momus, the classical figure who wanted human beings to have windows in front of their hearts so that he could see into their souls, the narrator explains that "to break into that wall would be to break into his breast," and that the Momus-like desire for "wall-breaking" is the "wish of a church-robbing gossip and knave" (p. 1325). His code of morality is squarely opposite that of the wife and the architect: what is immoral is exposure, not enclosure, and his mission is to ensure that the walls of his personhood are never cracked open. The "profound mystery" must remain closeted in the "profound masonry" (p. 1319), and the narrator insists that, "if there were a secret closet, secret it should remain, and secret it shall. For once I must say my say. Infinite sad mischief has resulted from the profane bursting open of secret recesses" (p. 1325).

If the exposure of secrets is "profane," privacy emerges from this tale as sacred (an anagram of Dacres, as readers often note); thus, a story that begins with apparent nostalgia for centralized domestic despotism ends up articulating a new, liberal "negative theology of the self." In contrast to D. A. Miller's argument that no value can be put on the "liberal hoard" of hidden subjectivity if it does not circulate intersubjectively, Melville here suggests that this hoard is valuable only on condition that it *never* circulates. "Peter Goldthwaite's Treasure," another tale by Hawthorne that influenced "I and My Chimney," features a protagonist who *does* yield to the "profane" temptation to break through his chimney, only to find a treasure chest filled with worthless, outdated colonial currency. Melville suggests in similar terms that the bursting open of hidden recesses represents not a validation but a devaluation and debasement of the self's vaulted core.

Rather than simply fret over the disappearance of one model of manhood, then, "I and My Chimney" dramatizes the ascension of another. The narrator's final withdrawal from the social world does not represent merely a resistance to the ethos of exposure but an achievement of the right to be alone, anonymous (we never do learn his name), and incommunicative. He is, of course, quite vociferous on the subject of this incommunicativeness; indeed, his withdrawal into the "rear room" (most likely a study) is also imagined by Melville as the condition that allows him to write his story, a story that, like "Wakefield," subsumes the feminine plot within a masculine mode of writing. Ann Douglas convincingly reads the tale as pertaining to the antebellum literary marketplace, where the architect, the "hired scribe," is "emblematic of the writers and litterateurs bribed by the feminine populace to invalidate and destroy the masculine experience."[51] The architectural conspiracy, then, stands for the assault on masculine literary talent by a combination of scribbling authors, greedy editors, and a philistine female audience. Bearing in mind that "masculine experience" in this tale connotes, first and foremost, the staking of a claim to privacy, we might wish to take Douglas's reading a step further. Melville is defending in literary terms an explicitly masculine aesthetics of concealment and disguising of private facts in cryptic symbolism, what William Charvat describes as Melville's "strategy of omission." Charvat argues that Melville became increasingly anxious in later years that, in his own words, "it [was] impossible to talk or write without apparently throwing oneself helplessly open." He thus developed an aesthetic style meant to conceal the relationship between sign and referent, to "thwart the common reader's tendency to identify the external action of a story with the story's meaning."[52] The narrator's steadfast refusal to find the secret closet, let alone break into it, represents not only the masculine view of the private sphere but also the literary conventions of concealment of meaning that are inseparable from it. "Sir! . . . do not be personal" (p. 1304), he warns an intruder who questions him about his chimney, and perhaps also generations of readers who will attempt to violate Melville's privacy by interpreting this domestic tale. By contrast, the combination of feminine authority and the forces of the marketplace, embodied in this story by the wife ("ever restless for newspapers, and ravenous for letters") and the architect, represents the opposite aesthetic code: the easily consumed clichés of newspaper exposés and the sentimental roman à clef that promote an ethos of the public's right to know and insist on the correspondence of literature to private life in order to justify intrusion, disclosure, and distortion of private life. (Appropriately, the wife's final strategy is to write, under a pseudonym, to the county's newspaper to criticize the chimney, thereby writing her own version of the exposés of domestic violence that she is so fond of reading.)

"I and My Chimney" indeed marks a new stage in Melville's writing, one that Richard Brodhead dates to his interest, expressed in a letter to Hawthorne, in his "London husband."[53] Like "Wakefield," it treats its domestic subject matter in what may be termed a sociofugal manner. Rather than draw the reader into the secret transgressions of the households it depicts, and rather than aspire to "reform" domestic life, it places a distance of unresolved ambiguity between fiction and the reader and thus caters to the values of the "book reading & and book writing men" who, like *Putnam's* readers, believed that the business of man's private life was his own. Significantly, neither Melville nor Hawthorne links the architecture of privacy with a verifiable secret. Wakefield's "petty secrets," as we have seen, are beyond enunciation, and Hawthorne stresses that the story is a self-declared invention. The point of Dacres's secret closet is that it may or may not exist, and the resistance to delving into this question is related to the narrator's own withdrawal from the realm of visibility by the end of the tale. By refusing to finalize judgment on the very presence of a secret, both Melville and Hawthorne bypass the possibility of its ever being "opened" and thereby, inevitably, distorted. What they describe as a singularly masculine condition is not, in this sense, secrecy but privacy—not a hidden, coherent subjective content but the ineffable remainder or excess that coercive social narratives, like middle-class domesticity and marriage, leave behind. Vincent Bertolini is thus right in suggesting that "I and My Chimney" zooms in on masculine personhood "*within* the institution of marriage and carves out a tiny space of freedom within its normalizing constraints," that it stages a "cultural conflict between the domestic regime and excessive male subjectivity."[54] But I would challenge Bertolini's attendant argument that this excess needs be linked to an alternative homoerotic subjectivity. While Melville unquestionably and hilariously associates the chimney

with a homosexual secret, he also associates it with secrets that are heterosexual (impotence, masturbation, and sexual exhibitionism) and
with secrets that are not sexual at all (failure of the creative powers,
hereditary mental disorder), thus depleting, through this semiotic
proliferation, the very structure of open secrecy.[55] The logic of the
story, and its ultimate point, is that any attempt to extract a secret from
it, be it homosexual or otherwise, immediately places the critic in un-
holy alliance with the "profane" wife and her unctuous sidekick,
Mr. Scribe.[56]

Of Carpets and the Domestic Hybrid

Despite the still-prevalent critical tendency to treat as separate the romantic and the sentimental traditions, one cannot help but notice the
similarities between "I and My Chimney" and Harriet Beecher Stowe's
"The Ravages of a Carpet" (1865). The first in a series of sketches
printed in the *Atlantic* and eventually published in book form as *House
and Home Papers*, the sketch appeared under the pseudonym "Christopher Crowfield," also the name of the fictitious narrator of the entire
series. Crowfield resembles Melville's narrator in his conservativism, in
his self-deprecating humor, in his love for quiet reverie, and in his
propensity toward philosophizing. Like the "Chimney" narrator, he is
confronted with a "pretty domestic conspiracy" within his household—
this time, the decision of the wife and two daughters to replace the
parlor's furniture (the sturdy pieces that were bought by the wife's old-
fashioned father, "granite foundation of the household structure"[57])
with a stylish new Brussels carpet and modern upholsteries (p. 19).
Here, too, the domestic man feels that modernization amounts to the
destruction of the domicile's "backbone" and steadfastly resists it. He
loses the battle to win the war: his vision of what a home should be finally triumphs as the spirit of the old parlor, though lost in the modern
one, is simply transported into his newly separated private study. Crowfield even alludes to "Fire-Worship," creating an explicit link with
Hawthorne's domestic tales and an implicit one with Melville, who, as
we have seen, was inspired by the sketch (p. 7).

Stowe's main theme in "The Ravages of a Carpet" and the sketches
that follow—the sense of division within the domestic sphere—is evident in the volume's title, which calls attention to the difference between "home" and "house." In what seems at first a distortion of
domestic ideology, Stowe associates the more affective term with the
husband and the material one with the wife. It is Crowfield who understands that the "building and arrangement of a house" merely serve the
higher purpose of influencing "the health, the comfort, the morals, the

religion" of "human existence" (p. 272), while women, as he explains, tend to restrict their vision to the physical: "there are many women who know how to keep a house, but there are but few that know how to keep a *home*" (p. 30).

The association of the ideal of the home with manhood by a writer who was herself a celebrated priestess of domesticity is tied to another surprising aspect of the sketches. Whereas her social-reform novels—*Uncle Tom's Cabin* and *Dred,* for example—are narrated in her own voice, Stowe masks herself with a male persona to narrate these sketches of middle-class domestic life (a persona she employs in *Little Foxes* and *The Chimney-Corner* as well). Critics explain this puzzling choice in two ways. First, as Joan D. Hedrick claims, "speaking in a male voice was the price of admission to the *Atlantic* club," a magazine that also featured a successful domestic series by Oliver Wendell Holmes. Second, and here Hedrick is joined by Lisa Watt MacFarlane, Stowe's late-years artistic choice signals the decline of domestic ideology after the 1850s "as a social model and as generative aesthetic." Women lost their authoritative voice, Hedrick and MacFarlane convincingly argue, as a new parlor culture separated middle-class women from work and from the communal world represented by the old-fashioned kitchen and parlor.[58]

What complicates these explanations, however, is that as early as 1850, and in the pages of the *National Era* (where *Uncle Tom's Cabin* first appeared), Stowe published sketches, such as "A Scholar's Adventures in the Country," that employed a similar domestic male narrative voice. Even if the new parlor of formal performativity and conspicuous consumption eventually had the effect of muffling women's authorial voice, the fact remains that as Stowe was working on her political masterpiece, she occasionally chose to present the inner affairs of the home through the perspective of the husband and father. But if we do not regard the home, even in the heyday of the cult of domesticity, as strictly a female sphere, if, instead, we understand its inner workings through its self-imposed divisions, Stowe's narrational choice is less puzzling. The rise of the middle class, I have been arguing, signaled not the end of patriarchy and the beginning of woman's reign in the home but a sharpening of a gendered bivalence within the private sphere and a new form of masculine privilege anchored in privacy. As we have seen, stories about the home were written from both a feminine and a masculine perspective, depending on their themes and goals. *Uncle Tom's Cabin*, written, in Stowe's description, "because, as a woman, as a mother, [she] was oppressed and heartbroken with the sorrows and injustice which [she] saw,"[59] could not have achieved its strong emotional effect were it narrated through a masculine voice, since the role of maintaining social morality and managing societal order was assigned by the ideology of the divided interior to the bourgeois woman. As Stowe ventriloquizes through Crowfield, "women have the centripetal force which keeps all the domestic planets from gyrating and frisking in unseemly orbits" (p. 30). But sketches such as "The Ravages of a Carpet," concerned as they are not with societal reform but with the isolated home, its conservation and protection from contaminating external influences, reinforce themselves by being narrated by the figure now explicitly associated with sociofugality and the value of privacy: the middle-class husband and father.

I will argue that Stowe does not use a male voice to create for herself a "prophylaxis" (Lauren Berlant's term), a persona meant to shield the fragile domestic woman's identity as she ventures out into the masculine public sphere.[60] By 1865, the successful Stowe hardly needed such protection. Rather, she uses a male voice in recognition of the overriding power of men within the newly organized domestic regime, their role in transcending and harmonizing domestic division and conflict and thus securing the home's well-being. But, crucially enough, Stowe imagines the performance of this role not through the *disavowal* of those values associated with parlor femininity (as Hawthorne and Melville do in the stories we have discussed) but through their *incorporation*. In shaping her male persona, she seeks to reform as well as to imitate the voice of middle-class manhood: Christopher Crowfield emerges, in the final analysis, as a hybrid voice combining elements from both sides of the domestic divide and inhabiting a fluid and malleable domestic space, one that simultaneously upholds privacy and empties the private of its uncanniness. Stowe, to borrow a phrase from Homi Bhabha, "mimics" the masculine voice of her male colleagues, and in sounding almost, but not quite, like Hawthorne and Melville, she manages to rewrite the liberal ethos of privacy in accordance with her "parlor" perspective, which stresses exposure, transparency, and intimacy.[61]

Complicating 1970s and 1980s feminist readings of Stowe that key in on her protofeminist glorification of the home as woman's separate sphere, *House and Home Papers* attributes the success of the well-managed household to the husband and father. Crowfield's views on home life are decidedly those that we have been associating with the space of the study and the ethos of individual privacy: "nothing makes a room so home-like," he writes, "and gives it such an air of refinement, as the presence of books. . . . It gives the appearance of permanence and repose" (p. 113). Crowfield describes himself as "reading for the two-hundredth time Hawthorne's 'Mosses from an Old Manse,' or his 'Twice-Told Tales,' I forget which, I only know that these books constitute my cloud-land, where I love to sail away in dreamy quietude, forgetting the war, the price of coal and flour, the rates of exchange, and the rise and fall of gold" (p. 125). Once again, we meet the upper-class man, for whom the home offers "repose" and "dreamy quietude," a fantasy land away from the bustle of politics and economics. Meanwhile, his "wife represents the positive forces of time, place and number" (p. 125), and one of her functions is to disturb her husband's reverie as she reminds him to get back to work. He mentions the "dismay that lodges in the bosoms of us males" when the wife enters the study on cleaning day, so that "who can say . . . what sins of ours may be brought to light; what indulgences and compliances, which uninspired woman has granted in her ordinary mortal house, may be torn from us?" (p. 14). Here Stowe, a writer who formerly devoted her career to the cleansing of the nation's closeted sins, places her sympathies not with the wife's energetic house-keeping but with the husband's desire to be let alone. Inspired by an etching "the subject of which was the gambols of the household fairies in a baronial library," Crowfield imagines the spirit of the home to take the form of a host of "library fairies," who represent an unambiguously masculine "feeling of security, composure, and enjoyment" (p. 15).

Stowe constructs the character of the wife as the husband's antithesis, his symmetrical but reversed reflection. "My wife," Crowfield writes, "resembles one of those convex mirrors I have sometimes seen. Every idea I threw out, plain and simple, she reflected back upon me in a thousand little glitters and twinkles of her own; she made my crude conceptions come back to me in such perfectly dazzling performances that I hardly recognized them" (p. 6). Surface without depth, representing sheer visibility, the wife is the perfect symbol of the social, a kind of elaborate parlor ornament that decorates her husband's thoughts for presentation while remaining, like Mrs. Wakefield or Mrs. Chimney, without interior depth herself. The problem is that her proper talent for "perfectly dazzling performances" would sometimes carry her too far and, "in parox-ysms of housewifeliness to which the women are subject," she "would declare that we are never fit to be seen" (p. 9). If a mirror, she is a two-way mirror, opening up a window to the world and exposing the home to public scrutiny. During one such "paroxysm" she puts pressure on her husband to purchase an elegant carpet for the parlor, one that will properly bespeak their social status; this inaugurates a shopping spree that eventually leads, in Crowfield's metaphors, to the banishment of the "baronial library spirits" from the family sitting room and intro-duces, instead, the "Brownies," evil spirits of consumption and status display. "There are certain crises in a man's life," Crowfield laments, "when the female element in his household asserts itself in dominant forms that seem to threaten and to overwhelm him" (p. 19).

Crowfield's two daughters, echoing those in "I and My Chimney," help trigger his sense of masculine crisis. Marian fully embraces her identity as a parlor girl, a natural-born shopper: as for "pretty things," she says, "I am made so that I really want them" (p. 81); and Jenny is the very voice of modern interior décor, complaining that "our parlor has always been a sort of log cabin,—library, study, nursery, greenhouse, all combined. We never have had things like other people" (p. 18). Their father's reclusive habits, they explain, prevent him from understanding social considerations: "he never goes into company; he don't know and don't care how the world is doing, and don't see that nobody now is living as we do" (p. 19). Like the daughters in "I and My Chimney," Marian and Jenny associate the multifunctional, old-fashioned parlor with outdated paternal tyranny, and their wish to upgrade the parlor is accompanied by a desire to remove their father from it: they wonder why "papa never had a study to himself" and talk him into turning the south room into his study so that they can have "a parlor fit to be seen" (p. 18). The patriarchal parlor that gathered family and friends together in the evenings in intimate conversation and shared activities will henceforth be divided.

Stowe follows the same cultural logic as Hawthorne and Melville, then, in showing men and women to have a naturally oppositional attitude toward the home. Like her male colleagues, Stowe sees the division of the spaces of the home as a potential loss of masculine control, and the redesigning of its interior as a battle between the sexes. In a sketch entitled "Our House," for instance, Crowfield's son-in-law is obsessed with his "favorite idea of a library," and when he and his wife plan their new house, he "resists like a Trojan" the wife's and mother-in-law's attempt to steal two feet from his library to benefit the bedroom and parlor (p. 267). There ensues a battle of pencils, where Bob fights to preserve the size of the library and the plan's "symmetry" against the women's agenda. It is important, however, that the meaning of this architectural war-zone in terms of gender and interiority is markedly different in Stowe's sketches and Hawthorne's and Melville's. Despite the dramatization of marital conflicts, Stowe's assumed masculine perspective does not pose privacy and intimacy as mutually exclusive terms. Nor, in the final analysis, are men and women as dichotomized or spaces as segregated in her ideal domestic plan as they are for Hawthorne and Melville. Stowe allows for a considerable fluidity between genders and spaces and thus imagines a different kind of middle-class masculinity and a different program for domestic unity. We saw in Chapter 1 how marital-advice novelists like Sarah J. Hale and Eliza Leslie, alongside domestic architects like A. J. Downing, attempted, somewhat paradoxically, to imagine a democratic, "symmetrical" household that is nonetheless unified under the overriding values associated with the husband and father. Stowe, by contrast, tries to imagine in her sketches a democratic household where unity is achieved by the father's incorporation of feminine values. Crowfield is the ideal domestic man for Stowe because he patently embraces both intimacy and privacy, both sociability and solitude. When he lists the attributes of the well-managed home for his wife and daughters, the liberal axiom "There can be no true home without liberty" is high on his list. Like Wakefield and the Chimney narrator (and like Ruskin and John Ware), he explains that "the very idea of home is of a retreat where we shall be free to act out personal and individual tastes and peculiarities, as we cannot do before the wide world" (p. 60). But, revealingly, this consideration is only second on his list, preceded by the maxim "No home is possible without love" (p. 57). Intimacy, for Crowfield, does not negate masculine liberty, and even precedes it in importance.

This merger of negative liberty and intimacy constitutes the spirit of the old parlor that he wishes to preserve. This room is a hybrid space, both the male and the female domain, both parlor and study: "it was written on the face of things that everybody was there to do just as he or she pleased. There were my books and my writing-table spread out with all its miscellaneous confusion of papers on one side of the fireplace, and there were my wife's great, ample sofa and work-table on the other; there I wrote my articles for the 'North American;' and there she turned and ripped and altered her dresses; and there lay crochet and knitting and embroidery side by side with a weekly basket of family mending, and in neighborly contiguity with the last book of the season" (pp. 6–7). As for the children, "the centripetal attraction drew every pair of little pattering feet to our parlor" (p. 8). The boys use their father's desk to hide their toys, and the girls keep their paper dolls in their mother's sofa. What characterizes this room is not the erasure of gender difference. On the contrary, gender difference is continuously emphasized and reemphasized by the room's strict separation into male and female domains.

But this dichotomy does not seem to generate conflict in Stowe's world. The husband's intellectual pursuits live in "neighborly contiguity" with the activities of the wife and children. Nor does the continuous "stream of visitors and loungers which was always setting towards our parlor" threaten its privacy (p. 9). When the wife and daughters separate the study from the parlor, then, Crowfield simply moves this bigendered, multifunctional room into his domain. "I had purposely christened the new room study," he explains, "that I might stand on my rights as master of ceremonies there, though I opened wide arms of welcome to any who chose to come" (p. 21). What the sketch ultimately upholds contra prevailing designs of the domestic sphere, then, is (a) that the function of space is considerably fluid; it can be manipulated and changed by the mere act of renaming a room, and (b) that while father undoubtedly knows best, what he knows about the proper management of the household is what every proper parlor woman would wish him to know.

I am arguing that, while Stowe cleverly retains the rhetoric of masculine privacy found in "Wakefield" and "I and My Chimney" in the character of Crowfield, she simultaneously empties that rhetoric of much of its import. Hers is a mode of privacy with nothing "odd" or "eccentric" about it, unthreatened by the invasion and exposure of intimacy, unburdened by traces of the uncanny. Crowfield's private space of writing and reverie is tame enough to welcome children and pets into it, normative enough not to be threatened by constant social observation. Stowe's version exemplifies the problematic logic (which we have already encountered in the case of Fanny Fern's "Mother's Room"; see Chapter 1) of a privacy awarded on condition that its contents be predetermined to be utterly coherent and safe. Appropriately, therefore, where both Melville and Hawthorne erect high walls around private space through a mode of representation that calls attention to its own fictionality, through allusive symbolism and ambiguity, Crowfield embraces the conventions of domestic realism. The language of these sketches is designed to create the illusion of the reader's actual entrance into the real household of real people (reinforced by the fact that Crowfield is presented as the real, living author of the tales), an illusion that accords with Crowfield's philosophy that the study welcomes with open arms "any who [choose] to come" (p. 21).

Stowe's sketches, like her narrator, are, in that sense, sociopetal, structured on open secrecy: they construct the home as private only to open it up to the inspection of the world. In Joan Hedrick's terms, they represent an example of "parlor literature," the kind of literature based on the realistic reporting of quotidian life, meant to be enjoyed in familial intimacy rather than in the solitude of the study, and aimed at drawing readers in and regulating their personal lives, even as they maintain an illusion of a "private" sphere.[62] The pedagogical writing Crowfield produces in the parlor/study, that is, is to be consumed communally in the same parlor/study by his wife and daughters, to whom he reads his work, and also by thousands of like-minded readers in their own homes. Despite her thematic similarities to Melville and Hawthorne, and despite the androgynous act of assuming a male voice, Stowe's writing is based on a different understanding of domestic fiction, one that is directly connected to women's particular relation to domestic space. In their full exposition of perpetually sunshiny interior spaces, mimetic detail, sentimental pedagogy, and intimate atmosphere, these sketches present, in fact, a contrasting, mirror image to "Wakefield" and "I and My Chimney" and their negative theology of privacy.

But this theology does surface in Stowe's writing on occasion, although, interestingly enough, not as a masculine prerogative but as a feminine desire. As Stowe contemplated launching a professional writing career, she (anticipating Virginia Woolf by many years) wrote to her husband, "If I am to write, I must have a room to myself, which shall be *my* room";[63] apparently, she, unlike her avatar Crowfield, found it impossible to think and write with spouse, houseguests, children, and pets clamoring for attention. It is noteworthy that, while she was writing the sketch, Stowe was planning her family's first house in Hartford, where she reserved a space designated solely for her own intellectual work, a sanctum of privacy and writing (in a letter to her editor, she refers to "our parlor" but to "my library").[64]

In *House and Home Papers*, the wife suggests that "one of the greatest reforms that could be, in these reforming days . . . would be to have women architects. The mischief with houses built to rent is that they are all mere male contrivances. . . . I don't see for my part, apropos to the modern movement for opening new professions to the female sex, why there should not be well-educated female architects" (p. 276). Of course, in a sense, there already were. Stowe's sister Catharine Beecher designed an interior plan for middle-class houses and published it in *Treatise on Domestic Economy*, and the two sisters collaborated in designing a similar plan in *American Woman's Home* (Fig. 7).[65] The differences in the conception of the domestic interior, its divergence from, say, Downing's blueprints, are subtle, but clear. In *Treatise*, for instance, Beecher describes "a retired parlor for the mother"; she injects the value of privacy into the same space that male architects describe as the realm of woman's self-effacing devotion to her family and to her social circle.[66] By the same token, Beecher and Stowe do not regard the presence of a masculine study as a necessity. They allocate an additional, multipurpose room that "is a parlor, [but] can be used for a study or library by the master of the family" and can triple its function as guest bedroom. Their plan not only prescribes a less-stringent segregation but also specifically allows for spatial fluidity: one of their important innovations is the introduction of moving screens that subvert the fixing of space and allow for its continual re-creation on an ad hoc basis. Moving the screen enabled the creation of private niches even within an essentially communal space, and now the same room could function as a bedroom, a sewing room, and a sitting room all at once. (The patrician central chimney, needless to say, Stowe and Beecher describe as "the most wasteful method, as respects time, labor, and expense. The most convenient, economical, and labor-saving mode of employing heat is by convection, as applied in stoves and furnaces" [p. 69].)

Overall, what is remarkable about the Beecher and Stowe design is

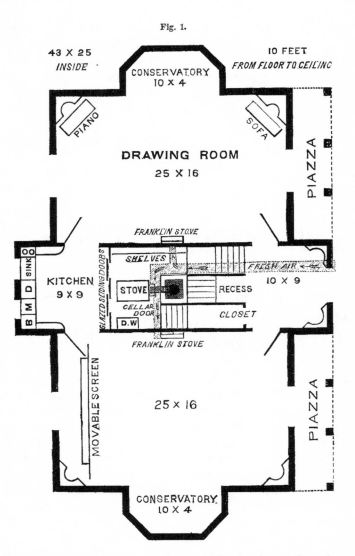

Figure 7. Beecher and Stowe's design for a middle-class home, featuring an unnamed multipurpose room with a movable screen. From *American Woman's Home.*

the way it revised, through a hybrid and relatively fluid understanding of space, the image of the home as a masculine preserve of privacy. Stowe's husband once complained to her (in a passage that could have been taken out of "Wakefield" or "I and My Chimney"), "and as for place, it seems to be your special delight to keep everything in the house on the move, and your special torment to allow anything to retain the same position a week together. Permanency is my delight,—yours, ever-lasting change."[67] In its dynamic design, challenging the static designs of Downing and his professional colleagues, Beecher and Stowe's plan made malleable the boundaries between privacy and intimacy, repose and performance of social duties, and if they allowed for individual privacy at all, they claimed it for the wife or mother rather than for the middle-class man.

If, as I have emphasized in this chapter, the designs and descriptions of the mid-century home regularly functioned as metaphors for subjective interiority, what kind of mental architecture did Stowe's conception of the interior imply? Unlike the liberal model of the divided self, which we have explored here at length, Stowe's blueprint imagines no stringent barriers within the self, no permanently obscure or incommunicable backstage regions in the mind. Her version of interiority is characterized by what Lefebvre calls the "illusion of transparency" (p. 124), where space is conceptualized and idealized as fully visible, cleansed of dark, hidden traps. It is an interior space where the uncanny does not exist: whatever is obscure or encrypted can easily be made coherent and visible by use of communication, just as the inner tensions of the middle-class home are brought into the public eye, and thus resolved, by sentimental writing itself. This suspicion of privacy and belief in the power of communication to heal somewhat resemble Freud's early ideas on psychoanalytic therapy. But unlike in Freud, where the crossing of the threshold between the back- and the front stage of the mind always involves fierce resistance and anxiety, here subjectivity has a smooth continuum between its social and private aspects. This ideal is also accompanied by a specific political program. "It was on the basis of this ideology," Lefebvre writes, "that people believed for quite a time that a revolutionary social transformation could be brought about by means of communication alone. 'Everything must be said! No time limit on speech! Everything must be written! Writing transforms language, therefore writing transforms society!'"[68] This is certainly true of many twentieth-century identity-politics movements, which proposed that emplotting the private self in public narratives was tantamount to social change; it is no less true, as I will argue in the next chapter, of Stowe's antislavery fiction.

Stowe's sketches were devised even as the Union Army was taking its heaviest blows in the middle years of the Civil War. The war provides the context for the sketches because, among other aspects, it created a boom in consumption and, especially, reduced the prices of carpet and upholstery textiles, which the women in "The Ravages" are so intent on purchasing. As she was first thinking about writing the sketches, Stowe hoped they would provide readers some relief from the horrors of the war, a kind of psychological displacement of political anxiety in favor of "household merriment."[69] The sketches thus eerily mirror the sharp segregation between man's public role as soldier and citizen and his private, domestic reprieve. That the national and the domestic are inextricably linked was by then a well-worn notion, buttressed by decades of political rhetoric that employed the metaphor of domestic architecture to describe the crisis in the federal union. The most famous example, of course, is Lincoln's 1858 "A House Divided" speech, in which he paraphrases the biblical quote and applies it to the state of the Union. "I do not expect the house to fall," Lincoln wrote, "but I do expect it will cease to be divided. It will become all one thing, or all the other."[70]

This rhetoric must have resonated with particular force for an audience that was simultaneously witnessing the actual divisions within the home and the challenges they posed to traditional values of centralized patriarchal control, a republican ethos of production and frugality, and masculine power. The divided plot, then, must have had significant political connotations for its readers. Although Stowe's sketches are too sentimental, too engaged in domestic realism, to have drawn critical attention to their possible national-political content, they clearly diverged (unlike Hawthorne's and Melville's) from Lincoln's promise that domestic affairs would become "all one thing, or all the other." Her view of the war of the sexes within the home (the new "south room" of the father accommodating as it does the "northern" residents as well) was meant to promise readers, perhaps, a form of national hybridity, or, at least, a "neighborly contiguity" on the political front as well, provided that the ethos of transparency was allowed to reign. It is to Stowe's and her contemporaries' use of the divided interior in national debates over slavery that I next turn.

Chapter 3

The Master's House Divided: Exposure and Concealment in Narratives of Slavery

"If people could only know the secrets of other lives, how differently they would judge," Martha said at last.
"Yes, I said, that would be Heaven—the exact knowledge of facts."
"That is a grand thing to say," said Martha. "I never heard that before, I always think—well there . . . I shall have justice."
"And eyesight," I replied, "that is what I want above all. . . . Indeed, doubt and uncertainty make hell."

—*Women's-rights reformers, 1869*

I write in silence, without the fierce distraction of my noisy voice. . . . My silence is observant, an open eye, a secret shelter, vulnerable and dangerous and always deadly accurate. It is the distance that speech rushes in to fill, it is the honesty that the lie of my speaking voice rolls over like water, like cream, like the dangerous slithering of a deadly, impassive neutrality.

—*Patricia Williams*[1]

In the previous chapter we saw how Freud uses the metaphor of domestic architecture to illustrate his notion of a divided interiority. In "The Unconscious" (1915), however, he chooses the metaphor of race instead. He explains that some elements of the unconscious, while seemingly coherent, are constitutively incapable of passing the threshold into consciousness. "*Qualitatively* they belong to the system of [consciousness]," he writes, "but *factually* to the [unconscious]." They are comparable to "individuals of mixed race who, taken all round, resemble white men, but who betray their coloured descent by some striking feature or other, and on that account are excluded from society and enjoy none of the privileges of white people."[2] Abandoning the metaphor of the divided house, Freud now imagines the difference between the unconscious and the conscious in terms of the broader opposition between the public and the private. Certain dreams and fantasies he likens to mulattos in a racialized society who, try as they may to shed their genealogy, pass as white and vie for public acceptance on a "qualitative" basis. They are nevertheless doomed by the "factuality" of their racially marked bodies to remain bound to the invisible private realm, forever barred from the privileges of the (white) public.

Freud's choice of a racial metaphor to describe the contents of an invisible private realm would certainly strike a familiar cord with students of antebellum culture. Priscilla Wald, for example, analyzes in depth the peculiar "uncanniness" of nonwhite American subjects who—much like Freud's dangerous impulses, which invade consciousness only to be forced back into invisibility—pass the threshold of white public discourse, momentarily destabilizing its fiction of neutral, equal rights, only to be pushed back into their privatized, embodied, and excluded existence.[3] The binary structure of private embodiment versus public disembodiment itself has received ample attention in recent years. Michael Warner and Lauren Berlant have each explored at length how in America acquiring public voice and recognition involves a process of self-abstraction and self-concealment: from the eighteenth century onward, going public has meant creating a "prosthetic," disembodied public persona, one that negates the specificities of one's embodied existence. This process (what Warner calls the "principle of negativity") has been construed as the basis of a just society, as that which ensures that equal rights will be granted neutrally, without regard to private differences. And, as Warner and Berlant both point out, this process means *protection* as well as rights: the disembodied public persona has functioned as a form of "prophylaxis" for the individual, whose vulnerable, local aspects remain shielded from the assaults of the public.[4] In the realm of literature, publishing—going public—meant constructing a prosthetic narrative voice, a voice that could relate information drawn from private life without placing the embodied author's privacy at risk (we have seen how "Hawthorne," the narrator in the preface to *Mosses from an Old Manse*, both opens up and deflects discussion of Hawthorne's private interiority, which remains shielded behind a "veil").

This process of self-abstraction and self-concealment, however, and its reward of rights and protection, was available first and foremost to white, male, and propertied subjects. As Warner and Berlant note (as have many others), the abstract, unmarked individual of the liberal public sphere is, paradoxically, in fact distinctly identifiable by gender, race, and class (in the sense that, for instance, the universal voice is always grammatically male), and only those who embodied this ideal could safely pass into the realm of public recognition; others, like the mulattos of Freud's metaphor, were barred from entrance, pulled back into the darkness of the private realm, held by the "factuality"—what Warner calls the "humiliating positivity"—of their bodies. In the realm of literature, publishing meant for female, nonwhite, and/or nonpropertied authors, unlike for their male, white, propertied counterparts, placing the most vulnerable aspects of their lives at risk. Since these authors lacked the "prophylaxis" of self-abstraction, the attack on their literary voice was often also a direct attack on their private selfhood.

What strategies, then, were available to such subjects? They could try to pass as white men (by, for example, using a pseudonym) and thereby claim the privileges and immunities of the public sphere. They could also challenge the very process of self-abstraction/self-concealment by venturing into public visibility unabashedly embodied, without use of a prosthetic persona (as did, for example, middle-class women writers who sought to gain public authority by writing openly as domestic women). To do the latter was to revise the very meaning of the public sphere, from a space where particularized identities are repressed to a space "for the formation and enactment" of particularized identities, for "speak[ing] in one's own voice."[5]

The liberal-public sphere's relegation of female, poor, and/or nonwhite subjects to the private realm was linked with another form of "privatization": that of slavery. While slavery was undoubtedly the most urgent and salient issue on the public agenda in the antebellum United States, it was simultaneously and repeatedly described as beyond the bounds of public discourse. Slavery, that is, was often described, much like domestic violence, as none of the public's business. It is worth taking a moment to return, in this context, to "I and My Chimney."

I argue in Chapter 2 that Melville's tale uses the domestic interior to imagine, decades before psychoanalysis, an internal space of irreducible privacy. The concealed recesses of the chimney, that is, stand for an inherently unreadable and immensely valuable aspect of personhood, an aspect protected by the privileges of normative masculinity. I further suggest that to read these recesses as an "open secret," to insist, for instance, that they signify latent homosexuality, is not to expose the dark secrets of liberal individualism from outside but to participate in its own game of hide and seek, to enter, that is, into its binary structure, a structure that forever pits revelation against concealment, expression against reticence, a normative identity against the residues of subjectification.

In making this argument, however, I ignored another prevalent reading of Melville's tale, one that "opens" the secret of the chimney to expose racial rather than sexual meaning. The domestic space over which Melville's married couple struggles for mastery stands, according to this reading, for another bitterly disputed territory: the "national house" (as Abraham Lincoln liked to refer to the Union in the 1850s).[6] Expanding on that most worn-out of metaphors in the debates over slavery and the union, Melville warns that a house divided, if it can stand, is at the least not very cozy: "In those houses which are strictly double houses—that is, where the hall is in the middle—" he writes, "the fire-places usually are on opposite sides; so that while one member of the household is warming himself at a fire built into a recess of the *north* wall, say another member, *the former's own brother*, perhaps, may be holding his feet to the blaze before a hearth in the *south* wall—the two thus fairly sitting back to back."[7] This design, Melville adds, probably well aware that "architects" was frequently used in mid-nineteenth-century public discourse to refer to the framers of the Constitution, must have "originated with some architect afflicted with a quarrelsome family" (p. 1299). What keeps the narrator's own house from being thus divided is that until now the hollowness at its midst, the private recesses of the chimney, have not been probed and demolished. Those dark spaces, critics have suggested, encrypt the uncanny existence of slaves in the national house, much as the Constitution's most crucial act of compromise (and most devastating moral blind spot) is the burying of the issue of slavery within its enlightened discourse for the sake of uniting a nation. The fact that the word "slavery" does not appear in the tale could support rather than dispute such a reading: if Melville's textual house is an allegory of that other "framed" text, it is only apt that it should refrain from inscribing the one word that is so conspicuously absent from the Constitution itself.[8]

I am not suggesting, contra my previous argument, that the chimney's secret can indeed be conclusively opened by critics, that reading the tale as an allegory of slavery clarifies once and for all the text's deliberate ambiguities. My argument, after all, has been that *any* allegorical reading undermines the text's construction of privacy; and, indeed, critics who have argued for the existence of such an allegory of slavery in "I and My Chimney" diverge widely on what that allegory precisely consists of. Some, implying that the narrator's refusal to break open the chimney allies him with the abolitionist cause, point out that Melville patterned the tale's house on his two residences in Pittsfield—Arrowhead and Broadhall—and that both had cellars that were rumored to have sheltered fugitive slaves.[9] Others have argued, however, that this refusal should more properly be associated with a Websterian spirit of compromise (favoring, as the narrator does, a design in which flues are "grouped together in one federal stock in the middle of the house" over the "egotistical, selfish" separatist design) while abolitionism is represented by the wife and Mr. Scribe. Still others equate the wife with southern liberals and the narrator with slaveholders, Melville's progressively belligerent and defensive tone echoing that of southern politicians in the 1850s, down to his final exclamation "that I and my chimney will never surrender" (p. 1327).[10]

While the force of the allegorical readings diminishes as the narrator circulates among every major position in the antebellum slavery debate, I do find compelling the one element that all these readings share: the association of masculine privacy and of textual ineffability with slavery. By 1856, the year in which "I and My Chimney" was published, it has indeed become customary to think about slavery as somehow the white man's *private* affair, even as, paradoxically, it persisted as the first item on the public agenda. When Melville's narrator, caught digging at the root of his chimney, cuts short an intrusive neighbor's questions by throwing down his spade and exclaiming, "Sir! do not be personal" (p. 1304), he is echoing such better-recognized figures as George Harris's owner in *Uncle Tom's Cabin*, who dismisses his neighbor's pleas in behalf of the slave with "I know my own business, sir. . . . It's a free country, sir."[11] He echoes, also, the rhetoric promoted by the Kansas-Nebraska Act of 1854, say the words of Illinois senator Stephen A. Douglas, chairman of the Senate Committee on Territories, who supported a "privatization" of slavery by evoking "the great fundamental principle that every people ought to possess the right of framing and regulating their own internal concerns and domestic institutions in their own way."[12] Douglas deployed the double meaning of "domestic," that is, to draw the issue of slavery (as George Harris's owner does) into the invisible and protective realm of privacy and freedom of choice.

What facilitated his proposal was another central aspect of the liberal public/private divide: the notion that private property offers immunity from public interference. In other words, the liberal individual's privacy is protected not only by self-abstraction in the public sphere but also by his ownership of the private sphere. This is what Philip Harper calls "proprietary privacy," the mutual dependence of proprietorship and the protection of personal life in American ideology. The public has no right to interfere with a man's relationship with his slave because both the slave and the space in which this relationship unfolds are owned by that man.[13]

These two aspects of the liberal public/private divide—its protection of the private (white, male) self and its protection of private property—are mutually supportive. They come together under a philosophical notion, one that C. B. Macpherson has famously shown to be at the core of classical liberalism, the notion of self-property. Macpherson explains that, from Locke's *Second Treatise* on, "the individual, it was thought, is free inasmuch as he is proprietor of his person and capacities."[14] We have already discussed a central metaphoric structure that performed the task of enmeshing selfhood with property: the metaphor of masculine selfhood as a house. The house provided concealment and protection of the owner's private self, itself imagined as a walled-off interiority, while the "sacred inviolability" of that private self provided a hallowed aura for his estate, protecting it from public appropriation. All the while, subjects who did not or could not own property, and those who *were* property, subjects like the domestic woman or the slave who were relegated to a private space that they did not own, were denied full personhood (lacking, as they did, both public voice and private reprieve). Trapped in the circular logic of self-possession, they could not publicly claim the right to own property in return. We have discussed at length how middle-class women were simultaneously relegated to the private sphere and denied a space for privacy, to the extent that even private spaces that were "theirs" were represented as so thoroughly performative, conventionalized, and disciplined that they can only be described as "dead" private spaces. This was even more pronounced in the case of slaves, whose living conditions rarely included unsurveilled private spaces, whether because they worked and lived in a white household or because their living spaces were meager and cramped. Orlando Patterson argues that a prominent feature of the slave's life was "social death," that he or she had no social existence outside the house and person of the master.[15] No less dehumanizing, however, was slaves' "private death," the fact that, though limited to the private sphere, they had no proprietary claim over the space that they inhabited, nor the availability of domestic retreat from surveillance, and therefore no viable claim to full personhood.

This serves to explain why radical social-reform groups such as abolitionists and women's-rights activists targeted precisely liberalism's mechanisms of privatization and concealment. A primary contra strategy used by these groups was what may be called a *strategy of exposure.* If the public/private divide, in the name of neutrality and equality, in fact denied recognition of both public and private selfhood to a large portion of the population, and if it enabled the perpetration of violence behind the doors of privately owned space without making allowances for public redress, the solution was to work against this divide, both by publicizing the personal and by personalizing the public. An aspect of this solution is described by William Leach as "the doctrine of no secrets," the systematic revelation of the furtive contents of the private sphere to public scrutiny. Leach brings the example of a conversation between two midcentury reformers that perfectly captures the motivation behind the strategy of exposure: "if people could only know the secrets of other lives, how differently they would judge," says one; "that would be Heaven," answers the other, "the exact knowledge of facts." "And *eyesight*," replies the first, "doubt and uncertainty make hell."[16]

Like the wife in "I and My Chimney," the doctrinaires of "no secrets" understood the complete transparency between the spheres as both a means of promoting social justice and a utopian end in itself (a "heaven") and equated invisibility and reticence, the shaded spaces of "doubt and uncertainty," with evil (or "hell"). By exposing the stories of private life in public, social reformers sought to achieve two important aims: first, to fight against proprietary privacy by demanding public interference into the covert abuses of the private sphere; and, second, to achieve public recognition of the voices of excluded, privatized subjects such as women or nonwhites.

Since the 1970s, readers of noncanonic antebellum literature have rightly celebrated the success of these texts in forcing into visibility the private stories and social identities on whose repression the liberal public sphere was constituted. I wish to complicate such readings, however. I claim that if we take into account not only the public/private divide but also the internal divisions within the private sphere, this success accrues an additional, more problematic, dimension. As Shane Phelan has correctly pointed out,

> The real danger facing us is not one of doctrine nor of behavior, but more fundamentally of the impulse of totalization. . . . By "totalization," I do not simply mean the urge to produce grand theory. Grand theory, which seeks to tie all the threads, to connect all oppressions or causes to one underlying point, is part of the totalizing process. However, beyond this the process of totalization is one that *traps its practitioners by commanding that every facet of life be measured by one yardstick that, in turn, is seemingly clear and authentic.* . . . The denigration of the public/private split must be rethought.[17]

The strategy of exposure, that is, can backfire on its users. In its ambition to erase distinctions between public and private, it also erodes the internal boundary between the externally geared, narrativized aspects of the self and its residual, less-coherent aspects, thereby reducing all subjects to their socially defined narrative of identity. The strategy of exposure helps elevate "privatized" social identities to the position of public recognition but simultaneously risks the disappearance of concrete individual differences into these identities. What practitioners of the strategy of exposure sometimes discovered was that, in translating the private self into a public voice, in stepping out into public visibility as embodied subjects (as women, as blacks), they thereby also denied themselves the possibility of relief from social narratives of identity, the crucial backstage of disembodiment and the relaxation of performance. This problem can be put in the terms of possessive individualism as well. As Macpherson reminds us, classical liberalism indeed recognized an internal division in the self beyond the public/private divide. While Locke and his followers regarded the self as a form of property, they did not claim that every aspect of the self could be reified. They regarded the self, instead, as encompassing *alienable* aspects. For Locke this meant primarily the body and its capacity to work, but with the growing sophistication of capitalism, this also meant every aspect of a person's life that was offered for public consumption, including one's image and personal narratives. But they also recognized the existence of *inalienable* aspects, those nonbodily components that defied objectification, components that, though protected by property, were not in themselves property. You can sell your body, Locke argued, but you cannot sell your *life*.[18] While the question of what Locke meant by "life" is outside the scope of our discussion, it is clear that he assumed the existence of aspects of the self that could not be traded on. The danger inherent in the strategy of exposure is that it reduces the self to sheer alienability and, in refusing to recognize the existence of inalienable private aspects, also mistakes the normative narratives of gendered and racial identity—those narratives that can be publicized, shared, traded in—for the entire scope of the self.

By the end of this chapter, I hope to have explored both the problem inherent in the strategy of exposure and the reaction against this strategy by the very subjects who relied on it for liberation. I begin, however, with a section on the house-divided metaphor in public discourse, a metaphor that was used by all sides of the debate over slavery. I show how political rhetoric drew on the material and symbolic division of the bourgeois private sphere to garner support in the slavery debate. More specifically, I show that the masculine view of the private sphere, a view that, as we have seen, stressed the values of privacy, defensiveness, and containment of internal differences, was used by Lincoln to imagine a form of national harmony sustained by the "concealment" of slavery.

I will then move to show how this logic of concealment and containment was countered by social reformists using the strategy of exposure, a strategy perfected in such narratives as *Uncle Tom's Cabin*. To combat the concealment of slavery, *Uncle Tom's Cabin* casts the figures of the slave and the bourgeois white woman as domestic informants who undermine the protection promised by proprietary privacy. It thereby achieves two aims: it threatens white property owners with the invasion and internal division of their bastion; and it forces into the public sphere the embodied voices of women and blacks. But this strategy, I argue, was based on acceptance of the problematic assumption that the "factualities" of race and gender are the elements closest to one's subjective core, and that this core can be smoothly translated into coherent and comprehensive narratives of social identity. Put in different terms, this strategy accorded private interiority to marginalized subjects only on the condition that nothing about that interiority defied normativity.

I shall then read Frederick Douglass's response to *Uncle Tom's Cabin*, "The Heroic Slave," as an attempt to liberate subjectivity from the politics of exposure. This novella is commonly interpreted as a challenge to

Stowe's depiction of passive, feminized black masculinity, a challenge issued through the construction of the publicly heroic black man who manages to escape "social death." No less important, however, is the fact that Douglass bases this construction on another project: staking for the black man a right to a vital private region beyond social identity, exposure, and narrativization. If in the context of voice politics silence is a mark of failure, Douglass shows why silence can also be the badge of achievement.

The National House Divided

As the political reading of Melville's quarrelsome "chimney" couple suggests, antebellum stories of private life often reached beyond the boundaries of the home to comment on public affairs. Indeed, in her influential essay "Manifest Domesticity," Amy Kaplan points out that adherence to the separate-spheres ideology in the interpretation of antebellum domestic fiction, the assumption, that is, that national concerns lie outside its imaginary realm, falls apart at the point where the two meanings of "domestic" converge. While the primary meaning of "domestic" relates to home life and is in opposition to "public," another one of its meanings relates to the nation (as in "domestic policies" or "domestic affairs") and is in opposition to "foreign." The convergence of these two meanings facilitates the notion, so central to the rhetoric of the modern state, of the nation as a home. Moreover, "when we contrast the domestic sphere with the market or political realm," writes Kaplan, "men and women inhabit a divided social terrain, but when we oppose the domestic to the foreign, men and women become national allies against the alien, and the determining division is not gender but racial demarcations of otherness."[19]

Oftentimes, however, the rhetoric of national domesticity did not depict the home as a front united against the threat of racial otherness; on the contrary, it employed the notion of an internal split within the home to allegorize political differences while deflecting the threat of racial otherness. Such is most clearly the case with the house-divided metaphor, one of the most prevalent metaphors in political rhetoric during the decades leading up to the Civil War. While the use of the paraphrase of the biblical "if a house be divided against itself, that house cannot stand" to describe a potentially fragile national unity can be traced to the early republic, it gained in popularity and frequency in the 1830s, and was eventually employed by all sides of the slavery debate, by abolitionists, African American activists, unionists, and supporters of slavery alike.[20] What surely lent particular force to this metaphor was the fact that the antebellum middle-class home was itself becoming a divided, contested, and gendered terrain, one that encompassed clashing sets of values. As the middle-class house became literally divided between different domains, and as cultural authorities devised strategies for maintaining patriarchal control over this divided space, a rich metaphor was created for discussing the growing rift between North and South and the possibility of maintaining federal authority despite this rift. No less important, the metaphor provided a way of discussing these issues without bringing the question of slavery itself into the limelight.

The house-divided metaphor encouraged a way of thinking about the nation as a home markedly different from the metaphor described by Kaplan. Kaplan's study focuses on the rhetoric of gurus of domesticity such as Sarah J. Hale and Catharine Beecher. Domestic writers, she shows, promoted the syllogism that, since women had a privileged position within the home, and since the nation was a "home," the domestic woman should have had a determining influence over the nation. Their language forged a tight link between the domestic woman's duty to reach out to the world beyond the home, to domesticate a disorderly exterior, and the ideology of manifest destiny, which declared it a national responsibility to civilize foreign lands and peoples. At the same time, these writers associated the woman's task of cleansing the home's interior of "barbarity" (say, the behavior of unruly children) with the national fantasy of ridding the homeland of its internal aliens, particularly "savage" blacks and Indians. Kaplan's analysis thus allows us to recast within a national context precisely those values that I have tied, in the previous chapters, into "parlor" domesticity: its commitment to sociopetence and transparency, to the expansion of the boundaries of the home, and to the exposure and eradication of its hidden, "uncanny" spaces.

But what Kaplan terms "manifest domesticity" represents only one way of linking the regulation of the home with the conduct of the nation. If we turn from the texts of domestic writers to those belonging to traditionally more masculine genres, we find the metaphor of the nation as home shaped not by the feminine but by the masculine perspective on the private sphere. That perspective, we have seen, emphasized not the sociopetence of the home, not its expansion out into the world, but its sociofugality, its defensive contraction down to a realm of impenetrable privacy. We have also seen how this view favored the containment rather than the expulsion of the otherness within, thereby prescribing a model of patriarchal governance through which the domestic other (most often the wife) was given her own space, but was also carefully monitored and delimited within that space, a model that is implied in the architectural recipes of Andrew Jackson Downing and his colleagues. This model was easily translatable into a vision of the nation as divided over the issue of slavery yet united by federal authority, and it

allowed the public to focus on the precarious "marriage" between a pa-
ternalistic North and an unruly South, rather than on the more vexing
issues of slavery and racism.

Consider, for example, an editorial that appeared in *Harper's* in January 1852 entitled "The Value of the Union." Raising the topic on the approach of the "natal day of Washington," the editorial asks its readers
"to consider the value of our national Constitution as *a work of art.*" "In
the department of architecture, especially," it continues,

> some of the favorite writers of the age are analyzing the elements of its ideal ex-
> cellence. The perfection of an architectural structure is its rhythm, its analogy,
> its inward harmonious support, its outwards adaptedness to certain ends. . . .
> One of the most popular and instructive works of the day is Ruskin on the dif-
> ferent styles of architecture. Would it be thought whimsical to compare with this
> the Letters of Madison and Hamilton on the Federal Constitution? . . . There is
> *analogy* of ideas, there is *harmony* of adaptation, there is *unity* of power. There
> is . . . the beauty of *rest*, the beauty of *strength in repose*, the beauty of action in *har-
> monious equilibrium*. . . . there is a perfect arrangement of mutually supporting
> parts, and a perfect *resolution of mutually related forces*, all combined with *harmo-
> nious* reference to a high and glorious end.[21]

While *Harper's* does not explicitly discuss domestic architecture, its vocabulary of "inward harmonious support," "strength in repose," "harmonious equilibrium," "mutually supporting parts," and "mutually related
forces" draws from Ruskin and his American followers' model for private homes. The editorial repeats one ideal in developing the metaphor
of the Constitution as the Union's architectural blueprint: that of "harmony," or the smooth management of internal differences. It thus precisely echoes architects such as Downing, who insinuated, as we recall,
that the master of the house should contain and control the domestic
other rather than violently suppress her and used the analogy of a
"Washingtonian," democratic style of governance, which was superior to
a "Napoleonic," despotic style. Rather than oust from the national
house those who "should traitorously conspire the death of our American Union, or even think of applying the torch to the glorious structure
of our Federal Constitution," the *Harper's* editorial proposes to make
them realize that they represent an integral part of the Union's structure, subservient to its larger design. All the while, and quite strikingly
for the contentious year of 1852, the term "slavery" is mentioned not
even once, as if that ideal harmony of the union depended also on silence concerning the main cause of domestic strife.

Harper's used President Washington's birthday not only to invoke the
Founding Fathers' spirit of consensus but also to underscore the notion
of "strength in repose." By the 1850s, the worship of Washington as
America's quintessential hero had come to focus, alongside his public

deeds, on his withdrawal into private life (it is not coincidental that this popular admiration chose as its cynosure not any public monument but the campaign to preserve Washington's private residence in Mount Vernon).²² Washington could have "made himself an emperor of the United States," wrote one commentator. "Why did he not do it? There can be no doubt that a love of home and native soil, and of the shade of retirement, was one of the master passions of his mind."²³ Indeed, it is precisely this notion of retirement as democratic patriotism, embodied in the legendary Washington, that is again and again raised in antebellum writing to describe the ideal American citizen. Designers of the private sphere insisted that "the love of country [was] inseparably connected with the *love of home*," and that the man who "render[ed] domestic life more delightful" was thereby also "strengthening his patriotism, and making him a better citizen."²⁴ The citizen benefited the nation not by seeking to launch from his home a campaign to domesticate a ruthless and alien world, like Hale's and Beecher's model domestic woman, but by wishing, above all, to *defend* this home from that alien world. "Thus, the man who has a home," wrote a home reformer, "feels a love for it, a thankfulness for its possession, and a proportionate determination to uphold and defend it against *all invading influences*. Such a man is, of necessity—we might say selfishly, a good citizen."²⁵ Rather than expansionism, the rhetoric of patriotism-cum-domestic retirement stressed the fortification of domestic boundaries and the resistance to movement, appropriation, and change: "and to this innate feeling, out of which grows a strong attachment to natal soil," wrote Downing, "we must look for a counterpoise to the great tendency towards constant change, and the restless spirit of emigration, which form a part of our national character; and which, though to a certain extent highly necessary to our national prosperity, are, on the other hand, opposed to social and domestic happiness."²⁶ In 1858, in defense of the Homestead Bill but already within earshot of the drumbeats of war, Andrew Johnson made a similar point: "who are more interested in the welfare of their country than those who have homes? . . . When you are involved in war, in insurrection, or rebellion, or danger of any kind, they are the men who are to sustain you . . . you will have a population of men having homes, having wives and children to care for, who will defend their hearthstones when invaded. What a sacred thing it is to a man to feel that he has a hearthstone to defend."²⁷

The house-divided rhetoric struck an emotional chord because it appealed to these twin sentiments: the desire to control internal otherness, and the desire to protect the home from external invasion. Such sentiments guided the most familiar usage of this metaphor, Lincoln's speech during his successful bid for the Republican nomination for the

Senate in 1858. The speech's famous opening sentences seem at first to oppose the notions of domestic containment and defensiveness and to resemble more the desire for "house cleaning" and domestic expansionism that Kaplan shows to characterize domestic writers. Lincoln states:

"A house divided against itself cannot stand." I believe this government cannot endure, permanently half *slave* and half *free*. I do not expect the Union to be *dissolved*—I do not expect the house to *fall*—but I *do* expect it will cease to be divided. It will become *all* one thing, or *all* the other. Either the *opponents* of slavery will arrest the further spread of it, and place it where the public mind shall rest in the belief that it is in the course of ultimate extinction; or its *advocates* will push it forward, till it shall become alike lawful in *all* the States, *old* as well as *new*—*North* as well as *South*.[28]

But Lincoln's rhetoric is significantly less bellicose than it may at first seem. While the promise that the house "will become all one thing, or all the other" seems to issue a threat of annihilation against the slave-holding South, Lincoln later pointed out that this was not his intention. As Don E. Fehrenbacher explains, the Lincoln of this speech is no abolitionist fighter; he is far from calling for the active liquidation of slavery. What he proposes, rather, is to "arrest the further spread of it, and place it where the public mind shall rest in the belief that it is in the course of ultimate extinction." His primary concern is to block the spread of slavery to the west, an expansion that would have been enabled by Stephen A. Douglas's campaign for popular sovereignty. Slavery can exist, the speech suggests, as long as it remains bound within the southern states, where the Founding Fathers first "let it alone," and where it will, as Lincoln's usage of the passive voice suggests, eventually perish with no need for active intervention.[29]

The model invoked by the house-divided metaphor, then, is one of containing rather than purging internal differences. The speech implies that the South (like the overstepping wife of the domestic-division narrative) should be neither ousted nor brutally subdued but allowed to adhere to its own set of values as long as these do not spread beyond its clearly bounded sphere of influence.[30] While the first two sentences of the speech seem to suggest that the division of the national house must give way to the triumph of one half over the other, Lincoln is in fact implying that *only* a house divided—but carefully controlled—can stand, at least for the time being.

George B. Forgie has argued persuasively that speeches like "The House Divided" capture Lincoln's conviction that only a change in public sentiment can affect political resolution and that such a change is best achieved through the language of domesticity. He thus reads Lincoln as closely allied with domestic writers such as Harriet Beecher

Stowe, whose antislavery fiction was based on the same premise.[31] But if we are attuned to the gendered multiplicity of voices *within* the language of domesticity, clear differences between Lincoln's rhetoric and that of Stowe and other domestic writers begin to emerge. In fact, Lincoln's language of domesticity in the examples that Forgie presents implicitly associates his political rivals—Stephen A. Douglas and Franklin Pierce, James Buchanan, and Justice Roger Taney—precisely with the misguided ambitions of the domestic woman, who is presented as the home's internal threat in so many antebellum stories and sketches. Like the fastidious wife of "I and My Chimney," who refuses to let alone the enclosed spaces preserved by the narrator's ancestors, or like the heroines of *Uncle Tom's Cabin* who (as we shall see) boldly pried into the covert spaces of the master of the house, "Douglas and his friends," conspire to move slavery "from the position in which our fathers originally placed it," and thus to put the entire domestic/national structure at risk. And like the domestic woman of Kaplan's analysis, who conflates the home with the world, forever seeking to expand her sphere of influence beyond its bounds, so do Douglas and his allies, in Lincoln's argument, desire to reach beyond the "national house" to annex additional territories to the south and the west, thus rendering its borders unstable and vulnerable.[32] Lincoln's use of domestic language, that is, places him both alongside and in opposition to writers like Stowe; like her, he is mindful of the special power of the home in popular imagination but, unlike her, he regards that home from the perspective of privatist, liberal masculinity.

Lincoln's domestic language appealed not only to anxiety over internal instability but also to anxiety over external invasion into the home. Like so many authors of domestic-division stories that portray the erring wife in cahoots with an external threat to the home (often figured by the "meddling confidante"), Lincoln portrays Douglas and his supporters as simultaneously an internal and an external threat to the national house. This is what Forgie describes as Lincoln's deployment of the "fantasy of the house besieged." We have mentioned that one of the most prevalent and emotionally productive refrains in the rhetoric of national domesticity was that of the true citizen's "determination to uphold and defend [his house] against *all invading influences*." Lincoln knew to garner this determination in support of his platform. Southern politicians had long used the metaphor of the besieged house in their speeches, claiming that a while northerners were "safely housed, enjoying all the blessings of domestic comfort, peace, and quiet in the bosom of their own families," southerners were defending their homes (from abolitionists and their supporters) "as if hordes of insatiable desperadoes threatened domestic securities."[33]

Lincoln attempted to play on his northern audience's similar siege mentality. As Priscilla Wald persuasively argues, Lincoln recognized the difficulty in drawing support from an audience whose own homes were not directly influenced by slavery; he thus repeatedly portrayed Douglas as the enemy, not simply because he opposed abolitionism, but because he opposed *the very ideal of liberty*. In that way, he was able to represent Douglas as a danger to the home of each and every one of America's white citizens, not only to the well-being of its black subjects. According to Lincoln, to accept Douglas's "privatization" of slavery, his idea that the existence of slavery should be left up to the decision of each citizen in his "domestic institution," was not to promote but to place at risk one's autonomy and personal liberty. "It does not stop with the Negro," Lincoln warned; "is the white man quite certain that the tyrant demon will not turn upon him too? . . . destroy the spirit of liberty, and you have planted the seeds of despotism *around your own doors*." Douglas, figured as a promoter of anti-Washingtonian, foreign-inspired despotism, threatened to invade the American house, or to "dig . . . under it that it may fall of its own weight."[34]

But while this kind of rhetoric characterizes the culmination of Lincoln's debates with Douglas, it also points to the logic that both positions share. Precisely where the two political rivals seem to be most at odds is arguably also where their positions begin to approximate each other. Each politician represented himself as the protector of the sanctity of the home, and each represented the other as the dangerous enemy of its freedoms. Douglas's popular-sovereignty doctrine proposed to leave citizens alone to form their own decision about whether slavery should be allowed in their private sphere of influence, and he railed against the meddlesome invaders of that sphere. As Lincoln puts it in the "House Divided" speech, Douglas suggests "that if any *one* man choose to enslave *another*, no *third* man shall be allowed to object" (p. 462); as long as the principle of private choice is maintained, Douglas "*cares* not whether slavery be voted *down* or voted *up*" (p. 463). Lincoln argues that this "care not" position is tantamount in practice to the support of the spread of slavery. He describes himself as holding the opposite view, as one of "those whose hands are free, whose hearts are in the work—who *do* care for the results" (p. 468). Lincoln thus equates freedom with the *refusal* to turn a blind eye to acts and choices just because they are taken in private. But in arguing for the "containment" rather than the purging of slavery, in playing on his audience's "fantasy of a house besieged," and in his substitution of the general issue of liberty for the concrete problem of slavery, Lincoln was in fact in accord with Douglas's privatist philosophy. Lincoln was willing, that is, to "let alone" pockets of slavery in the South in order to save the Union's domestic harmony, and his rhetoric's bottom line posed the liberty and privacy of the white home above and beyond the crime of enslavement. The use of the metaphor of the divided house itself is the rhetorical equivalent of "privatizing" the issue of slavery. Posed as the speech's central motif, it drew attention to the conflict between the different factions of the body politic and away from those who were altogether excluded from it.

It was precisely to this practice of reticence and concealment, one shared by arch political rivals, that Frederick Douglass fervently reacted in a speech four years later. Referring to the horrors of the now full-blown Civil War, Douglass's speech echoes the house-divided rhetoric of the previous decade. Like Lincoln, who played on the "fantasy of the house besieged," Douglass aimed to provoke emotional reaction by describing the Confederates as home invaders, as "the spoilers of the Republic [who] have dealt with the nation like burglars—stealing all they could carry away and burning the residue."[35] But the real target of his speech was not the criminal actions of the Confederacy; it was the use of language by the political leaders on both sides of the national divide. Douglass points out that future generations "will find in no public document emanating from the Loyal Government, anything like a frank and full statement of the real causes which have plunged us into the whirlpool of civil war. On the other hand," he adds, "they will find the most studied and absurd attempts at concealment. Jefferson Davis is reticent. He seems ashamed to tell the world just what he is fighting for. Abraham Lincoln seems equally so, and is ashamed to tell that world what he is fighting against . . . this concealment is one of the most contemptible features of the crisis" (p. 477). The concealment of slavery, which characterized both Lincoln's and Douglas's positions, in both cases legitimized by the promotion of white liberty, is here presented by Douglass as the mark of shame: slavery is concealed because it is the stain on the white man's hidden soul, the skeleton in his closet.

Douglass then goes on. "A house divided against itself cannot stand," he repeats the cliché;

We have endeavored to join together things which in their nature stand eternally asunder. . . . union by compromise is impossible. In order to have Union, either in the family, in the church, or in the state, there must be unity of idea and sentiment in all essential interests. . . . When a man and woman are lawfully joined together for life, the only conditions upon which there can be anything like peace in the family, are that they shall love or fear each other. Now, during the last fifty years the North has been endeavoring, by all sorts of services and kindness, to win and secure the affection of the South. It has stepped sometimes a little beyond the requirements of true manly dignity to accomplish this, but all in vain. (Pp. 479–81)

Expanding the house-divided metaphor into a mini domestic-division drama, Douglass critiques the notion of "harmonious equilibrium" popularized by antebellum commentators on both family life and the Union. The notion that the ideal marriage should be based on the husband's loving indulgence of his wife's differences is ineffective in the case of the North's union with the South. It is unmanly and undignified. To control a divided house, what is required is fear rather than love, not indulgence but coercion. Lincoln, Douglass implies, was wrong on two counts. He was wrong to believe that slavery could be concealed in public discourse, and he was wrong to think that slavery could be "let alone" within the national house. What is needed is not containment but purging, not concealment but exposure. What is needed is what Douglass calls the "busy tongues and pens" of the abolitionists (p. 478), whose strategy was precisely to erode the boundary between private concealment and public visibility, and to do so through storytelling.

Peeping Toms: *Uncle Tom's Cabin* and the Strategy of Exposure

In what has been called *Uncle Tom's Cabin*'s claptrap ending, Cassy, Simon Legree's chattel concubine, manages to escape the plantation by using a psychologically sophisticated scheme.[36] Cassy's main asset is her knowledge. Unlike her protégée Emmeline and unlike Uncle Tom, she has been living in the plantation house for some time and has been inspecting the conduct of its owner closely. "I could make any one's hair rise, and their teeth chatter, if I should only tell what I've seen and been knowing" (p. 420), she says to Tom; and to Emmeline, "You wouldn't sleep much, if I should tell you things I've seen" (p. 437). What Cassy knows, in particular, is that her master has two skeletons in his closet: his unspecified sinful behavior toward his mother; and an unnamed crime against a slave woman that led to her death. Tellingly, it is the villain Legree whom Stowe depicts as harboring personality aspects that are intensely private, beyond the scope of narration; it is he, in other words, who is depicted as having psychological depth in a novel in which most other characters (and certainly the good ones) are transparent and flat. Although he proclaims that "ye won't find no soft spot in me, nowhere" (p. 484), Cassy knows that his Achilles heel lies in the enclosed, uncanny space of the garret, which shelters the specters of his mother and an abused slave woman. Her plot is ingenious: she invades the innermost corners of his soul to harp on his conscience (even succeeding in entering his dreams) and, simultaneously, appropriates a space of reprieve within his house where he dares not enter. She is thus able, through the staging of an "authentic ghost story" that plays directly on Legree's twin fears, to manipulate her way into freedom.

Far from a claptrap ending, I read Cassy's "stratagem" as *Uncle Tom's Cabin's mise-en-abyme* and as a vivid instantiation of the strategy of exposure that characterized abolitionism and other reform movements embraced by middle-class women. Cassy's use of a "literary" plot that drags "hidden things of darkness" into the light to gain liberation (and an actual Gothic novel is one of her props), correlates with Harriet Beecher Stowe's strategy of effecting political change by exposing in public, through literary convention, the dangerously privatized relationship between master and slave.[37] It is Stowe, after all, who made her readers' "hair rise and their teeth chatter" by publishing what she had "seen and been knowing" about the concealed horrors of slavery. If proprietary privacy had become a definitive white, masculine prerogative in the decades before the Civil War, what distinguishes the writing of reformers such as Stowe and what made it a potentially powerful political tool is its repeated invasions—bolstered by claims of truth, presence, and authenticity—into the private sphere's most covert spaces and its exposure of the relations they conceal. As we shall see, however, this systematic violation of boundaries was accompanied by the desire for spatial appropriation, for the extension of the right to privacy to those to whom it was not extended. This attendant desire was problematic not only because it meant claiming for oneself the very right that one put into question (similarly, perhaps, to Cassy's self-imposed enclosure in the very house that imprisoned her for years) but also because, to legitimize this claim, its maker was forced to empty the concept of privacy of its most vital meaning.

Cassy's "stratagem" is a far cry from the "art of gentle suasion" that domestic writers often presented to their female audience as compensation for its privatized existence. The "art of gentle suasion" was the expression often used to describe the belief that women, by preaching the values of compassion and Christian virtue to their husbands and children, lovingly and unobtrusively, within the home, could exert immense influence on the world without venturing out into it. Stowe, however, repeatedly presents the *failure* of this "art." In the opening chapters, Mrs. Shelby, for all her "high moral and religious sensibility and principle" (p. 20), cannot convince her husband not to sell Uncle Tom and little Harry. Eliza's Christian rhetoric and "gentle system of ethics" (p. 28) do little to dissuade her husband from his perilous escape plan. Later, Mrs. Bird, long regarded as the book's perfect avatar of domestic angelhood, fails to reach her husband's heart in their ideological argument over the Fugitive Slave Act. The kind of suasion that succeeds in the plot is Cassy's, and it is far from gentle. Hers is an influence "of a strange and singular kind" (p. 466); she is described as exerting over Legree "the kind of influence that a strong, impassioned woman can ever keep over the most brutal man" (p. 431), "an influence over him from which he could not free himself " (p. 432) and that he is "greatly controlled by" (p. 466). Cassy's influence captures what Richard Brodhead describes as the grimmer implications of gentle suasion, the sheer manipulative coercion that lay beneath this disciplinary strategy's rhetoric of love and Christian morality.[38] Her control is devoid of any benevolent pretensions: it is the raw use of psychological weaponry available to a person who lives in close proximity to another, who knows the inner workings of the latter's most private spaces, both material and psychic.

By the time Cassy's "dark influence" appears in the book, Stowe has already established that, where abstract preaching of compassion, moral virtue, and Christian love fail in the plot, the introduction of the particular and embodied stories of abuse succeeds. In the Bird household, for example, the physical entrance of Eliza, her crossing the threshold into the white home, convinces the senator (who has, on the same day, campaigned for the passing of a fugitive slave bill and who has just rejected his wife's abstract moral preaching) to provide shelter to a runaway slave. Philip Fisher argues that the witnessing of the effects of slavery on slaves and their families plays an important role in this novel, that Stowe is concerned with the potentially devastating effects of this witnessing on the white home, as "the family of white witnesses collapses alongside the slave families in their midst."[39] Stowe recognizes that compelled witnessing has the power to force a change of mind even among those opposed to abolition in principle. Just as the witnessing of Eliza's plight succeeds in the Bird household, Stowe's novel continuously relies on a form of vicarious witnessing of the horrors of slavery—filtered through her narration—to change her audience's opinion.

It is crucial to note, however, that (excepting the "matriarchal" Quaker settlement, an exception that proves the general rule) the home that bears witness to the effects of slavery within *Uncle Tom's Cabin* is first and foremost a *masculine* space. Houses in this novel are the referents by which men, not women, are defined. Thus, on the first page, the physical description of the interior of Shelby's house supports his classification as a "gentleman": "Mr. Shelby had the appearance of a gentleman; and the arrangements of the house, and the general air of the housekeeping, indicated easy and even opulent circumstance" (p. 11). Good housekeeping attests to male status, not to female virtue. Similarly, St. Clare's mansion defines *his* character rather than his wife, Marie's. That the "appearance of the place was luxurious and romantic," for example, supports the characterization of St. Clare as a "poetical voluptuary" (pp. 194–95). And to establish her description of Legree as morally decadent, Stowe depicts his house as having "that ragged, forlorn appearance, which is always produced by the evidence that the care of the former owner has been left to go to utter decay" (p. 400). Influential architects of Stowe's generation argued that the house was an extension, reification, and mark of its owner's character. Ruskin, for example, went so far as to argue that one could read the nature of a man by analyzing the architecture of his home, in much the same way as phrenology and physiognomy revealed a man's character by studying the shape of his body.[40]

Thus, while many readers choose to find in *Uncle Tom's Cabin* evidence for the "feminization" of the American home, the novel, in fact, promulgates the linkage between masculine selfhood and private property, the objectification of masculine character in wood and stone. The novel, after all, is entitled *Uncle Tom's Cabin* and not *Aunt Chloe's Home,* and its primary trajectory is Tom's replacement of his earthly cabin with a home with Jesus. For Stowe, the tragedy of slavery is compounded by and channeled through spatial loss; Uncle Tom's misadventure begins when he is plucked out of his pastoral cabin in Kentucky, and his dream of liberation through the salvation of his soul is vested in the language of real estate. Jesus promises him that "in my Father's house are many mansions. I go to prepare a place for you" (p. 174), and a religious hymn he sings imagines salvation as a "title clear to mansions in the sky" (p. 458).[41] Important evidence that Tom has indeed reached hell on earth on Legree's plantation is his discovery that he is not to have a room of his own, not even a "place to be alone out of his laboring hours" (p. 403). And to reinforce the idea that his death is a form of triumph, Stowe explains that Tom now rests, in quintessential privacy and never to be molested again, under the roof of the green turf of his grave.

The subplot of George Harris's escape, which critics often contrast with Tom's story, in fact follows a similar, though secularized, logic. George's grievance against slavery is that he has "not a cent of money, nor a roof to cover [him], nor a spot of land to call [his] own," and all he asks for, repeatedly, "is to be let alone" in his own house (pp. 220–23). "The right of a man to be a man" means in this novel "the right to have a home of his own, a religion of his own, a character of his own, unsubject to the will of another" (p. 448). Manhood, liberty, and proprietorship emerge as coterminous, and a sure sign that George Harris has, toward the denouement, achieved the full status of "man" is that he now possesses "a small, neat tenement in the outskirts of Montreal," with his own little study, to boot (p. 497).

What white men have and blacks should have is their "own private little world of memories, hopes, loves, fears, and desires" (p. 391), ensured by the proprietorship of their own house. This tight connection between manhood and home is one that, as we saw in Chapter 2, Stowe retains in her later domestic sketches, such as "Ravages of a Carpet," where she chooses a male persona to narrate domestic stories. But if Mr. Crowfield, the reformed, sentimentalized father, "earns" his right to proprietary privacy, the male characters in Stowe's earlier political fiction present a problem with that right. The problem is that, while the house projects the man's persona to the public, it also allows him to hide whatever interferes with that projection. The right to be let alone, Stowe shows, in fact enables cruelty and, first and foremost, the cruelty of the master toward his slaves. To claim such a right, moreover, is to effectively block humanitarian interventions into the abuses of slavery. I mentioned earlier that, when George's employer tries to dissuade his owner from taking him back to the farm, the latter silences him with; "I know my own business, sir. . . . It's a free country, sir" (p. 25). Likewise, the basically kind but morally lacking St. Clare holds that privacy supersedes ethical obligation. Commenting on the case of Prue, a slave who was tortured to death by his neighbor, St. Clare explains to his concerned cousin, "the best we can do is to shut our eyes and ears, and *let it alone.* You've only seen a peep through the curtain, a specimen of what is going on, the world over, in some shape or other. If we are to be prying and spying into all the dismals of life, we should have no heart to anything. It is like looking too close into the details of Dinah's kitchen" (p. 259; emphasis added). St. Clare's logic assumes that, while slavery may be wrong, invasion of privacy is a greater wrong, one that may entail the loss of one's own "heart" (especially if the prying does not stop with one's neighbors but proceeds into one's own kitchen). The objection to slavery, for men like St. Clare, must remain on an abstract, disembodied, nonintrusive level. If St. Clare's moral position reminds us of Stephen Douglas's care-not position, his marriage resembles nothing so much as that symbolic marriage in Frederick Douglass's speech, where the husband (the North) indulges his wife's (the South's) acts of atrocity with "unmanly" and "undignified" patience. St. Clare's earlier proclamation that he is "one of the sort that lives by throwing stones at other people's glass houses, but . . . never mean[s] to put up one for them to stone" is proved false (p. 217): to preserve his own, he never throws stones at other men's houses.

It is ironic, then, that St. Clare's house, with its large verandahs and sliding doors, is largely made of glass (indeed, his private study is "a little glass-room" [p. 330]). The proverbial glass house, both transparent and fragile, is an apt symbol for anxiety about the permeability of man's proprietary privacy, an anxiety triggered by the mere presence of the other within the house. Women like Ophelia, who go around peeping through curtains, prying into closets, and spying on "all the dismals" of private life, show that the house of slavery is indeed a glass house, its internal and external boundaries unprotected from surveillance and exposure.

Stowe's stratagem is thus not limited to the introduction of harsh, individualized facts into the tranquil home that is forced to witness them, as Fisher maintains, but includes the greater threat of transparency and leakage, a threat that the presence of the other within the divided house—of women and slaves—entails. As Ophelia points out to St. Clare, the master's house is never private. "Your house is so full of these little plagues, now," she distastefully remarks, "that a body can't set down their foot without treading on 'em. I get up in the morning, and find one asleep behind the door, and see one black head poking out from under the table, one lying on the door-mat,—and they are mopping and mowing and grinning between all the railings, and tumbling over the kitchen floor!" (p. 279). Indeed, the threat to the homeowner's privacy is one of the plot's main refrains. Over and over again, Stowe describes scenes of peeping, spying, and eavesdropping that are shown to complicate and disrupt the normal transactions of slavery. In the first few chapters, Eliza overhears Shelby and Haley's plan to buy her son and begins to plot her escape. As Shelby and his wife discuss the purchase in the supposed privacy of their bedroom, "there was one listener to this conversation whom [they] little suspected" (p. 49)—again, Eliza—who is confirmed in her need to flee. Mandy reports to the other slaves that she "got into the closet" and "hearn every word" of her master's suppressed anger toward his slaves (p. 58). Andy decides to help Eliza—escape because he overheard a dispute between his master and mistress "dis blessed mornin', when I bring in Mas'r's shaving water" (p. 61), that suggested that his mistress would condone such aiding and abetting. In fact, Mrs. Shelby counts on the slaves' eavesdropping as part of her efforts to hinder the purchase, and later in the novel she takes her slaves' knowledge of private conversations for granted, "nothing doubting, from her knowledge of Chloe's manner," for instance, "that she had heard every word of the conversation that had passed between her and her husband" (p. 298). Tom learns of St. Clare's carefully hidden despair over the death of Eva by "listening in the outer Verandah" (p. 363), and Adolph knows of Marie's plan to sell the slaves because he "hid [him]self behind the curtains when Missis was talking with the lawyer" (p. 375).

Hence, the real risk slavery poses to the white household is not in forcing it to witness horror but in forcing it to *be* witnessed. As Stowe notes in "Concluding Remarks," however, southern law had succeeded in evacuating this risk of much its force: "Let it be remembered," she writes, "that in all southern states it is a principle of jurisprudence that no person of colored lineage can testify in a suit against a white" (p. 510). Stowe knew that, although the law made some provisions against abuses of slaves, these provisions were often useless, since no slave could testify in court against his or her master, and in some states, no black man could serve as a witness in a white man's trial at all.[42] As an 1853 book about the "law of slavery" explains, the law could not afford to indict the master for battery of his slave, because this indictment "would only prompt him to 'bloody vengeance, generally practised with impunity, by reason of its privacy.' "[43] Refusing to undo the gory link between privacy and slavery, the law's circular and morally distorted logic suggested that it was in the *interest of the slave* to conceal the abuses of slavery from the public, because this would prevent the wreaking of vengeance in private later on. In *Uncle Tom's Cabin*, Cassy reminds Tom that there is "not a white person here, who could testify, if you were burned alive,—if you were scalded, cut into inch-pieces, set up for the dogs to tear, or hung up and whipped to death. There's no law here, of God or man, that can do you . . . the least good" (pp. 419–20). George Shelby, at the end of the novel, learns the same truth. When he threatens Legree—"I will go to the very first magistrate, and expose you"—Legree answers calmly, "Do! . . . Where you going to get witnesses?—how you going to prove it?—Come, now!" (p. 488).

But where the law fails, the novel steps in to issue a corrective. If Legree cannot be exposed in court, he certainly can be in fiction, and Stowe's narrator is the supreme eavesdropper and bearer of testimony of her own novel. A full sixteen chapters out of the novel's forty-five begin with a detailed survey of interior spaces, creating the continuous illusion that the narrator is shedding light on zones commonly veiled in darkness. Here is where the domestic woman's relegation to the private sphere by domestic ideology becomes an advantage: not simply because of her purported moral superiority but because of her privileged vantage point into the inner workings of the home. *Uncle Tom's Cabin*'s primary tactic, then, is its revelation of what it insists is authentic fact, its claim to an extreme form of realism not only mimetic of reality but also identical to it, to the blurring of the boundary between fiction and reportage. Stowe makes this clear in "Concluding Remarks." The novel is not imaginary, she claims, but "authentic," using as its source "her own observations, or that of her personal friends," who "have observed characters, the counterpart of almost all that are here introduced; and many of the sayings are word for word as heard herself, or reported to her" (p. 510). The "terrible incidents" reported have "their parallel in reality" and are "sketches drawn from life." They are part of a bloody body of facts that, despite the law's restrictions, "occasionally force their way to the public ear" (p. 511).

This "desire to exhibit [slavery] in a *living dramatic reality*" (p. 513), so clearly antithetical, for example, to Hawthorne's repeated pleas in his prefaces for imaginative latitude and a break in relation between fact and fiction, is the context that dictated the novel's reception as well.

Rather than debate the novel's merits as a literary performance, the typical response was to question the truth of the facts it purported to expose, which induced Stowe to compose *A Key to Uncle Tom's Cabin; Presenting the Original Facts and Documents upon Which the Story Is Founded Together with Corroborative Statements Verifying the Truth of the Work*. In the introduction to *A Key* she explains that this novel, "more, perhaps, than any other work of fiction that ever was written, has been a collection and arrangement of real incidents,—of actions really performed, of words and expressions really uttered" and constituting a "mosaic of facts."[44] With this publication, *Uncle Tom's Cabin* openly declared itself a roman à clef, representative of the genre of fiction that hovered most precariously on the boundary between public visibility and domestic privacy.

Cassy, we recall, emplotted her own roman à clef, in which her master's secret life found correspondence in a staged Gothic drama. Her presence within his house and access to his mind allowed her to find the key that would unlock this hidden relationship between private fact and fictional convention. Stowe's stratagem approximates Cassy's again when she implies in "Concluding Remarks" that she is privy to the (southern) reader's own interior life: "Have you not, in your own secret soul, in your own private conversings, felt that there are woes and evils, in this accursed system, far beyond what are here shadowed or can be shadowed? Can it be otherwise? Is *man* ever a creature to be trusted with wholly irresponsible power?" (p. 513). Not unlike Cassy, Stowe claims knowledge of the secret feelings hidden in her readers' breasts. And not unlike Legree, her readers are, in turn, urged to confront the connection between her novel's terror-inspiring plot and their "irresponsible power" in the private sphere, a connection that she believed would open the doors to emancipation.

"A Plain Spoken Woman Is Always to Be Dreaded"

Stowe's strategy in *Uncle Tom's Cabin* of exposing private truths to public knowledge, her deliberate violation of the spaces of privacy to achieve a political goal, was by no means unique. It is precisely the principle that guided what Frederick Douglass called the "busy tongues and pens" of the abolitionists. If the house-divided metaphor of mainstream politicians enmeshed home, nation, and Constitution to help preserve the Union through the concealment and containment of slavery, radical abolitionists such as William Lloyd Garrison retorted with "accursed be it, from the foundation to the roof, and may there soon not be left one stone upon another, that shall not be thrown down."[45] A primary tool in bringing down the house's walls was the publication of private affairs. In her thoughtful analysis of the career of leading antislavery activist

Angelina Grimké, Katherine Henry shows how Grimké's language in her speeches and writing continuously undermined the image of the private sphere as a peaceful, safe retreat, describing it instead as a prison or tomb. "Repeatedly," Henry explains, Grimké's "emphasis is not just on confinement, but on concealment. Her object is not just liberty for the captive, for it is the exposure of slavery to public view that provides comfort and deliverance. Bringing the invisible and unknown violence of Southern domesticity into the public discourse—the central tactic of abolitionism—is, in Grimké's metaphors, opening the tomb, exposing the putrid and pestilent to fresh air and sunlight, liberating the prisoner, and bringing the dead back to life."[46]

This strategy was wielded by reformers in the struggle for other social causes besides abolition, including, eventually, women's rights. Indeed, it was used by Stowe herself throughout her prolific career, in one instance, to correct the injustice done to one woman in marriage. In *Lady Byron Vindicated* (1870), Stowe unveils the sexual transgressions of the famous English poet and thereby seeks to salvage the reputation of his mistreated and falsely defamed wife. As in "Concluding Remarks" and *A Key to Uncle Tom's Cabin*, Stowe asserts that this work, too, is a mosaic of facts and based on firsthand knowledge. "I claim for men and women," she declares, "our right to true history. . . . Let us have truth when we are called in to judge. . . . I have vowed to tell the truth."[47]

"True history" was evoked to contract the growing distance between private and public life, a distance that allowed powerful men like Byron to maintain their position even if, behind closed doors, they indulged in behavior that Victorian society would never have condoned in its heroes.[48] Once again, Stowe recognized that, if the cultural prescription on women's role as moral authority was to be taken seriously, then print could serve as the best means to mediate between private sin and public scrutiny, despite the public silence imposed on "proper women" by propagandists of domesticity. Etiquette manuals and conduct books warned female readers that "a plain spoken woman is always to be dreaded";[49] but this warning sent, inadvertently, the opposite message since it could be issued only when the advantages of speaking plainly about private life had already been recognized as a potent political strategy.

The reception of *Lady Byron Vindicated* was, not surprisingly, mixed. While many saw the exposé of Byron's sexual transgressions as a dangerous violation of the code of privacy (even George Eliot, an admirer of Stowe's work, admonished her that "the Byron question should not be brought before the public, because . . . the discussion of such subjects is injurious socially"),[50] others, like Phoebe Hanaford on the pages of the *Woman's Advocate*, praised Stowe for precisely the same principle: "your book shows that there is nothing hid that shall not be revealed."[51]

Indeed, by the time *Lady Byron Vindicated* was published, women advocates had already been using the violation of privacy and the strategy of exposure for several decades, initially, within the context of Evangelical reform associations. This strategy was inseparable, in fact, from the brand of Evangelicalism bred by the religious revivals of the 1820s and the 1830s, the theological upheaval that was to affect Stowe's own upbringing so strongly and to provide a rationale for women's critique of patriarchy throughout the century. Although the Evangelical message imported from England early in the century, particularly through the works of Hannah More, prescribed a rigid form of the separate-spheres ideology and insisted that woman's role was restricted to the domestic sphere, in the American Northeast, Evangelical revivals often encoded, paradoxically enough, the opposite message. The Finneyite revivals in New England, New York, and Ohio, for example, promulgated the notion that women's role included the public exposure of sins perpetrated in private. Women were encouraged to speak publicly in so-called promiscuous assemblies and to "bear witness" or "testimony" on the public platform in order to confront their own private sins and, more important, in order to inspire the conversion of others through public example and thereby to purge society as a whole of its sins. What threatened established Protestant authorities most about these revivals was their practice of "praying by name": the singling out of "sinful" individuals—husbands, relatives, notable citizens, or prominent ministers—within the context of mass prayer. This practice was inseparable from Evangelical theology.

The problem with established Christianity, and particularly with Catholicism, Evangelicalism posited, was its de facto condoning of sin in the name of the privacy of the conscience.[52] As one woman put it, if in the "antique world," crime was dealt with publicly, "after the introduction of Christianity, the world trembled before the more awful terrors of conscience. But as the consolations of Christianity left untouched the evils which had caused pain . . . both the antecedent and the consequence of crime were relatively overlooked; wrongdoing was not the offense against public order which it had been to the Roman law, the crime,—it was the sin which did not need to be public in order to be deadly,—indeed was liable to be more deadly the more it was secret and concealed. Hence sprang up the conception of unspeakable crime."[53] Evangelical revivals sought, therefore, to turn concealed, "unspeakable" sins into exposed, purgeable crimes by naming individual sinners in public.[54]

So too did the Evangelically inspired temperance movement of the 1830s and the 1840s, in which women were active in large numbers, and which was soon to provide one forum for the development of an embryonic women's-rights movement. The temperance movement, as Elizabeth Pleck has shown, came into being as a reaction against the increasing privatization of the home and the public loss of interest in punishing private transgressions of morality. As consumption of alcohol and resulting incidents of wife and child abuse were removed from legal scrutiny by virtue of their domestic setting, Pleck explains, women flocked in increasing numbers to associations that made it their duty to correct this legal oversight.[55] The temperance movement's main strategy was the writing and publishing of exposés of drunken husbands. If, as one woman advocate of temperance lamented, "intemperance assaults the wife at her domestic hearth, and there she must bear her sorrows until her heart breaks, shut up without the world's observation, and the world's sympathy," then the best way to counter its horrors was to force them into the public eye. One temperance writer explained in 1841 that while "men can deal in statistics and logical deductions . . . women can describe the horrors of intemperance—can draw aside the curtain and show us the wreck it makes of domestic love and home enjoyment—can paint the anguish of the drunkard's wife and the miseries of his children," much as Stowe painted the miseries of slavery.[56] Unsurprisingly, many women writers, including Lydia Sigourney, Mary Fox, and Stowe herself, lent their pens to the writing of temperance exposés.

Moral reform societies, another important forum for women's social action and context for protofeminist energy in the 1840s and the 1850s, likewise claimed the use of exposure tactics in the struggle for social improvement. Under the generic title of "moral reform," these societies focused on the problem of sexual "promiscuity." Although they made several attempts to appeal to the law to interfere with the transactions of prostitution, what little they achieved in terms of imposition of fines and threats of incarceration was temporary and without lasting effects. By the late 1830s, women were resorting instead to increasingly radical extralegal tactics, including public ostracism. Reformers called for the "discountenancing [of] all men reputed to be licentious, in excluding them from our society and by every other laudable means in our power."[57] Such "laudable means" gradually came to signify the exposing and public humiliation of men who solicited the services of prostitutes. By keeping their ears open and then reporting the facts they had gleaned from kitchen gossip and parlor heart-to-hearts, these women were able to steer men to the path of righteousness more effectively than through the imposition of fines, threat of prison sentences, or abstract moral preaching. Charges against women's intrusiveness and violations of privacy were countered by pointing out the hypocrisy of separating private life from public reputation. "This man has the charge of a paper the object of which is to criticize public morals," a reformer retorted in one case: "May we not ask how long shall men like these occupy responsible stations, and be tolerated among a Christian people?"[58]

When a women's-rights movement sprang out of such traditional women's causes as Evangelicalism, abolition, and temperance, invasion-of-privacy strategies had already proved themselves successful. It is hardly surprising, then, that the women's-rights movement espoused the "doctrine of no secrets" as a central pillar in its platform.[59] Reformer Zena Fay Pierce captured the spirit of this doctrine in a speech before the New York City Woman's Parliament in 1869: "Bad morals will exist only as long as virtuous women do not choose to look at all they see, to understand all they hear, and to tell all they know." It was woman's "duty," that is, to turn private facts into moral currency. Mary Putnam Jacobi, the celebrated feminist doctor, called on women to "live in the open air! A thing that one is not willing the whole world should know is wrong." Jacobi, explains Leach, was so adamant in her attack on the veil that surrounded private life that she came close to repudiating altogether the foundation of liberalism—the freedom of the private conscience—by insisting that "the essence of personal life—its private character—be open to public inspection." Feminist Ezra Heywood issued a similarly radical call (ironically, in the context of the alleged sexual scandal concerning Henry Ward Beecher, Stowe's brother) to hasten forth the "Great Universal Washing Day, when everybody's dirty linen will be paraded, and when the leaders of sham morality in high places will find it will cost more than $.75 a dozen."[60]

Indeed, bringing about that "Great Universal Washing Day" was often the motivation behind the writing of domestic novels as well. Since critical attention has focused largely on the way these novels idealized home life through their portrayal of saintly children, self-effacing mothers, and parental love, the fact that these conventions were regularly accompanied by realistic (and often autobiographical or, at least, "drawn from experience") sketches of the hidden abuses of the home is sometimes forgotten. The most successful domestic novels of mid-century, from Catherine Maria Sedgwick's *New England Tale* to Sarah Parton's *Ruth Hall*, from Susan Warner's *The Wide, Wide World* to Maria S. Cummins's *The Lamplighter*, all violated the codes of domestic privacy by exposing the cruelties of home life to the eyes of the reader. Elaine Showalter's description of Victorian sensationalist authors accurately applies to the novels of American domestic writers as well: "They wanted to persuade people that in almost every one of the well-ordered houses of their neighbors there was a skeleton shut up in some cupboard; that their comfortable and easy looking neighbor had in his breast a story which he was always trying to conceal."[61]

By understanding the breaking open of closets as its main undertaking, women's domestic fiction, on the one hand, affirmed the notion that what a woman knew best was the inner workings of the home, thus supporting her domesticated life; but, on the other hand, it transplanted the function of that knowledge from the self-contained ordering of household economy to the realm of the public, thus daringly crossing liberalism's deep moat between the home and the world. In doing so, the domestic novel issued a corrective to what Wai-chee Dimock describes as the contraction of the legal domain in nineteenth-century America. In the course of the nineteenth century, legal discourse increasingly drew a separation between the concept of sin and the concept of crime, leaving a wide range of moral transgressions, formerly punishable by law, outside its reach.[62] What the law now increasingly ruled out of its domain was not only cruelty to slaves but also "domestic tyranny": sexual misconduct, wife abuse, and cruelty to children.[63] The domestic novel's interest in moral transgressions in the private sphere, then, coextended with a vacuum in social surveillance occasioned by the law's abandonment of a range of moral misconduct within the home. Indeed, Foucauldian critics regard the nineteenth-century novel as an instrument of "policing" and "discipline," which ensured the invisible circulation of social regulation, even in the deepest recesses of the private, as institutional, ostentatious, and corporal methods of discipline were gradually abandoned.

But, as Dimock convincingly argues, this does not mean that the novel's aspirations to moral disciplining and institutional forms of "policing" are necessarily homologous. "It is equally possible to argue the opposite," writes Dimock, "locating the novel's function not in the extent to which it replicates social forms, but in the extent to which it complements, and hence diverges from those forms."[64] What particularly tends to be lost in the homology between the novel and the police is categories of social hierarchy. Regarding the domestic novel as one in a multiplicity of parallel discourses newly charged with disciplinary energy minimizes the historical fact that it was mostly (though not only) women who used this genre as an instrument of moral discipline. Nor is the Foucauldian approach always sensitive to the fact that white, propertied men were indeed able to enjoy a *degree* of relief from surveillance in the home where others did not. The domestic novel used the private against the public to question this privilege accorded by gender, race, and class.

The challenge to patriarchal authority implicit in the strategy of exposure was evident also in the reception of the writing of its wielders. Reviewers of Sarah Parton's roman à clef *Ruth Hall*, for example, while praising the book's moral sentiments, reacted against the writer's "unfemininely bitter wrath and spite," the hunting of "her persecutors so remorselessly." "As we wish no sister of ours, nor no female relative to show toward us, the ferocity she has displayed toward her nearest relatives," one reviewer wrote, "we take occasion to censure this book that might initiate such a possibility."[65] What was most menacing was that the domestic novel might turn into the literary equivalent of the Evangelical "promiscuous assemblies," where sisters, wives, daughters, and mothers named private offenders.

In the case of *Uncle Tom's Cabin*, this menace earned Stowe the threat of a lawsuit. At one point in the novel she makes the crucial choice of mentioning undisguised the name of Dr. Joel Parker, a Philadelphia Presbyterian minister, as a supporter of slavery. Parker's reaction was to threaten her with a $20,000 libel suit, and there ensued a lengthy exchange between Stowe and Parker on the pages of the *New York Observer* and in private letters, an exchange that brought to the forefront the question of violating the privacy of real persons in a work of fiction. "After painting a scene of shocking inhumanity," Parker charged Stowe, "you hold me up to the public, in an odious light, by representing me as uttering sentiments that seem to justify or, at least to palliate the cruelties which you have described." Stowe's reaction was typical of the strategy of exposure. While she rather ironically pleaded the feminine obligation to remain silent about the accusations in public, in her next novel, *Dred*, she includes the unpleasant character Dr. Packthread, a thinly disguised fictional portrait of Dr. Parker, as revenge against his attacks. "While other people look upon words as vehicles for conveying ideas," she writes, "Dr. Packthread regarded them only as mediums for concealment. His constant study, on every controverted topic, was to adjust language that, with the appearance of the utmost precision, it should always be capable of a double interpretation."[66] Stowe's criticism of Dr. Packthread's language of concealment captures the epistemological difference between the domestic novel and more masculine genres of writing. While the latter often used language to "conceal" and create "double interpretation," thus producing a region of irreducible privacy—Melville's convoluted sentences, Hawthorne's ambiguities, and Thoreau's elusive symbols come to mind—the sentimental novel used language to draw unambiguous connections between fact and representation, to create insistent parallels between life and fiction, denying, in the spirit of Evangelical reform, any man's right to be let alone.

Dead Private Spaces

As Dr. Parker's attack on Stowe demonstrates, writers wielding the strategy of exposure "came very close to exhausting the limits of the legitimate public exposé," and their revelations "often bordered on slander, frightening not only their victims but the reformers themselves" and leading to a dangerous backlash.[67] What was frightening about the use of exposure techniques was that it opened the doors to attacks on the writer's own private life, and thereby endangered the integrity of the very identity under which domestic writers claimed authority as public speakers. One of the strongest responses to *Ruth Hall*, for example, was an anonymous collection entitled *The Life and Beauties of Fanny Fern* (1855), a collection that reprinted Parton's newspaper columns accompanied by scathingly ironic commentaries that called attention to her own scandalous marriages.[68] The strategy of exposure, then, was a double-edged sword. On the one hand, it allowed women to voice criticism with authority; on the other, it threatened to undermine the very basis of that authority, women's reputed moral superiority in the private sphere.

To return to the terms set forth by Michael Warner and Lauren Berlant: women writers and other social reformers were vulnerable to backlash precisely because they often ventured into the public eye without use of the "prophylaxis" of a disembodied (read: white and male) public persona. In telling the stories of the cruelties of the private sphere, they often chose, as Stowe did in *Uncle Tom's Cabin*, not to hide behind a pseudonym, not to don a "prosthetic" male face. On the contrary: Stowe emphasized that she wrote the novel "because, *as* a woman, *as* a mother, [she] was oppressed and heartbroken with the sorrows and injustice which [she] saw."[69] Writing as an avatar of virtuous domestic femininity was not an incidental but a crucial aspect of the strategy of exposure, and one that serves to explain why it led so smoothly from the espousal of miscellaneous social causes to a crusade for women's rights. Speaking as women in public lent authority and authenticity to the private stories that these writers told: who, after all, knew more about the secrets of home life than the mistress of the house? But speaking as women in public undermined the "principle of negativity" on which that sphere was based; it destabilized the liberal public sphere's ruling fiction of neutrality by making audible the privatized, embodied voices excluded by it, thus preparing the ground for the eventual recognition of women's rights.

As Henry observes in regard to Grimké, "instead of confronting the 'public sphere' on its own terms," this woman "refigured publicity as something that exposed the 'private' rather than protecting it, and that drew upon her femininity rather than denying it." Rather than view the public as a place where particularized, embodied identities must be concealed, Grimké marched into the public eye, parading her identity as a proper, virtuous woman and using it as political currency to benefit slaves and, indirectly, other white women. At first, Grimké did not intend to do this. Her inaugural antislavery publication, a letter she wrote William Lloyd Garrison testifying to the evils of slavery in the white southern household, was published in the abolitionist paper *The Liberator* under her real name without her knowledge and consent, much to her chagrin. Garrison realized that the letter would have more impact "not as abstract reason, but as personal testimony." He, after all, was the orchestrator of some of the most famous personal testimonies of slaves who had escaped to the North, including Frederick Douglass's, and he was among the first to recognize the benefits of undoing the principle of negativity of the public sphere. "Instead of a critical publicity based in the exclusion of private interests from public discourse," Henry explains, "Garrison [drew] on a publicity of exposure, whose source and ground is ostensibly personal." What Garrison understood, and soon also Grimké herself, was that a crucial part of the strategy of exposure was the exposure of one's private identity to an eager public.[70]

But the transition from exposure of the other to exposure of the self was anything but smooth. In translating private identity into public voice, reformist writers were faced with a logical bind. Consider Grimké's case. As Henry argues, the most radical aspect of her strategic erosion of the public/private boundary was her recognition that the private identity of the domestic woman was always *already* public and performative. As we discussed in Chapter 1, the private identity of the proper domestic woman was never private in the more radical sense of the term, since the moral "essence" attributed to her was a carefully designed and staged social performance, no less so for taking place in the parlor rather than on the public podium. This Grimké understood. And taking her cue from this realization, she made use of that persona in public. Ironically, however, the performance of virtuous womanhood always relied on the very illusions of essence and authenticity that it seemingly dispelled. To be successful, it had continuously to feed the social narrative of essential feminine virtue. Henry writes, "For while Grimké's radicalism lay in her stubborn insistence on violating privacy, on treating everything—including her own domestic life—as potentially 'public,' her inescapable dilemma was in the necessity of performing a more conventional privacy in order to hold her public's attention, the necessity of playing to her public's prejudices even as she proceeded to empty them out."[71] In translating private identity into public voice, then, the strategy of exposure accepted (in some cases, was forced into accepting) conventional narratives of identity, the very narratives in the name of which the public *excluded* female, nonwhite, and unpropertied subjects.

To put the problem in different terms we might return to *Uncle Tom's Cabin*. As we have seen, the novel repeatedly works against the right of proprietary privacy. But at the same time, its entire thrust is to extend to disenfranchised subjects that very right. Cassy's scheme, we recall, involved more than the invasion of the dark recesses of Legree's private conscience: it also relied on the appropriation of a space within his house that would be barred from *his* invasion, a space where, long ago, a black woman died and that now would serve as the instrument and symbol of two black women's liberation. This is the symbolic culmination of the novel's overarching telos: to give blacks such as George and Tom a house of their own, even as it so diligently exposes the moral transgression to which the right to privacy inevitably leads. (Indeed, we have seen that Stowe extends for *herself* the right to privacy as well, for example, when she refuses to openly expose herself in public in the debate with Dr. Parker.) But what logic could possibly justify the claiming of the same right that one has so painstakingly and adamantly exposed as promoting immorality? Why should George have what Legree should never be allowed to have—his "own private little world of memories, hopes, loves, fears, and desires"? Stowe's answer is that George, Tom, and Cassy, as well as the Mrs. Shelbys, Mrs. Birds, and Mrs. Stowes of this world, earn the right to be let alone simply as blacks or women. Only an adherence to the notion of women as inherently, essentially, moral and an extension of that notion to blacks as well can put Stowe in a position to claim for them the right to privacy, on the premise that nothing about that privacy can possibly compromise social norms. Women and blacks may claim a space for hopes, fears, and desires only if it is shown that these hopes, fears, and desires are always prescribed by social narratives of identity and will never exceed those narratives. Being a domestic woman (and hence virtuous) and being a slave (and hence, like the domestic woman, virtuous) encompasses the entire scope of the self, a self that can then seek recognition for the stories it tells in the name of its unwavering virtue. It is to such a phenomenon that Wendy Brown refers when she describes the language of public recognition as the language of "unfreedom," where "articulation in language becomes a vehicle of subordination through normalization and regulation even as it strives to produce visibility and acceptance."[72]

As we saw in Chapter 1, once domestic ideology accorded women their own interior space, it clashed with traditional patriarchy in dangerous ways, since that space overlapped with a territory traditionally controlled by the paterfamilias and hence challenged the traditional distribution of familial power. The house divided by domestic ideology's insistence on the constitutional "moral" difference of women, a difference that, it claimed, warranted their own domain, raised the specter of conflicting interests and brewing dissent within the divided house. In that respect, the new emphasis on the home's invisibility, structured to protect the "man in his castle," could also be understood as potentially dangerous to social order, since it provided a shield from the law, as well, for other subjects besides the house's master.

The most dramatic example of this problem unfolded in relation to slavery, of course. The 1850 Fugitive Slave Act, in response to which Stowe wrote her novel, gave impetus to the Underground Railroad, an undertaking that relied for its success on concealing slaves on their way to Canada in private homes in the North. This undertaking depended for its existence on the growing respect for the privacy of the home and its newfound privilege to be shielded from both neighbors and the government. The Underground Railroad's hiding of slaves in closets, attics, and secret rooms captured the tension between the legally protected status of the house's interior and the resulting incapacity of the law to ensure obedience to those crimes that it did *not* rule out of judicial domain (unlike, say, domestic abuse and cruelty to slaves). In *Uncle Tom's Cabin*, this problem is carefully staged. In the Bird household, we recall, Eliza's physical entrance into the home forces the senator to alter his policy on slavery. But he continues to be threatened by the fact that in the name of his wife's "high Christian principles" the "confounded awkward, ugly business" of sheltering slaves is legitimized (p. 107), despite the risk to his public standing. The senator, then, fiercely objects to hiding Eliza overnight in their servant's room, his wife's pleas notwithstanding.

Indeed, *Uncle Tom's Cabin* abounds with examples of how private spaces can shield the potential transgressions of the subaltern. Eliza's private room, her "neat little apartment" within the Shelby estate (p. 26), protects George Harris's voicing of his hatred of his master and his radical antislavery agenda. When George rents a room of his own in the public tavern, he can afford to display his "improper state of mind" and impart dangerous ideas on slavery to Mr. Wilson. In Aunt Chloe's kitchen, her one unquestioned domain, Haley's attempts to capture Eliza are frustrated by the cook's deliberate delaying of his parting meal. Meanwhile, in the small public house on the riverbank, the hostess aids Eliza by hiding her in a small bedroom, away from the eyes of the tavern's slaver customers. Dinah's closed cupboards and drawers in the Louisiana kitchen conceal articles suggestive of voodoo ritual and witchcraft that represent an order defiant of her master's order. And, of course, the Quaker home, in a secluded settlement, illegally houses runaway slaves under the matriarchal supervision of Rachel Halliday.

The Quaker household, the only wholly "feminized" home in the novel, calls attention to the potential collision of legal authority and privacy for the disenfranchised. In constructing this home, Stowe experiments with a relatively novel idea of the domestic sphere as ruled single-handedly by the figure of the mother, the idea that the private sphere can be not merely stretched to include domains for women but also turned over in its entirety to women. The Quaker home can conduct the Underground Railroad because, in its position outside the bounds of patriarchal normalcy, it does so with no danger of internal collusion or implosion. This is a house undivided, ruled in its totality by the woman abolitionist. But, ironically, no space is more normative and less threatening than Sarah Halliday's home, with its consummate cleanliness and perfectly disciplined order. Precisely because the spaces extended to women and slaves are potentially dangerous, the novel appeases that threat through use of the normative and conventional. Stowe's repeated tactic is to allow the reader access to these other interior spaces in order to display the moral rectitude and essential benevolence that they house, placating the very anxiety their existence produces. She simultaneously constructs private spaces for women and blacks *and* implies that the boundaries of privacy are all but superfluous, because nothing within these rooms requires a protective veil to begin with.

Thus, Stowe invites the reader to "enter the dwelling" of Uncle Tom and discover that it hides nothing more than patriotism, family values, and piety: a portrait of George Washington, a few children playing, and a man studying the Bible. In this scene, the reader is encouraged to identify with young master George, the white male figure who feels at home in the plausibly transgressive private spaces of slaves. In Louisiana, she invites her readers to "accompany us up to a little loft over the stable" to learn of Tom's actions when in private (p. 275), and the reader discovers him doing nothing more than consorting with Eva over an affectionate letter to his family, utterly subdued in tone and comic in its naïveté. The reader's perspective joins that of St. Clare, who climbs to the loft to observe and admire the sentimental scene from a short distance, assuring himself that all is well on the "other" domestic front. Indeed, in such scenes Stowe strives to do what Rachel Halliday does to the slave hunter Tom Locke. Rachel takes Tom into the heart of the Quaker home and thus allays his paranoia and hatred by letting him see with his own eyes the inner workings of this space. The point is not to "convert" Locke—the Quakers try to convert him, as he relates, and fail—but to alleviate his violent fear of the other. And so Stowe's sentimental descriptions of such domestic interiors do not necessarily mean, as Gillian Brown argues, that she is trying to convert her readers to an acceptance of utopian matriarchy. Rather, through making the reader feel at home within the private spaces of women and blacks, she placates the potential anxiety produced by the proposal to extend spaces of privacy to other kinds of human beings.

A good example of this structure of threat and appeasement takes us back to Aunt Chloe's kitchen, where Shelby's slaves voice indignation over the sale of Tom and Harry. The kitchen, as Chloe's domain, is an emblem of the possibility of a man's house turning against his interests. Following Eliza's escape, a group of slaves gathers in the kitchen to discuss the successful defeat of Haley's chase and the frustration of Shelby's plan to sell little Harry. The slave Sam turns the occasion political by imitating partisan rhetoric: " 'Yer see, fellow-countrymen,' said Sam, elevating a turkey's leg, with energy, 'yer see, now what dis yer chile's up ter, for fendin yer all,—yes, all on yer. For him as tries to get one o'our people is as good as tryin' to get all' " (p. 95). But the uncomfortable spectacle of slaves gathering in private to assert their solidarity is simultaneously deflated by Stowe, as she turns the scene into a veritable minstrel show: Black Sam's political rhetoric lapses more and more into pathos, as he gradually conforms to the well-worn and benign figure of the jester Sambo. The revolutionary potential of the slave's space is thus simultaneously exposed and deconstructed, and, encountering the familiar stereotype, Stowe's ideal reader would feel both tension and relief. Similarly, when readers are invited to join "an evening in Uncle Tom's cabin" and observe the slaves' "meetin'," what they find is a scene that depicts in highly sentimentalized language the slaves' hidden interiority: their deep devotional feelings, their tears and laugher from pure religious joy, their singing of hymns and reading of scripture. Like Uncle Tom himself, the "meetin' " is discovered to be "an organization in which the *morale* was strongly predominant" (p. 43), emptied of any political content, and as harmless as children's play.

This architecturing of interiority for women and slaves only to fill it with well-rehearsed social narratives of identity is part of what David Reynolds calls Stowe's "rhetorical deflation of the subversive."[73] As we have seen, the very essence of human status, "the right of a man to be a man," equals "the right to have a home of his own"; but for Stowe's novel to claim this status for other subjects, it must empty out the spaces it extends to the disenfranchised of any individualized, counteridentitarian, and potentially transgressive contents; they must be exposed to contain nothing beyond sheer convention.

It is worth returning for a moment to Stowe's assertion that her book exposed the "*living* dramatic *reality*" of slavery, for we are now in the position to point out that this phrase includes a strange contradiction: do the spaces of the home hide "life" and "reality," or do they hide "drama," performance, convention? The strategy of exposure's unfulfilled potential lies in its collapsing of the difference between the two and showing, as at one point Grimké did, that what society attributes to privatized subjects as private essence is in fact artificial and performative. But Stowe, like so many of her contemporaries, chose to overlook this potential and to claim instead that the hidden "truths" of women and slaves, part of the body of private truths that the novel exposes, were thoroughly defined by convention. In marked contrast to a story such as "Wakefield," where Hawthorne deliberately chose the most lifeless, bland, conformist male protagonist in order to show that some queerness always exceeded his socially defined identity, Stowe paints the portrait of exceptional and heroic figures only to reveal their deadened and clichéd interiority.

This is especially clear in the description of Eva's room, the fullest and most conventionalized interior in the novel. The minute details in the description of Eva's room are at the same time an extension of her character in space and a promise that every aspect of that character has been cataloged and is transparent, legible, and readily open to the reader's inspection. Everything in this interior is "rose-colored," every decorative element is based on a floral motif, every object radiates innocence and religious devotion—from the "beautiful sculptured angel . . . with drooping wings," through the "exquisite paintings of children, in various attitudes," to the "beautifully wrought statue of Jesus." "In short," Stowe writes, "the eye could turn nowhere without meeting images of childhood, of beauty, and of peace" (pp. 333–34). Even as the heroic Eva is given a room of her own (and the notion that children are a distinct human category and merit separate rooms was only a few decades old in 1851),[74] this space is defined by the absence of any individuality or singularity outside the constraints of sentimental convention. Each article in Eva's room is part of a simple, monochromatic sign system that attests to the purity of its occupant and leaves no residual or unaccounted-for corners. It is a profoundly uninhabitable space, a *dead* space, a museum or shrine rather than a bedroom. Inevitably, then, when we enter Eva's room, it is only literally to witness her death.

This logic can again be related to Evangelical reform movements (as Eva's name rather unsubtly suggests). If Evangelicalism demanded the public exposure of private sin, its more central departure from Calvinist tradition was its idealistic promise that perfection was attainable in private life on Earth and need not be postponed to the afterlife. This "doctrine of Christian perfection" defied the Calvinist notion that people were born with original sin and insisted that sin, as well as sinlessness, was an ethical and moral choice. Earthly perfection, moreover, was a sure way to achieve the more important state of perfection in the next world. Women Evangelists' use of the tactics of exposure, therefore, was accompanied by a commitment to purge their own inner lives of any sin, and their claim to equality rested on that commitment: "Human beings have rights," one woman wrote, "because they are *moral* beings. . . . the mere circumstance of sex does not give to man higher rights and responsibilities, than to woman."[75] If men's rights could be justly violated when men were immoral, then women's rights were guaranteed as long as their morality was left unquestioned. In the context of privacy, this led to an uneasy conclusion: women merited a space away from society's surveillance only on condition that Christian morality was so profoundly internalized that privacy became, in effect, a depleted concept.

"Speaking of Marks, Traces, Possibles, and Probabilities, We come before Our Readers"

In 1853, a mere year after the earth-shaking publication of *Uncle Tom's Cabin*, Frederick Douglass published an antislavery novella of his own, the only work of fiction he would ever compose. "The Heroic Slave" cannot be read apart from Stowe's novel, whose strategy Douglass both adopted and critiqued. A fictionalized version of an actual historical event—the 1841 rebellion aboard the slave ship *Creole*, led by the slave Madison Washington, who disappeared in British-ruled Nassau following the successful revolt—the novella opens with a direct presentation of the problem of the "privatized" status of slaves. "The State of Virginia is famous in American annals for the multitudinous array of her statesmen and heroes," Douglass begins. "History has not been sparing in recording their names, or in blazoning their deeds." But not all the great men of Virginia have enjoyed public recognition. "By some strange neglect, one of the truest, manliest, and bravest of her children . . . holds now no higher place in the records of that grand old Commonwealth than is held by a horse or an ox." "Strange neglect" is, of course, an ironic phrase. It is as clear to the narrator as it is to the reader that the reason for Madison Washington's "public death" is his race, the only reason why "a man who loved liberty as well as did Patrick Henry,—who deserved it as much as Thomas Jefferson," and who was as valiant as the two Founding Fathers after whom he was named, was relegated, like a domestic animal, to the invisibility of the private sphere, why his name was found only in the "chattel records of his native state."[76]

With these opening lines, Douglass declares his intention to adopt Stowe's strategy of exposure: like Stowe, he is writing fiction based on true stories; like her, he uses this fiction to reverse the lethal privatization of slaves, to disturb the silence imposed on their experience by white public discourse. But no later than in the next paragraph do clear differences between Stowe's and Douglass's narrative techniques begin to emerge. For whereas Stowe repeatedly insisted that what appeared to be fiction in *Uncle Tom's Cabin* was really a "mosaic of facts," "a collection and arrangement of real incidents,—of actions really performed, of words and expressions really uttered," Douglass immediately draws attention to the *fictional* status of his novella, to the fact that the story of Madison Washington that follows is little beyond an exercise in imagination:

Glimpses of this great character are all that can now be presented. He is brought to view only by a few transient incidents, and these afford but partial satisfaction. Like a guiding star on a stormy night, he is seen through the parted clouds and the howling tempests; or, like the gray peak of a menacing rock on a perilous coast, he is seen by the quivering flash of angry lightning, and he again disappears covered with mystery.

Curiously, earnestly, anxiously we peer into the dark, and wish even for the blinding flash, or the light of northern skies to reveal him. But alas! He is still enveloped in darkness, and we return from the pursuit like a wearied and disheartened mother, (after a tedious and unsuccessful search for a lost child,) who returns weighted down with disappointment and sorrow. Speaking of marks, traces, possibles, and probabilities, we come before our readers. (Pp. 175–76)

The passage is worth quoting in full because it presents some intriguing questions. Given the strategy of exposure's reliance on claims to the factuality and authenticity of the private stories it reveals, what could motivate Douglass's immediate disclaimer that the truth must remain unknown? And how to account, moreover, for the fact that the obscure nature of Madison Washington's story is presented not as this story's weakness, but as its *strength*, described, as it is, through the images of a blinding flash, a howling tempest, and a menacing rock? Far from expressing regret or issuing an apology, I would argue, this passage prepares us for one of the text's most important achievements: its recognition of the limits of the strategy of exposure as well as its bold revision of that strategy. What "The Heroic Slave" presents from its very beginning is the triumph of the black hero in defying the intrusive invasions of both the narrator-informant and his white, middle-class audience, the power enfolded in his "disappear[ance] covered with mystery," a disappearance that frustrates our "curious," "earnest," "anxious" (and, as the text will later illustrate, morally questionable) desire to know the inner details of the slave's story. If *Uncle Tom's Cabin* is told through the voice of the northerner who sheds light on the darkened corners of the slave-ridden South, here the "light of northern skies" fails fully to illuminate its subject. And if *Uncle Tom's Cabin* is told through the voice of the omniscient mother who knows the private stories of slaves as well as she knows her own child, here the narrator is more like "a wearied and disheartened mother," whose child eludes her loving but controlling gaze.

Stressing that the novella is based on "marks, traces, possibles, and probabilities," rather than on a "mosaic of facts," Douglass's narrative technique approximates more that of Melville in stories such as "Bartleby, the Scrivener" (published later in the same year) than that of Stowe. Melville's narrator also begins his story with stating his departure from the kind of intrusive domestic story "at which good-natured gentlemen might smile, and sentimental souls might weep," explaining that "no materials exist, for a full and satisfactory biography of [Bartleby]."[77] The similarity between these two gambits hints that we can read Douglass's novella in relation to the ethos of privatist, liberal masculinity that we discussed in Melville's and Hawthorne's short fiction in the previous chapter, and not singly in relation to the ethos of exposure articulated by women's reform fiction. Richard Yarborough and Robert Stepto persuasively argue that in "The Heroic Slave" Douglass's goal was to attribute to his hero the standards of middle-class masculinity prevalent in his time, and thereby to amend Stowe's often-belittling representations of black manhood. If Stowe's ideal black man is passive, self-sacrificing, and ultimately feminine, Douglass's black hero embodies the qualities attributed to white, middle-class manhood: intelligence, articulateness, courage, self-control.[78] Maggie Sale argues, along similar lines, that Douglass patterns his protagonist—providentially named after George Washington, the Revolution-era paragon of manhood—on the republican ideal of masculine virtue, stressing again his "bravery, eloquence, moral restraint," but also his "concern for common good, and willingness to die for a cause."[79]

While all of these interpretations are undoubtedly correct, I wish to show that Douglass was no less mindful of the mid-nineteenth century liberal ethos of manhood, claiming for his hero, as he did, the right to be let alone, the same right to a protected, inviolable, private selfhood that Melville and Hawthorne claimed for their white male characters. Douglass's point was not simply to gain public recognition for the "privatized" black man but to construct simultaneously for him a space of retreat, without which, he shows, public visibility becomes yet another form of unfreedom. I have mentioned that by the 1850s the heroization of President Washington emphasized his "love of home and native soil, and of the shade of retirement" alongside his heroic public deeds; Douglass's heroic slave, like his eponym, achieves full manhood by both acting heroically and retiring to privacy, by appearing *and* disappearing in public.[80]

There is critical consensus that Douglass's fictionalization of Madison Washington's story was shaped by his own experiences as a former slave and abolitionist activist. It is crucial to note, in particular, that "The Heroic Slave" was composed after Douglass's disillusionment and break with Garrisonian abolitionism. The year 1841 witnessed both Madison Washington's disappearance in Nassau and Frederick Douglass's first public appearances as spokesperson for abolitionism. This year, Henry Louis Gates argues, marks Douglass's symbolic birth, his rescue from the social death inherent in the experience of the slave and the beginning of his self-construction in narrative.[81] But it is also the year in which he began his at times uplifting, at times tumultuous relationship with Garrisonian abolitionism. As Robert Stepto writes, Douglass's feeling that this movement hindered "his full development not just as an antislavery agent but also as a human being" eventually prompted him to relocate to Rochester, New York, after his return from Europe in 1847, because he preferred to be among "strangers" than with "New England friends." It was in Rochester that he composed and published "The Heroic Slave," a text that interprets Madison Washington's disappearance from narrative as a declaration of freedom that mirrors Douglass's own self-imposed exile from his New England abolitionist friends.[82]

As William L. Andrews explains, Douglass turned to the writing of fiction in 1853 as part of his revolt against Garrisonian narrative technique. It was Garrison who first offered Douglass the opportunity to rescue his story from privacy, to testify in public to his harrowing experiences as a slave, and thus to speak and, later, to write himself into public recognition. But what Douglass and other former slaves sponsored by the abolitionist movement soon realized was that the structure of the slave narrative as defined by Garrison and his supporters, a structure that relied on the presence of the black man in public and on the relating of true personal anecdote, demanded the *distortion* of private experience. "White abolitionists encouraged ex-slave narrators to conform to the conventions that had proved successful," writes Andrews; but, ironically, "to *sound* authentic to whites required them to adopt a mask, to play a role, to feign authenticity in and through a carefully cultivated voice."[83] The slave narrative, that is, produced the same double bind that I describe in the previous section: it exposed privatized stories and introduced embodied voices into the public sphere, but, in order to authorize and authenticate these stories and voices, it filled the space of individual interiority with performative, conventionalized narratives of socially defined identity. The black private self constructed by the abolitionist narrative was wholly alienable, an object for public consumption, fully legible and ultimately *safe*.

Houston Baker remarks that in Douglass's abolitionist-sponsored autobiographical narrative, *The Narrative of the Life of Frederick Douglass*, "the light of abolitionism is always implicitly present, guiding the narrator into calm, Christian, and publicly accessible harbors."[84] Along the same lines, in order for the Madison Washington story to have been useful to Garrisonian abolitionism, it, too, would have needed to be illuminated by what Douglass calls "the light of northern skies," the guiding conventions of the abolitionist-sponsored narrative. It is not surprising that *The Liberator* urged its readers to try to get the true facts of Madison Washington's story "from his own lips" in order for it to be published, and it is in some sense fortunate that no reader has succeeded. In the *Liberator*'s hands, his story would have most likely turned into the kind of exposé that uncovered the horrors of slavery even as it provided the reader access to the proper and safe inner constitution of the slave who revolted against it. Douglass's refusal to claim authenticity of speech and presence (he does not claim to have met Madison Washington or to have heard the story from "his own lips"), his drawing attention, instead, to the fictional status of his novella, liberates his hero's story from the mill of abolitionist narrative convention, from its propensity to reify its subjects, at the same time as its hero is liberated from the bonds (and records) of chattel slavery. Baker points out that, as no such thing as private language exists, the former slave narrator faced tremendous difficulties in "transmuting an authentic, unwritten self—a self that exists outside the conventional literary discourse structures of a white reading public—into literary representation."[85] But as we saw in Chapter 2, if there cannot be private language, "there can be a sense . . . conveyed in language, of a person's irreducible privacy."[86] This sense of private interiority is what "The Heroic Slave" ultimately captures.

Madison Washington's drama of appearance and disappearance in public is staged in four acts. The four parts of the novella follow the course of Washington's escape from slavery, but also from the abolitionist narrative of exposure. Indeed, the novella opens with what may be read as a parody of this very strategy. Part One takes us to a disturbing scene of violation. We meet Madison Washington in a Virginia forest near the slave plantation from which he has just escaped the violent wrath of his overseer. He speaks to himself, thinking he is alone. But Washington is, in fact, not alone: Mr. Listwell, a white gentleman from the North who is visiting Virginia, happens by and, being "intensely curious to know what thoughts and feelings, or, it might be, high aspirations" the black man might here unwittingly reveal, "he stealthily drew near the solitary speaker; and, concealing himself by the side of a huge fallen tree" (p. 176), eavesdrops on the soliloquy. Mr. Listwell (whose entire character is defined by this act of listening, as his name suggests), "almost trembled at the thought of his dangerous intrusion." Still, he "could not quit the place. He had long desired to sound the mysterious depths of the thoughts and feelings of a slave. He was not, therefore, disposed to allow so providential an opportunity to pass unimproved. He resolved to hear more" (p. 179). What he hears, however, is not what we might expect; he hears not the fragmentary ideas and associative sentences that characterize interior monologue but the slave's highly

rhetorical and eloquently formed thoughts on liberty and his valiant desire for it, dressed in the "now bitter, and now sweet . . . heart-touching
narrations of his personal suffering, intermingled with prayers to the
God of the oppressed for help and deliverance" (p. 180). What he
hears, that is, is a version of George Harris's speeches on liberty in *Uncle
Tom's Cabin*, or a version of the speeches of former slaves on the abolitionist podium. Parading as "the mysterious depths of the thoughts and
feelings of a slave," Washington's words are anything but mysterious;
they are pure surface, public and performative in character, as if he is
conscious of an audience that he has to persuade of his safe inner constitution (indeed, at one point, "the thought of being overheard had
flashed across his mind" [p. 181]).

But it is precisely this illusion of depth that serves to convert Listwell
to Madison Washington's cause: "Here is indeed a man," he decides, "of
rare endowments,—a child of God,—guilty of no crime but the color of
his skin, hiding away from the face of humanity, and pouring out his
thoughts and feelings, his hopes and resolutions, to the lonely woods"
(p. 181). Since he has gained access to the slave's interiority through his
voice, through what Douglass calls the "unfailing index of the soul" (p.
179), and since what he found in there is nothing beyond suffering
piety, patriotic love of liberty, and moral restraint, Listwell declares:
"from this hour I am an abolitionist" (p. 182).

Gates points out that this episode is "a model of the function that all
of the slave narratives were to have upon their American and European
audiences." Washington's soliloquy is, in this reading, a version of the
slave narrative, and Listwell a stand-in for the reader of this narrative,
who, ideally, would be converted to the cause, just as he himself had
been.[87] But what I take to be of crucial importance is that Listwell is not
in fact listening to a public speech or reading a published story; he is
stealing upon a private scene supposedly not designed for his audience.
While Douglass is undoubtedly commenting here on the power of personal narrative to affect political change, he is simultaneously offering
an ironic commentary on the strategy of exposure, on the white audience's insatiable desire and assumed privilege to enter the mind and
soul of the slave and on the posing of such intrusions as precondition
for enlistment for the cause. In its theatrical and highly rhetorical style,
Washington's speech also ironizes the very notion that the slave's speech
is "an unfailing index of his soul," one that exposes the full contents of
his private being, leaving no unassimilable remainders. Mr. Listwell indeed stands in for the reader of the story: recall that in the opening
paragraphs Douglass has already established what motivates the reader:
"Curiously, earnestly, anxiously we peer into the dark," he writes. This is
now echoed by Listwell, who "long desired to sound the mysterious

depths of the thoughts and feelings of a slave." But Douglass has also already established that such a desire for intimate knowledge of the slave's story is doomed to failure in his novella, leading us to read the satisfying of Listwell's curiosity with a touch of irony. If, in the opening scene, Washington has not yet managed to evade the intrusion of the listener/reader (even as he is still under the foot of his master), Douglass has already told us that he eventually will.

It is therefore apt that Part Two opens with a contrasting scene. The time is five years later. The setting is no longer Virginia but "the fireside of [the Listwells'] own happy home, in the State of Ohio" (p. 182). The warm, protected interior of white, middle-class northerners is offered as contrast to the vulnerable privacy of the slave in the forest. And if Madison Washington was introduced through the exposure of his interiority in speech, "the happy pair seemed to sit in *silent* fascination, gazing on the fire," engaged in quiet "*reverie.*" "A whole wilderness of thought might pass through one's mind during such an evening," Douglass writes, but he never presumes to enter the potentially "wild" corners of the white man's inner space, the "subtle chambers of the mind" (p. 183). The Listwell home accurately captures the privileges of proprietary privacy: Listwell is a homeowner and is thus protected in his thoughts; his mind, in turn, is imagined as a house, one that even the narrator dares not fully enter.

Soon, however, the house *is* entered, and by no other than Madison Washington himself, who has managed to escape the plantation and cross the border into the free state. Listwell immediately recognizes him and, based on this recognition, offers him shelter, explaining to Washington: "*I know all,*" a statement that "rather disconcerted and disquieted the noble fugitive" (p. 185). Listwell's declared omniscience does not smother his desire to know yet more, and he prompts Washington to tell him of the events that led to his surprise appearance. The rest of the chapter is devoted to Washington's narration of his escape, interspersed with the Listwells' interrogations and comments. The narration nonetheless represents the next stage of the slave's withdrawal from narrative visibility. It is now *he* who has entered another's private space, and it is now *he* who assumes narrative control, choosing what to relate and what to withhold. It is thus significant that Madison Washington opens his story precisely with the problematic status of the slave's speech. Flashing back to the lashing he suffered at the hands of the overseer just before the earlier scene in the forest, he explains, "my crime was that I had stayed longer at the mill, the day previous, than it was thought I ought to have done, which, I assured my master and the overseer, was no fault of mine; but no excuses were allowed. 'Hold your tongue, you impudent rascal,' met my every explanation. Slave-holders are so imperious when their passions are excited, as to construe every word of the slave into insolence" (pp. 188–89). The master's silencing of the slave is offered in direct contrast to Listwell's generous attentiveness. But the problem of distorted interpretation attributed to the slaveholder, who, when his passion is roused, misconstrues every word as evidence of the slave's essentially rebellious constitution, is one that could be attributed to the (com)passionate abolitionist listener as well, albeit in reverse: it is Listwell who has and will take every word uttered by Madison Washington as evidence of his moral rectitude, a benevolent form of misrecognition that nonetheless traps the slave in a distorting interpretation of his experience.

And nobody seems to be as mindful of this distortion as Washington himself. In an important but rarely commented on section of his story, he tells how, on his way North, he was forced into hiding in a forest, where he secretly observed a group of black workers chopping down trees. At the end of the workday, as the men leave, he eavesdrops on the prayer of the only worker left behind, a "most fervent, earnest, and solemn" address to God. The old slave, a sketchy version of Stowe's Uncle Tom, calls out to God, "take pity on poor me! O deliver me! O deliver me! In mercy, O God, deliver me from the chains and manifold hardships of slavery!" (p. 198). The scene is an ironic duplicate of the primal scene in the Virginia forest. Now it is Madison Washington who eavesdrops on the slave's private speech, only to learn of his profoundly pious nature. The words "I knew enough of religion to know that the man who prays in secret is far more likely to be sincere than he who loves to pray standing in the street" could have been uttered earlier by Listwell (p. 198), but belong to Madison Washington. Crucially, however, the outcome is reversed. Having gained knowledge of the old man's "secret" piety, Madison Washington decides to trust him with his life, only to be promptly betrayed by him.

The point of the scene is not to prove that the black man is inherently treacherous (as Mrs. Listwell is quick to suggest), but that construing private speech as an "unfailing index of the soul" is a fatal mistake. Ironically, moreover, it is precisely his "truthful" and "sincere" nature that leads the old man to betray Washington: "I can easily believe," the latter says, "that the truthfulness of the old man's character compelled him to disclose the facts; and thus were these blood-thirsty men put on my track" (p. 199). In relating this anecdote, Washington implicitly warns against a politics based on the exposure of interiority and the "sincerity" of the black man. Sometimes, the scene suggests, silence is a better strategy than revelation.

What may seem, then, a digression—the opening paragraphs of Part Three, which take us to an old tavern in Virginia—in fact develops further the theme of violation of privacy that Douglass has woven into the first two parts. The narrator now abandons Madison Washington's story and describes at length the poor white "loafers" who people the tavern. These men's main attributes are intrusiveness and gossip. Having no occupation aside from biding their time in the tavern, they are "as good as the newspaper for the events of the day, and they sell their knowledge almost as cheap. Money they seldom have; yet they always have capital the most reliable. They make their way with a succeeding traveller by intelligence gained from the preceding one. . . . He must be a shrewd man, and well skilled in the art of evasion, who gets out of the hands of these fellows without being at the expense of a treat" (pp. 207–8). One such shrewd man is Listwell himself, who returns to Virginia and stays at the tavern.

Listwell's gentlemanly discretion is contrasted with the poor southern whites' cunning inquisitiveness. But the reader cannot miss the irony embedded in this contrast. What the loafers like most to do—trade in surreptitiously gleaned stories—is what Listwell himself has done in intruding on Madison's Washington's scene of privacy and in using his story (a story that, we are told, Listwell often trades with his circle of friends) as political currency. That is why Listwell manages not simply to evade the loafers' skilled interrogations; he beats them at their own game. He secretly listens in on their private conversation, exposing the "vulgarity and dark profanity" that hide behind their white exterior (p. 213), just as he has earlier uncovered the profound virtue that lurks behind the slave's mysterious façade.

Ever "our informant" (p. 216), Mr. Listwell's first wish on reencountering Madison Washington, now a slave again and chained in a slave gang on its way to the market, is, once more, to hear the full story. There is something disturbing in the fact that Listwell's first words, at his arranged meeting with Madison Washington later that day, are, "Now *do* tell me all about the matter" (p. 218), as if his desire to know supersedes the imperative to act. It is completely in line, however, with the construction of Listwell's character up to this point. Madison Washington's story thus resumes, but with the important indication that he has withdrawn even farther from Listwell's, and the reader's, insatiably curiosity: "I must be short," he says, "this then is the story in brief " (p. 219). Madison Washington's curtness is dictated by circumstances; he can no longer afford the leisurely pace that characterized his first narration in Ohio. But it also signals what will be his ultimate silence in the last part of the novella, for in Part Four, which tells of the actual revolt aboard the *Creole*, we will no longer have the privilege of hearing his story from his own mouth. Madison Washington, like Bartleby, or like Babo in Melville's novella of maritime slave revolt, "Benito Cereno," will "prefer not to" speak, becoming, instead, a silent, disembodied presence in the midst of the dramatic events. These events will be told from a distance, after the fact, through a dialogue between the ship's first mate, a witness to the events, and a fellow sailor. Part Four offers a reversal of the scene that opens the story: the reader now eavesdrops on the private conversation of two white men, not the soliloquy of a slave. And what the first mate Grant emphasizes in the course of this conversation is precisely the strategic illegibility of Madison Washington's character: "he seldom spake to any one, and when he did speak, it was with the utmost propriety. His words were well chosen, and his pronunciation equal to that of any schoolmaster . . . none of us knew the extent of his intelligence and ability till it was too late" (p. 233). As happens with Listwell, Grant's encounter with Madison Washington persuades him of the just nature of the slave's bid for freedom. But unlike Listwell, he learns to admire Washington, not by invading his interior space, but by catching glimpses of him from a protective distance. I therefore disagree with Yarborough's claim that Part Four represents Douglass's failure in the representation of heroic black manhood, since Washington ends up relying on the white storyteller, himself reduced to silence.[88] I read Grant's narration, instead, as a "prosthesis" in Warner and Berlant's sense, as a voice that relates information about a person without placing that person's privacy at risk. It is precisely Washington's silence, his liberation from the requirement to lay himself bare to white readership, that finally allows him to emerge with full force, "like a guiding star on a stormy night," or "like the gray peak of a menacing rock on a perilous coast." Douglass's decision to let Grant tell the last portion of Washington's story protects the latter's private self even as it "grants" that story a public audience.

If, as Andrews argues, "there is a fluctuating distance between narrator and the narrated world" in works of fiction such as "The Heroic Slave," one "that was unprecedented in the African American narrative tradition,"[89] this distance is one that gradually and consistently opens up in the course of the narrative as it proceeds from providing access to "the unfailing index of the soul" of the slave to witnessing the former slave's "disappearance shrouded in mystery." The heroic slave's resurrection from demeaning privatization leads first to a problematic and distorting exposé that precludes true recognition of his full and equal humanity. But it ends with his triumphant evasion of the strategy of exposure, one that enhances our recognition of his value rather than erases his existence from record. Put in different terms, the movement of this novella is from privatization and enslavement (captured in the format of the "chattel records"), to exposure of the private story based on presence, ironically represented as another form of objectification (the abolitionist-sponsored narrative), and finally to a Melvillian text based on "marks, traces, possibles, and probabilities" that free Washington from both forms of appropriation.

I argue in the previous chapters that the construction of the concept of privacy in the first half of the nineteenth century was dual in nature. On the one hand, it was taken to mean intimacy, domesticity, and family life; on the other, it connoted solitariness, withdrawal from intimacy, and reprieve from social narratives of identity. What the writing of antebellum African American former slaves often shows is the degree to which they were painfully deprived of privacy in *both* of these meanings, even as their existence was so degradingly privatized. For many of these writers, America was indeed a house divided. As slaves in the South, they could, occasionally and precariously, be physically and emotionally close to their families and friends, but they were denied both shelter from the eye of power (whether individually or as a family) and a public voice. In the North, they were offered considerably more autonomy and public visibility, but at the price of both their former intimate life (having typically been forced to leave their families and friends behind) and recognition of their more fragile and complex inner privacy (having to subdue their private experience to prescripted convention).

It is in this context that an additional aspect of "The Heroic Slave" is important. It is worth noting that the linear course that I have charted in my reading of the novella, from slavery to freedom and from exposure to concealment, is in fact disturbed in the middle of the narrative. Madison Washington's ultimate disappearance from the narrative, strictly speaking, is not his first. He previously disappears from our eyes during the five years between Parts One and Two. We are later told that, having tried to escape to the North after his altercation with the overseer, Madison Washington found himself back on the plantation where his wife, Susan, remained. He then decided to remain close to her and reside in the forest rather than continue northward. He thereby attempted to evade the devastating choice faced by the escaping slave, the choice between family in the South and liberty in the North. For five years, Washington explains, he managed to have at least a minimal version of both, seeing his wife on a regular basis ("our meeting can more easily be imagined than described" [p. 191]) while eluding the supervision of the slaver. These five years are summed up in a few sentences: "I had partly become contented with my mode of life, and had made up my mind to spend my days there" (p. 192), as if the privacy he achieves during this time is textually performed by the absence of a more detailed description. After he reaches Canada (a forest fire has brought an end to this mode of existence), he nonetheless attempts to return once more to Susan ("with her in slavery, my body, not my spirit, was free" [p. 220], he explains), and this is when he is caught and sold to the slave gang, and the narrative resumes.

As several critics have pointed out, the plot element of the "return south" is one that distinguishes African American slave narratives, both fictional and nonfictional, from those of white abolitionists. In the latter, the plot typically follows a direct course from enslavement in the South to freedom in the North, a course that would have been disturbed by the slave's choice to return to his or her family in the South and by the critique of the kind of freedom experienced in the North ("my body, not my spirit, was free") implied in the act. *Uncle Tom's Cabin*, for example, never digresses from this direct course, solving the problem of the familial price of liberty by having Eliza and her son escape at the same time as George Harris does. Yet versions of Madison Washington's five years in the forest, scenes in which the slave manages to secure a niche of privacy within the South, appear over and over again in African American narratives: Henry Bibb, faced with the awful choice—"I must forsake friends and neighbors, wife and child, or consent to lie and die a slave"—secretly returns to his wife more than once; Harriet Jacobs spends seven years in her "loophole of retreat," the garret in her grandmother's house, in close proximity to her children yet outside the ravenous gaze of her master; Hanna Craft imagines a few precious months in a forest cabin in the South with her "sister" escaping slave.[90] All these scenes testify to the horror of a system that forces the slave into inhuman living conditions when she or he pursues the most elementary of desires. But all also represent a moment of qualified triumph: it is in those episodes that the slave manages to achieve a degree of both familial intimacy and individual privacy unmatched by the former experience as a slave and by later experience in the North (ultimately, the price of liberty is presented as a heavy one: Washington's wife dies; Bibb's betrays him; Jacobs remains separated from her children). It is in those always sketchily drawn episodes, also, that the action of the narrative temporarily comes to halt, as if to keep the reader, too, at bay. Perhaps more than the narratives' denouement, then, it is those transitional episodes in their midst where the slave is both absent and present, both with family and alone (not unlike Wakefield in his twenty years of exile next door to his wife) that fully capture the painful claim to a right to privacy on its range of meanings, as well as the qualified success of achieving some version of that right.

In *The Alchemy of Race and Rights*, Patricia Williams tells of her personal recognition that the distant and formal vocabulary of rights continues to be an object of desire and a source of hope for black subjects such as herself, despite contemporary theorists' deconstruction of that vocabulary. Theory's counterlanguage of "circumstantially defined need, of informality, solidarity and overcoming distance," she writes, "sounded dangerously like the language of oppression to someone like me who was looking for freedom through the establishment of identity, the formulation of an autonomous social self." To the theoretician, she grants, "my insistence on the protective distance that rights provide seemed abstract and alienated." But the task of theory should not be "to discard rights but to see through or past them so that they reflect a larger definition of privacy and property: so that privacy is turned from exclusion based on self-regard into regard for another's fragile, mysterious autonomy." "Give to all of society's objects and untouchables the rights of privacy, integrity, and self-assertion," she concludes; "give them distance and respect."[91]

What Patricia Williams recognizes is what I claim African American authors such as Douglass articulated more than a century earlier. The reform movement's strategy was the deconstruction of the right of proprietary privacy through the strategy of exposure, favoring, like Williams's theoretician, "informality, solidarity and overcoming distance" as a mode of relating to the other. "The Heroic Slave" expresses a yearning for the opposite, for the most profound meaning of the right to privacy, what Williams calls "regard for another's fragile, mysterious autonomy." It encodes that yearning at first by use of irony and then of silence and protective distance.

Not surprisingly, it is precisely the figure of the slave deprived of both senses of privacy that served as one catalyst for the articulation of a legal right to privacy in the United States. Peggy Cooper Davis argues that the modern right to privacy has its roots in the Fourteenth Amendment, whose drafters had "vivid impressions of what it meant to be denied rights of family, for the denial of those rights was a hallmark of slavery in the United States."[92] In her account, the legal protection of privacy first shielded *family* life from public interference, based on the post–Civil War amendments, and only in the twentieth century did it move to articulate an *individual* right to privacy, based on the Bill of Rights. But, as we shall see in the next chapter, the right to privacy in fact began to appear in the decades before the Civil War, and it appeared shrouded in a rhetoric mindful of class status more than of slavery. From its inception, moreover, the right to privacy involved the protection of both individual and family privacy and struggled to balance these two claims. This struggle, I will suggest, shaped the core of that genre of writing that Hawthorne would call "romance."

Chapter 4
Hawthorne's Romance and the Right to Privacy

*The home ought not to be open to the casual eye, or the secrets of it liable to
the prying or the propinquity of neighbors. . . . How much greater the harm
which comes from always living so near to others so exposed front and rear,
and both sides, that inevitably, in spite of you, the daily life . . . is subject to
influences you would gladly be rid of.*

—John F. Ware

*an ante
more private than a bedroom even, for neither lovers nor
maids are welcome, but without a
bedroom's secrets . . .
Devoid of flowers and family photographs, all is subordinate
here to a function . . .
reached by an
outside staircase, domestic
noises and odors, the vast background of natural
life are shut off. Here silence
is turned into objects.*

—W. H. Auden[1]

At the heart of the American canon stands a room. It is the room where
Nathaniel Hawthorne conceived his greatest romance: suffering from
the "wretched numbness" that dulled his imagination in the Salem Custom House, unable to find relief in his walks on the seashore and the
New England countryside, and intimidated by the spirits of his predecessors in the Old Manse's study, Hawthorne entered the parlor, deserted
at night by wife and children and turned into a makeshift study, to find
the ideal place for bringing *The Scarlet Letter* to life. If the archetypical
study, as in Auden's poem, is defined in opposition to domesticity—it
shuns women and sexuality, shutting its door to lovers and refusing
to accommodate familial portraits—Hawthorne's makeshift study described in "The Custom House" does not oppose domesticity so much as

transform it. The "little domestic scenery"—with "the chairs," "the center table," "the sofa," "the picture on the wall," "a child's shoe"—lose their "actual substance, and become things of intellect." The parlor as the scene of domestic events is turned into a space within Hawthorne's mind, an uncanny space, "invested with a quality of strangeness and remoteness." Thus appropriated and defamiliarized, this room serves as the backdrop to his most famous definition of romance as "a neutral territory somewhere between the real world and fairy-land, where the Actual and the Imaginary may meet, and each imbue itself with the nature of the other."[2] Romance, we might say, is born when domestic life is subsumed under the intractable privacy of the mind.

In the preface to *The House of the Seven Gables*, however, Hawthorne defines romance not in relation to domestic space but in relation to law. Romance, he writes, must "rigidly subject itself to laws," even as it claims for itself—in contradistinction to the novel—"a right," or "privileges" of representational latitude and of the freedom of the imagination.[3] This famous definition is at this point misleadingly simple: what precisely is that system of "laws," "rights," and "privileges" to which the romance writer must adhere? Are those laws that delimit and determine the genre, that is, strictly aesthetic?

The last paragraph of the preface suggests otherwise. Here, in a judicious disclaimer (that has since become standard in fictional works), Hawthorne cautions his readers not to bring "his fancy-pictures . . . into positive contact with the realities of the moment" and thereby expose the romance "to an inflexible and exceedingly dangerous species of criticism." In different terms, "he trusts not to be considered as unpardonably offending, by laying out a street that infringes upon nobody's private rights, and appropriating a lot of land which has no visible owner" and urges that the book be read "strictly as a Romance" (pp. 352–53). Hawthorne's definition of romance thus spills over from the purely literary into the legal domain: the "laws" that regulate its mode of representation involve those that safeguard the right of individuals to keep their affairs private while the "privilege" of the imagination claimed by the romance writer protects his work from charges of "unpardonable" infringement on that right.

Indeed, this contiguity of the legal and the literary in the preface has inspired some of the most important work on the Hawthornian romance in recent years. Critics such as Walter Benn Michaels, Brook Thomas, and Gillian Brown have argued that the system of "laws" and "private rights" through which the romance is defined and that it is anxious to protect is the primary, yet residual, right of property.[4] "Residual" because, as these critics explain, by the time Hawthorne wrote his romances, the near-mythical eighteenth-century legal paradigm of the right of property was no longer regarded as either philosophically indisputable or rhetorically sound. If the late eighteenth-century patrician class marked the limits of governmental and societal intrusion on the individual and secured his liberty and autonomy through rights of property and, first and foremost, through real estate, the rise of the middle class and of modern capitalism in the first half of the nineteenth century considerably complicated this model. The logic of the modern marketplace no longer assumed the intrinsic value of real estate; consequently, the Lockean notion that property based on labor and natural use of land secures the inalienability of personhood could no longer offer a stable legal foundation for the definition of personhood. As the "age of contract" gradually replaced the "age of property," that is, personhood became dangerously alienable, potentially appropriable by market relations.[5] According to critics, Hawthorne's romance, "appropriating a lot that has no visible owner" and placing the disputed seven-gabled estate at its hermeneutical crux, tries to resecure the vestigial definition of personhood based on property and to create a middle-class foundation for the right of property, in Michaels's words, "based neither on labor nor wealth and hence free from the risk of appropriation."[6]

What this critical emphasis tends to overlook, I think, is that in *The House of the Seven Gables* Hawthorne seems to abandon rather than grapple with the problem of property rights. Although at the beginning the question of landownership seems central, by the denouement it has become almost irrelevant. Neither the aristocratic Pyncheons nor the plebeian Maules are finally explicitly declared to be the rightful proprietors of the seven-gabled house; instead, an amalgam of people enjoys its fruits: Pyncheons and Maules, old generation and new, the propertied and the homeless. The claim to the Maine land is forgotten, and, as the characters move from the disputed property to a more neutral location, we sense that the question of the right of property itself is displaced and neutralized. This transference of attention away from the right of property, I would argue, is as telling as its initial introduction.

What I wish to argue in this chapter is that the Hawthornian romance takes its shape from and contributes to a transition from the older, patrician paradigm of property rights toward an emerging middle-class legal paradigm of the right to privacy. When, in the preface, Hawthorne describes his romance as "laying out a street that infringes upon no body's private rights, and appropriating a lot of land which had no visible owner," he is suggesting that romance, unlike a deed, possesses the power to appropriate only metaphorically, but that it has a literal ability to infringe on one's right to privacy by making public the stories concealed within the house's walls. The contested plot at the center of the romance is, in that sense, not the physical but the literary one: Hawthorne asks who has the right to the private stories that haunt the gabled house's interior, rather than simply who has the right to own the land on which the house was built.

By the mid-nineteenth century, middle-class thinkers had begun to base the autonomy and inviolability of the individual on a right to secure one's privacy, to withhold information from the public, to avoid, in Ware's words, being "exposed front and rear." As Brook Thomas argues, the right to privacy was invented precisely to counter the problem of the alienability of personhood that emerged with modern capitalism, to keep stories about the self from circulating in the market, and hence to resist the risk of appropriation by the market.[7] The articulation of that right, one might add, involved not only the recognition of privacy as a viable legal category, distinct from and even inhospitable to property rights, but also an expansion of the very boundaries of privacy. Middle-class subjects not only came to regard their thoughts and beliefs as sanctified by privacy, as their ancestors did, but also regarded their domestic affairs, their actions in the home, the narratives around which family life was organized as protected from public visibility and knowledge by right. Typical of the class "which does not want to be named,"[8] the middle-class right to privacy appeared more democratic and universal than the right of property, to be enjoyed by all alike, regardless of financial status. If the right of property accorded a limited number of citizens a limited degree of relief from governmental and societal interventions, the right to privacy offered a more abstract, general, and symbolic protection to domestic life.

But the right to privacy, I will argue, had class distinctions built into it. The concept of privacy always implies the threat of intrusion by others and is therefore a thoroughly political concept: it tends to set one group of people against another. The intrusion against which the middle-class home shut its doors was not only that of the government but also that of what Hawthorne habitually called "the multitudes," revealing privacy to be a specifically middle-class privilege, shaped by anxieties of intrusion from the top and the bottom of the social spectrum.

Of course, the relationship between the novel and a middle-class insistence on the value of individual and domestic privacy has been the subject of several critical works. D. A. Miller and Richard Brodhead, for instance, have shown that, while the creation of domestic privacy is among the conditions of the novel, and while the novel regularly reproduces an ideology of privacy, it simultaneously invades the very space it sanctifies, operating as an instrument of social discipline and "policing." Miller tests this argument through British mid-Victorian novels; Brodhead is interested primarily in American sentimental fiction.[9] But to what degree are their hypotheses applicable to other subgenres of the nineteenth-century novel? Or, rather, do all genres of the novel invade what Miller calls the "sheltered space" of privacy in the same way or to the same degree and effect? Does the American romance, a genre traditionally defined through its self-removal from the domain of the private family, intimacy, and sexuality, share the efficacy of British and sentimental fiction in disciplining the middle-class subject? Using the example of *The House of the Seven Gables*, I will suggest that romance branches away from the novel precisely over the issue of the right to privacy: an anxiety over the potential intrusiveness of fiction and a desire to shield the domestic interior from governmental and societal policing dictate the very form of the Hawthornian romance, endowing it with its distinctive ambiguity and imaginative latitude.

From Head to House

Only since about 1950 has the right to privacy become central to constitutional debates in the United States. Seldom explicitly articulated in legal discourse prior to Samuel D. Warren and Louis D. Brandeis's famous 1890 *Harvard Law Review* article, "The Right to Privacy" (to which I shall return), and relatively marginal in constitutional law in the half-century that followed, the right to privacy began to emerge in the 1950s and the 1960s not only as a distinct right but also as the most fundamental right that Americans possess. In 1950, Erwin Griswold, dean of Harvard Law School, described the right to privacy as nothing less than "the underlying theme of the Bill of Rights," a radical assertion that was endorsed in the next two decades in Supreme Court cases such as *Griswold v. Connecticut* (1965) and *Roe v. Wade* (1973).[10] Such controversial and publicly debated cases elevated the right to privacy to the position of a legal "trump"—a concept that often overshadows all other aspects of the legal debate—a position similar to the one occupied by the right of property in its heyday.[11]

In the face of this diffusion of the right to privacy, legal scholars have to struggle with a definition of the concept of privacy itself, despite there being no such definition readily available in the founding texts of American constitutional law. The right to privacy is based on an indeterminate concept of privacy, a "concept in danger of embracing everything" and thus "in danger of conveying nothing."[12] Other disciplines, notably anthropology, sociology, and philosophy, have attempted since the 1970s to define privacy, to taxonomize privacy issues, and to determine the cultural standing of the concept.[13] In the effort to define "privacy" coherently and distinctively, attention is drawn to both the immanence and the relativity of the concept: while in most cultures we are likely to find a sphere that is partially free from direct societal intrusion on the individual, the borders of that sphere and its uses and meanings depend on historical and cultural contexts. Therefore, in order to discuss meaningfully the development of a middle-class rhetoric of privacy in America, we need to look at the particular historical conditions that produced and surrounded Hawthorne's use of the term.

A glimpse at the range of meaning the term "privacy" encapsulates is offered by anthropologists who compare the expanse and shapelessness of the boundaries of privacy in postindustrialized America with privacy in nonindustrialized cultures. The African Tuareg, for instance, is a culture so small, in which anonymity is so impossible and rigid social control so necessary for survival, that the private sphere is limited to the individual's mind. This sphere is symbolically demarcated by the veiling of one's face, an act that "bestows facelessness and the idiom of privacy upon its wearer."[14] The veil limits privacy to the head, the space where individual thought, but not individual action, takes place.

Hawthorne's ancestors in Puritan New England tended to restrict privacy to the similarly limited sphere of the mind. Indeed, Jürgen Habermas pinpoints the Protestant reformation as the very origin of our modern notion of privacy. As divine authority was taken away from the church and given to the individual, Habermas argues, the religious conscience became the "first sphere of private autonomy."[15] Drawing its energies from the reformation, Puritan theology stressed the importance of solitary reflection and recognized the human conscience or mind as "a haven, where man and his God were alone."[16] The Puritans also recognized, for the most part, that one's thoughts were beyond the power of government or church to control directly and fully. But in the collaborative venture to create "the new Jerusalem," privacy had to cease outside the borders of that mental haven. The space immediately beyond was subject to invasion from legal authorities—who exercised residency laws; regulated visitors, lodgers, and tenants; and supervised marital relationships—from church authorities, meticulously concerned with every overt manifestation of personal life; from other members of the congregation, constantly on the alert for offenses committed by their neighbors; and even from other members of the household (including servants and lodgers), since Puritan home life was often characterized by mutual surveillance. Members of colonial communities did not hesitate to invade their neighbors' homes in order "not to Suffer Sin in My Fellow Creature or Neighbour."[17] As we saw in Chapter 1, the hall-and-parlor house design popular throughout the seventeenth century created a domestic interior that facilitated this regular and rigorous vigilance, since it lacked a distinct division between public and private spaces, and since, with its minimal partitions, it did not offer individual privacy to single members of the household.

Writing during the years of his self-imposed seclusion in his study in Salem, Hawthorne returns to Puritan New England in order to explore imaginatively the origins of his culture's idea of privacy. Appropriately, he uses the emblem of the veiled visage. "The Minister's Black Veil" (1836) imagines a fictional moment wherein a Puritan congregation is forced into the explicit recognition of the head as a realm of absolute privacy. When the eponymous minister covers his face in the beginning of the story, he creates "a type and a symbol" for a space of private autonomy, now conspicuously shielded from "the gaze of multitudes."[18] The Reverend Mr. Hooper's act serves as an apt reminder that in his society the "head," or "conscience," is private, and that, "on every visage," metaphorically, there is "a Black Veil" (p. 384). The veil protects the head from the intrusions of authorities (the "deputies"), from the inquisitive gossip of the congregation (the "multitudes"), and even from the sympathetic queries of his fiancée, family, and friends. All desire to lift the veil and probe its mystery in the course of the tale, and all fail.

More revealingly, the narrator never unveils the minister's visage, nor does the reader discover what it is, if anything, that the minister is concealing under the black crepe. Refusing to appease the reader's "hermeneutic desire," Hawthorne implicates the act of writing and the act of reading in the reification of privacy.[19] He creates a fictional private space that is extremely confined but absolute and impenetrable to the degree that neither writer nor reader probes beyond its apparent surface manifestation. It is important that the minister refuses even to acknowledge that the veil hides a specific "secret sin"; such an admission would reduce the interpretation of the tale to the "opening" or decoding of this secret. A symbol without a concrete referent, the veil comes to stand for privacy itself, for that which is forever immune even from the writer's and the reader's authoritative perspectives. Read in this context, the problem that Hawthorne's text poses is not *what* the signified secret behind the signifying veil is, but *where* the text draws its limits, what area the writer is going to hide, self-consciously and purposefully, from knowledge. It is a problem that belongs more to Hawthorne's New England, middle-class, mid-nineteenth-century milieu than to the Puritan village. "The Minister's Black Veil" is a product of the widening of the borders of the private sphere in Hawthorne's time and the problems of authoritative intrusions into that sphere that are entailed, problems that Hawthorne more explicitly negotiates, as we shall soon see, in future writing.

In the course of the eighteenth century, the borders of the private sphere in the northern colonies gradually widened to encompass the domestic sphere. Although the (originally feudal) idea of the house as "man's castle" was imported from Europe by the Puritans, not until

Puritanism waned was it extensively elaborated on. The home's emergence as a secluded, protective sphere is reflected in the history of colonial town planning: toward the eighteenth century, New England "compact towns," which prohibited living beyond a half-mile range from the meetinghouse, became increasingly scattered, and many residents, turning their fields into homelots, now lived away from the center. Each house was now protected, by distance if nothing else, from public surveillance. In Chapter 1, we saw how, as the eighteenth century gave way to the nineteenth, the house provided a better shield for domestic privacy: the colonial hall-and-parlor design was gradually replaced with the two-story house, a model more spacious and better partitioned than its predecessor. The introduction of the hallway into the standard house helped provide privacy for its inhabitants. In addition, servants and lodgers were now occasionally separated in outbuildings.[20] The house newly created the possibility of an individual private space within and also strengthened its walls against intrusions from outside.

Indeed, the idea of entitlement to domestic privacy and resistance to intrusion worked its way into the rhetoric of the American Revolution. In 1761, the Superior Court in Massachusetts debated issuing a writ filed by Charles Paxton, collector of customs, to authorize officers to search any home. Prominent Boston attorney James Otis stated as part of his argument against the writ that "one of the most essential branches of English liberty, is the freedom of one's house. A man's house is his castle; and while he is quiet he is as well guarded as a prince in his castle." Otis relied on a growing emphasis on domestic privacy in English common law, which stipulated, in Blackstone's summary, that "the law of England has so particular and tender a regard to the immunity of a man's house, that it stiles it his castle, and will never suffer it to be violated with impunity."[21] Otis lost the case, but John Adams, who was present in the courtroom, wrote years later that "American Independence was then and there born."[22]

Not surprisingly, then, the best rhetorical expression of the desire to expand the borders of privacy from "head" to "house" during the early republic we find in the U.S. Constitution. Although, as I have mentioned, the Bill of Rights fails to address the issue of privacy as such, contemporary constitutional law scholars nonetheless detect a "penumbra" around the amendments "where privacy is protected."[23] This penumbra defines the contours of a mental zone of privacy in the First Amendment's freedom of thought and conscience and in the Fifth Amendment's self-incrimination clause, which allows citizens not to surrender their thoughts to their own detriment. But it defines a broader zone as well, one that encompasses the domestic sphere, in the Third Amendment's prohibition against the quartering of soldiers without the consent of the owner, and in the Fourth Amendment's prohibition of unreasonable searches and seizures. Relying on notions of limited government imported from Hobbes, Locke, and Blackstone, rather than on the value of personal privacy as such, early American legal discourse nonetheless strengthened and shaped the rhetoric that designated the house as a sphere of privacy, a rhetoric that became more and more elaborate in the course of the nineteenth century.[24]

We now recognize a number of economic and sociological factors as contributors to this development: the ideal, if not real, enclosure of the home to separate it from modes of production; growing secularization and weakening of religious authorities' involvement with the inner functioning of the family; urbanization and the anonymity it created; an increase in work mobility; the crystallization of the nuclear family—all eased the pressure on the home from both administration and community and allowed the expansion of the "sanctity of the heart" into the "sanctity of the home" ideology. These factors are recognizably those that also molded the middle class in the North; and, indeed, the sanctification of domestic privacy, as Habermas reminds us, is uniquely a middle-class phenomenon.[25] The wealthier class had a relatively large private space from the early colonial period, since, for example, its members often lived in the physical seclusion of larger houses and homelots. The emerging working class, on the other hand, did not enjoy privacy in the home (to the extent that the middle class did) even in the nineteenth century: dense living conditions and multifamily housing, and the control that economic factors continued to exert over personal life (consider, for example, life organized around a factory schedule or life as a servant) limited the ability of the working-class home to serve as a sphere of individual privacy.

It is important to note that increasing privacy in the middle-class home necessarily corresponded to an increasing pressure on its walls, and that the desire to shield was accompanied by a growing desire to expose. Puritan authorities' restricting of individual privacy to the mind had all but eliminated the potential for seditious action, as any action, theoretically, had to take place within a publicly controlled space. These authorities had little need, therefore, to cross the privacy borders that they themselves helped institute. Although torture, public confessions, and oaths were attempts to probe mental privacy and are often associated with the Puritans, they were not as common as we may tend to think.[26] The middle-class expansion of the boundaries of privacy to the house, and thus to a sphere of actions and associations as well as of thought, enhanced the possibility of active subversion in the private sphere. Michel Foucault describes a fear that, from the end of the eighteenth century, haunted the public imagination: "a fear of darkened spaces, of the pall of gloom which prevents the full visibility of things, men and truths . . . [of] the unlit chambers where arbitrary political acts . . . were fomented."[27] Thus, the widening of the boundaries of privacy entailed not only the creation of an enshrined home sphere but also an anxiety that this sphere contained an unnamed danger or horror. While exalting domestic privacy in its rhetoric, such a society needed simultaneously to generate mechanisms that threatened to destroy it.

Foucault's work on the rise of the European modern state, and particularly his work on penal and medical institutions, shows, of course, how surveillance of the private individual did not ease with the appearance of the nineteenth-century bourgeois state but was replaced with invisible mechanisms of power that were no less intrusive, if less conspicuous. The simultaneity of an ideology of privacy and the amplification of ways to invade privacy certainly applies to the United States as well. The same catalysts, in fact, that served to expand the private sphere—urbanization, changes in the form of government, market and technological developments—also rendered these borders vulnerable. A self-regulated economy helped enlarge the private sphere but also demanded intrusion into it: economic relations in the city, for example, became distant and less reliant on personal acquaintance and trust, thus requiring intrusion into the private lives of business partners to provide the missing information needed for that trust. The rise of representative government similarly demanded information about private life, whether of persons aspiring to public office or simply to characterize a constituency. Statistics and bureaucracy developed as a means of retaining information about private life,[28] and technological advances, specifically, in the field of communications, further rendered the private sphere vulnerable. The development of regularized postal services and of the telegraph, for example, while allowing personal communications to pass through an impersonal, anonymous medium for the first time, simultaneously increased the possibility of surreptitious interceptions of private communications.[29] The expansion of privacy into the home therefore coextended with an immense growth of information about the domestic sphere and of modes of getting at that information. A new form of power was thus engendered: the power of invasion.

Foucauldian historiography's emphasis on state policing, however, may obscure the fact that the power of invasion was not understood as or imagined to be limited to institutional control. In his early fantasy about the problems of privacy, Hawthorne hid the minister's face not only from the deputies but also from "the gaze of multitudes." The concept of "watchfulness," of control exercised by ordinary citizens over each other through mutual observation and through the exposing of private information, did not connote precisely an invasion in colonial New England.

The term "gossip," for example, had few negative connotations. In the sixteenth and seventeenth centuries, gossip, to the extent that it was seen as negative, was related to religious "sins of the heart." It was not committed against one's neighbor but involved the relationship of an individual to his or her God. Only in the late eighteenth century did gossip come to be regarded as a social problem, a "failure in social responsibility."[30] As the house became a realm of privacy, as it began to claim protection for action as well as thought, gossip became a form of popular power that threatened to intrude on the house from its back entrance.

The power of this "popular" form of invasion, like that of the "official" one, was greatly enhanced during the nineteenth century. The rise of the popular press, which from its beginning made it its business to report incidents from the private lives of citizens, multiplied the power of gossip a thousandfold. The printed word added authority to that oral form of invasion, as gossip was now reproduced in thousands of copies. Thus, only with the emergence of newspapers (and, later, other means of mass communication) did "degradation of personality by true public disclosure of private intimacies become a legally significant reality."[31] Gossip developed from a mere nuisance early in the century to a real threat by 1900. The invention of early instantaneous photography added to that threat: the camera enhanced the concept of "watchfulness" as it allowed not only the capturing of intimate scenes but also their accurate representation and their potential for seemingly infinite dissemination in public.[32]

Even as it was defining itself as a private sphere, then, the middle-class home was subject to invasion on at least two fronts: the front-door intrusion by official authorities and institutions, forever suspecting the privacy of the house to be a cover-up for potential fragmentation; and the back-door intrusion by the "masses," who regarded the very invasion of that sphere as a mode of exercising power, especially by exposing hidden depravity carefully concealed in the middle-class home. In the face of this two-pronged attack, legal discourse slowly devised a dual response. Constitutional law, which protects the privacy of the individual against governmental action, awaited the twentieth century to formulate its answer. But common law, protecting privacy against invasion by other private parties, made significant attempts to articulate a right to privacy decades before Warren and Brandeis offered an explicit definition of that right in 1890.

Inventing a Right

Courts began to struggle with the articulation of a right to privacy as early as the first decades of the nineteenth century. As G. Edward White explains, during the nineteenth century, privacy emerged as a residual category of law, covering cases that teased the boundaries of traditional legal categories.[33] A rhetoric of a right to privacy began to appear, in other words, in miscellaneous cases in which the category of property and other primary legal categories could no longer provide a satisfactory resolution to new social demands.

Among its earliest appearances were those in cases involving charges of trespass. The right of the inhabitats to protect themselves from both official and unofficial intrusion was absolute and undisputed when the persons in question also owned the house. But from early in the century, courts occasionally chose to protect domestic privacy from trespass even when such protection undermined the right of property. In 1822, for example, a court discussed a householder's "right of shutting his own door" even in the face of justified property claims by others. In the course of the next three decades, other courts questioned the right of landlords to enter their property without the consent of residents and the right of owners of property to retrieve it from the house of others without permission. Further, they asserted occupiers' right to domestic privacy even if they were mere tenants or lodgers. "The purpose of the law," wrote one judge, "is to preserve the repose and tranquility of families within the dwelling house" beyond property interests. Moreover, judges now sometimes recognized that compensation for trespass should not be limited to harm to property but should also take into consideration "injury, insult, invasion of privacy, and interference with the comfort of the plaintiff and his family."[34]

The right to privacy also began to be articulated in cases involving libel and slander charges. Until the mid-nineteenth century, American common law recognized truth as constituting a defense in civil defamation cases. Following Blackstone, who claimed that a plaintiff could not collect damages in civil suits for statements that were true, because the plaintiff had "received no injury at all," courts refused to recognize harm done to a person by publication of facts that he or she had striven to keep private. In 1843, Lord Campbell suggested to the British Parliament that it eliminate truth as an absolute defense for libel, and, around the same time, Thomas Starkie revised Blackstone's explanation of lack of injury caused by truthful publications. From that point on, both British and American judges, increasingly favoring privacy over truth in resolving civil defamation suits, began to identify the harm done to a plaintiff by the mere act of exposure.[35]

Moreover, courts often ruled out an investigation into the truth or falsity of allegedly libelous statements, because they wished to prevent the exposure of citizens' private lives in public courts that such an investigation would necessarily entail. The very structure of the trial, that is, was increasingly conscious of the citizen's right to privacy in domestic affairs.[36] A consciousness of the role language plays in the violation of privacy characterized slander suits as well. Here, judges explained, one must pay attention to the language used by the defendant to determine whether a slanderous act had been committed. A mere innuendo, one court ruled, "cannot extend the sense of words spoken, beyond their natural meaning, unless something is put upon the record, to which the words spoken may be referred, and, by which, they may be explained in the *innuendo.*" Therefore, a plaintiff could claim a violation of privacy and reputation only when the language used was "actionable": unambiguous, mimetic (or "natural"), and specific in its details and references. A use of language characterized by insinuation rather than by direct accusation, and lacking in specific reference, would not be considered actionable in slander cases.[37] What emerged from court rulings in trespass, libel, and slander suits, therefore, was a new language of privacy: detaching itself from the rhetorical foundations of property rights, it prescribed that the statement of truth was potentially harmful to private life and that an ambiguous use of words created the possibility of talking about private life without endangering the value of privacy.

Significantly, one of the primary legal domains within which the right to privacy made an appearance was intellectual property. In 1848, for example, the highest court in the State of New York heard *Hoyt v. MacKenzie and Others.*[38] MacKenzie and his associates obtained Hoyt's personal correspondence by breaking open a chest in which it was kept. They then published the letters, and Hoyt decided to take them to court, arguing that "he alone had the right to publish the letters he had written."[39] Although the lower court agreed with Hoyt, the chief judge of the New York Court of Appeals canceled the injunction issued by the lower court and allowed MacKenzie to continue publication, claiming that "this court cannot restrain and punish crimes, or enforce the performance of moral duties, except so far as they are connected with the rights of property." Since the private contents of the letters had no "literary value," they could not be considered "property" and therefore be offered legal protection.

This case points to a problem that would continue to plague publication cases in the next decades: if a text was protected by law only insofar as it had "literary value" (assuming that courts were competent to make such a call), then any report of a citizen's private life could be published without the possibility of legal intervention, provided that report was not "literary." In other words, as long as the right to a text was bestowed on its author—on the person who wrote it and endowed it with literary merit, which made it valuable—the subject of the text had no rights to control its publication at all. Paradoxically, then, the more private a text was, the easier publishing it would be, because, as it was not written for the public eye, it would tend to have less value as a commodity.

A bit more flexibility was shown by the same court seven years later. The case this time involved a Mr. Woolsey, who complained that the New York *Chronicle* got hold of a copy of "a certain letter—wholly private in character" and intended to publish it.[40] The court now recognized that the publication might "involve whole families in great distress from the public display of facts and circumstances" that were originally intended to "remain forever inviolable secrets." But the judges did not go beyond the rhetorical expansion of the right of property in their decision. "We must be satisfied," they wrote, "that the publication of private letters, without the consent of the writer, is an invasion of an exclusive right of property which remains in the writer, even when the letters have been sent." Furthermore, "the exclusive right, which alone a court is bound to protect . . . is [the] right of property in the words, thoughts and senti-ments, which [the] manuscript embodies and preserves," even if the text has no literary value. The court prevented the *Chronicle* from pub-lishing the letters, but it did so by stretching the definition of property to include private feelings, events, and thoughts, not by postulating that Mr. Woolsey and his family were entitled to a right to privacy, regardless of whom the writer of their personal stories might be.

We might say, then, that when Hawthorne recognized that the writing of *The House of the Seven Gables* potentially infringed on the private rights of those "inhabitants" and "communities" associated with its plot and that he would need to create literary mechanisms—"construct[ ] castles in the air"—to bypass such an intrusion, he acknowledged a value that the law was still struggling to articulate: the value of a text as an account of its subjects' private lives, unrelated to literary forms that might imbue it with aesthetic and hence monetary value (p. 353). To be sure, Hawthorne is writing about a fictional family, not real people who might actually be violated by his narrative. But in deliberately creating an aura of truthfulness for his story, using real locales, and pretending, at times, that he had heard rather than invented it, Hawthorne was able to ex-plore the notion of a right to privacy, a right that precisely dismisses, as we have seen, the question of the truth of a given story.

Since no firm legal boundaries were yet constructed to guard the domestic story as private, the occurrences described in Hoyt's and Woolsey's letters could hardly be protected under the claim to privacy. As I mentioned earlier, the right to privacy remained a residual category of law until later in the century, and neither the Constitution nor com-mon law explicitly and consistently articulated such a right, although both offered a basis on which these discussions could rely once they emerged.[41] The first explicit argument for the legal recognition of a specific right to privacy was made by Warren and Brandeis in 1890, in an article entitled "The Right to Privacy." The article was triggered by the yellow *Saturday Evening Gazette*'s continual and embarrassing coverage of Mrs. and Mr. Warren's private social events, especially a family wedding.[42] It was specifically directed, therefore, toward creating legal protection against back-door intrusions into the private sphere. With new media technology, complained the writers, "what is whispered in the closet shall be proclaimed from the house-tops," and domestic privacy would be seriously jeopardized.[43]

But Warren and Brandeis recognize in the article that the private sphere needed protection from "official" forms of invasion as well. Postulating that "political, social and economic changes entail the recognition of new rights" (p. 75), they conclude: "The common law has always recognized a man's house as his castle, impregnable, often, even to its own officers engaged in the execution of its commands. Shall the courts thus close the front entrance to constituted authority, and open wide the back door to idle and prurient curiosity?" (p. 90). By using the door metaphor Warren and Brandeis acknowledge the house as a private zone and propose the right to privacy as a means of assurance that both doors of that house are shut. Not only should one's thoughts be regarded as private, they argue, but "man's family relations [should become] a part of the legal conception of his life" (pp. 75–76) and thus must be protected as well.

Aside from reaffirming the borders of the private sphere, Warren and Brandeis present a list of legal arguments aimed at distinguishing and defining a right to privacy. The most important of those is that the right to privacy is qualitatively different from the right of property: "the principle which protects . . . personal productions," they argue, "is in reality *not the principle of private property*, but that of an inviolate personality" (p. 82; emphasis added). In order to constitute a new right to privacy, Warren and Brandeis needed to rhetorically unmoor it from the idea of property and thus illustrate its independence as a philosophical concept. By "personal productions," Warren and Brandeis are referring explicitly to written texts and works of art; and, indeed, throughout the article the right to privacy is inextricably tied to common-law cases involving libel and publication rights. They, too, make the important distinction between protection against the publication of lies and protection against publishing truthful but personal information, defended by a right to privacy.

Laws concerning artistic creation (for example, copyright laws) provided a second important legal premise. Recognizing a continuous tension between the private act of writing and the public act of publishing, Warren and Brandeis point to these statutes as offering a principle on which a right to privacy can be based (p. 79). Unlike the judges in Woolsey's and Hoyt's cases, they argue that the publicizing of private writing should be recognized as involving personal discretion and consent, again, not because writing is "property," but because it constitutes a textual extension of the domestic zone. If a man records in a letter to his son, for instance, that he did not have dinner with his wife on a certain date, it is not "the intellectual act of recording the fact" that is being protected by the right to privacy, nor is the actual product or letter, but "the domestic occurrence" itself (p. 79). The signified contents were now detached from the actual letters on the page, and whereas a writer or publisher might "own" the text, the right to its contents rested with the person, or family, whose occurrences were represented. The legal right to privacy was defined through this distinction.

Although the American legal system was slow in incorporating this new right into its debates, the force with which it finally has suggests that the ground was well prepared. The subtitle sometimes added to Warren and Brandeis's article—"The Implicit Made Explicit"—indicates that the right to privacy was already present in mainstream American rhetoric by the end of the nineteenth century and that their role was merely to translate that right into explicit constitutional theory. This, combined with the connections they draw between the right to privacy and the act of writing, leads us back to Hawthorne and to a search for the emergence of that right in nineteenth-century literary works. How does Hawthorne help ingrain the expansion of the sphere of privacy in the imagination of his readers? What characterizes the tension between describing the interior household and simultaneously insisting on its right to privacy? And what is the relationship between novels, specifically, the Hawthornian romance, and the invasion of privacy?

The Corpse in the House

Hawthorne's participation in the conceptual expansion of the boundaries of privacy is most salient in *The House of the Seven Gables* in the recurrent metaphorical juxtaposition of the house and the human mind. His characters' psyches are symbolized by architecture: Hepzibah's brain, for instance, is like "poor, bare, melancholy chambers"; it is "impregnated with the dry rot of its timbers" (p. 408).[44] But Hawthorne goes beyond this. Like Poe in "The Fall of the House of Usher," he inverts the metaphor and anthropomorphizes the house: "The aspect of the venerable mansion has always affected me like a human countenance," he tells us at the outset; or "[the house] was itself like a great human heart, with a life of its own, and full of rich and sombre reminiscences" (pp. 351, 374).[45] The reciprocity of this metaphorical structure implies the complete interchangeability of house and mind in his story: the house does not merely symbolize the mind but has, somehow, become the mind. The anatomized house expresses a fantasy of the somatic impermeability of domestic space, while the architectured mind expands the space that the individual is entitled to claim as veiled from public vision.

A veiled space creates an obsession with unveiling, as the narrator admits, for the house "has been an object of curiosity with him from boyhood" (p. 359). The tension that this obsession instigates is apparent from the very beginning: we are informed that the "long lapse of mortal life, and accompanying vicissitudes, that have passed within" the house, though remarkable, have no space in this narrative. Instead, we must be satisfied with "a rapid glimpse at its quaint exterior" (p. 355). At once reproducing in us his own curiosity and restricting our vision to external surfaces, the narrator begins to sketch the ambiguous hermeneutic borders of this text. With "invincible reluctance," he (and we) will "loiter faintheartedly on the threshold" of the old house of the narrative, sometimes looking in, mostly substituting speculation for drama and fantasy and innuendo for fact (p. 381).

The imagined history of the house contains within it a history of private space as well. On the occasion of its inauguration in seventeenth-century Puritan Salem, the House of the Seven Gables stood open to members of all social castes: under its doorway "trod the clergymen, the elders, the magistrates, the deacons and whatever of aristocracy there was in town or county"; in came also, carefully segregated by the doormen, "the plebeian classes, as freely as their betters and in large number"; and finally, the high sheriff and the lieutenant governor (standing in for King William) crossed the threshold and made themselves "free to intrude" into the innermost chamber of the house: its master's study (pp. 361, 363). There, amid piles of his letters and correspondence—which aptly enmesh personal writing with private space—the corpse of Colonel Pyncheon was discovered by the lieutenant governor, the "multitudes" pressing on the official's back with "the eagerness of their curiosity" and creating "many rumors" and a "vast deal of noise" that spread the news of death throughout Salem (p. 364). The dark secret hidden in the house, the corpse in the house's great human heart, was promptly exposed by a coalition of officials, the masses, and the narrator.

Generations later, Hepzibah, the present tenant of the house, finds herself vulnerable to the attacks of this very coalition. Although she lives in comfortable seclusion, Hepzibah's decline from gentility forces her to open a cent shop in her home, and by introducing the market into her private life, she becomes a target both of town gossip and the physical intrusion of the town's people, who go "prying with vague eyes about the shop" (p. 409). Hepzibah's largest menace, however, is the constant scrutiny of Judge Pyncheon, "a personage of mark, influence and authority," the embodiment of officialdom, whose "eye rested on the shopwindow . . . [and] minutely surveyed Hepzibah's little arrangement of toys and commodities" (pp. 400, 401). Long barred from entering the house by its front door, the judge will now try the other. This backdoor opening into her private domain stimulates Hepzibah to fantasize about building a palace, where, protected on her literal and metaphorical pedestal, she would "look down from its highest tower on hill, dale, forest, field and town" (p. 408). But, lamentably, Hepzibah's real estate–based fantasies of patrician seclusion are no longer realizable.

The Puritan owner of the House of the Seven Gables issued an open invitation; Hepzibah opens the door with reluctance and suffering. The ancestral guests have bred pernicious intruders, and the whole scene is now tainted with paranoia: Hepzibah tiptoes to the window, imagining "some bloody-minded villain to be watching behind the elm-tree, with intent to take her life" (p. 385). This complicates the narrator's own crossing of the threshold (could *he* be that stalker?); thus, for instance, on our first introduction to Hepzibah, we are barred from directly watching her and have to make do with imagining her from behind the closed door of her chamber. The narrator smiles: "Far from us be the indecorum of assisting, even in imagination, at a maiden lady's toilet!" while, in the same breath, he minutely surveys the scene within (p. 377). This moment of gentlemanly, vicarious voyeurism is, in a sense, a prototype for the romance's rhetorical code throughout. Gordon Hutner has identified in Hawthorne's writing a "dual process of promising and deferring disclosure," which "lends his rhetoric its characteristic tension."[46] In *The House of the Seven Gables* the tension of the rhetoric may be described as the product of the reversed strategy: Hawthorne repeatedly discloses information even as he refuses to own up to his act of disclosure. In the narrator's description of the details of the store's interior, for instance, we do not learn that its stock includes barrels of flour, apples, and Indian meal. We learn, rather, that were "a curious eye, privileged to take an account of stock and investigate behind the counter," to exercise its privilege, such would be its findings (p. 381). Hawthorne's use of language, that is, reveals what he calls a "reluctance to disclose," as if the crossing of the threshold into the story involves an unpleasant and even morally ambiguous duty (p. 381).

It is not until Phoebe arrives that the walls of the House of the Seven Gables begin to ossify. Phoebe, as Joel Pfister points out, "serves as an advertisement for middle-class domesticity and the emerging middle-class itself "; under her blessed influence, the house becomes both joyful and protected.[47] The problem of privacy seems to reach a comfortable equilibrium: gossip ceases; the judge's attempts to invade the house are obstructed. Into Phoebe's angelic frame Hawthorne channels his middle-class ideals of the sanctity of personal life, ideals that he tried to realize in his own life and for which he has earned the title of "shaman of domesticity."[48] Pfister, T. Walter Herbert, David Leverenz, and others have shown how *The House of the Seven Gables* contributed to the shaping of the middle-class by dramatizing the separate-spheres ideology and prioritizing, in accordance with that ideology, gender dichotomies over class distinctions.[49] The value of privacy, however, exceeds the prescriptions of the separate-spheres ideology, which allies the private with the feminine and the public with the masculine. While domesticity is perfectly captured in the character of Phoebe, the concept of domestic privacy is not easily or simply interchangeable with domesticity and is not associated only with female characters. On the contrary, the character that most needs to learn his entitlement to domestic privacy is Clifford.

Whereas the women of the house naturally thrive in the newly protected home, Clifford has a harder time adjusting. A relic of an older time, his adult mind shaped in the restricted space of a prison cell, Clifford is baffled by changes that time has brought and, although he does his best to "kindle the heart's house-hold fire," the walls seem constantly to melt around him (p. 442). Referred to as "the guest" for a large part of the book, Clifford's private mental sphere refuses to expand into domestic privacy. He sustains "a dim veil of decay and ruin betwixt him and the world," beneath which "far more of his spirit [is] hidden than revealed," even under Phoebe's benign influence (pp. 442, 475). For Clifford, the alternative to seclusion in one's mind is a complete lack not only of privacy but also of personhood, a suicidal submergence into a "broad mass of existence—one great life—one collected body of mankind" that new technologies, such as the train and the telegraph, seem to have produced in the world outside his window (p. 494). These technological innovations, forming an "all-pervading intelligence," attempt to make the whole globe "one vast head" and thus, by expanding the private sphere indefinitely, threaten to eliminate privacy altogether (p. 578). Only by the end of the book, after Clifford actually takes the plunge into the outside world and experiences the homelessness of the city and the train, does he manage to lift his solipsistic veil and expand his identity to correlate with the domestic sphere. Hawthorne instructs Clifford in the course of the novel that proper masculine identity is residential, that a man without a home is a potential criminal.

A crucial element in the narrative puts a twist into the process of the emergence of a middle-class right to privacy that the text traces, for the domestic haven is tainted with the presence of an in-built dark secret, and that secret is at once the crux and the burden of the rhetoric of privacy. In his most elaborate use of the house-head metaphor, Hawthorne describes how a person (Judge Pyncheon, in this case) would build up "a tall and stately edifice" around the self. "Behold, therefore, a palace!" he exclaims in an oft-quoted passage: "Its splendid halls and suites of spacious apartments are floored with a mosaic-work of costly marbles; its windows, the whole height of each room, admit the sunshine through. . . . Ah! but in some low and obscure nook—some narrow closet on the ground floor, shut, locked and bolted, and the key flung away—or beneath the marble pavement, in a stagnant water-puddle . . . may lie a corpse, half-decayed and still decaying, and diffusing its death scent all through the palace!" (pp. 549–50). Like Mr. Hooper's veil, the walls of the house that the Pyncheons have built symbolically shield from public view a potential threat, a possible horror. The sole rightful penetrator of these walls is "a seer, before whose sadly gifted eye the whole structure melts into thin air, leaving only the hidden nook . . . and the decaying corpse within" (p. 550). The questions that Hawthorne implicitly addresses are who that "seer" might be, and what he should do once he finds the nook in which the metaphorical corpse is entombed. In other words, who had the ability, the responsibility, and the right in nineteenth-century America to melt down the walls and expose the private to public view?

The beginning of *The House of the Seven Gables* seems to suggest that "the multitudes," Salem's people, are assigned the role of "the seer." Through gossip, rumors, and whispers, they attempt to undermine the standing of the House of the Seven Gables and of the patrician Pyncheons. By participating in the tradition of rumors about the edifice, by creating the illusion, in fact, that his entire story is an end product of decades of gossip and popular legend, Hawthorne seems to align his narrative with such intrusions. The domestic novel, Patricia Meyer Spacks has shown, has indeed stemmed from "gossipy" genres as such as the epistolary novel and the biography, and it shares with gossip a "kind of intense interest in personal detail" and "may attempt to establish with . . . readers a kind of relationship approximating that of gossip."[50] By making the private sphere of the middle-class home their subject, novelists found themselves collaborating with oral gossips and with popular-press journalists against the powerful upper crust of that class. If gossip became a form of expository power in the nineteenth century, as Warren and Brandeis postulate, then novelists may have found themselves identified with social agitation. Indeed, some American novelists have made conscious use of the power implied in the role of the gossip, what I call in Chapter 3 the "strategy of exposure." The urban exposé novel of the mid-nineteenth century, for instance, attempted to undermine the political power of the growing middle class through deliberate acts of exposure. George Lippard, for example, one of the first spokesmen for the working class in America, employs actual sensational newspaper items in his novel *Quaker City*. Another story featuring a house—"Monk Hall"—this novel's entire structure relies on short anecdotes from the private lives of Philadelphia's upper class, drawn from the press and aimed at undermining this class's growing political strength. Monk Hall, again a structural metaphor for the skull of its resident "Devil Bug," contains a dead man buried in its cellar whom, in the course of the novel, Lippard exposes, literally and as a symbol of inherent upper-class corruption.

Similarly, the antebellum sentimental novel attempted to exploit the connection between fiction and gossip to challenge gender politics. For example, in Fanny Fern's *Ruth Hall* (although the house is only implied, perhaps, in this title) the plot again relies on the unauthorized entrance into the middle-class private home. Fern's rhetorical strategy, like Lippard's, is to gossip: she tells private anecdotes about characters who could easily have been identified by contemporary readers as real-life personages. Moreover, Fern (as well as her heroine, Ruth) writes for the popular press, and the "dead corpse" that she exposes is the small-mindedness of the middle-class home.

But Hawthorne, unlike the socialist Lippard or the protofeminist Fern, has no conspicuous agenda concerning the middle-class home. On the contrary, while recognizing gossip as an existing form of social discourse, he is careful both to stress what he perceives as the limitations of this form and to separate from it his own writing. "Tradition," or gossip passed on through the ages, Hawthorne explains, is by no means a dependable narrative source: "tradition sometimes brings down truth that history has let slip but is oftener the wild babble of the time, such as was formerly spoken at the fireside, and now congealed in newspapers" (p. 365). He further hopes not to be "belied by some singular stories, murmured, even at this day, under the narrator's breath" (p. 457). Clearly attracted to these legends, Hawthorne also rejects them as babble, unfit by their very nature to represent what he calls "truth."

This is one motivation, therefore, for Hawthorne's invention of the term "romance" to separate his writing from the novel. The desire to lay bare the home, according to Jonathan Arac, lies at the very heart of the nineteenth-century novelistic enterprise. Arac argues that the novel in its heyday was closely allied in its aesthetic vision with both "writers of journalism and social polemic" and "the activities of the central agencies of government." The novel, that is, joined forces with both forms of intrusion into middle-class privacy. Hence, for instance, Charles Dickens's invocation of Le Sage's *diable boiteux*—the diabolic intruder

Asmodeus—as his mentor and muse. He calls for "a good spirit who would take the house-tops off" to expose corruption within London's homes, "for men, delayed no more by stumbling-blocks of their own making . . . would then apply themselves . . . to make the world a better place!" What Hawthorne's romance reveals, by contrast, is an ambivalence toward this reform-through-exposure novelistic principle. In "Sights from a Steeple," for instance, Hawthorne engages in an implicit conversation with the novelist, who sees Asmodeus as his hero. "Oh, that the limping devil of Le Sage would perch beside me here," the narrator exclaims, "extend his wand over this contiguity of roofs, uncover every chamber and make me familiar with their inhabitants! . . . But none of these things are possible; and if I would know the interior of brick walls or the mystery of human bosoms, I can but guess."[51] Romance, while desiring to penetrate the privacy of the home, nonetheless carefully distances itself from such a penetration by claiming for itself the supremacy of the imagination. It will ideally retain the novel's ability to see through the middle-class home without infringing on its privacy and endangering its very existence.

Hawthorne is further anxious to separate his writing from another form of intrusive power, that which I have referred to as "official." The "authorities" in his narrative are embodied in Judge Pyncheon, the public man who intends to run for governor of Massachusetts, who is loyal to public service, devoted to his party, and involved, with "remarkable zeal," in a number of organized institutions, such as the Bible Society and the Widow's and Orphan's Fund (p. 550). Judge Pyncheon repeatedly attempts to invade the House of the Seven Gables, and his constant presence on the threshold of the house poses at least as much of a threat to its inhabitants as the talk around town. If gossip is associated with tales, rumors, and the novel, Judge Pyncheon's public surveillance is associated with public records. The official portrait of the judge's Puritan ancestor, who bears an uncanny resemblance to the judge himself, hangs in the central chamber of the house, surveying its inhabitants and reminding them of the patrician threat to their domestic privacy.

But official records, Hawthorn stresses, are even less capable than the "babble" of the masses of maintaining discursive integrity. Writers in an official capacity—the clergyman, the legal critic, the historian—are not better qualified to tell the story of the house, for they write "cold, formal and empty words . . . for the public eye and for distant time . . . which inevitably lose much of their truth by the fatal consciousness of so doing" (pp. 456, 457). Intended for the distant future, such official acts of representation, whether oil-painted or textual, are analogous to the powerful men whose reputation they attempt to perpetuate. The latter, Hawthorne explains in the preface, are guilty of the "folly of tumbling down an

avalanche of ill-gotten gold, or real estate, on the heads of an unfortu-
nate posterity, thereby to maim and crush them" (p. 352). Similarly, the
cold words of the chisel handed down from previous generations would
maim the story, as the centuries-old portrait of the Puritan Pyncheon literally threatens to tumble down on the residents of the house. Here, too,
Hawthorne is careful to dissociate his romance from official records, as
he has from the novel. Precisely by refusing to implicate itself, eventually,
in a discussion of property and real estate, by not clinging to the avalanche of ill-gotten gold, the romance critiques official writing and its ruling interest of conserving power and property interests.

In the representational world of Judge Pyncheon and his ancestors,
the right of property is a privileged signifier, and the judge derives his
very raison d'être from his great possessions. It is, Hawthorne tells us, a
"counterfeit of right," but its false representational power is so strong
that it imposes its control even on the "secret minds" of the less endowed (p. 372). The right of property is thus antithetical to—and even
subsumes—the right to privacy in the beginning of the narrative, because under its name the very sanctity of the mind is violated. The
judge, after all, is the real owner of the House of the Seven Gables and
thus assumes he should be granted free access to its interior. Consciously rejecting this empire of property rights aided by public record
and real-estate titles, Hawthorne's romance is an attempt to disturb and
reverse the relationship between property and privacy.

When Hawthorne imagines a "seer," one before whose powers of observation the house's walls melt and its secrets become exposed, he has
neither the gossip nor the official in mind, neither the novelist nor the
clerk. In the chapters that lead to the climactic discovery of the corpse,
both kinds of intruders try to collaborate and create a united front
against the House of the Seven Gables. Judge Pyncheon, having tried
the front door in vain, now enters the house from the back. He manages
to penetrate its interior physically, aided by Hepzibah's neighbors, who
"have been eye-witnesses to whatever has passed in the garden." "The
butcher, the baker, the fishmonger, some of the customers of [the]
shop, and many a prying old woman" have told the judge "several secrets of [the] interior," armed with which he now hopes to destroy
the domestic haven of Hepzibah, Clifford, and Phoebe (p. 555). But
whereas in Puritan Salem such collaboration managed to expose the
dead body in the house's innermost chamber, this time it fails. The
judge himself becomes the dead body, and neither the authorities nor
the town's people (although the butcher comes close) will finally be the
ones to discover the bloody corpse.

The person who does find Judge Pyncheon's body is Holgrave. Allied
neither with officialdom nor with the rest of the town—he is "lawless"

and an out-of-towner—Holgrave possesses the strongest invasive po-
tency of all (p. 424). He is a "lodger" in the House of the Seven Gables
and roams free in its very heart; he is a photographer, whose technology
invades both the house and its occupants and "actually brings out the
secret character with a truth that no painter would ever venture upon";
he is, finally, a mesmerist—one who has the ability to penetrate that inner and most private sphere of all, the human mind (p. 425). The combination of these elements turns Holgrave into the largest threat,
perhaps, to the privacy of the house, so large, in fact, that Phoebe initially fears that "he may set the house on fire!" (p. 424).[52]

Holgrave's supreme visual powers are comparable only to those of the
narrator, the other presence in the book whose privileged point of view
allows free travel in both the heads and the house of the narrative. A
connection is often drawn between Holgrave and Hawthorne in his
younger days: Holgrave's experience in a community of Fourierists,
which led him to believe that "a family should be merged into the great,
obscure mass of humanity" and that houses "ought to be purified with
fire," reminds us of Hawthorne's unsuccessful experiment with utopian
collectivism on Brook Farm, a few years prior to his writing *The House of
the Seven Gables* (pp. 510–11). Holgrave learns in the course of the narrative, though, what the older Hawthorne believes from the outset: that
the power of the seer needs to be used for the protection, and even for
the construction, of domestic privacy, rather than for its violation and
destruction. He learns, that is, to be a romancer rather than a reforming
novelist.

The embedded story of "Alice Pyncheon" dissolves the borders between narrator and character, between Hawthorne and Holgrave, between fact and fiction. The lodger's story duplicates that of the book as a
whole: Alice's mind, that "sphere impenetrable" that embodies domestic privacy, itself harbors an unmentionable secret, a "treachery within,"
that critics have linked with forbidden sexual desire. This "sphere
impenetrable," rendered fragile by internal transgression, is invaded
through the collaboration of her powerful patrician father and the
lower-class carpenter, both eager to substitute their property interests
for her right to privacy (p. 526). This story of invasion told by Holgrave
is indistinguishable in terms of language from that of Hawthorne. Holgrave, too, describes, for instance, the house's "pleasant aspect of life,
which is like the cheery expression . . . in the human countenance"
(p. 516). The main difference is that Holgrave's story poses a much
larger threat to the House of the Seven Gables, for, whereas Hawthorne
stresses in the preface the fictionality of his tale, Holgrave is openly writing about characters that in the ontological world of the book are real.
And whereas Hawthorne defines his story as romance, Holgrave intends

to publish *his* in a newspaper, to inject his text with the power of gossip, and thus to merge the Pyncheon household into the "obscure mass of humanity" (p. 511). Unlike Hawthorne's romance, this exposé "essentially follows" the "wild, chimney-corner legend" (p. 522). Moreover, Holgrave's story provides precisely the missing generational links between Colonel Pyncheon and Hepzibah, the inside information that the narrator, as we recall, decided to rule out of his narrative at the outset and to substitute with the exterior description of the house. It is thus especially significant that Holgrave learns, through the telling of his story to Phoebe, "reverence for another's individuality," that he contemplates burning the manuscript, and that, indeed, he never publishes it (p. 535). Rather than subvert the private haven, his story leads him to desire it. The invasive narrative potential of "Alice Pyncheon" has managed momentarily to penetrate Phoebe's mind and, symbolically, the fragile domestic sphere that she embodies. But Holgrave decides to make an exit, not to carry this mesmerizing effect further, and to begin to contemplate building a home with Phoebe instead. The masterful intruder of the feminized private sphere would become its protective master.

When Holgrave discovers a literal corpse in the house, he is faced with two options: to publish the crime by turning the evidence over to the authorities ("Let us throw open the doors!" Phoebe urges him, again illustrating the point that it is men, rather than women, who are the primary protectors of the right to privacy), or to keep the horror concealed in the house to himself. This moment is replete with legal implications: What right or duty does one have to reveal information? Does that duty surpass one's concern for another's private affairs? It is thus particularly important that Hawthorne has Holgrave opt for silence and for keeping the criminal evidence to himself, and that, having matured into understanding of the value of privacy, Holgrave uses this knowledge to protect rather than destroy the House of the Seven Gables. The daguerreotype that he takes of the dead judge will not be put to use by either the police or the press; it will serve merely for Holgrave's private use and for the protection of Clifford and Hepzibah. The moment of supreme invasion into the dark secrets of the house becomes, thus, an occasion for the strengthening of its borders—"the Black moment [becomes] at once a blissful one"—as Holgrave confesses his love for Phoebe and promises to establish a new middle-class home (p. 615). A domestic secret, therefore, creates the foundations for familial privacy and fixes the couple within an impenetrable circle all their own.

But Holgrave, strictly speaking, is not the first one to find the dead judge; preceding him, the narrator himself dissolves the walls of the house to gaze at the corpse. The strange and ontologically ambiguous "Governor Pyncheon" chapter disrupts the narrative and contains almost no action. Uncharacteristically for this romance, the chapter provides an entrance into the mind of the judge in the hours before his death and gives us direct access to his thoughts. Also uncharacteristically, it addresses readers directly and continuously, urging us to participate in the intrusion into the judge's mind and abode. With the narrator, we become the "enemy or mischief-maker" stalkers, who "taking him thus at unawares . . . peep through these windows into his consciousness, and make strange discoveries" (p. 582). This chapter does what Holgrave will refuse to do: it slowly and painstakingly exposes the corpse to public gaze. From his lofty, "owlish" perspective, the narrator surveys the house and the corpse in minute detail. But as twilight begins to obscure the contours of the house, he begins to acknowledge the dangers inherent in his own power of vision and in the unveiling of the corpse: "There is no window! There is no face! An infinite, inscrutable blackness has annihilated sight! Where is our universe? All crumbled away from us; and we, adrift in chaos, may hearken to the gusts of homeless wind, that go sighing and murmuring about, in quest of what was once a world!" (p. 589). The nightly intrusion into the mystery of the house has melted both the walls and the skull of individual privacy. Hawthorne elegizes the privacy of the well-protected home from a position in a potential future when technology and modernity's "all-pervading intelligence" (p. 578) will annul the world, will turn it into a homeless place where no privacy exists, a kind of an apocalyptic relapse to pre-Genesis chaos. His power as a writer, the potential he exhibits for penetrating the private to its innermost reaches, participates in the proliferation of this "inscrutable blackness" (p. 589) and in the constitution of a universe empty of meaning.

Hawthorne does not allow this momentary vision to take over his narrative, however. He insists that this part "must by no means be considered as forming an actual portion of our story," and therefore fulfills his earlier promise that, when the "sadly gifted" seer confronts the corpse, he will leave intact the nook in which it is hidden (p. 593). In the pages immediately following his weird exposé, he returns to a detailed, strikingly calm description of the house's exterior. Like Holgrave, who turns the moment of blackness into a promise of domestic joy, Hawthorne musters the remaining chapters for the task of rebuilding those walls that momentarily crumbled. When Hawthorne described the last days of work on the book to his publisher in terms of "hammering away a little on the roof," he had patching up rather than an Asmodian lifting of the rooftop in mind.[53] He ends the book, thus, by uniting Phoebe and Holgrave and constructing a new and better home for them, for their intimate friends, and for their close relatives: "A house of stone, indeed!" as Phoebe exclaims, far away from the town's prying eyes, as well as from "the eye of yonder portrait," who "rendered himself so long the Evil Destiny of his race" (p. 623).

The two moves at the end of *The House of the Seven Gables*—the move to penetrate the domestic haven even to its innermost reaches, and the consecutive move to build a new house away from public gaze (and away from our gaze as well, as the story ends, implying that part of the happiness in the cliché "they lived happily ever after" comes from our letting the heroes alone)—evince the relationship imagined by Hawthorne between the writer and the right to privacy. Hawthorne's story is filled with tension that arises from the desire to stress the writer's inclusive vision, on the one hand, and his self-proclaimed responsibility to participate in the production of privacy, on the other. This uneasy coexistence leads Hawthorne to invent his romance genre, a genre that he defines in the preface as conveying "subtle" rather than "ostensible" truth. The romance is an attempt to do away with the fundamental problem of representing the unpresentable, of simultaneously invading and protecting. Unlike the newspaper, the camera, or the novel, which ostensibly try to expose domestic truth and "thus at once deprive[ ] it of life," Hawthorne's genre wishes to recognize truth, but to control its representation (p. 352). The romance occupies a kind of penumbral zone "where the real and imaginary may meet," neither a fully lit nor a precisely shaded space, surrounding a dark spot of absolute, inviolate, privacy. Its "subtlety" is in its ability to take with the one hand what the other has given: to acknowledge the writer's power of invasion while gallantly refusing to negotiate its deployment as a weapon.

The celebration of domestic privacy at the end of *The House of the Seven Gables*, of course, has been often described in a disappointed tone. The marriage of Holgrave to the boringly pure Phoebe, critics have suggested, signifies not only the domestication of one of Hawthorne's most radical figures but also Hawthorne's failure to own up to some of the radical implications of the very genre he has invented. Ultimately, the argument goes, Hawthorne swerves away from romance and precisely toward the novelistic tradition that he began by critiquing.

To the extent that I am correct in reading the book in relation to privacy laws, this sense of disappointment can be tied to a different critique, that of the right to privacy itself, a critique that gained momentum especially after the infamous *Bowers v. Hardwick* Supreme Court decision. In 1986, the Supreme Court upheld Georgia's antisodomy laws, claiming that the right to privacy is one that protects only "family, marriage or procreation" from state interference. The *Hardwick* decision, as its critics correctly point out, determines that privacy is offered as protection in the United States only provided the public already defines in advance that which it agrees to protect: normative subjects engaged in heterosexual, reproductive acts.[54] The right to privacy, in that sense, is the most domesticated of rights. In support of that argument, we might return to Warren and Brandeis's article to recall that what motivated their invention of that right was, after all, their wish to protect the privacy of a wedding, and that their example of the "domestic occurrence" that requires protection is nothing more menacing than "a man not having dinner with his wife."

Still, I would argue, both senses of disappointment—that over the happy ending of *The House of the Seven Gables* and that over the policing uses of the right to privacy—are not entirely justified. The force of the Hawthornian romance lies in the insinuation that every house has a corpse in the cellar, that even the most domesticated of scenes, such as the domestic parlor in "The Custom House," harbors the strange and uncanny. Even Holgrave's marriage to Phoebe does not exactly promise the purification of the Gothic house, for who's to know what it is that Phoebe's own interior hides? Just as Alice Pyncheon's story exposes the forbidden desires that lurk behind the virtuous woman's façade, so does Holgrave's very refusal to trespass into Phoebe's soul imply that even this avatar of normative domesticity is bound to be hiding something in the closet (else why was Phoebe so mesmerized by Alice's story?). It is precisely the radical potential of the right to privacy, a potential *betrayed* by the 1986 *Hardwick* decision, that this right recognizes that even the most normative identities are always queer.

It is perhaps this recognition that Brandeis became anxious about in the years following the publication of his landmark article. In a letter to his future wife (who else?), Brandeis admits that he is worried about the right to privacy's collision with the First Amendment's guarantee of freedom of speech and that he should have published a "companion piece" on "the duty of publicity." These doubts resurfaced later, when the now Supreme Court justice speculated, in decidedly Hawthornian language, that "if the broad light of day could be let in upon men's actions, it would purify them as the sun disinfects."[55] This lingering insistence on the duty of exposure attests to the power of the right to privacy and of its underlying wish *not* to be pure.

Chapter 5

Thoreau in Suburbia: *Walden* and the Liberal Myth of Private Manhood

You know that no American, who is at all comfortable in life, will share his dwelling with another. Each has his own roof, and his own little yard.

—*James Fenimore Cooper*

A man is a housekeeper,—yea, verily, he builds a house, and it is his task thenceforward whilst he lives to paint, shingle, repair, enlarge & beautify that house.

—*Ralph Waldo Emerson*[1]

In April 1849, Henry David Thoreau was in the midst of a lecture tour on what would, five years later, become *Walden*, when he earned the prized endorsement of the *New York Tribune*. Thoreau, wrote Horace Greeley, the *Tribune*'s editor, "has built him a house ten by fifteen feet in a piece of unfrequented woods by the side of a pleasant little lakelet, where he devotes his days to study and reflection. . . . If all our young men would but hear this lecture, we think some among them would feel less strongly impelled either to come to New-York or go to California."[2] For Greeley, in building the cabin Thoreau had also con- structed a new model for manhood, one that could inspire an entire generation of restless young men to make a home and stay in it rather than escape to the cities or answer the call (at one time, Greeley's own) to "Go West." By following Thoreau's example, Greeley believed, young men could manage "to preserve their independence without starving their souls,"[3] to be free by avoiding the exterior world of competitive labor.

But not all *Tribune* readers were equally impressed. Five days later, Greeley published a response from the improbably named "Mr. Timo- thy Thorough." "I notice in your paper of this morning a strong com- mendation of one Mr. Thoreau for going out into the woods and living in a hut all by himself," wrote Mr. Thorough;

I felt a little surprised at seeing such a performance held up as an example for the young men of this country, and supposed I must have mistaken the sense of your article. Accordingly I called in my wife, Mrs. Thorough, and we studied it over together. . . . Mrs. T. is more clear in her mind than I am. She will have it that the young man is either a whimsy or else a good-for-nothing, selfish, crab-like sort of chap, who tries to shirk the duties whose hearty and honest discharge is the only thing that in her view entitles a man to be regarded as a good example. She declares that nobody has a right to live for himself alone, away from the interests, the affections, and the sufferings of his kind. Such a way of going on, she says, is no living, but a cold and snailish kind of existence, which, she maintains, is both infernal and infernally stupid.[4]

What seems to have infuriated the reader is Thoreau's rejection of the duties and pleasures of the private sphere. A young man who lives "snailishly," shirking both familial intimacy and empathy with "his kind," should not be upheld as a paragon of manhood, he protests. Telling, however, is his choice to call in his wife to voice this protest ("she declares," "she says," "she maintains," he insists). This allows him to absolve himself of the critique and at the same time highlights the gendered subtext of the clash in values between "Mr. Thoreau" and "Mrs. Thorough." It is the "clear-minded" domestic woman who is appalled by Thoreau's rejection of what she perceives to be the essence of private life: familial and social intimacy.

Her reaction was not singular: it would soon be reiterated in the early reviews of *Walden* ("It is difficult to understand that a mother had ever clasped this hermit to her bosom; that a sister had ever imprinted on his lips a tender kiss," wrote one reviewer in 1854, confirming Mrs. Thorough's view of Thoreau as the adversary of intimate domesticity).[5] Ironically, in ceding full authority to his wife, Mr. Thorough unclasps *himself* from the bosom of domesticity, thus indicating that Thoreau's "hermitism," if not "an example for the young men of this country," nevertheless is a representative example *of* them.

Indeed, it is precisely what Mrs. Thorough found most objectionable about Thoreau's experiment, his self-proclaimed "right to live for himself alone, away from the interests, the affections, and the sufferings of his kind," that earned him the esteem of other readers. Bronson Alcott, for example, called his friend Thoreau "the best republican citizen in the world; always at home minding his own affairs . . . dropping society clean out of his theories, while standing friendly in his strict sense of friendship."[6] For Alcott, Thoreau was not the adversary of the private sphere; on the contrary, he was its most stringent proponent, "always at home minding his own affairs." And his disregard for the social does not preclude friendship, provided friendship is defined in the "strict sense" of the term; it certainly does not make Thoreau a "crab-like sort of a chap" but, rather, "the best example of an indigenous American" or "the best republican citizen in the world."

In going to Walden, then, did Thoreau rebel against the most cherished values of the home, or build the best model of it? These radically divergent early responses illustrate how Thoreau's experiment entered right into the crux of antebellum conversations on the meaning of the private sphere and its relation to the social. As we have seen, what we often assume was a univalent middle-class private sphere in the nineteenth century was in fact a divided, gendered, and contested terrain. The discourse of domesticity tended to collapse the distinction between public and private by producing a privileged intermediary zone of social intimacy and self-exposure defined in opposition both to individual privacy and to the abstract, impersonal public sphere. It is in the name of this discourse that Mrs. Thorough was summoned to critique Thoreau's abandonment of family and society.

The liberal discourse of the home, on the other hand, tended to flatten the trilateral structure of the public, the social, and the private by advocating a strong binary pull between the loose, abstract association of the public sphere and the monadic, interiorized man. It desired to protect both the individual and the public from the intrusion of the social, with the meaning of the latter ranging from familial intimacy to the intrusive "masses." It is from this perspective that Thoreau is upheld as a model for the integrity of the private sphere; the value of his example lies precisely in his "drop[ping] society clean out of his theories."

The existence of these competing discourses can explain why three of the most elaborate theorists of the modern public/private divide— Hannah Arendt, Jürgen Habermas, and Richard Sennett—all describe the nineteenth century in terms of both the rise *and* the decline of the social sphere. According to Arendt, the nineteenth century witnessed the dangerous coupling of the social with the intimate, the demand that individuals act "as though they were members of one enormous family which has only one opinion and one interest," a demand that grated against both individual privacy and the agonistic public sphere. Habermas recasts this observation to describe the rise of the "pseudo public or sham private world of culture consumption" in the nineteenth century, the "superfamilial zone of familiarity" that threatened the existence of interior life and brought about the demise of the Enlightenment's critical public sphere. Sennett likewise describes the rise of the modern "intimate vision of society," which destroyed the impersonal social sphere of the eighteenth century.[7]

Their different terminology notwithstanding, all three discuss two interrelated phenomena: the decline of an older (and, in their view, more estimable) social realm; and its replacement by a powerful new realm that, in collapsing the social and the intimate, corroded the public/private divide. All three, however, neglect to highlight the *gendered* aspect of this transformation. While Arendt, Habermas, and Sennett (to varying degrees of explicitness) associate the residual social sphere with manhood, they largely overlook the link between the rise of the "familial" or "intimate" social sphere and the formation of domestic womanhood. At least in the United States, however, where the middle of the nineteenth century witnessed what Ann Douglas has famously called "the feminization of American culture," the realm of "pseudo public or sham private world of culture consumption" (in Habermas's description) was closely associated with femininity. At the same time, the decline of the older paradigm of the social (which some historians argue was comparatively weak in America even during the early republic)[8] coextended with a strengthening liberal ideal of masculinity, one that defined itself *against* this feminizing, intimate social sphere. Thus, paradoxically enough, the association between men was newly perceived as a *loss* of manhood, or, as Emerson famously put it, "society everywhere is in conspiracy against the manhood of every one of its members."[9]

In this and the next chapter I argue that Thoreau is one of the most elaborate theorists of this privatized masculine ideal. In this chapter, I argue that *Walden* joined a variety of antebellum texts in suturing "natural" or "true" masculine identity to private space, a space designed to resist the threats of permeability from within (domestic womanhood) and from without (homosociability). The antebellum home, in this discourse, is not perceived as "entirely the domain of wives," a space from which "men were increasingly exiled . . . unable to return without fear of feminization," as historians nowadays sometimes describe it.[10] On the contrary, it is seen as a signal of the achievement and protection of manly independence. In building his cabin, Thoreau both realizes this liberal ideal of the home and takes it to an extreme. Unlike the homes we have examined thus far, the cabin is a house *un*divided: emptied of the accoutrements of domesticity and social ostentation, it is a study without an accompanying parlor, an interior that cancels internal divisions by declaring its sole function to be the expression and shielding of man's autonomous, interior life. Undivided within, the cabin is also defined by distance from the social realm and the dangerous proximity to other men that it imposes. Thoreau's cabin showed men how to, as Greeley put it, "preserve their independence without starving their souls," partially because it was removed from homosocial spaces (in Greeley's terms, the marketplace [the city] and the frontier [the West]).

It is in this sense, I argue, that Thoreau can be discussed as one of "the original creators of the suburb." Lewis Mumford has eloquently described the fantasy that subtended that creation: "To be your own unique self; to build your unique house, mid a unique landscape, to live in this Domain of Arnheim a self-centered life, in which private fantasy and caprice would have license to express themselves openly, in short— to withdraw like a monk and live like a prince—this was the purpose of the original creators of the suburb."[11] *Walden*, I argue, is an experiment in realizing this liberal fantasy of independence qua withdrawal into the private sphere.

In Chapter 6 I ask whether this "suburbanization" of middle-class manhood simply destroyed social intimacy between men, as some critics assume, or, instead, *redefined* it. I suggest that the latter is correct. As we have seen, Mrs. Thorough objected to Thoreau's experiment because he shunned intimacy, a form of intimacy defined as the "interests" that people take in each other's personal life. But Thoreau develops instead an alternative logic of intimacy, one that allows for masculine relations while avoiding the dangers of this "feminizing" self-exposure. Throughout his career—in texts such as *Walden*, *A Week on the Concord and Merrimack Rivers*, and the lesser-known essay "The Landlord"—Thoreau repudiated the feminine form of intimacy, defined as the exchange of stories about personal life, and developed an alternative, masculine definition of intimacy, based on concealment rather than revelation, on distance rather than physical proximity, on silence rather than speech. I demonstrate that this form of "depersonalizing" intimacy is not merely schematized but also performed in Thoreau's texts, which idealize intimacy between (male) writer and (male) reader, an idealization found also in the writing of Hawthorne, Melville, and Emerson. I thus propose resisting reading Thoreau's abstract relations and spare personal revelations simply as affective foreclosures; rather, I propose seeing that, given liberalism's construction of the private, isolated masculine self, such relations might satisfy a desire for reciprocal (and potentially politically effective) fraternal intimacy.

I wish to take seriously, then, Greeley's and Alcott's perception of Thoreau as a *model* for middle-class manhood. If this perception is often lost in our own time it is because Thoreau has been read largely through two dominant critical frames: first, the critical tradition that regards him as an antibourgeois dissident, a writer whose value lies in his ability to stand outside of the petty and oppressive middle-class life that he so adamantly critiqued; and, second, the tradition that views *Walden* as an ur-text in the "melodrama of beset manhood," a prime example of the male American's overriding desire to *escape* from a coercive, feminine domestic sphere and into a mythical, redeeming "wilderness."[12] But as Laurence Buell and Nina Baym each show, these two critical traditions have their roots less in any essential quality inherent in Thoreau's writing than in the historical process of his canonization.[13] In fact, for a large part of its history, Thoreau's writing was read precisely as an *expression* of middle-class, domestic values.

From his death in 1862 until the end of the nineteenth century, Thoreau enjoyed a limited but stable position in the emerging American canon as a second-tier writer, a minor supplement to the major sextet of Longfellow, Emerson, Hawthorne, Whittier, Lowell, and Holmes. He was read not in contrast to but in tandem with this group of writers dominated by the Fireside Poets, a group that was hailed as solidifying liberal bourgeois notions of the primacy of the private sphere for the middle-class man. The Fireside Poets embodied these notions in a number of ways. They regarded the "homestead hearth" as the site of the writer's imagination and pictured the hearth's flickering light as generating a neutral ground where writer and reader "met" safely and intimately. Their poetry conveyed that "sweet home feeling" regarded as the source of truth and morality; its virtues, as Whittier wrote, consisted "in its simplicity, and genuine, unaffected sympathy with the common joys and sorrows of daily life. It is a home-taught, household melody . . . the poetry of home, of nature, and the affections."[14] In their very lifestyle, moreover, the Fireside Poets were models of the emergent suburban ideal. As Robert Penn Warren writes, these poets "could have emerged only from a society that had made the first, irreversible step from agrarian life to the urban, industrial pattern."[15] This was partially because they were "Sunday poets": they worked as lawyers, politicians, doctors, or journalists in their public role but pursued their true calling, writing, after work, within the confines of the home, in the tamed, natural environment of the urban fringes. It was of significance to their contemporaries that they worked in the "spiritual suburbs of Boston"— Concord and Cambridge—"withdrawn" yet "within easy reach of a great city."[16] And the very metaphors used to describe the six major writers in the second half of the nineteenth century point to their conception as models of middle-class homosocial intimacy: they were described as a family of writers or as an intimate group of friends who were more important in their relationship to each other than in any manifestation of iconoclastic, isolated individual genius.

Thoreau was regarded as enhancing this familial portrait of the great American writers even as he became a more dominant figure in the canon in the last two decades of the century. Between 1880 and 1900, sales of his works quadrupled, and in 1906, Mifflin supported Thoreau's gain in popularity by issuing an expensive twenty-volume edition of his writing.[17] His popularization coextended, that is, with the rapid growth of suburbia and the stabilization of the figure of the private, suburban man.[18] His gradual canonization at the end of the century, it is important to note, did not depend on a cultural revision of the figure of the

Great American Writer. Thoreau was accepted as reinforcing the ideal of the respectable middle-class citizen, as the incarnation of liberal, Emersonian values. Emerson's own description of Thoreau as "a bachelor of thought and nature" still governed his image,[19] where "bachelor" defined his position *within* the bourgeois "grand narrative of connubiality" rather than expressed a defiance of it, and "nature" connoted the tamed, inhabited landscape of Concord rather than the "wilderness." Emerson's efforts to enshrine Thoreau in the pantheon of polite values have been recently analyzed as a kind of middle-class plot to erase from the record his essential "queer radicalism,"[20] and no doubt Emerson's editorializing flattened many of Thoreau's sexual and political challenges. I would emphasize two points, however: first, the degree to which a "bourgeois" version of Thoreau was embraced by middle-class men until the twentieth century (as Emerson put it, nineteenth-century "young men of sensibility" did not deem it problematic to pursue Thoreau as a kind of a model, a "man of men, who could tell them all they should do")[21]; and, second, the fact that the alternative, "radical" Thoreau is no more essential than the Emersonian version—he, too, is a flattened product of a later process of critical enshrinement and interpretation.

The radicalization of Thoreau was begun after the First World War by such early modernist critics as Waldo Frank and Van Wyck Brooks. This generation, which transported the task of canonization to academia and which also introduced Poe, Melville, Whitman, and Twain into the canon at the expense of the Fireside Poets, rewrote their predecessors' narrative of the "family" of great American authors as an antinomian romance featuring the alienated and ill-understood American genius, intransigent in his rebellion against middle-class values. In that context, Thoreau was consciously transformed into a major figure of antibourgeois revolt. Waldo Frank explained this transformation in 1919: "When we were boys, we all had tedious uncles who professed to be very fond of Thoreau. . . . These uncles were typical good citizens of old America: Altogether dull-minded and sober paragons. We decided that their favorite author could be no favorite of ours. We took it for granted that Thoreau also was a stuffy bore. We left him alone. Thoreau was killed by his good name. It is time, however, that we wake up to the wicked, destructive fellow Thoreau really was: give him the bad name that is his due."[22] For Frank and others of his generation, this revision of Thoreau was implicated in the very process of coming of age, of finding their own masculine identity through a critique of fin-de-siècle bourgeoisie, of polemically explaining the new modernist generation to itself. In this polemic lie the seeds of the post–World War II "melodrama of beset manhood," because for the early modernists manhood was conditioned by what Georg Lukács called, in 1920, "transcendental homelessness," the great fissure between the estranged masculine intellect and the domesticated, bourgeois *mentalité*.[23]

When the task of canonization was picked up by F. O. Matthiessen, R. W. B. Lewis, and others (and later by such critics as Joel Porte), Thoreau's reputation as an intransigent Young Turk had already been established. This perspective was now elaborated on and refined. Matthiessen, in the culminating chapter to *American Renaissance*, revealingly entitled "Man in the Open Air," compares Thoreau's "myth making" less to antebellum novels and poetry and more to the great heroes of modernism: Thomas Mann, T. S. Eliot, Freud. He also draws a parallel between Thoreau and the "American Demigods" of the wilderness like Davy Crockett and Sut Lovingood. For Lewis, Thoreau is a prime example of the "American Adam," the "frontiersman" who escapes from the constraints of socialization into the wilderness. Joel Porte's comparison between a conservative Emerson and a radical Thoreau is supported by his claim, also made by others, that the domestic sphere symbolizes death in *Walden*, and he elaborates on Thoreau's "aching need to escape" from it. Thoreau was thus increasingly viewed as a dissident, not only in relation to the Fireside Poets but also in relation to Emerson and Hawthorne, now regarded as more conservative.[24] Overlooking the fact that nature in *Walden* is more suburban than wild, an annex of society rather than its antithesis, as Philip Fisher has correctly pointed out,[25] such critics admire the untamed Thoreau, who drank from the "tonic of wilderness" and was tempted to devour a woodchuck raw, and forget about the Thoreau who dreamed of owning a home and living "the steadier for it."[26]

Given this canonization history, it is hardly surprising that feminist criticism's reaction to Thoreau has often been one of alienation, a result more of the way Thoreau was packaged in the twentieth century than of any specific passages in his writing. If Thoreau's texts were to be read as an articulation of an inherent desire to escape from domesticity into the wilderness, then women readers were bound to feel, in Judith Fetterley's terms, "lost in the masculine wilderness" of this great "American Masterpiece." If Thoreau's legacy were indeed of "the family and home as symbol of that which keeps man from being independent, an artist, human," and "the family and home" were interchangeable with "the feminine," then his interest for feminist critics could come about in only one of two ways: either as yet another expression of a deep-seated misogyny inherent in American literature, to be dismantled and exposed; or—if his interest in "home-making" is taken into account—as a "feminized" writer, an androgynous figure who traverses the gender boundaries instituted by his own culture.[27]

But, as we shall see, for Thoreau and his generation the home was not what kept man from being independent but what ensured his independence vis-à-vis the "wilderness" of the exterior, social world. This does not mean that Thoreau's writing is not often clearly tainted by misogyny; it does suggest, however, that the root of this misogyny may well be located precisely in the friction between the two gendered understandings of the home and its relation to the social—liberal and domestic, Thoreau's and Mrs. Thorough's—ideally compatible, but often clashing.

The Liberal Myth of Private Manhood

Walden is indeed a melodrama of beset manhood. But what impels this melodrama, we sometimes forget, is Thoreau's rejection of homosocial intimacies as well as of domestic womanhood. In "The Village," Concord appears to Thoreau as a "great news room" where men examine each other "with their bodies inclined forward and their eyes glancing along the line this way and that . . . with voluptuous expression, or else leaning against a barn with their hands in their pockets, like caryatides, as if to prop it up." It is from the "dangers" posed by these men, whose description is haunted by both feminization and homoeroticism, from the vulnerable self-exposure they demand, that he "escaped wonderfully" (pp. 456–57). "What do we want most to dwell near to?" he asks in "Solitude." "Not to many men surely, the depot, the post-office, the barroom, the meeting-house, the school-house, the grocery, Beacon Hill, or the Five Points, where men most congregate" (p. 428). "The value of a man is not in his skin, that we should touch him" (p. 431). Thoreau's experiment thus begins precisely with the disavowal of homosocial intimacy, understood as a violation of privacy and coerced visibility. Relation to other men, he posits, must be based on distance and boundaries: "it would be better if there were but one inhabitant to a square mile, as where I live" (pp. 430–31).

Emerson wrote that "Union is only perfect when all the Uniters are absolutely isolated. Each man being the Universe, if he attempts to join himself to others, he instantly is jostled, crowded, cramped, halved, quartered, or on all sides diminished of his proportion."[28] The society of men must rely on physical distance from each other, since proximity threatens each with the loss of whole, self-contained manhood; any sign of closeness between men is, counterintuitively, detrimental to the creation of a community of men. Echoing Emerson's jostling, crowding, cramping, halving and quartering of manhood in association, Thoreau warns in *Walden* that "we live thick and are in each other's way, and stumble over one another" (p. 428), and he therefore escapes *into*, not away from, the private sphere.

This linkage between independent manhood and the private sphere is, of course, nothing new. It is at least as old as the aphorism "A man's home is his castle," a phrase that points to its even older manifestation under feudalism. It is, one might say, the very foundation of patriarchy. But the seemingly continuous term "patriarchy," as Eve Sedgwick reminds us, conceals important discontinuities.[29] In fact, the home that Thoreau "escapes wonderfully" into is described as *antithetical* to that of the patriarch of the previous generation. In "Sounds," Thoreau boasts of the "deficiency of domestic sounds" in his cabin, where he hears "neither the churn, nor the spinning-wheel, nor even the singing of the kettle, nor the hissing of the urn, nor children crying, to comfort one," and remarks that "an old-fashioned man would have lost his senses or died of ennui before that" (p. 424). The cabin, emptied of family, tools of production, and, first and foremost, women's labor (the spinning wheel, the kettle, children), is thereby defined in opposition to the home of "old-fashioned man."

Cleansed of both women and labor, Thoreau's cabin reflects a major redefinition of the meaning of the private sphere for masculine self-fashioning. The old-fashioned man's home represents the residual, republican model of the private sphere, drawn from the classical model. This model perceived the private sphere as the site of productive and reproductive necessity, the existence of which freed man to pursue his higher, less-material calling away from it, in the public company of other men. As Hannah Arendt explains, under the classical model, "the distinctive trait of the household sphere was that in it men lived together because they were driven by their wants and needs." As the sphere of women and slaves, the household was synonymous with dependence and bodily needs, signifying both the precondition for and the opposition to manly independence.[30] The change introduced by the rise of bourgeois liberalism was that now the *private* sphere was conceived as the site of freedom, choice, and independence; the exterior world, where men worked together for a living, was now often described as the realm of necessity and subjugation (where "you are the slave-driver of yourself" [p. 328]), as Thoreau famously put it). The "new fashioned" man's ideal home, therefore, was defined by minimizing the traces of dependence, labor, and need. In Thoreau's extreme version, the cabin rids itself altogether of the domestic woman and the kind of (re)productive labor she represents.

One could attribute both these features of the cabin—its distance from homosocial spaces and the ridding of its interior of domestic womanhood—to Thoreau's biographical idiosyncrasies: his famous dislike of Concord's farmers or his prolonged bachelorhood and ambiguous sexuality. But a strictly biographical reading would cancel out what Dana

Nelson has correctly identified as Thoreau's "representative isolation-ism," the way his experiment reflects and promotes a general model of manhood based on solitariness and boundedness.[31] Indeed, it is hard to ignore the fact that the above two features of the cabin are very close to the ones that psychoanalytical theory places at the very core of the con-struction of masculine identity. As is well known, the orthodox Freudian narrative about the formation of the bounded masculine ego has been revised in recent decades. While Freud attributed this formation prima-rily to the son's Oedipal confrontation with his father, an attribution that left a scant role for women beyond being the object of desire, femi-nist psychoanalysis proposes, instead, that masculine self-formation is founded on the disavowal of femininity, a femininity associated with the absence of boundaries. Since the mother connotes for the boy depend-ence on the other, argue such theorists as Nancy Chodorow and Cather-ine Keller, he needs to reject both her and the femininity she instills within him. Only then can he develop a strong independent, separatist identity. More recently, however, queer theory has moved the originat-ing moment of masculine self-formation farther back. Judith Butler, for instance, argues that the (already heterosexualized) disavowal of femi-ninity is preceded by an earlier foreclosure—of homosexual attach-ment. For Butler, the phantasmatically separate masculine ego is formed at the moment of the prohibition (though not the disappearance) of this attachment, and to sustain itself, the ego needs continuously to negate its introjected presence.[32]

Both revisions could inform a reading of *Walden*. If the book is, in-deed, as Greeley, Alcott, and Emerson implied, about the shaping of model, independent manhood, feminist psychoanalysis would argue that this project begins with Thoreau's cleansing of the interior of femi-nine dependence; queer theory would trace its beginning to the escape from Concord's voluptuously gazing, hand-pocketing men.

But it might be more accurate to read psychoanalytical theory through *Walden*, rather than vice versa. The isolationist masculine ideal that psychoanalysis often regards transhistorically, in other words, is, in fact, a historical construct, one that dates to the early annals of liberal thought. At the time in which Thoreau was writing, there already existed an account of masculinity that naturalized the state of isolation and re-pressed its formative dependency on both the feminine and the mascu-line other. As Seyla Benhabib has lucidly shown, early liberal thinkers such as Locke, Hobbes, and Rousseau developed a myth of the original man in the state of nature, a myth based on a "simple and profound message: in the beginning man was alone." These thinkers posed soli-tude, independence, and boundedness as man's *original* condition, thus erasing the double disavowal that produced this condition. Hobbes, for example, asks us to "consider men . . . as if but even now sprung out of the earth, and suddenly, like mushrooms, come to full maturity, without all kind of engagement to each other." He asks us to imagine men who come into being as self-contained, separate, and fully formed entities. The metaphor of mushroomlike men depends precisely on the repression of childhood as a state of dependence on the other. In this myth, masculine independence is not carved from a complex mass of relations to other beings but precedes these relations. It does not originate with the negation of dependence on women, as the mother's role is altogether erased in the Hobbesian metaphor of self-generating "mushrooms." Nor does it emerge from the disavowal of relations to other men but "without all kind of engagement" of men "to each other." Rather, man's original, natural state is that of being completely, gloriously alone. Only then does this autonomous state become endangered, at the moment in which man enters into domestic and social relations. Man is endangered from within his sphere by the presence of the domestic woman, who signifies reliance on the other and need; and he is endangered from outside by the male other, who presents the dangers of invasion and appropriation. To ward off these threats, Benhabib explains, as man enters domestic and social relations, he devalues, limits, and controls women and devises laws that define and protect his sphere as property and his relation to other men as contracts.[33]

This liberal myth of natural manhood, I argue, was revived in Thoreau's time with the rise of the middle class and its fantasy of man's return to nature. One of the most important sociospatial developments of the nineteenth century, the creation of the suburb, can be read as the continuation of the myth of the naturally bounded, independent man, who, by owning and controlling a space of isolation and privacy, wards off the threats imposed by both domestic womanhood and his peers. And it is in this context that Thoreau's seemingly radical, idiosyncratic experiment in *Walden* emerges as truly representative.

Thoreau in Suburbia

In the first few lines of *Walden*, Henry David Thoreau introduces himself as a suburban writer. Not that he often uses the term—as *Walden* was composed, "suburbia" was only beginning to accumulate the pile of connotations, wistful or contemptuous, that eventually combined to define it as the hallmark of the American middle class—but Thoreau positions himself along a series of coordinates that we have since come to associate with suburban geography and mentality. "When I wrote the following pages, or rather the bulk of them," Thoreau begins, "I lived alone, in the woods, a mile from any neighbor, in a house which I had built

myself, on the shore of Walden Pond, in Concord, Massachusetts"
(p. 325). His opening literary (and literal) move encapsulates a number
of emphases also promoted by those "original creators of the suburb"
that Lewis Mumford describes. Among them are privacy ("I lived
alone"), relation to nature ("in the woods"), distance between men (although a whole mile between neighbors is the suburbanite's fantasy, not
reality), making one's own home ("in a house which I had built myself"),
and living on the periphery of common space (Concord, which itself was
fast transforming from a farming village into a Boston satellite). All these
specifications introduce a new kind of space onto the antebellum social
grid, a territory that defies traditional divisions into "town" and "country," "urban" and "agrarian," an opportunity for the middle-class man to
"return" to nature and its promise of independent, solitary manliness.

Thoreau's book is, of course, suffused with the language of domestic
architecture, from his experiments in masonry in "Economy" to the descriptions of his dream home in "Housewarming." I wish to focus on the
web of resemblances between Thoreau's spatial language and the body
of prescriptive literature that orchestrated the middle-class move to the
first suburbs.[34] Emerson's description of Thoreau as a "man of men"
who could tell "young men of sensibility" "all they should do" places
Walden in relation to two powerful contemporaneous discourses: the
young man's behavior manual, and the architectural pattern book. Behavior manuals, written and published with increasing popularity between 1830 and 1860, were not intended as guides to financial or
political success, like their late nineteenth- and twentieth-century de-
scendants. On the contrary: written not by successful businessmen but
by clergymen and educators like John Todd, Henry Ward Beecher,
William A. Alcott, and Horace Mann, these manuals defined ideal manhood in relation to the private sphere and in opposition to the world of
commerce and politics. Addressing young men in the liminal stage before mature adulthood, and centering on the metaphor of "character
building," they encouraged their readers to secure their position within
the middle class by buying a home and withdrawing as much as possible
from the social spaces of fraternal association: taverns, political clubs,
and lodges.[35]

The sequel, as it were, to the behavior manuals, the architectural pattern books of Andrew Jackson Downing, Gervase Wheeler, and others,
entered the market with increasing vigor in the 1840s and the 1850s,
and provided practical advice on how to achieve the newly woven dream
of a home of one's own while remaining within one's means and thus retaining one's independence. They developed and elaborated on the behavior manuals' equation of masculine identity with the appropriation
of an isolated home in nature.[36]

Despite the book's philosophical and aesthetic sophistication, there are a number of indications that *Walden* was both written and read with the popularity of this prescriptive literature in mind. Thoreau's writing to an audience of "poor students" (p. 325), and his proclaimed mission of "prescrib[ing] rules" for the "mass of men who are discontented," particularly those who are "seemingly wealthy" but are the "most terribly impoverished class of all" (p. 335), implies a readership of young men of relative means who suffered from anxiety and spiritual malaise rather than dire material need, and who required guidance to get them over the threshold into secure, content manhood. The image that seems to have carved the deepest impression in the minds of his contemporaries is that of Thoreau "brag[ging] as lustily as chanticleer in the morning, standing on his roost, if only to wake [his] neighbors up" (p. 389). The domestic virility exemplified by the rooster, which, somewhat like a behavior-manual writer, cries out from his own home to arouse the sensibilities of others, was a powerful enough image for the publisher to reprint it on the title page of *Walden*'s first edition, embellished by a bucolic sketch of Thoreau's cabin.

As we have seen, much of the early response to Thoreau's experiment centered around the feasibility of his prescriptions for young men, whether readers concluded that he was "a very wholesome example" for those who could learn through him "how, by chastening their physical appetites, they may preserve their proper independence," or doubted that his prescriptions were feasible or even desirable. This kind of response came so early (when *Walden* was still presented in lecture form) and so prevalently that Thoreau incorporated a passage into the final version to assure his readers that his experience was not meant to be copied verbatim—"I would not have any one adopt *my* mode of living on any account," he wrote (p. 378)—but only followed in spirit.

A number of critical studies establish a connection between Thoreau and the architectural pattern book as well. In *American Renaissance*, Matthiessen highlights Thoreau's thematic connections to the aesthetic dictates of Horatio Greenough, the famous antebellum architectural theorist. Theodore Brown places *Walden* firmly within contemporary domestic architectural discourse, pointing out the shared sentiments of *Walden* and such popular pattern books as Orson Fowler's *A Home for All*. Richard and Jean Carwile Masteller examine at length the internal dialogue in *Walden* between Thoreau and pattern-book authorities such as Andrew Jackson Downing, the arbiter of taste for the antebellum middle class, proving that, despite some fundamental divergences, "some of Downing's assumptions and rhetoric are strikingly similar to Thoreau's." More recently, Cecelia Tichi points out the similarities between *Walden* and such domestic guidebooks as Catherine Beecher's *Treatise on Domestic*

Economy.[37] Thoreau's interest in the minute details of domestic masonry, his discussions of "ornament" versus "foundation," his detailed account of the cost of building and maintaining a house would all have been familiar to his readers from their reading of pattern books. (It was not entirely as metaphor, then, that he earned the nickname "Transcendental architect" from Emerson's son.)[38]

What both the behavior manual and the pattern book kindled in their middle-class readers was the dream of owning a home away from the violent bustle of the growing cities. Unlike in continental Europe, where the bourgeoisie, as even its name reveals, traditionally defined itself in relation to the centralized urban centers and sought proximity to the cities' increasingly elaborate social spaces, the American middle class instead translated the older Jeffersonian rural ideal into a suburban ideal, and thus decentralized social urban spaces even as they were forming. As early as 1815, the phenomenon of the middle-class suburb began to be conspicuous in the North, and the move to suburbia gained momentum in proportion to the progress of urbanization in the second third of the nineteenth century.[39] The binary pull between public and private that diminished the homosocial sphere was captured and reinforced by the creation of the suburb, which literalized the distance between man and society and idealized a private realm walled off from the social world. In an article meant to promote buying real estate in Highland Terrace, a suburb of New York City, Nathaniel Parker Willis prophesizes that soon "New Yorkers will be ready for a startling and most revolutionizing change"—life in the suburb—and adds that "industry, necessity, or vice, could alone prefer a house in a 'block,' among disturbances and gutters, to a home unencroached upon, amid fresh air and gardens."[40]

Downing, arguably the single most influential person to orchestrate this decentralization, wrote in 1848, "In the United States nature and domestic life are better than society and the manners of towns. Hence all sensible men gladly escape, earlier or later and partially or wholly, from the turmoil of cities."[41] Both influenced and appreciated by Emerson and the transcendental movement (Emerson imagined the ideal "readers and thinkers of 1854 as suburban commuters on the morning train to the city"),[42] Downing prescribed the same principles that Thoreau experimented with in building his cabin: appropriating a space for individual privacy; "naturalizing" the domestic sphere; separating interior life from labor; and digging a wide moat between the private and the social realms. What Leo Marx calls Thoreau's "middle landscape"[43]— neither city nor wilderness—bears a striking resemblance to the kind of space appropriated by the suburbs, and the appearances of the train in *Walden* remind us that the main vehicle for suburbanization was already in place by the time Thoreau was writing. "Five times a day," Thoreau notes in his journal, "I can be whirled to Boston within an hour."[44] Although he was far from being a fan of this new technology, Thoreau did recognize that the railroad created a "link" between his seclusion and society and thus allowed the opening up of new livable spaces "on the confines of towns, where once only the hunter penetrated," and that people "live steadier for it" (pp. 414–16).[45]

Indeed, in 1854, Concord itself was in the midst of a change from a largely self-sufficient farming community to one dependent on its proximity to the fast-growing urban center of Boston. This is true not only in the sense that Concord's farmers, as Thoreau repeatedly lamented, became engulfed in the antebellum wave of agricultural capitalization and were increasingly dependent on the city's market for their livelihood but also in regard to the growing ranks of Concord residents who were not farmers but were engaged in business (like Thoreau's family) and in other middle-class occupations (like the group of transcendentalist intellectuals who gathered around Emerson); for these men, the rural environs of Concord were a life-style choice rather than something required by the nature of their labor.[46] Combined with the pastoral tranquillity it offered, Concord's distance from Boston allowed men like Emerson to separate their private lives from their public performance and to "withdraw like a monk and live like a prince" in the privacy of their suburban homes.

Transcendental Property

For the behavior manual and the pattern book, then, this withdrawal into a home of one's own signified the achievement of independent manhood. The home was not only a reprieve, an "elysium to which [men] can flee and find rest from the stormy strife of a selfish world," but also the clearest evidence of man's liberty and virtue. When a young man built and owned a suburban home, he also built and owned himself as an autonomous man. A popular behavior manual metaphorized, "a good character must be formed, it must be made—it must be *built* by our individual exertions."[47] That proper manliness and suburban home-ownership were intimately intertwined was obvious to such observers as Russell Conwell, who, in a lecture tour in the 1860s, explained, "My friend, you take and drive me . . . out into the suburbs of Philadelphia . . . and I will introduce you to the very best people in character as well as in enterprise in our city, and you know I will. A man is not really a true man until he owns his own home, and they that own their homes are economical and careful, by owning a home." Catharine Beecher concurred: "implanted in the heart of every true man, is the desire for a home of his own," the root and rationale for all his endeavors. Even Walt Whitman emphasized the importance of homeownership for the achievement of manhood: "A man is not a whole and complete man," he attested, "unless he owns a house and the ground its stands on."[48] As Clifford E. Clark argues, the emergent antebellum middle class may be defined precisely through the criterion of homeownership, which testifies not merely to a certain level of income but also to a specific definition of autonomous personhood.[49]

The ambition to reach this goal of self-making through homeownership steered the life of the young, middle-class man throughout his adolescence. Because manhood was coupled with homeownership, the achievement of the status of manhood for a young man of Thoreau's generation and class was, for the first time, delayed, often postponed until his thirties.[50] The various advice manuals entered a man's life precisely during this prolonged period of liminality, to direct his desires toward homeownership and to make sure that his energies did not diverge from this telos. "Much of that feverish unrest and want of balance between the desire and the fulfillment of life," the dictum went, "is calmed and adjusted by the pursuit of tastes which result in making a little world of the family home."[51]

The young Thoreau's building of the cabin on Walden's shores was an act of following rather than shunning this teleology. Underlying his project was the deferred fantasy of owning a home, of ceasing to be a "*sojourner* in civilized life" by affixing himself firmly within it. "At a certain season of our life we are accustomed to consider every spot as the possible site of a house," he writes. "In imagination I have bought all the farms in succession. . . . Wherever I sat, there I might live, and the landscape radiated from me accordingly. What is a house but a *sedes*, a seat?—better if a country seat" (p. 387). His fantasies encompassed not only the buying of land but also the building of the house that would stand on it: "I sometimes dream of a larger and more populous house, standing in a golden age, of enduring materials, and without gingerbread work" (p. 516), he writes. "I intend to build me a house that will surpass any on the main street in Concord in grandeur and luxury, as soon as it pleases me as much and will cost me no more than my present one" (p. 361).

To be sure, Thoreau's tone is much more complex than the behavior manuals'. His words serve at once to parody the possessiveness of his contemporaries (who enslave themselves to own gingerbread-work country homes) and to remove his own fantasies to the realm of symbol and the imagination. But it is precisely this symbolic abstraction that provides the philosophical foundations for the equation between manhood and homeownership. Thoreau says to his reader, "If you have built castles in the air, your work need not be lost; that is where they should be. Now put the foundations under them" (p. 580). The metaphor of "building castles in the air" to signify masculine self-realization captures the idealized connection between personhood and real estate in *Walden*.

Why must men dream of owning houses? In "Solitude" Thoreau asks; "For what reason have I this vast range and circuit, some square miles of unfrequented forest, for my privacy, abandoned to me by men?" The answer, of course, is provided as part of the question. The appropriation of a piece of nature in *Walden* is "for my privacy," for returning man to his true, original state of solitude and independence of the other. The cabin, much like the ideal suburban home, has no other house "visible from any place"; it provides a "little world all to [him]self," not "profaned by any human neighbor." As such, it allows Thoreau to imagine himself back in the state of nature, to imagine himself, as he puts it, "the first or last man." Appropriation is necessary for the securing of privacy, even as subjective interiority is imagined as a suburban homelot, a "clearing, familiar and worn by us, appropriated and fenced in some way, and reclaimed from nature" (p. 426). C. Wright Mills has written (in relation to the twentieth century) that the middle-class man was "the man for whom wealth was not necessarily an end in itself but rather a means of continuing his unruffled way of life . . . who [owned], like a territorial prince, a fenced-off reserve of his share."[52] Property, in this description, is not an end in itself, nor a means for securing class status; rather, both property and class are tools for achieving an "unruffled" privacy, for withdrawing from society, history, and economy into a mythical territory.

To be sure, from a Marxist perspective, appropriation for the sake of protecting isolation and independence illustrates precisely how privacy is used as an abstraction meant to conceal and justify private property and class status. Privacy, in Raymond Williams's definition, is a "record of legitimation" of middle-class economic privileges.[53] In Jürgen Habermas's more detailed formulation (which I discuss in Chapter 1), the liberal invention of private selfhood both relies on economic privileges and repeatedly conceals them. Habermas argues that the prerogative of ownership is what allowed the bourgeois man to mark off his home as the site of autonomous interiority. Property, therefore, is indeed a means for the attainment of privacy. But this attainment depends precisely on the concealment of property; on the pretense that this realm of interiority is universal, natural, and inalienable; and on the repression of any reminders of the home's status as alienable property or as a marker of class. If the home is to function as symbol and protection of man's independent interiority, it cannot, at the same time, evoke the contingencies of the marketplace or bespeak class mobility. Hence the function of the home in terms of privacy both depends on and collides with its status as property.

This explains why the antebellum pattern book insisted both that a young man own a home for the achievement of manhood and that this home not loudly testify to that man's material success. The *Atlantic Magazine* explained, for example, that, while building a home was man's ultimate goal, building lavishly was a mistake: "not to be conspicuous, and to that end, to respect the plain fundamental rules of stasis, of good construction . . . and to resist sacrificing any solid advantage to show, these are our safest rules at present."[54] Building for "show," for the sake of social appearance rather than for escaping the social, undid the very project of creating self-possessed, natural, private manhood that the move to the suburbs was meant to ensure.

What appears, then, to be a glaring inconsistency in Walden—the way Thoreau both insists on owning a home (and opposes its alternative—renting) and seems to recoil from the very concept of property—in fact, accompanies the discourse of suburbanization as well. For Thoreau, houseownership ideally ensures an independent existence and factually threatens to deprive man of that independence when it supersedes the requirements of privacy and isolation, what Sherman Paul calls "the perversion of the rights of personality by the rights of property."[55] Thus, Thoreau laments the love of real estate for the sake of real estate, the "avarice and selfishness . . . from which none of us is free, of regarding the soil as property, or the means of acquiring property chiefly" (p. 454). "Superfluous" and "unwieldy" property, which goes beyond the appropriation and fencing of personal space, "imprisons" rather than "houses" (p. 349). The ideal house, like the cabin, would be an exercise in self-control and restraint and would defy architectural excesses. Much in the spirit of the pattern book, Thoreau dreams of a future ideal of the simple, frugal "suburban box" (p. 360), which would be defined in opposition to both the poor man's rented apartment and the rich man's showy architecture. A poor man, rather than rent, is better off housing himself in a box that he can own for a dollar, "and so have freedom in his love, and in his soul be free" (p. 345). But the rich build so excessively that their houses erode their privacy and their very humanity; their houses are "so vast and magnificent that the latter [the rich] seem to be only vermin which infest them" (p. 434). Thoreau's frugal suburban box is located on an ideal middle ground, where "on the one side is the palace, on the other [is] the almshouse"; on the one hand, the "degraded poor" and, on the other, the "degraded rich." The young man should exercise "Yankee shrewdness" in house building, to obtain a home "for a lifetime at an expense not greater than the rent which he now pays annually," and, in the process, secure his privacy, free from the "inconvenience of many and noisy neighbors" (p. 362). Hence, Thoreau does not "mean to prescribe rules to strong and valiant natures, who will mind their own affairs whether in heaven or hell, and perchance build more magnificently and spend more lavishly than the richest, without ever impoverishing themselves" (p. 335). Such model men have already struck the ideal equilibrium between privacy and property.

On the one hand, then, Thoreau's middle-class, suburban box is defined through the sharpening of class difference, defined in opposition to both the poor's lack of property and the rich's lack of privacy. On the other, underlying Thoreau's experiment is the belief, on which the rise of the suburbs was hinged, that if every man owned such a house, social frictions between classes would disappear. Pattern-book writers, like Orson Fowler, Henry William Cleaveland, and William and Samuel D. Backus, strove to "cheapen and improve human homes, and especially to bring comfortable dwellings within the reach of the poorer classes."[56] If every man, they posited, through frugality and self-constraint, owned a semirural cottage, America would fulfill its promise as a free and equal nation. Architect William Ranlett explained: "The republican equality of our institutions, offers to all, the opportunity of being the proprietors of their own houses; and it cultivates a laudable ambition to enjoy the *independence* of such a position."[57] This idea plays itself out in *Walden* in the scene with the poor Irishman, John Field, whom Thoreau urges to imitate his experiment in order to achieve freedom and the American dream: "I tried to help him with my experience telling him that . . . I lived in a tight, light and clean house, which hardly cost more than the annual rent of such a ruin as his commonly amounts to; and how, if he chose, he might in a month or two build himself a palace of his own" (p. 486).

The middle class defined itself by abstracting and naturalizing its principles, by insisting that whatever it prescribed for itself it demanded universally, without class distinction, and the discourse of suburbanization was no exception. But just as we sense a certain blindness, if not irony, in Thoreau's preaching to the Irish family (they do not have friends to provide them with land, nor a family in Concord to fall back unto; for them the shanty is not a temporary experiment but a way of life), so also the move to the suburbs did more to reify class structure spatially than to erase class from the social map. Downing's books, for example, were carefully divided into three sections: villas for the rich; cottages for the middle class; and modest housing for the poor. So while advocating "a home for all," Downing helped ossify class differences through architectural style. Similarly, architectural-reform books like Cleaveland's often based their argument on a hierarchy that ran from animals and "savages" (including poor whites) to the virtuous "average

American,"[58] thereby doing more to cohere the definition of the forming middle class than to incorporate the working poor into its suburban
vision. Nathaniel Parker Willis, in his "Highland Terrace" article, promises "the class of seekers for sites of rural residence" that "what may be
understood as 'Cockney annoyances' will not reach" that New York suburb, and takes "pains to specify, once more, that it is to a certain class, in
view of a certain new phase of the philosophy of life, that these remarks
are addressed."[59]

The early version of the "home for all" ideology concealed, in effect, a
process of displacement. In the presuburban socialscape, social status
was determined partly by proximity to the village or town center: the
wealthy lived closest to the crux, while the fringes were left for the socially marginal—such as poor immigrants and blacks. This spatial
schema appears residually in *Walden*, when Thoreau describes the poor
farmers' dream to "sell their houses in the out-skirts and move into the
village" (p. 349), and in the listing of the "former inhabitants" of
Walden on the margins of Concord: a freed slave; a colored woman; the
poor potter squatter. The rise of the early suburb appropriated these rural fringes for middle-class use, displacing and then excluding their former inhabitants. Thus, for example, in Brookline, one of the first
Boston suburbs, deeds included a provision that forbade the sale of land
to "any negro or native of Ireland."[60]

Despite its universalist claims, then, the discourse of suburbanization
clearly became a vehicle for class distinction. In *Walden*, Thoreau famously renders James Collins's family homeless by buying his shanty
and using the wood to build his own cabin. His vision of the future of
Walden's shores is more suburban than utopian, more futuristic than
residual. Just as Willis imagines a day when "the river-banks will have become a suburban avenue,"[61] so does Thoreau speak of the "ornamented
grounds of villas which will one day be built here" (p. 466), a change for
which he is a precursor: "The future inhabitants of this region, wherever
they may place their houses, may be sure that they have been anticipated" (p. 387).

Naturalizing the Suburban

In displacing the former inhabitants of the urban fringes—particularly
the farmers, whose homes the pattern books suggested could be bought
and renovated into "country villas"—the architects of suburbanization
risked exposing the artificiality of the suburban home. The invention
and idealization of the suburban home, that is, came precisely at a time
when the private, monadic household was no longer automatically considered "natural," when, for the first time, withdrawing to nature no

longer seemed a self-evident way of life. In the first part of the century, as production increasingly left the household and the northeastern middle class gradually abandoned agrarian occupations, the single-family rural or semirural house ceased to be a meaningful economic unit. Urbanization introduced, for the first time, alternative forms of habitation: apartments, boardinghouses, and other forms of shared residences. Only in such a period of transformation of the private sphere could radical movements like socialism and feminism build themselves using the critique of the middle-class private home as "unnatural" and "oppressive" and claiming that the "isolated household is a source of innumerable evils, which association alone can remedy."[62] The challenge confronted by middle-class authorities was to renaturalize the isolated house, to root it in the very state of nature. As Henri Lefebvre explains, "when an institution loses its birthplace, its original space, and feels threatened, it tends to describe itself as 'organic.' It 'naturalizes' itself, looking upon itself and presenting itself as a body. . . . This physical analogy, the idea of an organic space, is thus called upon. . . . The ideological appeal to the organism is by extension an appeal to a unity, and beyond that unity (or short of it) to an *origin* deemed to be known with absolute certainty, identified beyond any possible doubt—an origin that legitimated and justified."[63]

Precisely such somatic metaphors, invocations of organic ideals, and myths of origins underlay the rhetoric of the move to the suburbs. Acquiring a cottage in a natural setting was explained as an inherent masculine impulse, an instinctual urge. If the Fourierist revolt against the semirural cottage described it as "wasteful in economy, . . . untrue to the human heart, and . . . not the design of God, and therefore it must disappear,"[64] Thoreau's response was that "I had rather keep a Bachelor hall in hell, than go to board in heaven. . . . The boarder has no home."[65] One pattern book, arguing against such "new fangled philosophers" as the Fourierists, claimed, "while self-preservation remains an instinct and our sensations are individual, man will always prefer living cottagely to living in a phalanstery." "Living cottagely" meant owning a house in a rural setting, designing it to blend with the natural landscape, and drowning it in foliage. "The main beauty of a rural dwelling," the book continues, "is its harmonizing with the scene *of which it forms a part.*"[66] Orson Fowler evoked the "great home law," under which every animal seeks first and foremost to build itself a home, and of which man is "the most perfect exemplification." A phrenologist as well as pattern-book writer, Fowler explained that man was "endowed with the primitive faculty called 'inhabitiveness' created for the express purpose of *compelling* him to provide an abiding place, which shall be the instrumentality and focus of most of life's sweetest pleasures."[67] Despite "circumstance most adverse and repressing," an architectural review claimed, "the home affections . . . belong to our nature."[68] One should build, Thoreau concurs, considering "what foundation a door, a window, a cellar, a garret have in the nature of man, and perchance never raising any superstructure until we found a better reason for it than our temporal necessities even. There is some of the same fitness in a man's building his own house that there is in a bird's building its own nest." Building a private home was more natural than any other manly occupation: "I never in all my walks," Thoreau continues, "came across a man engaged in so simple and natural an occupation as building his house" (pp. 358–59).

Precisely when technology and economy severed the agrarian connection between man and the rural home, Thoreau and his contemporaries constructed a narrative of origins in defense of the modern man's desire for suburban living. Thoreau locates the desire to own a home in the primitive past, *before* marriage and reproduction: "man did not live long on the earth without discovering the convenience which there is in a house, the domestic comforts, which phrase may have originally signified the satisfactions of the house more than the family" (p. 344). And this original story repeats within every individual: "Every child begins the world again, to some extent, and loves to stay outdoors, even in wet and cold. It plays house, as well as horse, having an instinct for it. Who does not remember the interest with which when young he looked at shelving rocks, or any approach to a cave? It was the natural yearning of that portion of our most primitive ancestor which still survived in us. . . . At last, we know not what it is to live in the open air, and our lives are domestic in more senses than we think" (pp. 344–45). Although he laments the loss of our ability to be outdoors, Thoreau regards this loss as natural and inevitable and draws on the state of nature to support this contention: "In the savage state every family owns a shelter as good as the best, and sufficient for its coarser and simpler wants" (p. 346).

Thoreau thus reiterates one of the most frequent conventions of the pattern book: using analogies to both the animal world and the "savage" state of man to justify the building of the semirural cottage. But this naturalization goes a step farther to equate the detached, single-family house with the male body. One of the most popular schoolbooks for boys of Thoreau's generation, William Alcott's *The House I Live In* (Fig. 8), illustrates the use and politics of this analogy. After surveying animal habitations and the history of human dwellings, Alcott lays out an extended conceit:

Now, my young friends, I am going to tell you about the house I live in. . . . There are several hundred millions of them in the world, very *much* like mine; and yet there is not one in the whole number that resembles it *exactly*. . . .

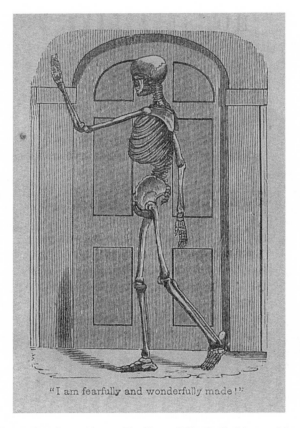

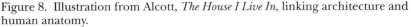

"I am fearfully and wonderfully made!"

Figure 8. Illustration from Alcott, *The House I Live In*, linking architecture and human anatomy.

Several people usually live together in one house; sometimes four or five; some-times ten; and sometimes a great many more. In cities, such as Paris, Vienna and St. Petersburg, there are from twenty to fifty people in one house. Even in New York and Boston, there are often a great number of poor people huddled to-gether in the same building. It is said that one house in New York, only two sto-ries high, contains 144 people! But I live entirely alone. . . . So you see, that I live in all parts of my house; even in the frame of it: yes, even in the underpinning—you must know, too, that I am always at home."[69]

With one stroke, Alcott trains his young readers to think of the isolated house as an organic extension of the individual self and criticizes the unnaturalness of foreign shared dwellings and the housing of the urban classes. He implies not only that the suburban home is the only natural form of habitation, thus privileging both the middle class and the American way of life, but also that, in its most natural state, that home is the place where man is *alone.*

While the comparison between body and architecture is nothing new, interwoven as it is into the history of architecture from Vetruvius to modernity, here the body is newly compared, not to temple or Parthenon, but to the bourgeois private cottage, at once naturalizing single homeownership and reinforcing the myth of an original state of privacy. Such analogies are everywhere to be found: George Wightwick explained in 1850 that in domestic architecture "what the skin is to the body, the hair to the head, the eye-brow and lashes to the eyes, and the lips to the mouth,—such is the marble casing to the walls, the cornice to the facade, the pediment and architrave to the windows, and the porch to the door."[70] The solitary house for Downing has an organic quality, "the predominance of one single feeling, one soul, one mind in every portion . . . the same spirit is recognized throughout the whole," and "construction is to buildings what bones are to the human body . . . and if this connection does not appear, the whole is vicious."[71] *Walden* combines such rhetoric with analogies to the animal world. According to Thoreau, the house relates to man like "the tenement of the shellfish" (p. 354). It constitutes his exterior skin, "a sort of crystallization" around him (p. 390), and should reflect his person, as "the tortoise got his spotted shell, or the shellfish its mother-o'-pearly tints" (p. 359). The house should thus grow "from within outward, out of the necessities and character of the indweller." If this organic relation does not exist, the house is like a body from which the spirit has departed or, rather, like the "coffin" that would contain that body. "Better paint your house your own complexion," Thoreau suggests; "let it turn pale or blush for you" (p. 360).

Moreover, for Thoreau nature itself reflects the values of the private home. As Douglas Anderson has illustrated, the natural phenomena that Thoreau observed around him confirmed the ideals of domestic virtue that a man must seek. When Thoreau built his cabin, Anderson argues, nature came to reflect domesticity, and "the result is a dramatization, on a suitably small scale, of some of those finer qualities in our nature . . . to which the Walden experience is most deeply committed. . . . He is part of a living household at Walden and is close to household events."[72]

But while for Anderson nature in Thoreau speaks the language of family and intimacy, I would argue that it reflects, first and foremost, the values of isolationist manhood. Walden Pond itself is the best example of that. It is a kind of house for Thoreau: he not only seeks the "builder" of the pond, or "*Walled-in* Pond" (p. 468), as he calls it, but also detects, in the great thaw of spring, distinct architectural shapes, "a sort of architectural foliage" (p. 565) in the mud, the same "drop" shape that he also locates in the form of the human body (p. 567). This metaphorical collapsing of architecture, body, and pond is the climax of a series of analogies that Thoreau constructs throughout *Walden*: the cabin is like the shell of the body; the body is like an "individual lake, cut off from the ocean" (p. 554); and the pond is like the cabin, housing, as it does, pure, transparent waters just as the house shelters its owner's interiority. In this triangular structure lie both the significance of and the justification for Thoreau's walling himself off from the rest of the world. Finding validation for his project in nature itself, Thoreau infuses his move with natural imperative and makes its logic appear self-evident and universal.

Spiritualizing the Suburban

While nature, the male body, and the privately owned house were often enmeshed in the discourse of suburbanization, this discourse then typically moved on to elevate the home *above* nature and the body to tell a story of evolution as well as a return to origins. As I remark at the beginning of this chapter, whereas in the classical model the house was perceived as the realm of the body and of labor, for the middle class, it was the "unnatural" *city* that connoted "industry, necessity, or vice" (as Willis puts it), and the suburban home needed to be cleansed of these functions to serve as the site of manly virtue and freedom. Downing, for example, conceded that the first principle to guide men in relation to the domestic sphere was "utility"—that is, the catering to the "most imperative wants of the body." But this principle, he explained, was "savage" and must be complemented by a process of intellectualization and spiritualization of the house, its emergence as the site of a man's "spirit," "mind," "soul," and "feeling."[73] It was claimed in the *New Englander*, in the same vein, that the new domestic architecture "indicate[d] an advance in thought and feeling from a lower to a higher stage of development . . . it show[ed] that the many [were] inclined to think, as never before, that the body [was] more than meat. . . . The world of ideas, thoughts and feelings, [was] most intimately connected with the world of matter [that the house embodied]."[74]

This "higher stage of development" is exactly what Thoreau sought in his move to the cabin. Little wonder, then, that the cabin was often described by his contemporaries as "Thoreau's study." The cabin for Thoreau was primarily the site of intellectual escape and reverie, a space "free and clear for study" (p. 377), whereas bodily necessities were satisfied through physical labor *outside* of it. But even the manual work performed on the cabin's grounds—the cultivating of beans—was etherealized for Thoreau into an intellectual pursuit, performed "for the sake of tropes and expression," a hobby or "rare amusement" (p. 451). The labor associated with the displaced farmhouse is evoked in *Walden* only to be spiritualized: Thoreau imagines his ideal domestic "crops" as abstract manly virtues and "will not plant beans and corn with so much industry another summer, but such seeds, if the seed is not lost, as sincerity, truth, simplicity, faith, innocence, and the like" (p. 453). Like his contemporaries, who saw the semirural house as the site for man's "repose," "leisure," and "virtue," Thoreau spent his cabin days, having dispensed with necessary labor, "rapt in a revery" amid its natural surroundings (p. 411).

The threat to the more spiritual function of the house is bodily pleasure, defined by Thoreau, in opposition to spiritual pursuit, as "sensuality . . . the sluggish habit of the mind" (p. 498). Paradoxically, as much as nature serves to legitimize his experiment, "Nature is hard to be overcome, but she must be overcome" (p. 498). Before we can adorn our houses with beautiful objects," Thoreau argues, "the walls must be stripped, and our lives must be stripped, and beautiful housekeeping and beautiful living be laid for a foundation" (p. 353). Masculine housekeeping, which Thoreau calls "man's morning work" and describes as the dusting of the "furniture of [the] mind" (p. 351), requires a purification of the domestic interior of its function of addressing bodily needs and desires. This is why Thoreau so admires the purification rites of the Mucclasse Indians and the Mexicans, during which "they abstain from the gratification of every appetite and passion whatever," burn domestic utensils, and cleanse their houses (p. 376). Thoreau imagines the ideal private life of "John Farmer" like this: having finished his labors, he bathes himself to purify his mind, "still running on his labor." He then sits down "to recreate his intellectual man." He enters a state of reverie, induced by the harmony of a flute that comes "home to his ears out of a different sphere from that he worked in," and gently does away "with the street, and the village, and the state in which he lived." In this condition, he thinks of how "to practice some new austerity, to let his mind descend into this body and redeem it" (p. 499). At home, away from the space of labor, the mind expands and, through the denial of need, it redeems the body itself.

Thoreau's contemporary Karl Marx laments that with the rise of capitalism "the worker feels at ease only outside of work, and during work he is outside himself. He is at home when he is not working and when he is working he is not at home."[75] Thoreau embraces this separation. He criticizes men who "come tamely home at night only from the next field or street, where their household echoes haunt, and their life pines because it breathes its own breath over again" (p. 489). His response is not

to escape the home but to protect it from labor. As in the life of the suburban commuter, who returns home after a long day of work in the far-
off city, a clear separation between work and leisure is essential to
Thoreau's ideal conduct of life.

The Suburban Box and Feminine Clutter

If the suburban home signified the achievement of solitary, naturalized,
middle-class manhood, what room could women occupy? How did suburbanization relate to the cult of True Womanhood, which tied domesticity to womanhood rather than to manhood? Margaret Marsh and
Dolores Hayden each illustrate how, although urban decentralization
and the ideology of domesticity arose coextensively in the second third
of the nineteenth century, they developed not only independently but
also in conflict with each other. Domesticity was propagated primarily by
and for women and centered on the social, familial, and material goals
of the home, whereas the move to the suburbs was orchestrated by men
and centered on the primacy of isolated privacy. As a matter of fact,
middle-class women often opposed the move to the suburb. Their lives
were not governed by the binary pull between social and private, work
and leisure, nor did they perceive the urban social spaces as a threat to
the home. On the contrary, the physical proximity of services and other
women offered by the city made it convenient for them to fulfill their social and consumer roles.[76]

For middle-class men, on the other hand, the presence of wives in the
household constituted both a requirement and a certain complication.
As we saw in Chapter 1, since women were thought of, and taught to be,
the promoters of social intimacy and the harbingers of fashion and society, their presence in the private sphere endangered the impermeable
privacy by which men wished to define themselves. They introduced social considerations, family, and domestic labor into the private sphere
and hence threatened to expose precisely that which the middle-class
man desired to conceal: the home's less-spiritual and more-mundane
economic and social functions.

Thoreau, of course, never brought a wife to share his cabin. But although his antimarital sentiments are famous,[77] in *Walden* he does not
seem to oppose marriage so much as to postpone it. Domestic partner-
ship is part of man's life for Thoreau but, chronologically delayed, is an
appendix to the primary act of establishing a home. As in the liberal
myth of private manhood, where "in the beginning man was alone," domesticity for Thoreau is a state that follows that pure, original condition.
Thus, "domestic comforts . . . originally signified the satisfactions of the
house more than of the family," and "man wanted a home, a place of

warmth, or comfort, first of physical warmth, *then* the warmth of the affections" (p. 344; emphasis added).[78] There is nothing unusual about
this chronology: it was the message magazines like *A Voice to Youth* conveyed to young men. In order to maintain his class position, a young
man was urged to postpone the gratifications of marriage until he
could, through hard work, purchase a house; he was urged to "maintain
a delicate imbalance between his sexual needs and his career objectives,
postponing gratifications of the former to enhance the latter."[79]

Houseownership rewarded the middle-class man's hard work with the
coveted prize of manhood, but as alienable property a house demanded
continued regimens of self-control, economic calculations, and denials
of physical pleasure in order not to lose the very object on which manhood was staked. The entry of the domestic woman into the house at
marriage, then, constituted both the anticipated sexual and emotional
reward and the dangerous introduction of consumption and increasing
expenses, the looming threat of dependence. That Thoreau's experiment in *Walden* does not include the rearing of a family is thus both an
intensification of his culture's gender prescription and a deviation from
it: an intensification because the cabin embodies a distilled masculine
household, "purified" of its familial and procreational functions, and
thus a stable symbol of independent manhood; a deviation because
Thoreau does not take the next necessary step of marriage and the incorporation of domesticity into privacy.

Thoreau, as I have mentioned, follows the conduct book in advocating a "Spartan-like" way of life for young men (p. 394). And his experiments in radical physical denial are explicitly tied to the threat of
feminine excess and materiality. The yeastless Indian rye bread that
Thoreau invents, for example, shocks the pampered Concord housewives. The "young man" he heard of, who "tried for a fortnight to live on
hard, raw corn on the ear," would, he imagines, gain the approval of the
"human race" but the disapproval of "a few old women who are incapac-
itated for them" (p. 374). And if the masculine principle is that of
denial—of "simplicity and nakedness"—consumption, excess, and waste
in the household are explicitly bound up, for Thoreau, with femininity.
Like fashion in clothing, which women like "Madam Pfeiffer" or
Thoreau's female tailor falsely believe measures a man's character,
household luxuries not only are feminine but also threaten to render a
man "completely emasculated" (p. 351). The "modern drawing-room,
with its divans and ottomans and sunshades and a hundred other orien-
tal things" was invented "for the ladies of the harem and the effeminate
natives of the celestial Empire;" the true American "Jonathan" would
shun them (pp. 351–52). Thoreau poses the "stripping" of the house to
create "beautiful housekeeping and beautiful living" against a feminizing

principle of consumption and social ostentation, or the "adorn[ing] of our houses with beautiful objects" that "clutter and defile" them (p. 351). What his cabin will feature is, of course, a "withdrawing" rather than a "drawing" room (p. 392).

If the house is grounds for the dispute between man's physical denial and woman's consumption, it also combines, problematically, man's "morning work" and woman's "morning work." We have seen that Thoreau regards the private sphere as the site of intellectual reverie rather than of physical labor. Both the exhausting physical labor of housekeeping and the work produced by the social functions of the house are outside of man's realm. Thoreau has a particular aversion, for instance, to dinner parties and, instead, "naturally practiced abstinence" in entertaining. "Let company come and company go," he advises his reader, "let the bells ring and the children cry . . . let us not be upset and overwhelmed in that rapid whirlpool called a dinner" (p. 399).

Thoreau is particularly bothered by the idea that the labors of housekeeping and the rituals of sociability divide the house up, create off-limits, uncontrolled spaces within it, and thus ruin its organic "integrity": "There is as much secrecy about the cooking as if [a host] had a design to poison you . . . the parlor is so far from the kitchen and workshop," he laments, "how can the scholar, who dwells away in the Northwest Territory or the Isle of Man, tell what is parliamentary in the kitchen?" (p. 517). The division of the house between mental and physical labor, between manly isolationism and feminine housekeeping, suggests for Thoreau a certain loss of control over the interior.

If "domestication," or the adding of marriage and family to the house, problematizes masculine privacy, intellectual repose, and economy, then it is hardly surprising that Thoreau wants his "chanticleer" to be "naturalized without being domesticated"—or "privatized" without sacrificing masculine control. The "naturalized" cockerel would have complete dominion over the roost while allowing "the cackling of the hens to fill the pauses when their lords' clarions rested" (p. 423). Accordingly, the ideal house that he imagines in "Housewarming" would not necessarily exclude women but would control the threat they embody. Like the cabin (and like Hawthorne's and Melville's favored architectural blueprint), it would center around the phallic structure of the chimney, "to some extent an independent structure [which] even after the house is burned . . . still stands sometimes, and its importance and independence are apparent" (p. 515). Like the cabin, it would have "all the attractions of a house . . . concentrated in one room," thereby defying internal divisions; it would be a "kitchen, chamber, parlor, and keeping-room" all at once, and "whatever satisfaction parent or child, master or servant, derive from living in a house" would coexist in harmony. Thoreau's dream house, "standing in a golden age," would consist of "one room, a vast, rude, substantial, primitive hall" with no luxuries, no social ceremony, with "all the essentials of a house, and nothing for housekeeping," where "you can see all the treasures of the house at one view," "where the washing is not put out, nor the fire, nor the mistress." In short, "a house whose inside is as open and manifest as a bird's nest" (p. 516). Thoreau's fantasy of the naturalized house expresses a longing for complete interior control; with no competing interests, no multiplicity, divided plots, hidden nooks, room for bodily functions or carnal pleasures, or any other aspect of the household that its "domestication" would imply.

Gregory S. Jay has analyzed Thoreau's politics in terms of gender and argues that, in "Civil Disobedience," "the failure of virtue is figured as a failure of masculinity." Thoreau's politics, he argues, cannot be separated from gender anxiety: he equates the state to the feminine—"I saw that the State was half-witted, that it was timid, a lone woman with her silver spoons"—which threatens to emasculate the citizen. Thus, in Jay's interpretation, "the cure for emasculation lies in disobedience."[80] This is a complete overhaul of the ideology of the separate spheres, in which masculinity is associated with the public and femininity with the private. Because Thoreau idealizes the close bond between manhood and the private sphere, and because the domestic woman, in her rare appearances, is figured in his writing as a threat to this sphere rather than as its symbol, the metaphor of the state as a silver-spooned woman makes sense. In *Walden* the state is imagined precisely as a "feminized" (or "domesticated") house: "an unwieldy and overgrown establishment, cluttered with furniture and tripped up by its own traps, ruined by luxury and heedless expenses, by want of calculation and a worthy aim," the only cure for which is "rigid economy, a stern and more than Spartan simplicity of life and elevation of purpose" (p. 395). The image of the nation as a house not divided but cluttered, spun out of control and feminized, is the contrasting image to the integrity of Thoreau's model cabin.

Stanley Cavell mentions the fact that "Poe's and Hawthorne's worlds, or houses and rooms, have other people in them, typically marriages, and typically show these people's violent shunning, whereas Emerson's and Thoreau's worlds begin with or after the shunning of others."[81] I have been arguing that the shunning of the domestic woman as the symbol of dependence and social visibility is the act on which the Walden cabin was founded. But I have also been arguing that this act of shunning is imagined by Thoreau to follow, rather than precede, an original state of manly isolationism. As in the Hobbesian metaphor of mushroomy men who come into being without dependence on the mother, Thoreau, as a "first and last man," constructs a wholly masculine, "natural" private sphere that domestication would only kill. Thus, the domestic woman—that timid woman with her silver spoons—is expelled from the ideal private sphere, only to reappear as the symbol of a defiled exterior world: the nation or the marketplace, the world of labor, materialism, and dependence, where men lose their autonomy. This is a complete revision of the "melodrama of beset manhood" through which *Walden* has been inaccurately read: it is when men *leave* the home that they enter the subjugating empire of the mother. Ironically enough, the exterior worlds of work and citizenship, precisely the spheres of association between men, are the ones that emerge from Thoreau's writing as feminizing.

But if "society everywhere is in conspiracy against the manhood of every one of its members," as Emerson charged, can true men form any associations among themselves? Does the myth of liberal manhood preclude the possibility of intimacy and empathy between men? And, if so, could any form of political identification be imaginable? To return, finally, to our point of departure: we have seen Alcott insist that, if Thoreau "was always at home minding his own affairs . . . dropping society clean out of his theories," he nonetheless stood "friendly in his strict sense of friendship." For Alcott, Thoreau's disavowal of society does not necessitate the demise of intimacy, albeit an intimacy defined in a very "strict sense." Nor does it preclude, *pace* Alcott's statement, social and political involvement. Thoreau is no less remembered today for his brave stand on the issue of slavery, for example, than for his program for private life. But what I intend to argue in the next chapter is that Thoreau's definition of intimacy, and his idea of masculine association in the social sphere, are founded on, rather than contradict, his prescription for a privatist, "suburban" form of masculinity.

To anticipate that argument briefly here, I wish to turn, finally, to one of Thoreau's most poignant and impassioned political essays, "A Plea for John Brown." Delivered on the eve of Brown's execution, the essay accuses the American public of being blind in condemning the Harpers Ferry attack and the figure who led it. Thoreau makes use of the same cliché that, as I discuss in Chapter 3, dominated the debate over slavery: "Our foes are in our midst and all about us," he writes: "There is hardly a house but is divided against itself."[82] What he means by the divided house is not that the nation is split over slavery, but that many individuals are split between their virtuous private core (which may be repelled by slavery) and their relationship to social or public life (which benumbs this repulsion). Thoreau's principal target in this essay is the institutions of the public sphere—the church, the state, and, especially, the newspapers—which, for reasons of expediency, condemn John

Brown and, by infiltrating the sphere of private discretion, destroy each individual's potential identification with the Harpers Ferry hero. Against this invasive public tyranny (as in "Civil Disobedience," figured as female: Brown confronted the country "herself" when "*she* was in the wrong," the state will have "to pay the penalty of *her* sin" [pp. 138, 151; emphasis added]), Thoreau presents the figure of Brown, built on the same principles of privatist masculinity that we find in *Walden*. Indeed, Brown in this essay resembles no one so much as Thoreau: "a transcendentalist above all, a man of ideas and principles," "a volcano with an ordinary chimney-flue," who always "spoke within bounds" and "was a man of Spartan habits, and at sixty was scrupulous about his diet at your table, excusing himself by saying that he must eat sparingly and fare hard" (p. 140).

Brown practiced "Spartan habits," Thoreau explains, to save himself from the dangers of "a life of exposure" (p. 140). In an essay devoted to a critique of agents of the public sphere, Thoreau uses "exposure" as a pun: physical exposure to the hardships of nature but also forced, distorting publicity. What is killing John Brown, Thoreau's pun implies, is not exactly the state but the appropriation of his story by the state and "her" agents—"the herd of newspapers and magazines"—an appropriation contrasted with Brown's elegant reticence ("In his case there is no idle eloquence, no made, nor maiden speech, no compliments to the oppressor" [p. 149]) and also with Thoreau's own sparse mode of exposition ("Little as I know of Captain Brown, I would fain do my part to correct the tone and the statements of the newspapers. . . . I will endeavor to omit, as much as possible, what you have already read. I need not describe his person to you" [p. 137]). Against the "politician," who believes that political action consists in "the quiet diffusion of the sentiments of humanity" and that these sentiments represent "the pure article" (p. 147), Thoreau suggests an alternative model of identification. Our "sympathy with, and admiration of" (p. 137) Brown would ensue not from his "exposure," not from the "pure article" of a co-opted, sentimental press, but from our recognition of his distance, invisibility, and intractable difference:

We dream of foreign countries, of other times and races of men, placing them at a distance in history or space; but let some significant event like the present occur in our midst, and we discover, often, this distance and this strangeness between us and our nearest neighbors. . . . Our crowded society becomes well spaced all at once, clean and handsome to the eye—a city of magnificent distances. . . . The thoughtful man becomes a hermit in the thoroughfares of the market-place. . . . It is the difference of constitution, of intelligence, and faith, and not streams and mountains, that make the true and impassable boundaries between individuals and between states. None but the like-minded can come plenipotentiary to our court. (P. 145)

The "suburban" landscape of this description, in which each individual's difference and strangeness is protected by distance from other human beings, is precisely what allows for a *true* identification between radically different but ethically "like-minded" individuals. And it is this identification through distance that forms the basis for joint political resistance (for coming "plenipotentiary to our court"). Whereas journalists and politicians deal with public sentiments as if they are "articles" or commodities "in the throughfares of the market-place," Thoreau's identification with John Brown, a fellow hermit, can serve as the core for a new kind of social and political identification, based on respect for boundaries rather than on exposure.

Chapter 6
"The Manliest Relations to Men":
Thoreau on Privacy, Intimacy, and Writing

You are the fact in a fiction. . . . This is what I would like,—to be as intimate with you as our spirits are intimate,—respecting you as I respect my ideal. Never to profane one another by word or action, even by a thought. Between us, if necessary, let there be no acquaintance.

—*Henry David Thoreau*

Some thirty inches from my nose
The frontier of my Person goes.
And all the untilled air between
Is private pagus or demesne.
Stranger, unless with bedroom eyes
I beckon you to fraternize,
Beware of rudely crossing it:
I have no gun, but I can spit.

—*W. H. Auden*[1]

If persons are walking houses, as Auden imagines, then every jab at intimacy becomes a form of trespass. If persons are defined by privacy, as Thoreau implies, a trifling conversation becomes a profane violation. Privacy and intimacy: what exactly is the relationship between these two terms? Are they interchangeable, as some have suggested, or at least interdependent, the one constituting a prerequisite for the other? Or are they, as the epigraphs suggest, in conflict, even mutually threatening? To the extent that intimacy is understood in terms of the emotional exchange of affairs of the self, privacy has often been imagined as its savings account, as the reservoir where personal information is accumulated, to be expended in intimate relations. As Charles Fried imagines it, "privacy creates the moral capital which we spend in friendship and love."[2] But even by the same logic, intimacy can be seen as privacy's violation and depletion. Richard Sennett, for instance, while sharing, as Fried does, the liberal view of the self as constituted first in privacy and only then in relation to the other, argues that the "market exchange of confession," an attribute of modernity's "tyranny of intimacy," erodes the personal boundaries on which both privacy and social life rely. Originating with the Victorian ideology of the separate spheres, the modern stress on pouring out feelings, desires, experiences robs the self of its privacy, and hence also of meaningful sociability.[3]

I have discussed in the previous chapters how the antebellum middle class characteristically grappled with the ambivalences of privacy and intimacy: through gendering. For the white, northern middle class, intimacy was figured by the "true woman" and her "natural" capacity for emotional expressivity. The "cult of True Womanhood" not only placed women in charge of the family's intimate relations but also encouraged them to cultivate a world of intimate bonds with each other through confessional exchanges and outpourings of sentiment. Thus, while symbolizing privacy, middle-class womanhood was construed in contradistinction to privacy: ideally, the "true woman" thrived in intimate society, kept little or nothing from her family and confidantes, and was never alone.[4]

Meanwhile, the same social realities that gave birth to the cult of domesticity bolstered an affianced but opposite masculine ideal of isolationist individualism. This ideal highlighted an ethos of privacy, bounded self-containment, affective restraint and reticence, all at the expense of emotional expressivity and intimacy. As we saw in Chapter 5, antebellum manhood was defined in relation to a social sphere that allowed for little or no intimacy between men: since middle-class gender ideology carefully channeled affection into heterosexual courtship, marriage, and the family and opposed it to the (now described as "heartless") masculine world of competitive work, laissez-faire economy, and hard-core politics, any sentiment between men became a prima facie violation of boundaries, a leaking of affection out of its designated sphere. As David Leverenz points out in *Manhood and the American Renaissance*, "male rivalry looms under fraternity" in this period; writers suggested again and again that, in Hawthorne's words, "between man and man, there is always an insuperable gulf. They can never quite grasp each other's hands; and therefore man never derives any intimate help . . . from his brother man, but from woman—his mother, his sister, or his wife."[5] Masculine intimacy threatened the "insuperably-engulfed" man with erosion of boundaries and deindividualization; it was perceived—and disavowed—as feminizing, infantilizing, and sexually transgressive. Social historians have shown that becoming a man in antebellum America meant shedding the male intimacies of childhood and early adolescence and replacing them with the more distant, ritualized, and rigidly hierarchical relations of the place of business, the club, or the political party. The competitive regime of such masculine spaces triggered anxiety about intimate friendship between men and, indeed, had homophobia built into it.[6] Moreover, as Christopher Newfield argues, other, more open kinds of public spaces—streets, urban crowds—likewise provoked fears of erasure of boundaries and loss of self-differentiation and were even bound up with anxieties over sodomy.[7] It is hardly surprising, then, that conduct-manual writers lured their middle-class readers away from spaces of potential male intimacy—barrooms, lodges, streets—and carefully directed their steps from the daytime workplace to an evening of private bliss in the suburban home.

I have been arguing that this gendered separation of intimacy and privacy was both thematized in and performed by the dominant fictional forms of the antebellum period. The form most often associated with True Womanhood, the sentimental/domestic novel, evolved from nonfictional and confessional modes such as journals, diaries, and personal letters and, like them, was designed to be read aloud, in an intimate social or familial setting. Mimicking a conversational tone of voice and based on sharing anecdotes from personal life, the sentimental novel found its natural habitat in the middle-class parlor, where an assemblage of family and friends, united by the figure of the domestic woman, was drawn together by the experience of shared reading.

Whereas for women the home constituted a space of sociability and intimacy, the governing principles of the home for men were privacy and seclusion. It was perceived, indeed, as an enclosure where "moral capital" could be produced, to be exchanged in intimacy with others outside of it. As we have seen, privacy was seen as essential and primary to masculine space, as *preceding* intimacy, even as it was, in fact, achieved by the (not so moral) shunning of intimacies that preceded it. The study as symbolic space, in other words, was carved out by the rejection of the emotional world of the parlor. "I shun father and mother and wife and brother, when my genius calls me," Emerson famously declared.[8] And if the parlor constituted the ideal setting for the sentimental/domestic novel, the study was linked to the masculine romance. If the sentimental novel relied on conventions of intimacy between reader and writer, the romance promoted the masculine ethos of boundedness, individualization, and reticence. If the former capitalized on the exchange of personal life, the latter fostered a desire for social invisibility and withdrawal and drew a thick line between the writer and his public.

The romance, then, can be read as the genre of escape from social intimacy, whether intimacy with the domestic woman or with the male other.[9] And perhaps no writer is more closely associated with that escape than Thoreau. Thoreau, who fled "civilization" into his cabin, who chose solitude over mother and sister, who loved a "broad margin to

life" and wrote "silently and reservedly," is a particularly distilled prototype of the masculine cult of privacy and rejection of intimacy. It was he,
after all, who penned, in *A Week on the Concord and Merrimack Rivers*, such
lines as "Pathless the gulf of feeling yawns— / No trivial bridge of
words / Or arch of boldest span, / Can leap the moat that girds / The
sincere man" (p. 235), lines that portray the "sincere man" as an impenetrable bulwark surrounded by an emotional gap unbridgeable by "trivial" words or deeds.

Yet, precisely because of his representative status, I wish to revisit
Thoreau in order to interrogate some of the assumptions we make
about manhood, intimacy, and privacy. Does bounded, liberal manhood
always signify a decisive break from intimacy? Must male intimacy always
connote the dangers of invasion, deindividualization, and loss of self
and agency? In the lines above, for instance, do we have to read Thoreau
as celebrating unfeeling manhood, or could he be expressing a yearning for an emotional bond, albeit one that would not compromise "sincerity"? The metaphor of the "pathless gulf of feeling," after all, could
signal the typically romantic desire to explore uncharted terrain, particularly as it is embedded in *A Week on the Concord and Merrimack Rivers*, a
narrative devoted to the art of navigating the pathless wilderness. In *A
Week*—which recounts Thoreau's travels with a beloved brother—and
particularly in its "Wednesday" chapter, Thoreau repeatedly expresses a
desire for intimacy with other men of his class and race and actively
seeks a path of emotional connectedness that will bypass the strictures
imposed on bounded manhood: the pitfalls of femininity and obstacles
of homoeroticism. The escape to the wilderness, then, is not necessarily
a flight from intimacy; as Thoreau states a few lines after the ones
quoted above: "There's nothing in the world I know / That can escape
from love" (p. 235).

In this chapter I first want to argue that throughout his writing
Thoreau busily imagines and articulates what he calls in *Walden* "the
manliest relations to man," a consistent logic of manly intimate relations. In making that argument, I am not suggesting, as some critics
have, that Thoreau is at times "feminized," nor that he posits a "queer"
alternative to the "grand narrative of connubiality" of his (and our own)
time. Such arguments sometimes seem to be not only decontextualized
but also needlessly reproductive of Victorian gender and sexuality bina-
risms.[10] They assume, that is, the very thing I wish to question: that intimacy can take only one form, one from which normative masculinity
excludes itself. I argue that Thoreau, as well as other antebellum romantic writers, while tacitly accepting (by escaping from it) the hegemonic,
confessional, "feminine" definition of intimacy of the separate-spheres
ideology, simultaneously create, from *within* that ideology and its

prescriptions, an alternative, contesting logic of intimacy, thus complicating the familiar binary of womanhood/intimacy versus manhood/privacy. Thoreau's logic, I will claim, is based on physical distance rather than proximity, on concealment rather than revelation, on silence rather than speech. It may be termed, following Candace Vogler, "depersonalizing intimacy." Perhaps the fact that this logic has been largely ignored is testimony to our own culture's, at times, monolithic understanding of intimacy as a capital exchange of affairs of the self. But, as Vogler claims, "not all intimacies are affairs of the self and . . . the fact that some intimacies are *not* affairs of the self is what makes people want them."[11]

The second part of my argument is that Thoreau's writing does not merely contain but also stylistically performs this logic of intimacy, fixing the relationship between (male) writer and (male) reader as an ideal. The intimate merger between writer and reader is for him not predicated on the kind of transgressive and bodily identification highlighted in the sentimental/domestic novel but on the obfuscation of personal experience and the production of an unmediated space, at once trans-subjective and intensely private, at once masculine and beyond gender, sexuality, and the body. Thus, while writing versions of the liberal myth of the self as constituted first in privacy and only then in intimacy, Thoreau nonetheless finds potential for intersubjective relations at the core of the private, masculine self.

The Veil of Ignorance

Thoreau began exploring the problems of masculine intimacy early in his writing career. In a lesser-known essay entitled "The Landlord," he imagines a homosocial utopia in the space of the tavern, the social antithesis of the private Walden cabin. That this "public house," "where especially men congregate" is a haven of fraternal love and intimacy is due to the figure that presides over it: the landlord or "publican."[12] The landlord is the closest approximation to the "perfect man," since he abandons private interests for the sake of an all-inclusive masculine friendship. Because he is "general," "open," of "universal sympathies" and "general sympathies, "public and inviting," "open and public," "wide," "broad" (pp. 188–90), he stands for the possibility of a masculine bond at once inclusive and democratic: "while nations and individuals are alike selfish and exclusive, he loves all men equally, and if he treats his nearest neighbor as a stranger . . . the farthest traveler is to some measure kindred to him" (p. 189).

The problem is that the intimacies of the tavern render individual difference fungible. In the world of the publican, where the distinction between kin, neighbor, and stranger is erased, the "tender but narrow ties of private friendship" are sacrificed "to a broad, sunshiny, fair-weather-and-foul friendship for his race" (p. 188). What the landlord loves, then, is mankind, not individual men.

Indeed, as the essay progresses, the landlord becomes more of a comic, or even monstrous, caricature, than a viable ideal. Unable to see the other as particular, he is likewise unable to maintain a sense of differentiated selfhood: "His sentiments on all subjects will be delivered as freely as the wind blows; there is nothing private or individual in them . . . but they are public" (p. 192). Unlike the "man of genius," who "says, by all possible hints and signs, I wish to be alone,—good-by,—farewell," the landlord "can afford to live without privacy. He entertains no private thought" (p. 193). The publican is, in fact, "abstractly offensive" (p. 192). In his open and unbounded exhibitionism, both his house and his body cease to function as barriers. All his secrets are "exhibited to the eyes of men, above and below, before and behind," and while "there can be no *pro*fanity where there is no fane behind," one senses that Thoreau is somewhat disturbed by the fact that "the whole world may see quite round him" (p. 193).

And if his behind is exposed, so are his insides: "when he eats, he is liver and bowels and the whole digestive apparatus to the company, and so all admit the thing is done" (p. 192). The imagery shifts from democratic equality to mastery: whosoever "steps across the threshold" of the tavern (imagined as a huge body with "heart," "left ventricle," and "vital part") becomes its "master" (pp. 190–91). What initially seemed a paradise of intimate fraternalism turns out to be a perverse image of servitude and loss of privacy to the dissolution of both self and other.

As we saw in Chapter 5, the view that intimacy with the male other, and not only with the female, is a principal threat to the masculine self predates American romanticism and can be traced at least to the appearance of autonomy and privacy as preconditions of selfhood in the founding texts of liberalism. What liberalism's early annals reveal, in Seyla Benhabib's summary, is "the fear of being engulfed by the [male] other" or the "brother," "the anxiety that the other is always on the look to interfere in your space and appropriate what is yours." This anxiety makes imperative liberalism's construction of the "disembedded and disembodied" generalized other, the view of the other solely based on the nonconcrete and universal. Such a view allows individuals to relate to other individuals without interfering with their privacy or risking interference with their own. The invention of the generalized other relies, therefore, on the suppression and concealment of private differences, on an "epistemological blindness" to the particulars of private affairs of the self, now deliberately hidden behind a "veil of ignorance" (recall Hawthorne's "so far as I am a man of really individual attributes, I veil my face"). The veiled, generalized other is what allows for the existence of a social contract, despite liberal individualism's emphasis on privacy, since it allows men to relate to each other from an epistemological distance that obscures seeing into private, embodied existences. The disembodied generalized other, while traditionally a masculine subject, in fact, tends to erase gender differences as well—the abstracted other is not treated as a gendered body (as even the androgynous metaphor of the veil underscores)—and hence helps relax the rigid heterosexual codes that forbid masculine proximity.[13]

In light of this description, Thoreau's "abstractly offensive" landlord makes sense: as the principle of public fraternity, the landlord cultivates universality but fails to patrol his own boundaries, which results in deterritorialization and (literal) disembodiment. The "publican" has generalized himself out of existence. For Benhabib and other feminist theorists, such fantasies reveal the inadequacies of the liberal model, its inability to co-maintain private selfhood and human connectedness. Benhabib thus suggests an alternative, feminine, mode of relations, one that highlights the empathic knowledge of the concrete facts of the other's private life— the removal of the veil of ignorance—as its basis. If we refuse to generalize the other but view her or him, instead, as a "coherent narrative" or as "the protagonist of a life's tale," human bonds could depend on the mutual sharing of stories of the concrete, embodied self.[14] Benhabib thus echoes the conception of privacy with which we began, as a reservoir of affairs of the self there only to be consumed in intimate relations. She also echoes the separate-spheres ideology from which this definition evolved: it is once again in the hands of women—who putatively are uniquely endowed with the capacity to feel for and know the other—that the job of maintaining intimacy is placed. But Benhabib wishes to expand that model, from parlor to public, as it were, since she believes that the sharing of affairs of the self could guarantee the coexistence of equality, difference, and an ethics of care. For Thoreau, however, nothing could be farther from the truth. The model whereby the self is constantly emplotted in "coherent narratives" and "life tales" to use as currency in relationships with others results, in his view, in the demise of intimacy, in the eradication of difference, and in potential tyranny.

"True though Incomplete Intercourse"

The verb "to intimate," to which "intimacy" is etymologically linked, connotes two seemingly conflicting actions: "to make known," to "notify," "to communicate openly," in its older use; "to signify indirectly," "to imply," "to hint at," in its more current use—a lavish impulse to publicize on the one hand, a frugal sparseness of signs on the other.[15] This duality is interlaced in Thoreau's meditations on intimacy in the "Wednesday" chapter in *A Week on the Concord and Merrimack Rivers*. Close to the chapter's middle, Thoreau tells of his relationship with a woman who embodies the "feminine," or self-exposing, mode of intimacy: "I know a woman who possesses a restless and intelligent mind," he writes. "Yet our acquaintance plainly does not attain to that degree of confidence and sentiment which women, which all, in fact, covet" (p. 227). Women like her, he explains, expect a regime of mutual confiding to which he refuses to succumb, opting instead for a different, more impersonal, mode of exchange. He explains that he "feel[s] as if [he] appeared careless, indifferent, and without principle to her," because she fails to recognize that his model of "true though incomplete intercourse" is "infinitely better than a more unreserved but falsely grounded one, without the principle of growth in it" (p. 227). Intimacy based on an unreserved revelation of the private is falsely grounded, partially because it is destined for a short life: once the parties to the exchange deplete their reservoir of personal stories, such intimacy exhausts itself. Moreover, while his "true though incomplete" mode of intimacy makes "equal demand" on both parties, the confessional mode connotes a surrendering of self to other. "We often forbear to confess our feelings, not from pride, but for fear that we could not continue to love the one who required us to give such proof of our affection" (pp. 226–27): the one who demands confession, according to Thoreau, exercises undue power.

The shorthand term that Thoreau habitually uses to describe this "unreserved" type of intimacy is "sympathy." In his journal, he describes sympathy as a "loosening" of emotional "gates," as begetting "a certain softness to which [he is] otherwise and commonly a stranger."[16] Sympathy is the "loose," "softening," "diseased" emotion that characterizes, for instance, social reformers, who loosen the gates of privacy in the name of doing good. "If I knew for a certainty that a man was coming to my house with the conscious design of doing me good," Thoreau writes, "I should run for my life, ... for fear that I should get some of his good done to me, some of its virus mingled with my blood." Such sympathy is "dyspepsia": it comes not from the head or heart, but from the "bowels"—"for that is the seat of sympathy" (*Walden*, p. 383). As Donald Yacovone has shown, antebellum reform societies rebelled against contemporaneous definitions of bounded manhood by emphasizing close male bonding, a Christianized form of androgyny, and interpersonal merger ("You are mine and I am yours. God made us one from the beginning" exemplifies their rhetoric).[17] For Thoreau, interventions into his private space, however well intentioned, are analogous to a passive form of molestation: reformers "would not keep their distance," he complains, "but cuddle up and lie spoon-fashion with you, no matter how hot the weather nor how narrow the bed. . . . it was difficult to keep clear of [the reformer's] slimy benignity, with which he sought to cover you before he swallowed you and took you fairly into his bowels" (*Journals*, 5: 264–65). Michael Warner has brilliantly analyzed such passages in terms of Thoreau's simultaneously strict abhorrence of and luxurious pleasure in erotic anality, an instance of his ability to forcefully bring forth the tension inherent in liberal capitalism between ascesis and waste, self-integration and self-dissolution. I wish to stress the degree to which self-integration—imagining the self in terms of a well-defined bounded space—is inherent in the discourse on middle-class masculinity. Where masculinity is defined as bounded, sympathy, as erosion of boundaries, triggers fantasies of bodily consumption and subsumption that resonate with unfulfillable desire, with gender anxiety and even with sexual panic.[18]

Thoreau's "true though incomplete intercourse," by contrast, "consists with a certain disregard for men and their erections, the Christian duties and humanities, while it purifies the air like electricity" (*Week*, p. 224). How is such antiseptic intimacy to be construed? Consider a poem Thoreau wrote in 1839 (apparently for his eleven-year-old star student, Edmund Sewall).[19] The poem was first entitled "Sympathy" but later was reproduced in *A Week on the Concord and Merrimack Rivers* without the title (perhaps because "sympathy" had by then acquired its dyspeptic connotations for Thoreau). It begins by describing "a gentle boy" whom "virtue," figured (despite its etymological roots) as a woman, "manned . . . for her own strong-hold," and who "on every side . . . open was as day" (pp. 211–12). This is a portrait of childhood: the boy is enfolded by virtue's "strong-hold" as a child by his doting mother and has not yet developed the "walls and ports" of adult manhood. But, though passive, the gentle boy is by no means weak: he is so appealing, in fact, that his power of attraction is unlimited; as "Caesar was victorious," so "this youth was glorious. . . . No strength went out to get him victory/when all was income of its own accord." Not even the speaker can resist this imperial, alluring force, and he is "taken unawares by this," as "each moment . . . we nearer drew to each." But this intimacy produces unhappy results: "I might have loved him had I loved him less," the speaker says. "We two were one while we did sympathize,/So could we not the simplest bargain drive." The merger of two into one, the too-thorough knowledge of each other brought about by the boy's magnetic openness, demolishes intimacy, because it prevents what Thoreau metaphorizes as "driving the simplest bargain," the distance required for equal commerce.[20] Indeed, as the speaker is sucked into the gentle boy's realm (not unlike being swallowed by the reformer), the two seem "less acquainted than when first we met" (p. 212). Soon the poem drifts into an elegiac mode: the boy is "irrevocably gone," ringing the "knell of departure," and the speaker is left to "celebrate [his] tragedy" by singing this "elegy" (p. 213), thereby hinting that the boy is dead (young Sewall simply left Thoreau's school). The poem can be read, then, as a lament over the impossibility of male-to-male intimacy, which momentarily surfaces in childhood but cannot survive beyond.

And yet the poem does not end there. Two more stanzas are added:

Is't then too late the damage to repair?
Distance, forsooth, from my weak grasp hath reft
The empty husk, and clutched the useless tare,
But in my hands the wheat and kernel left.

If I but love that virtue which he is,
Though it be scented in the morning air,
Still shall we be truest acquaintances,
Nor mortals know a sympathy more rare. (P. 213)

These lines suggest why the gentle boy's tragic absence may indeed be celebrated, and what "true though incomplete" intimacy could mean. It is plausible that the boy did not die after all, but simply grew up: as the boy in feminist psychoanalytical theory who introjects the mother in order to develop a demarcated ego, Thoreau's boy is no longer in the motherly "virtue's strong-hold"; he now holds virtue *within* him, as his "wheat" or "kernel." No longer "open as the day," but walled-off and distant, he can now engage in mutual, equal commerce with the speaker. (A friend, Thoreau pursues the commercial metaphor in the next pages, is he "we give the best to, and receive the best from"; friendship is "the state of the just dealing with the just, the magnanimous with the magnanimous, the sincere with the sincere, man with man" [pp. 218, 217].) What friends exchange, however, is not the concrete affairs of the embodied self—the "empty husk" or "useless tare"—but a universal, trans-subjective, metaphysical "kernel" that is imagined to constitute the self's innermost, essential core. This kernel, because abstract and universal, is not even strictly masculine (recall that "virtue" is feminine in this poem); it seems to tend toward gender neutrality. Physical separation, disembodiment, abstraction are thus the conditions on which "truest acquaintance" can be constructed. In the spirit of Plato's *Symposium*—which, as Caleb Crain has shown, dominated the transcendentalists' understanding of friendship—"as love ascends it purges itself of attachment to any single human being," so that what matters is not that friends love each other but that they both love virtue.[21] Thoreau says to an imaginary friend, "I love thee not as something private and personal which is *your own*, but as something universal and worthy of love, *which I have found*" (*A Week*, p. 219).

The "gentle boy" poem (in Emerson's opinion, "the purest strain & the loftiest, I think, that has yet pealed from this unpoetic American forest")[22] thus falls under the rubric of what Dana Nelson calls the "melancholy of white manhood." Nelson points to the fact that, at least in the nineteenth century, "white men seem able to achieve the equalitarian reassurance of unmediated brotherhood only with dead or imagined men." The distancing and generalizing impulses of white brotherhood, she argues, while appearing to promote democracy, instead "entail[] a series of affective foreclosures that block those men's more heterogeneous democratic identifications and energies."[23]

As I hope is by now clear, Thoreau's logic of intimacy is no exception. He seems interested only in intimacy with "the brother" of his own color and class, and his understanding of fraternal bonds is predicated on the disavowal of femininity and homoeroticism, both seen as threatening masculine privacy. I am wondering, though, whether, by dismissing this logic on the basis of its "affective foreclosures," we do not thereby foreclose our own reading of the text and its political potentialities. Take, for example, the way Thoreau binds his logic of intimacy together with an implicit critique of expansionism. In an extended and well-worn metaphor of bounded manhood that runs throughout "Wednesday," Thoreau imagines the self as "some fair floating isle of palm" containing "richer freights . . . than Africa or Malabar." But although "prince and monarchs will contend" who will first "call [this] distant soil their own," this territory of the self forever eludes the violence of the conquering other: "Columbus has sailed westward of these isles . . . but neither he nor his successors have found them" (p. 214). As in the "gentle boy" poem, the distance that thwarts imperial ambition is metonymically that which safeguards male intimacy.

Nowhere is this metonymy more fully instantiated than in the story of the friendship between the Indian Wawatam and Henry the fur trader, "Wednesday"'s most elaborate example of male intimacy. Adapted from William Henry's *Travels and Adventures in the Canada and the Indian Territories*, the story opens with the "imperturbable" Wawatam, who, "after fasting, solitude, and mortification of body, comes to the white man's lodge and affirms that he is the white brother whom he saw in his dream." The two become great friends, "and they hunt and feast and make maple-sugar together." Moreover, "If Wawatam would taste the 'white man's milk' with his tribe, or take his bowl of human broth made of the trader's fellow countrymen, he first finds a place of safety for his

Friend." Finally, "after a long winter of undisturbed and happy inter-course," the two must part. " 'We now exchanged farewells,' says Henry, 'with an emotion entirely reciprocal. . . . All the family accompanied me to the beach; and the canoe had no sooner put off than Wawatam commenced an address to the Kichi Manito, beseeching him to take care of me, his brother. . . .' We never hear of him again" (pp. 223–24).

Thoreau's version of the story, torn from its original context and embedded in a chapter of abstract thoughts about friendship, infuses his logic of intimacy with a fantasy of complete and affective equality between races. Once again, it is based on disembodiment: Wawatam's "fasting" and "mortification of body," not to mention his symbolic trans-formation into a "white brother" (whiteness signaling, perhaps, as it so of-ten does in American literature, racial neutrality and *dis*-embodiment), precondition the friendship. That the two men are able to develop a bond "entirely reciprocal" depends on the Indian's abstention from a cannibalistic appetite for bodily merger (this Indian will not taste this "white man's milk"), and on the white man's restraining his appetite for colonization of the other (this white man leaves rather than settles). Un-like that of more famous nineteenth-century interracial male couples, this fantasy, disembedded of its original narrative context, manages to sidestep the narratives of conquest, empire, and slavery and to cultivate, instead, a vision of complete equality based on disembodiment, respect for boundaries, and, ultimately, territorial isolationism.

But Thoreau's interest in "Wednesday" is indeed an interest in friend-ship with his social and racial equal, and only metaphorically with men of color. Wawatam is there to illustrate the notion that intimate knowl-edge of the other can amount to subjugation whereas "incomplete intercourse" promotes equality.[24] This precisely counters the notion pro-moted by Benhabib that listening to the other's concrete, "coherent narratives" and "life tales" naturally results in empathy, equality, and re-spect for difference. (It is enough to consider the contemporary culture of confessional talk shows to put that idea in question.) Indeed, Thoreau mistrusts speech as a mode of communication exactly because it is the medium of physical proximity and of self-exposure. Speech is, by defini-tion, antithetical to the principles of isolationist masculinity: it is the "commonly transitory" and "almost brutish" language of the public sphere, the parlor, and the mother and does not withstand the litmus test of man's private space; "what is commonly called eloquence in the forum is commonly found to be rhetoric in the study," Thoreau writes (*Walden*, p. 404). Rather than serve as a masculine adhesive, speech en-dangers intimacy, because it tends to drift to the concrete facts of per-sonal life rather than to the universal, to the "husk" rather than the "kernel." "All words are gossip," Thoreau writes in his journal, "what has speech to do with [friendship]. When a man approaches his friend who is thus transfigured to him, even his own hoarse salutation sounds prosaic and ridiculous and makes him least happy in his presence. . . . There is friendship—but without confession—in silence as divine" (*Journals*, 2: 380). Speech transfigures the other precisely by embedding him in a concrete narrative, by reducing him to "gossip." In "Wednesday" Thoreau explains, "persons, when they are made the subject of conversation, though with a Friend, are commonly the most prosaic and trivial of facts. The universe seems bankrupt as soon as we begin to discuss the character of individuals. Our discourse all runs to slander, and our limits grow narrower as we advance." Speech is, by definition, slanderous, because discussing persons empties them of universal essence and reduces them to a trivial and conventionalized prose. "I say," Thoreau concludes, "let us speak of mushrooms and forest trees rather" (p. 211).

Mushrooms and trees: tolerable speech between men displaces the personal and unites the speakers in an impersonal, exterior, third subject such as nature. This displacement of speech from the personal to the neutral has been described by Julie Ellison as an important aspect of the relationship between antebellum middle-class men. Emerson, for example, to protect what he called the "metaphysical isolation" of the individual man, supported a taboo on personal remarks and encouraged conversation on topics such as "culture." "Culture was required," Ellison argues, "so that people may talk about things other than themselves."[25] For Thoreau, of course, nature was the topic capable of sustaining intimacy through speech. But even such an impersonal conversation, we learn in *Walden*, is still framed by too close a physical proximity between men:

One inconvenience I sometimes experienced in so small a house was the difficulty of getting to a sufficient distance from my guest when we began to utter the big thoughts in big words. . . . Individuals, like nations, must have suitable broad and natural boundaries, even a considerable neutral ground, between them. I have found it a singular luxury to talk across the pond to a companion on the opposite side. . . . If we speak reservedly and thoughtfully, we want to be farther apart, that all animal heat and moisture may have a chance to evaporate. If we would enjoy the most intimate society with that in each of us which is without, or above, being spoken to, we must not only be silent, but commonly so far apart bodily that we cannot possibly hear each other's voice in any case. . . . As the conversation began to assume a loftier and grander tone, we gradually moved our chairs farther apart till they touched the wall in opposite corners, and then commonly there was not room enough. (Pp. 434–35)

"Intimate society," then, is predicated not only on speaking "reservedly" about "big thoughts" and "loftier" subjects; it can be freed from the

threat of contaminating bodily proximity, from "animal heat and moisture," only if it is protected by physical distance. And more: paradoxically, intimate conversation is possible only through silence,
as real speech between friends is about that which is "above being spoken to."

Indeed, if speech is "mother's tongue," silence for Thoreau is a constitutive of manhood: "It takes a man to make a room silent" (*Journals*,
2: 67); and elsewhere, "For where man is there is silence, and it takes a
man to make any place silent" (2: 112). Prefiguring a long succession of
silent masculine types in American culture, Thoreau suggests that sentiment between men is best expressed through the withholding of any
speech altogether: "silence is the ambrosial night in the intercourse of
Friends," Thoreau explains in "Wednesday," "in which their sincerity is
recruited and takes deeper root" (p. 221). If speech tends always to violate boundaries by exposing and trivializing the personal and by demanding closeness, silence allows men to bond without the threat of
merger. Friends, Thoreau explains, "will be most familiar, they will be
most unfamiliar, for they will be so one and single that common themes
will not have to be bandied between them, but in silence they will di-
gest them as one mind; but they will at the same time be two and double, that each will be to the other as admirable and as inaccessible as a
star" (*Journals*, 2: 7). Silence, then, allows for sentiment without de-
forming mediation; it allows both familiarity and unfamiliarity, both
oneness and doubleness, both metaphysical proximity and physical
separation; it allows for consumption (for digesting the "common")
without depletion of self. It is the medium, that is, of the intimate generalized other.

The only full dramatization in *Walden* of an encounter between two
middle-class men of equal social position appears in "Brute Neighbors,"
in which Thoreau recounts a meeting between his friend, the "Poet,"
and himself, the "Hermit." This encounter is striking because it never
really happens: it is both an evasion of an encounter and a hint of an encounter yet to happen. It begins with the Hermit rapt in private reverie
only to be interrupted by the arrival of the Poet. The former tenderly
asks him to "leave [him] alone, then, for a while," but his line of thought
is irreparably damaged by the intrusion. When the Poet returns, they
leave the scene together to go fishing, and the rest of the scene happens
in the realm of our imagination. This scene, more a conjoining of two
monologues than a dialogue, encapsulates Thoreau's ideal intimacy: always intrusive on one's privacy; approximated to be immediately
shunned; when it finally takes place, it takes place in silence, outside the
boundaries of the text (pp. 501–2).

The Manliest Relations to Men

Thoreau's writing often centers, then, on the problem of establishing and sustaining sentiment between men, despite a gender ideology that imagined the ideal man, in Clinton Rossiter's words, as "the private man, the man who keeps some of his thoughts and judgments entirely to himself, who feels no overriding compulsion to share everything of value with others, not even those he loves and trusts."[26] If mutual self-revelation, according to Thoreau, is not only unnecessary for intimacy but also destructive to it, then his own "reserved" and "deliberate" writing style performs this idea as well as presents it. In antebellum America, writes Caleb Crain, "literature came forward as a way to exchange emotions between increasingly separate men."[27] In that sense, I would argue, books such as *Walden* may be described as emotionally expressive, or even "sentimental," despite a long critical tradition of drawing a thick border between "classic" romantic American literature and the sentimental novel. One need only consider the deep affections triggered by *Walden* in enthusiastic Thoreauvians from F. O. Blake to Stanley Cavell to acknowledge that the book creates an intimate emotional tie with its (particularly male) readership that is perhaps no less powerful than that of, say, *Little Women* with generations of (particularly female) readers. This not because it follows any of the conventions of the sentimental novel: on the contrary, Thoreau poses his writing in contradistinction to this genre. The sentimental novel conforms to a specific understanding of sentiment that we have seen Thoreau refer to as "sympathy," the kind of identification that blurs the boundaries between public and private; highlights bodily-ness, consumption, and physical proximity; and aspires to arouse empathy by recounting a basic human *sameness.* Conversely, the kind of "masculine" sentiment that Thoreau propagates and *Walden* exemplifies is such that forges a bond between men not through the cancellation but through the concealment of private differences, through the displacement of affairs of the self, through *intimation.* The "reservedness" with which Thoreau says he wrote the book and urges us to read it is the aesthetic equivalent of what I have described as his depersonalizing intimacy. The relationship between the male writer and the male reader, each ensconced in his solitary study, epitomizes that mode of intimacy.

Stanley Cavell's reading of Thoreau in *The Senses of Walden* provides a good example. Cavell acknowledges the feeling shared by *Walden*'s readers that Thoreau has withdrawn "from the words on which he had staked his presence," the feeling of his "words' indifference to us, their disinterest in whether we choose to stay with them or not." He attributes this

sense to the fact that "every new clarity makes the writer's existence ob-
scurer to us" and to "his willingness to remain obscure." Cavell describes
the experience of reading *Walden* as an "almost unbearable sense of his
isolation," since "we find ourselves, perhaps, alone with a book in our
hands, words on a page, at a distance." But this feeling is overcome—or,
rather, accepted—once we realize that in the world of Thoreau "what is
most intimate is what is furthest away," and that separateness is the very
condition of kinship, an idea that Cavell is able to embrace. His sentiments toward Thoreau grow, not in spite of this obfuscation of the personal, but, ultimately, *because* of it, since this obfuscation points to the
text's "sincerity," defined as "the capacity to live in one's own separateness, to sail the Atlantic and Pacific Ocean of one's being alone." Only in
isolationist writing, in that sense, can one be sincere.[28]

We have seen that Thoreau mistrusts speech (and regards it as feminine and maternal) because, immediate and transitory, it always risks exposing the personal and slipping into "slander" and "gossip." Writing,
on the other hand, is "our father tongue, a reserved and select expression" (*Walden*, p. 403). Writing—"silent" speech—is paternal and masculine because of the writer's control over its contents, his ability to check
and edit himself rather than be swayed by the personal contingencies of
the moment. These qualities allow writing and reading to bring men
closer together. Writing "speaks to the intellect and heart of mankind"
and is "at once more intimate with us and more universal than any other
work of art" (*Walden*, p. 404), Thoreau claims, because, through reservedness and self-control, it can be at once universal and personal, at
once general and intimate. The reader, on the other hand, can be
"with" the writer without that writer asking for anything in return. "Being able to enjoy being alone along with another person who is also
alone," writes Winnicott, the most liberalist of psychoanalytical theorists,
"is in itself an experience of health." And nowhere is this experience
better captured than in the space of reading, a space that contains the
paradox of both separating us from other people and connecting us to
them. It is in the experience of reading that one achieves the optimal
state, in Winnicott's theory, "of being alone which (though paradoxically) always implies that someone else is there," someone who makes
absolutely no demands on the self.[29]

But this is not true of all experiences of reading, of course. Thoreau
warns against the way sentimental novels contaminate private existence
by invading, publicizing, and conventionalizing it, the way "the happy
novelist rings the bell for all the world to come together and hear"
(*Walden*, p. 406). Men read novels out of a sickened intrusiveness, not for
genuine "universal intimacy." Like the men in Concord's street who gaze
at Thoreau with "voluptuous" expression, they read "with saucer eyes,

and erect primitive curiosity, and with unwearied gizzard," not to form a
bond between "the heart and intellect of mankind" but for bodily, sensual pleasure (p. 407). In a language similar to that used by contemporaneous conduct manuals to describe the effects of masturbation on youth,
Thoreau describes the result of reading novels as the "dulness of sight, a
stagnation of the vital circulations, and a general deliquium and slough-
ing off of all the intellectual faculties" (p. 407). Like the intrusiveness of
social reformers, the conventions of sentimental fiction are based on
false, sickly, bodily sympathy. "I laughed at myself the other day to think
that I cried while reading a pathetic story," Thoreau writes in his journal;
"I was no more affected in spirit than I frequently am, methinks. The
tears were merely a phenomenon of bowels, and I felt that . . . I should
be ashamed to have the subject of it understand" (*Journals*, 4: 176–77).

The problem of sentimental fiction, like that of speech, is that, by
publicizing and narrativizing private life, it turns it into type, into a conventionalized story. It reifies the private into an artificial, typecast plot,
denies idiosyncrasy, and thus turns both itself and its readers into affective "machines" (*Walden*, p. 406). And the same is true of newspapers:
"To a philosopher," Thoreau writes, "all news, as it is called, is gossip,
and they who edit and read it are old women over their tea" (p. 397).
The newspaper article, like novels and speech, is "effeminate" because it
conventionalizes the private by mechanical-like repetition: "if we read of
one man robbed, or murdered, or killed by accident, or one house
burned, or one vessel wrecked, or one steamboat blown up . . . we never
need read of another. One is enough. If you are acquainted with the
principle, what do you care for a myriad instances and applications?"
(p. 397). "Reserved" writing and reading, conversely, displace individual
instances and applications, the particularized stuff of personal life, in favor of abstraction. Precisely because Thoreau's own essays and books reject the conventions and types of sentimentalism and news in favor of
depersonalization, they are capable of triggering the sentiments of the
reader and striking a genuine emotional cord.

We might say, moreover, that Thoreau's economy of friendship and
attendant aesthetic of intimation, or economy of words, mirror the kind
of extramarket economy he idealizes in *Walden*. Intrusive, confessional
intimacy is homologous to relations in the capitalist marketplace: using
personal stories, rather than money, as its currency (recall Fried's definition of privacy as "moral capital"), it has the effect of enslaving and de-
essentializing the self and robbing it of its autonomy and privacy. The
narrating of concrete stories is analogous to the consumption and reification of self in capitalist economy. Depersonalizing intimacy, by contrast, reflects the self-reliance and unmediated relations of the *Walden*
experiment. In "driving the simple bargains" of friendship, one does

not rely on the mediation of speech and personal stories as one's affective currency. Instead, silence or the sparest exchange creates a relatively unmediated economy of friendship that, like the alternative economy of *Walden*, preserves privacy, essence, and equality. Counterintuitively, then, writing is seen by Thoreau as a *less*-mediated form of communication than speech: it is precisely its reservedness that enables direct and intimate identification.[30]

Walden, therefore, famously refrains from self-exposure and self-emplotting. As autobiographical works go, it relates surprisingly few facts about its subject's daily existence. Throughout the book, Thoreau insists on describing his private "business" as his own, for him only to mind, and he uses private incidents only to generalize on what he regards as universal truths. For *Walden* to be successful under Thoreau's terms, it must be like the cabin/study in which it was produced: defying clear visibility, protected by wide boundaries, and shielding its own interiority. For *Walden* to bond writer and readers, it must conceal as well as reveal or, through partial revealing, suggest that much remains concealed. In his journal (itself even less of a "life tale" and more of a series of generalized fragments than the books based on it) he writes that "men should hear of your virtue only as they hear the creaking of the earth's axle and the music of the spheres. It will fall into the course of nature and be effectually concealed by publicness" (1: 263). The obscuring of the personal in *Walden*, its "concealment by publicness," is a *mode* of communication, not the end of communication.

This deliberate obfuscation of the private informs Barbara Johnson's insight that *Walden* "delights because it baffles." Johnson argues that Thoreau's language is characterized by catachretic symbolism that deliberately obscures its own tenors. She cites as an example a famous and poignant passage—"I long ago lost a hound, a bay horse, and a turtle dove, and am still on their trail. . . . I have met one or two who had heard the hound, and the tramp of the horse, and even seen the dove disappear behind a cloud, and they seemed as anxious to recover them as if they had lost them themselves" (*Walden*, p. 336)—to convincingly argue that any attempt to fill the symbolic "hound," "horse," and "dove" with concrete meanings destroys the passage's affective power. What is symbolized is loss itself, rather than anything specific for which it stands. The obscurity of the passage is thus its very purpose, as well as the key to our affective identification with it. The power of Thoreau's prose lies in its ability to "wake us up to our own lost losses, to make us participate in the transindividual movement of loss in its infinite particularity."[31]

This link between intimacy and intimation, I would hasten to add, is not limited to Thoreau but representative of American romanticism more generally. It finds an accurate articulation, for instance, in

Melville's description, in "Hawthorne and His Mosses," of his experience of reading Hawthorne's romances. To read Hawthorne, Melville writes, a reader would ideally be positioned, like his narrator, within "a papered chamber in a fine old farm-house—a mile from any other dwelling, and dipped to the eaves in foliage." Such Thoreauvian, suburban isolation is the kind of space that the narrator imagines Hawthorne himself to occupy and, moreover, to *embody*: he describes the "enchanting landscape in [Hawthorne's] soul," bound by an "intervening hedge" that blocks this interior space from the view of the other.[32] That both writer and reader are thus fixed in private isolation and separated by distance is what allows Hawthorne to "seize" the reader in his "seclusion" (p. 1154), whereas physical proximity and personal acquaintance would have prevented a bond between them. Books must be "foundlings," Melville claims; "on a personal interview no great author has ever come up to the idea of his reader. But that dust of which our bodies are composed, how can it fitly express the nobler intelligences among us?" (p. 1154). Disembedded, disembodied, and separated in space, the writer penetrates the very depth of the reader's being: "I feel that this Hawthorne has dropped germinous seeds into my soul. He expands and deepens down, the more I contemplate him; and further, and further, shoots his strong New-England roots into the hot soil of my Southern soul" (p. 1157). Replacing Thoreauvian kernels with Hawthornian seeds, Melville fantasizes about complete and eroticized intimacy between men, made possible only on condition that a map of isolated studies, intervening hedges, and nationwide distances has been formerly guaranteed. His erotic language would have perhaps repelled the more ascetic Thoreau, but the principle of intimacy through separation in reading is nonetheless similar.

Perhaps no passage in *Walden* captures the contours of this masculine trans-subjective merger better than one that appears in "Solitude": "I only know myself as a human entity," Thoreau writes, "the scene, so to speak of thoughts and affections; and am sensible of a certain doubleness by which I can stand as remote from myself as from another. However intense my experience, I am conscious of the presence and criticism of a part of me, which, as it were, is not a part of me, but spectator, sharing no experience, but taking note of it; and that is no more I than it is you. When the play, it may be the tragedy, of life is over, the spectator goes his way. It was a kind of fiction, a work of the imagination only, so far as he was concerned. This doubleness may easily make us poor neighbors and friends sometimes" (pp. 429–30). The lingering sense of what is here described as "doubleness" makes *Walden* the precise articulation of liberal masculine intimacy. Thoreau imagines himself as leading a schizophrenic existence, simultaneously operating within the hermetically circumscribed theater of his personal life, the realm of his thoughts and affections, and outside of it, where the contingencies of personal life appear a mere fiction—a "coherent narrative" or "life tale," in Benhabib's terms—no more important, in the final analysis, than the "husk," or a fleeting theater performance. A certain remoteness from this fiction is precisely what allows Thoreau to be a writer: to universalize the particular and thus make it meaningful to others across time and space. And although this "doubleness may easily make us poor neighbors and friends sometimes," because it denies the significance of the "concrete other," it nonetheless produces a trans-subjective space where intimate bonds are forged, despite individual difference. The writerly part of Thoreau is no more "I" than it is "you": removed from the affairs and burdens of the particularized self, it allows, finally, for an intimate merger between man and men, between Thoreau and his readers. "You are a fact in a fiction," says Thoreau to his friend. Within his romantic construction of bounded masculinity, then, lies a domain that is the hard fact of contingent, particularized life stories, at once its core and external to it, at once beyond concrete articulation and fully nonsubjective, a domain where privacy and intimacy can finally be reconciled.

Afterword

Today, or so we are told, Americans no longer have privacy. "We are persistently bombarded by reports of people's most intimate affairs by way of celebrity gossip and human-interest stories, confessional talk shows and soul-baring interviews, and by omnipresent television series and movies that treat the most banal incidents of ordinary life with the utmost gravity," writes Rochelle Gurstein.[1] Contemporary culture, she suggests, has canceled the boundary between the public and the private. And if few aspects of private life remain shielded from the media, none seem to be protected from high technology. From computerized medical records to electronic credit-card data, every private movement, sensation, or desire now seems to leave a public trace. "You have zero privacy anyway. Get over it," Scott McNeally, CEO of Sun Microsystems, pithily tells us.[2]

What's more, we are told, Americans no longer seem to *care* about privacy. Those commentators who lament the "destruction" of privacy invariably also express concern over the indifference with which this destruction has been met. "To the frustration of professional privacy advocates," writes Jeffrey Rosen, "Americans don't always seem terribly concerned." "The point is," agrees Robert Post, "that we should actually care about privacy, and it's not clear that we do."[3]

Those who write jeremiads about the decline of privacy often long for the past. In *The Repeal of Reticence*, for example, Gurstein dates the decline of privacy to the end of the nineteenth century and expresses nostalgia for a Victorian golden age that knew how to respect private boundaries. But what I would like these final comments to evoke, instead, is a certain continuity between the nineteenth-century understanding of privacy and that of the present. Rather than look to the Victorians in search of a lost ideal, that is, we might think of the way their tension-riddled conceptualization of privacy lingers in today's debates and concerns.

Throughout this study I have argued that the nineteenth-century liberal definition of privacy was multivalent and, at times, even self-contradictory. I suggested that the newly conceived definition of privacy comprised at least two separate notions. The first, which may be described as "affirmative" privacy, claimed for individuals the right to actively construct their private identity. It allocated the domestic sphere as the space where subjects cultivated and expressed a unique, autonomous selfhood, whether by designing their home or by telling their stories. From the beginning, however, this affirmative understanding of privacy was tethered to social performance. Recall Habermas's insight that "subjectivity, as the innermost core of the private, was always already oriented to an audience."[4] As such, we have seen, it has been critiqued in several ways. Both nineteenth-century critics, such as Thoreau, and contemporary theorists have pointed out that in constructing private identity the liberal subject also *reifies* this identity. Imagining one's relation to one's identity in terms of ownership (we own our life story as we own our house), the liberal subject also renders itself alien and alienable, open to appropriation by the public and the marketplace. Indeed, from a poststructuralist perspective, the right to privacy has always been a particularly insidious illusion. It is precisely where subjects think they most exercise their autonomy—in the formation of private interiority—that powers external to them work most busily and effectively to determine that formation. The self-constructed subject is unceasingly policed by social discourse/power and, most aggressively, by him- or herself.

Poststructuralist critics thus find themselves in cahoots with high-tech CEOs in declaring, "You have zero privacy anyway. Get over it." But, I have been arguing, this approach neglects to treat seriously a second understanding of privacy that developed in the nineteenth century, what we might call "negative" privacy. This understanding imagines an interior space in which the subject is left alone. Instead of the active laboring toward the construction of a coherent private identity, this kind of privacy protects a reprieve from that policed labor, a space of passivity, disorder, and silence. It harbors that which exceeds or resists smooth translation into a disciplined narrative of identity. In *The Psychic Life of Power*, Judith Butler recognizes that "the subject produced as continuous, visible, and located is nevertheless haunted by an inassimilable remainder, a melancholia that marks the limits of subjectiviation."[5] This "inassimilable remainder," produced by the very process of identity formation, need not be romantically imagined as a space of resistance— indeed, since it is incoherent or, in Winnicott's terms, "incommunicable," it *cannot* be imagined simply as such; but it nonetheless demands protection from social visibility and intrusion. Decades before psychoanalysis would theorize this kind of privacy as an aspect of the psyche, literary authors wrote it into being.

I argue in this book that this duality of the affirmative and the negative understandings of privacy influenced much of nineteenth-century cultural discourse and, in particular, contributed to the shape of antebellum literature on the levels of style, plot, and genre. But this duality also plagues contemporary debates over privacy. It subtends, for example, debates over whether the right to privacy is distinct from the right of property, or debates over the desirability of using the liberal right to privacy in feminist or queer politics. It may well offer, as well, a way to think about the complacency about privacy with which contemporary commentators are charging the American public. Rather than regard this complacency as a form of obtuse blindness or collective denial, one might ask to what degree media and technology invasions merely challenge privacy, affirmative and negative, and to what degree they in fact bolster its logic.

When participants on talk or reality shows flaunt their intimate lives for the camera, for instance, are they forgoing or affirming their privacy? To be sure, often they are victims of a cynical and profit-hungry enterprise that cares little, if at all, for their well-being. But at the same time, they enter that spiral of power and pleasure that, while subjecting them to disciplinary narratives of identity ("the black welfare mother," "the promiscuous preadolescent"), also endows them with a sense of autonomy and coherence that results precisely from the articulation/exposure of their private story. This is particularly true, since these participants are often members of disenfranchised social groups, subjects who lack other venues for self-construction. Just as Habermas's historical subject needed to pour out her heart in letters in order to become a private person, their public confessions may be construed, somewhat paradoxically, as a claim to affirmative privacy. More important, talk show participants are bound to experience that self-alienation that is the product of the very nature of the media. They are bound to feel and register, that is, the sense of misrecognition that social interpellation always entails, the sense that "I am not *really* the person I performed for the camera." Ironically, the more conventionalized, caricaturized, and clichéd their performed identity is (and the talk show format demands utter conventionality), the more lively that sense of an inassimilable remainder, of that negative space of interiority, becomes. In that sense, today's media "victims" may not be all that different from the domestic woman or the former slave who used writing to construct and make visible a private self, only to deepen their sense of self through silence and *dis*appearance.

The same might be suggested in relation to electronic infringements of privacy. When a company like Amazon.com makes commercial use of information about its consumers' private habits, tastes, or preferences, shoppers may feel something beyond sheer violation: there is a certain pleasure that comes from the seductive notion that shopping produces a solid identity, and that this identity is, moreover, *valuable*. It is not surprising, then, that Web users resort not only to software that erases traces of that identity from cyberspace but also to software that allows them to organize and *market* that identity. One Web-based enterprise advertises, "We work for you, the consumer, as an agent to extract the maximum value for your identity. We help you copyright your profile. Not only that, we take your click trail and consider that a unique work of authorship."[6] Cyberspace thus becomes the postmodern parlor, where one performs a social identity and translates it into material terms.

At the same time, consumers recognize the gap between this reified identity and other aspects of their personhood. If they "don't always seem terribly concerned," it is because their understanding of privacy is multilayered and complex. Certain, most crucial, zones of privacy, we feel, are untouched, and untouchable, by Amazon.com. Rather than indifference, contemporary culture, like its nineteenth-century predecessor, displays a keen regard for privacy, both for the kind of privacy that fosters a coherent, marketable identity, and for the kind of privacy that shields the lack of any identity whatsoever.

Notes

Introduction

1. Franzen, "Imperial Bedroom," in *How to Be Alone*, p. 42.
2. Hixon, *Privacy in a Public Society*, p. xv.
3. The dating of the formation of the middle class in America to the first half of the nineteenth century continues to be subject to debate, especially in light of work that suggests that the term was not put into use until after the Civil War. In locating the shaping of middle-class values in the decades before the Civil War, I am relying on works such as Blumin, *The Emergence of the Middle Class*, and Ryan, *The Cradle of the Middle Class*.
4. Historians such as Gordon Wood show that as early as the 1780s American political rhetoric shifted in the direction of liberal democracy and away from republican ideals (see, for example, Wood, *The Creation of the American Republic, 1776–1787*). Indeed, the claim of this book is not that the liberal concept of privacy was "invented" in 1830 (as my references to early liberal thinkers such as Locke or to the Bill of Rights should make clear), but that it reaches its full and ubiquitous articulation in America—and not just in political rhetoric but also in the discourses that regulate everyday life—in the middle decades of the nineteenth century.
5. Lefebvre, *The Production of Space*, pp. 33–39.
6. Lefebvre, p. 39.
7. Certeau, *The Practice of Everyday Life*, p. 117.
8. See Woods, "The First American Architectural Journals." Alexander Jackson Davis is commonly considered to be the first professional American architect. His important role in the creation of the profession is discussed in detail in Rebora, "Alexander Jackson Davis and the Arts of Design."
9. Some Pattern-book examples are M. Field, *City Architecture; or, Designs for Dwelling Houses, Stores, Hotels, etc.* (1854); Orson Fowler, *Home for All* (1848); David Henry Arnot, *Gothic Architecture Applied to Modern Residences* (1849); Gervase Wheeler, *Homes for the People in Suburb and Country* (1855); William H. Ranlett, *The Architect* (1849); Alexander Jackson Davis, *Rural Residences* (1837); and Andrew Jackson Downing, *A Treatise on the Theory and Practice of Landscape Gardening* (1841), *Cottage Residences* (1842), and *The Architecture of Country Houses* (1850). Downing's success was indeed impressive: *Treatise* went through nineteen printings and eight editions by 1879, *Cottage Residences* thirteen printings by 1887, and *Architecture* nineteen printings by 1886. See Woods, p. 119.

10. "Architecture in the United States," pp. 438–39.

11. Tocqueville's amazement at the sight of the "considerable number of palaces of white marble, several of which were built after the models of ancient architecture" is quoted by Downing in *Cottage Residences*, p. 10. Dickens is quoted in Lynes, *The Domesticated Americans*, p. 5.

12. Quoted in Lynes, *The Art-Makers*, p. 57.

13. See, for example, Arnot, p. 2, and Downing, *Cottage Residences*, p. 10. The list of Davis's works illustrates this change. Starting in the early 1830s, his designs clearly branched into the Greek style for banks, town halls, courthouses, and so on, and into the Picturesque/Gothic style for private houses, schools, and churches. This does not mean, of course, that the Greek style disappeared from the physical landscape: many private houses, particularly in the South, continued to make use of this style into the next century. But *prescriptive* architectural literature attacked this style with amazing unanimity.

14. Harbison, *Eccentric Spaces*, p. 19.

15. Downing, *The Architecture*, p. 25.

16. Sargent, *Our Home, or the Key to a Nobler Life*, p. 26. Sargent's words come later in the century but sum up quite well the arguments of Downing and his antebellum colleagues (see my discussion in Chapter 5).

17. Mill, *On Liberty*, p. 5.

18. Brooks, *The World of Washington Irving*, pp. 277–78.

19. Poe, "The Masque of the Red Death," p. 458. Subsequent references are provided parenthetically in the text.

20. Quoted in Brow, *American Art to 1900*, p. 280, emphasis added.

21. Renza, "Poe's Secret Autobiography," p. 71. For the idea that the Red Death is symbolic of the act of writing fiction, see also Kennedy, *Poe, Death, and the Life of Writing*, p. 203. "[T]he cerements and mask," he writes, "are signs without a proper referent; they mark the semiotic impasse in which writing has begun to locate its own activity."

22. Foucault, *The History of Sexuality: An Introduction*.

23. D. A. Miller, *The Novel and the Police*, p. 20; see also Brodhead, "Sparing the Rod."

24. Renza, *Edgar Allan Poe, Wallace Stevens, and the Poetics of American Privacy*, p. 11. I borrow the term "radical privacy" from Renza's provocative and immensely useful introduction. In thinking about the notion of radical privacy, I was also inspired by Dean, "Hart Crane's Poetics of Privacy." In a brilliant study, Dean shows how this poet's language inference captures an intensely subjective experience that is at once irreducibly private and potentially transpersonal. This radical form of privacy is then contrasted with the form of reified, discursively determined personhood that the privacy doctrine often postulates.

25. Holbrook, *Ten Years among the Mailbags*, p. xv. Subsequent references are given parenthetically in the text.

26. See Honig's discussion of Arendt in "Toward an Agonistic Feminism"; Habermas, *The Structural Transformation of the Public Sphere*, p. 49, emphasis added.

27. Gillian Brown, *Domestic Individualism*, p. 188.

28. Melville, "Bartleby, the Scrivener," pp. 653–55. Subsequent references are given parenthetically in the text.

29. Phillips, *On Kissing, Tickling, and Being Bored*, p. 65.

30. Morris, "Privacy in Public," pp. 16–17. See also idem, "Privacy, Privation, Perversity."

31. Butler, *The Psychic Life of Power;* Bernauer and Mahon, "The Ethics of Michel Foucault," pp. 141–47; Foucault, "Interview with Stephen Riggins," p. 122.

32. Benhabib, "Models of Public Space," pp. 86–87.

33. Raymond Williams, *Keywords*, p. 242; Harper, *Private Affairs*. See also G. Brown, *Domestic Individualism;* Michaels, "Romance and Real Estate," in *The Gold Standard and the Logic of Naturalism*.

34. Weintraub, "The Theory and Politics of the Public/Private Distinction," pp. 27–29.

35. See, for example, most of the articles collected in Davidson, *No More Separate Spheres*.

36. Sanborn, "Keeping Her Distance," p. 1336.

37. Kimmel, *Manhood in America*, pp. 52, 58.

38. Ware, *Home Life*, p. 24.

39. Berlant, "The Subject of True Feeling," pp. 60–61.

Chapter 1

1. *Appleton's* (1870) is quoted in Wright, *Moralism and the Model Home*, p. 99; Auden, "The Cave of Nakedness," in *About the House*, p. 32.

2. Fryer, *Felicitous Space*, pp. 31–32; Smeins, *Building an American Identity*, p. 18.

3. Lefebvre, *The Production of Space*, pp. 33–39.

4. Lukacs, "The Bourgeois Interior," p. 624.

5. Pleck makes a similar point in *Domestic Tyranny*. She claims that critics confuse "the family ideal with the reality of domestic life" and reminds us that "the household was comprised of individuals who had divergent goals and points of view. The interests of the husband were not the same as those of his wife" (p. 12).

6. Now-classic studies of the cult of domesticity include Cott, *The Bonds of Womanhood*; Douglas, *The Feminization of American Culture*; and Ryan, *The Cradle of the Middle Class*; Welter, "The Cult of True Womanhood"; Sklar, *Catherine Beecher*.

7. On the link between liberal individualism and the rise of the middle class, see, for example, Zaretsky, *Capitalism, the Family and Personal Life*, esp. pp. 54–78. Tocqueville's quote is from *Democracy in America*, bk. 2, chap. 8. For examples of the feminist critique of liberal individualism, see the essays collected in Landes, ed., *Feminism, the Public, and the Private*; MacKinnon, *Feminism Unmodified*, esp. pp. 93–102; and Yeatman, "A Feminist Theory of Social Differentiation," esp. pp. 283–89. The observation about the way liberalism and feminism interpret the divide between public and private differently is elaborated on in Weintraub, "The Theory and Politics of the Public/Private Distinction."

8. The most influential study in this second category is Tompkins, *Sensational Designs*.

9. Gillion Brown, *Domestic Individualism;* Kaplan, "Manifest Domesticity"; Merish, *Sentimental Materialism*. See also Romero, *Home Fronts* and the essays collected in Samuels, ed., *The Culture of Sentiment*.

10. Scott, "Gender," p. 43. Scott rightly argues against the tendency of historians to treat the cult of domesticity as if it were first created whole and only then reacted to. Rather than as a solid product of consensus, she explains, we should examine the small particles of this (and any) ideological construct, and such an examination would defy an oversimplified celebration of the private sphere as the space for a separate women's culture.

11. Habermas, *The Structural Transformation of the Public Sphere*, pp. 45–51.

12. Laslett, "The Family as a Public and Private Institution," p. 480.

13. Quoted in Lynes, *The Domesticated Americans*, p. 43. The quote refers specifically to the practice of bringing lodgers into the home but exemplifies

the more general threat that I will later discuss as the "permeability" of domesticity.

14. Quoted in Lynes, *The Domesticated Americans*, p. 50.

15. Quoted in Wright, *Moralism and the Model Home*, p. 13.

16. For a description of the origins, development, and uses of colonial domestic architecture, see, for example Bushman, *The Refinement of America*, pp. 100–138; Clark, *The American Family Home*, pp. 4–36; and Wright, *Building the Dream*, pp. 3–18. For a more detailed discussion of regional variations, see Gowans, *Images of American Living*, pts. I and II.

17. Clark, *The American Family Home*, p. 12.

18. Bushman, pp. 105–9.

19. Crevecoeur, *Letters from an American Farmer*, p. 67. See also Wright, *Building the Dream*, p. 22.

20. Demos, *The Little Commonwealth*, esp. pp. 82–99. Demos maintains that, although the legal and societal conception of women's role was extremely limiting, within the private sphere women had some decision-making power.

21. Flaherty, *Privacy in Colonial New England*, p. 57.

22. Robert Kerr, *The Gentlemen's House*, is quoted in Fryer, p. 62 (emphasis added). For discussions of the British precedents after which American architects modeled their plans, see Franklin, *The Gentleman's Country House and Its Plan, 1835–1914*, and Girouard, *The Victorian Country House*. Girouard explains that spatial segregation and specialization conformed well to a culture that also organized "government . . . into departments, the middle classes into professions, science into different disciplines, and convicts into separate cells" (p. 19).

23. Girouard, p. 10. See also Franklin, pp. 393–48, and Spain, *Gendered Spaces*, pp. 111–40. Spain argues that the American sexually segregated interior, imported from Britain, helped define a social reality in which women were denied basic rights like the vote, keeping their own wages, or owning property. Throughout history, she shows, the segregation of space on the basis of gender has coincided with limits on the knowledge available to women, and hence has resulted in a lower status for them.

24. Franklin, p. 39; Kasson, *Rudeness and Civility*, pp. 174–75; Chase and Levenson, *The Spectacle of Intimacy*, p. 167.

25. Bushman, p. 275.

26. Thus, Gervase Wheeler, for example, in his popular *Homes for the People in Suburb and Country*, distinguishes between gentlemen of leisure and their families, suburban families of professional commuters, and those who live in the country for reasons of economy, and designs "mansions," "villas," and "cottages" for them, respectively. The mansions and villas he designed included studies or libraries; the cottages did not.

27. Downing, *The Architecture of Country Houses*, pp. 96, 138.

28. Downing, *The Architecture of Country Houses*, p. 138.

29. On privacy in the working-class home (in the British case), see Hewitt, "District Visiting and the Constitution of Domestic Space in the Mid-Nineteenth Century."

30. Cott, p. 98.

31. Lefebvre, p. 11. The sociological position on space and social formation is summarized in Ardener, *Women and Space*, pp. 1–6. David Harvey, quoted in Spain, suggests that in looking at space and social formations we should "translate results generated in one language (say a social process language) into another language (the spatial form language). . . . both languages amount to different ways of saying the same thing" (p. 6). Similarly, Hillier and Hanson

argue in *The Social Logic of Space* that, "by giving shape and form to our material world, architecture structures the system of space in which we live and move. In that it does so, it has a direct relation—rather than a merely symbolic one—to social life since it provides the material preconditions for the patterns of movement, encounter and avoidance which are the material realization—as well as sometimes the generation—of social relations" (p. ix).

32. Vaux, *Villas and Cottages*, pp. 85–86.

33. Hall, *The Hidden Dimension*, p. 108.

34. The description of the parlor as a social "front" appears in Bushman, p. 251, who further describes the middle-class home under the regime of the parlor as "a house divided against itself," accommodating the mutually contradictory values of materialism, refinement, and consumption, on the one hand, and a republican ethos of hard work and frugality, on the other. See also Halttunen, *Confidence Men and Painted Women*, esp. chap. 3.

35. Vaux, "Parisian Buildings for City Residents," p. 810.

36. Kasson, p. 174.

37. Goffman, *The Presentation of Self in Everyday Life*, pp. 22–24.

38. Kasson, p. 176.

39. Quoted in Welter, p. 173.

40. Haven, "Mrs. Bowen's Parlor and Spare Bed-Room," p. 136.

41. Goffman, p. 252, emphasis added.

42. Rybczynski, *Home*, p. 5.

43. Quoted in Welter, p. 162.

44. Quoted in Fryer, p. 12.

45. On the space of the parlor as a combination of status and familial intimacy, see Wright, *Moralism*, p. 35.

46. Merish, e.g., pp. 2–3; Warner, "The Mass Public and the Mass Subject." See also Chase and Levenson, who analyze how the British middle class problematically conjoined the values of seclusion and display.

47. Tomes, "Houses We Live In," p. 737.

48. Cabot, "House Building," p. 429.

49. Quoted in Halttunen, *Confidence Men and Painted Women*, p. 109.

50. Leslie, *Miss Leslie's Behaviour Book*, p. 52.

51. Quoted in Halttunen, *Confidence Men and Painted Women*, p. 110. Halttunen discusses the role of etiquette manuals in monitoring the boundaries of the middle-class home and its relation to gender politics on pp. 92–123.

52. Quoted in Allen, *Uneasy Access*, p. 84.

53. Goffman, p. 112.

54. Leslie, "Mr. and Mrs. Woodbridge," p. 28, emphasis added.

55. Quoted in Degler, *At Odds*, pp. 53–54. In her European travelogue, *Sunny Memories of Foreign Lands*, Stowe likewise voices this desire for privacy: "at last I have come into dreamland," she writes of her sojourn in Paris, "into the lotus-eater's paradise, into the land where it is always afternoon. I am released from care; I am unknown, unknowing. . . . My time is all my own. I may at will lie on a sofa, and dreamily watch the play of the leaves and flowers, in the little garden into which my room opens" (vol. 2, letter XXXI). Stowe is here rejoicing in the relief from housework, of course, but also in the opportunity to plunge into reverie, to enter what I describe in the next section as the masculine prerogative of escaping performative identity.

56. Chesnutt, *A Diary from Dixie*, pp. 122–23.

57. "The Education of Girls," p. 140.

58. Quoted in Cott, p. 16.

59. Fern, "Mother's Room," in *Ruth Hall and Other Writing*, pp. 288–90.

60. Hedrick, *Harriet Beecher Stowe*, pp. viii, 76. Ann Douglas writes about the blend of privacy and spectacle in sentimental literature in *The Feminization of American Culture*: "Sentimentalism is a cluster of ostensibly private feelings which always attains public and conspicuous expression. Privacy functions in the rituals of sentimentalism only for the sake of titillation, as a convention to be violated. Involved as it is with the exhibition and commercialization of the self, sentimentalism cannot exist without an audience. It has no content but its own exposure, and it invests exposure with a kind of final significance" (p. 254).

61. Merish, p. 2.

62. Habermas, p. 50.

63. Wigley, "Untitled," p. 347.

64. Quoted in Paul, *The Shores of America*, p. 94.

65. Quoted in Spain, p. 123.

66. Downing, *The Architecture of Country Houses*, p. 404. The isolated function of the library developed gradually. It initially served as a sitting room for the family but soon "came to form a masculine contrast to the drawing room"; see Franklin, p. 46.

67. Girouard, p. 35.

68. Downing, *Cottage Residences*, p. 5.

69. Cabot, p. 427; Wheeler, *Rural Homes*, p. 22, emphasis added.

70. Leslie, "Mr. and Mrs. Woodbridge," p. 22.

71. Clark, "Domestic Architecture as an Index to Social History," p. 51.

72. Benjamin, "Paris, Capital of the Nineteenth Century," p. 154.

73. "The End of Prudence."

74. Barker, *The Tremulous Private Body*, pp. 3–14. Barker opens his book with a passage from the diary of Samuel Pepys in which he finds traces of a sexuality that was "banished" or "displaced" by the text. While I find the link he draws between subjection, writing, and private space most useful, I take issue with the ontological certainty with which he reads the hidden contents of the diary, what it *really* says. My argument, particularly in the next chapter, would be that the construction of all these three domains of privacy marks also the invention of an ontological *in*security, of the notion of subjective *ineffability*, which contemporary (particularly Foucauldian) critics too often ignore.

75. Butler, *The Psychic Life of Power*.

76. Bachelard, *The Poetics of Space*, p. 6.

77. Ware, pp. 15–23.

78. Quoted in Wright, *Moralism*, p. 13.

79. Emerson's shunning of his family to engage in intellectual production appears in "Self Reliance" and is quoted and discussed by Cavell, in "Being Odd, Getting Even," p. 304.

80. Quoted in Fryer, pp. 63–64.

81. Nedelsky, "Law, Boundaries, and the Bounded Self," p. 165.

82. Luria, "The Architecture of Manners."

83. Hawthorne, "The Old Manse," p. 1123. Subsequent references are given parenthetically in the text.

84. But something of the forbidden nature of his masculine reserve resonates in Sophia's journals: on a particularly hot day when Hawthorne was away, she and the children "were quite uncomfortably hot sitting perfectly still, & finally were obliged to go into Papa's study [which I keep shut up generally] as the only cool spot." As Herbert points out, "every phrase here is laced with accusation"; see *Dearest Beloved*, p. 25.

85. Leslie, "Mr. and Mrs. Woodbridge," p. 63.

86. Pateman, *The Disorder of Women*, pp. 119–24.

87. Lefebvre, p. 41.

88. Downing, *The Architecture of Country Houses*, pp. 11–19 (further references are given parenthetically in the text). The fifth principle, "Variety," is aberrant on this list.

89. Downing, *Cottage Residences*, 22.

Chapter 2

1. Freud, "Resistance and Repression," p. 288; Winnicott, "Communicating and Not Communicating Leading to a Study of Certain Opposites," p. 186.

2. Jung, *Memories, Dreams, Reflections*, pp. 158–59; subsequent references are given in parentheses in the text. See also Clare Cooper, "The House as Symbol of the Self," p. 139.

3. Freud, "Symbolism in Dreams," p. 153.

4. Bachelard, pp. xxxii–xxxiv.

5. Pfister, *The Production of Personal Life*, p. 27.

6. Freud, "Resistance and Repression," pp. 295–96. Subsequent references to this essay are given parenthetically in the text.

7. Schafer, "Narration in the Psychoanalytic Dialogue," p. 37.

8. Freud, "The 'Uncanny,' " p. 224. Subsequent references to this essay are given in parentheses in the text.

9. Vidler, *The Architectural Uncanny*, p. 23.

10. While Lacan is absent from my discussion of psychoanalysis and privacy, others have chosen to discuss privacy precisely in Lacanian terms. Renata Salecl, for example, argues that privacy means "respect" for the other, where "respect . . . concerns the subject's relation to the lack in the other, which also means that respect is just another name for the anxiety the subject feels with regard to this lack." If, in Lacanian terminology, the subject is marked by lack at the moment in which he or she becomes a speaking being and undergoes symbolic castration, then the right to privacy means that we avert our gaze from the fact that the other does not have full bodily integrity. Hence, "what privacy protects is not the subject's identity but the very lack of it" ("The Exposure of Privacy in Today's Culture," p. 8). This account helps situate a Lacanian discussion of privacy between the Freudian and the Winnocottian accounts I provide above: in Salecl's version, privacy involves an absence and an anxiety (as in Phillips's discussion of Freud) but also the realization that privacy allows for a certain reprieve from identity, the realization highlighted by Winnicott.

11. Phillips, *On Kissing, Tickling, and Being Bored*, p. 27.

12. Schafer, p. 43.

13. Phillips, p. 7.

14. Winnicott, "The Capacity to Be Alone," p. 34 (emphasis added).

15. Phillips, p. 60.

16. Winnicott, "Communicating and Not Communicating," p. 179, emphasis added. Subsequent references will be given parenthetically in text. Compare this with Pontalis's aphorism, "The speaking subject is the entire subject" (Le sujet parlant est tout le sujet), quoted in Khan, *Hidden Selves*, p. 46.

17. Winnicott, *Playing and Reality*, pp. 55–56.

18. Phillips discusses Khan on perversion and dreams on pp. 59–67; quote is on p. 65. See also Khan, pp. 42–50.

19. Laing, *The Divided Self.*
20. Miller, *The Novel and the Police*, p. 207.
21. Miller, *The Novel and the Police*, p. 204.
22. Sedgwick, *Epistemology of the Closet*, p. 1.
23. Lane, The *Burdens of Intimacy*, p. 235.
24. Borges, *Other Inquisitions, 1937–1952*, p. 56 (emphasis in original)
25. Hawthorne, "Wakefield," p. 290. Subsequent references are given parenthetically in the text.
26. Brodhead, *The School of Hawthorne*, p. 46, emphasis added.
27. The intended readership of *New England Magazine* was unlike, say, that of *Godey's Lady's Book*, established a year earlier. *New England Magazine* published, for example, the first two installments of "The Autocrat at the Breakfast Table," a series of sketches narrated by a genteel patriarchal voice and later picked up by *Atlantic Monthly*. The magazine's appeal to a male audience is evident particularly after Park Benjamin took over as editor and introduced regular features such as "Politics and Statistics" and the "United States Senate" as well as articles on topics such as "smoking" alongside its more literary pieces. See also Hoover, *Park Benjamin*, pp. 44–66.
28. Among the critics who have pointed out this symmetry are Weldon, "Wakefield's Second Journey."
29. Berlant, "Live Sex Acts," p. 280.
30. Khan, pp. 183–88.
31. Khan, p. 185.
32. Gatta, in " 'Busy and Selfish London,' " comments on the role of the new urban landscape in this tale. Laffrado, in " 'Far and Momentary Glimpse,' " analyzes the figure of Mrs. Wakefield in detail and argues that she comes to stand for the freedom and independence available to widows but not to married women.
33. Polk makes a similar point in "Welty, Hawthorne, and Poe."
34. Borges, p. 57.
35. See Edwin Miller, *Salem Is My Dwelling Place*, p. 87.
36. Emerson's words are quoted and discussed in Chapter 1.
37. Quoted in "The Wayside."
38. Quoted in Edwin Miller, p. 86.
39. See Newman, *A Reader's Guide to the Short Stories of Herman Melville*, p. 233. Melville's interest in "Wakefield" is also on record. For example, in the Agatha letters, Melville recounts a story that he heard about another husband who abandoned his wife and explains that, since the story was similar to "Wakefield," Hawthorne might be interested in turning it into a tale. See Davis and Gilman, eds., *The Letters of Herman Melville*, pp. 154–55.
40. Hawthorne, "Fire-Worship," p. 841. Subsequent references are given parenthetically in the text.
41. Melville, "I and My Chimney," p. 1298. Subsequent references are given parenthetically in the text.
42. Vidler, p. 42; Rogin, *Subversive Genealogy*, p. 231.
43. Brueckner, "Bachelor Hall."
44. See, for example, "A Word for Man's Rights"; "Household Skeletons"; "New York Daguerreotyped."
45. Readers who have interpreted the tale as political allegory include Browne, *Melville's Drive to Humanism*; Sowder, "Melville's 'I and My Chimney' "; and Woodruff, "Melville and His Chimney". Biographical readings have been offered by, among others, Arvin, *Herman Melville*; Rosenberry, *Melville and the Comic Spirit*; and Sealts, *Pursuing Melville, 1940–1980*.

46. See Dahl, "Arrowhead and the Razeed Roof." Other studies of Melville's use of architecture in his fiction include Adams, "Architectural Imagery in Melville's Short Fiction," which argues that architecture allows Melville to convey his theme of limited perception of reality, and hence that he rebels against contemporary architectural prescriptions of "transparency" in design; Dahl, "The Architecture of Society and the Architecture of the Soul," which claims that, unlike Hawthorne, Melville used architecture not to launch a critique of social developments but to explore the universal theme of the human soul; and Litman, "The Cottage and the Temple," which traces the connections between the development of antebellum architecture and literary representations.

47. The anatomical interpretation is offered by Chatfield, among others, who argues that the chimney stands for the penis, and the wife's tunnel-like hallway symbolizes the vagina (the womb, in Douglas's reading), and that the tale as a whole may be read as a Freudian castration drama of "the wife's desire to remove the man's penis" ("Levels of Meaning in Melville's 'I and My Chimney' ").

48. Slater, "The Domestic Adventurer in Melville's Tales," p. 272.

49. Quoted in Pleck, p. 2.

50. Sealts, p. 174.

51. Douglas, p. 318.

52. Charvat, *The Profession of Authorship in America, 1800–1870*, pp. 260–62.

53. In *The School of Hawthorne*, Brodhead shows that "I and My Chimney" was written during a period in which Melville's initial misreading of Hawthorne's aesthetics as concerned with revelation of hidden metaphysical truths was revised, as was his own aesthetic style. Melville had given up on the notion of transgressive truths encoded as open secrets in his texts. "The 'Agatha' letters," writes Brodhead, "show Melville paying attention to a new part of Hawthorne's work: to what Melville calls 'your London husband,' or the early tale 'Wakefield.' . . . in 'Wakefield' daimonization is a process almost perfectly opaque. Wakefield's personal program . . . has no motivation even suggested for it. His program leads to no symbolic counter-expression: Wakefield is the hero as literally uncommunicative man. If his special fate makes Wakefield seem like a 'figure' for some unknown truth of our condition, that truth remains almost perfectly elusive . . . it builds power through the secrets it keeps, not those it tries to tell" (pp. 46–47).

54. Bertolini, "Fireside Chastity," pp. 723–25, emphasis added.

55. See, for example, Pearce, "Secret Closets and Ashes."

56. I am inclined to agree here with an older generation of critics who point out that "one dislikes to probe into the interior of this almost wholly charming piece. . . . One feels Melville's reserve in it, which one feels called upon to respect" (William Ellery Sedgwick, quoted in Sealts, p. 175). My reading differs in not accepting this "reserve" as a universal ethos but, rather, historicizing and gendering it.

57. Stowe, *House and Home Papers*, p. 5. Subsequent references are given parenthetically in the text.

58. Hedrick, p. 314; MacFarlane, "The New England Kitchen Goes Uptown," p. 273.

59. In an 1853 letter to Lord Denman, quoted in the introduction to the 1967 reprint of *House and Home Papers* (New York: AMS Press), p. vii.

60. Berlant, "National Brands/National Body," p. 176.

61. Bhabha discusses mimicry in *The Location of Culture* as that which is almost the same but not quite the same in the context of postcolonial subjectivity, but his discussion is relevant in the context of other subalterns, women included.

62. Hedrick, *Harriet Beecher Stone: A Life*, pp. viii, 76.

63. Quoted in Hedrick, p. 139. And five years later she reinforced that wish by moving her papers to a separate room and writing, "The whole boarding establishment I have left to take care of itself, casting it off in a lump & just disconnecting my little wing suppose myself to be keeping house alone" (quoted in Hedrick, p. 163).

64. Quoted in Hedrick, p. 316.

65. The call for female architects was not limited to the Beecher sisters. Consider a letter by a woman to the famous architect A. J. Davis: "The mistress of the mansion is to be consulted, the tastes of all its destined occupants must be known and respected—there must be a room here and pantry there—this dressing [*sic*] must be made larger—this bedroom must look out in this direction and the drawing room in that. In short, neither the architect nor the proprietor can tell what he wants till the lady, and perhaps her daughters or nieces have seen the plans" (in Amelia, Peck, *Alexander Jackson Davis*, pp. 84–85).

66. Beecher, *Treatise on Domestic Economy*, pp. 272–73.

67. Quoted in Hedrick, p. 124.

68. Lefebvre, pp. 28–29.

69. In 1864 she wrote, "I feel I need to write in these days, to keep me from thinking of things that make me dizzy and blind. . . . I mean such things as are being done where our heroes are dying as Shaw died. It is not wise that all our literature should run in a rut cut through our hearts and red with our blood. I feel the need of a little gentle household merriment and talk of common things, to indulge which I have devised the following" (quoted in introductory note to the reprint of *Household Papers* (New York: AMS Press, 1967, p. ix).

70. Lincoln, "A House Divided," in *The Collected Works of Abraham Lincoln*, p. 461.

Chapter 3

1. The first epigraph (from a conversation in 1869) is quoted in Leach, *True Love and Perfect Union*, p. 43. The second is from Patricia Williams, "Meditations on Masculinity," p. 249.

2. Freud, "The Unconscious," p. 191 (emphasis in original).

3. Wald, *Constituting Americans*, esp. pp. 1–13.

4. See esp. Berlant, "National Brands/National Body"; Warner, *The Letters of the Republic;* and idem, "The Mass Public and the Mass Subject."

5. Fraser, "Rethinking the Public Sphere," pp. 125–26.

6. Lincoln's most famous use of the metaphor is the 1858 "House Divided" speech. But he used the metaphor frequently both before and after that speech, calling the government "national house-keeping," referring to the United States as "our national homestead," calling slavery "an element in the division of the house," and so forth. See Lincoln, vol. 2, pp. 237, 238, 241, 258, 362–63; vol. 3, pp. 18, 211, 213, 309; vol. 4, p. 13; vol. 5, p. 529; vol. 7, pp. 259–60.

7. Melville, "I and My Chimney," p. 1299, emphasis added. Subsequent references are given parenthetically in the text.

8. Emery, "The Political Significance of Melville's Chimney"; Sowder.

9. Arrowhead's previous owner, as a matter of fact, used his next lodging as an underground railroad station, as Melville was surely aware. See Robertson-Lorant, *Melville*, p. 353.

10. Emery associates the narrator with Webster, Sowder, with the southern proslavery position.

11. Stowe, *Uncle Tom's Cabin*, p. 25. All subsequent citations are given parenthetically in the text.

12. Quoted in vol. 2 of Blackmar, ed., *Kansas*, p. 732. Douglas was arguing for the right of states and territories to determine their own policy on slavery, but the language of domesticity that he uses—echoed by other supporters of popular sovereignty (e.g., in his inaugural address on March 4, 1857, President Buchanan said, "Congress is neither to legislate slavery into any territory or state, nor to exclude it therefrom, but to leave the people thereof perfectly free to form and regulate their domestic institutions in their own way, subject only to the constitution of the United States")—suggests that this political position drew force from the language of the privacy of the home.

13. Harper, pref. and chap. 1.

14. Macpherson, p. 3.

15. Patterson, *Slavery and Social Death*.

16. Leach, p. 43.

17. Phelan, *Identity Politics*, p. 138 (emphasis added).

18. Macpherson, p. 219.

19. Amy Kaplan, p. 582.

20. Wald, pp. 54–55.

21. "The Value of the Union," p. 415, emphasis added in the extract.

22. Mount Vernon become a national monument following the crusade for its preservation in 1853 by the Ladies of Mount Vernon Association, which sought to fix and preserve the estate in the hope that it would offer a symbol of national unity. See Handlin, *The American Home*, pp. 84–85.

23. Quoted in Forgie, *Patricide in the House Divided*, p. 187.

24. Downing, *A Treatise*, p. ix.

25. Quoted in Clark, "Domestic Architecture," p. 41.

26. Downing, *A Treatise*, pp. viii–ix.

27. Quoted in Forgie, pp. 180–81.

28. Lincoln, *The Collected Works*, vol. 2, p. 461. Subsequent citations are given parenthetically in the text.

29. Fehrenbacher, *Prelude to Greatness*, pp. 70–95. Wald analyzes at length Lincoln's rhetoric of historical inevitability, pp. 47–73.

30. Lincoln's marriage to Mary Todd, who was both from a southern slave-owning family and a fervent supporter of abolitionism, presented him with similar challenges in his private life, which is perhaps relevant to this linkage of the domestic and the national.

31. Forgie, esp. chap. 7.

32. Forgie, p. 262.

33. Quoted in Forgie, p. 274.

34. Quoted in Forgie, p. 265, emphasis added; and Wald, pp. 47–73.

35. Douglass, "Fighting the Rebels with One Hand," p. 476. Subsequent references are given parenthetically in the text.

36. Halttunen, "Gothic Imagination and Social Reform." Halttunen sees Stowe's final use of Gothic convention as important to the understanding of the novel as a whole and ties it to Stowe's agenda of social reform (as I do in Chapter 4). She emphasizes, however, a psychohistorical explanation of Stowe's Gothicism, finding in it traces of the anxieties produced by Stowe's father's staunch Calvinism.

37. In her superb biography of Stowe, Hedrick makes a similar point, arguing that this practice of exposing private slave/master relationships "broke down the ideological barriers between the public and the private sphere, a revolutionary

244 Notes to Pages 115–122

act that had the potential to free white women as well as male and female slaves" (p. 218).

38. Brodhead, "Sparing the Rod."

39. Fisher, *Hard Facts*, p. 104.

40. See, for example, Wright, *Moralism and the Model Home*, p. 12.

41. The juxtaposition of Christian rhetoric and house ownership is central to Walter Benn Michaels's and Gillian Brown's readings of the novel. Michaels is interested in the way antebellum literature supplements emerging property relations by establishing a closer and more secure relationship between personhood and property. The promise of a "clear title to mansions in the sky" therefore compensates for a legal reality in which slaves are denied personhood through a denial of property rights (see his "Romance and Real Estate," in *The Gold Standard*, esp. pp. 101–6). Brown argues in similar terms that such passages offer an alternative to possessive individualism, a kind of "sentimental property" not hinged on desire and the arbitrary forces of the marketplace (in *Domestic Individualism*, chap. 1 and 2).

42. Friedman, *A History of American Law*, pp. 226–27.

43. Goodell, *The American Slave Code in Theory and Practice*, p. 164.

44. Stowe, *A Key to Uncle Tom's Cabin*, p. 5.

45. Garrison, "The American Union."

46. Henry, "Angelina Grimké's Rhetoric of Exposure," pp. 336–37.

47. Stowe, *Lady Byron Vindicated*, p. 327, and Stowe to Sarah Parton, quoted in Leach, p. 58.

48. Of course, Byron owed his success, to a large extent, to the romantic image of his outrageous private life; but the image of the romantic hero was clearly regulated by its own moral economy, an economy that relied on the suppression of information like his incestuous love affair.

49. Leslie, *Miss Leslie's Behavior Book*, p. 207.

50. Quoted in Hedrick, p. 369.

51. Quoted in Leach, p. 40.

52. See Hardesty, *Women Called to Witness*, pp. 40–51.

53. Mary Putnam Jacobi, as quoted in Leach, p. 40. Jacobi made her comment in a lecture delivered to the New York City Positivist Society, not in an Evangelical context, but her insistence on the exposure of sin, her opposition to the Calvinist notion of bearing sin with patience in lieu of immediate and active repentance, and her attack on Catholicism all express the sentiments of Evangelical reform accurately and suggest the extent to which even the more radical brands of feminism, like Jacobi's, were influenced by Evangelicalism.

54. If the individual conscience was to be thrown open, so was the individual home. In one of the earliest examples, dating from the 1820s and the 1830s, Evangelical Bible societies (administered by men but run mostly by women) took it on themselves to counter the threat to Christian morals induced by the growing privacy of the home in two ways: they distributed Bibles to households, thus ensuring that their message crossed the threshold into the home; and they physically entered households to inspect whether they contained a family Bible. Such societies, according to Mary Ryan, signaled "the emergence of a new sector of social life, intermediary between the household and the corporate institutions of church and town meetings," which were "poised precariously on the fragile axis between public and private life" (p. 53). Bible societies, that is, helped shape a realm of action that was based on the growing tension between the public and the private, a realm of action in which women could participate in the name of Christianity and antebellum ideals of "moral" womanhood. From

the 1840s on, such religious associations made increasingly bold attempts to penetrate the family under the cover of religious morality. The established reaction to these societies, Ryan shows, was a mixture of praise and tremendous anxiety induced by their intrusive tactics.

55. Pleck, pp. 49–66.

56. Both are quoted in Pleck, pp. 52–53.

57. Quoted in Ryan, p. 119.

58. Quoted in Ryan, p. 120.

59. Leach, pp. 38–63.

60. Leach, pp. 40–43.

61. Showalter, "Family Secrets and Domestic Subversion," p. 113.

62. Dimock, "Criminal Law, Female Virtue, and the Rise of Liberalism."

63. Pleck, pp. 3–66.

64. Dimock, p. 217.

65. The reviews for *Ruth Hall* are quoted and discussed in Joyce W. Warren's introduction to *Ruth Hall and Other Writing*, pp. ix–xvii.

66. For a discussion of the Parker controversy, see Hedrick, pp. 225–30. The connection between *Dred* and that controversy is also made by Hedrick; see esp. p. 261.

67. Leach, p. 58.

68. See Berlant, "The Female Woman," pp. 265–66.

69. In a letter to Lord Derman, quoted in the introduction to *House and Home Papers* (New York: AMS Press, 1967), p. vii, emphasis added.

70. Henry, pp. 342–43.

71. Henry, pp. 349–50.

72. Wendy Brown, "Wounded Attachments," p. 215.

73. Reynolds, *Beneath the American Renaissance*, p. 79.

74. See Aries, *Centuries of Childhood*.

75. Hardesty, pp. 52–69; the quotation is on p. 65.

76. Douglass, "The Heroic Slave," pp. 174–75. Subsequent references are given parenthetically in the text. All emphases are in the original.

77. Melville, "Bartleby, the Scrivener," p. 635.

78. Yarborough, "Race, Violence, and Manhood"; Stepto, "Sharing the Thunder."

79. Sale, "To Make the Past Useful."

80. I borrow this phrase from Philip Fisher, who uses it in the context of his reading of Henry James's *The Bostonians*; see "Appearing and Disappearing in Public."

81. Gates, *Figures in Black*, p. 102.

82. Stepto, "Storytelling in Early Afro-American Fiction."

83. Andrews, "The Novelization of Voice in Early African American Narrative," p. 24.

84. Baker, *The Journey Back*, pp. 38–39.

85. Baker, p. 39.

86. Phillips, *On Kissing, Tickling, and Being Bored*, p. 65.

87. Gates, pp. 107–8.

88. Yarborough, p. 182.

89. Andrews, p. 26.

90. Goldsby reads *Incidents in the Life of a Slave Girl* in terms similar to my reading of "The Heroic Slave," emphasizing Jacobs's choice of silence when faced with the demands of the abolitionists (Jacobs wrote in a letter to Amy Post: "I had determined to let others think of me as they pleased but my lips should be sealed

and no one had the right to question me for this reason when I first came North I avoided Antilsavery people as much as possible because I felt that I could not be honest and tell the whole truth" [quoted on pp. 17–18]), and her choice of writing and fictionalization over speaking and an authenticity of presence.

Burgett's fascinating reading of *Incidents* in relation to liberalism's treatment of obscenity interprets the "loophole of retreat" as part of a series of ellipses in the text that signal not Jacobs's success in securing a private reprieve but her complicity with a liberal/sentimental culture that conjoins sexuality with private subjectivity. While I find much of his reading compelling, I would claim that there are different *kinds* of ellipses in *Incidents*. Some, especially in the first chapters, indeed reproduce the sentimental "open secret" of sexuality. But others, like her experience of being in the garrett, capture a different kind of silence, one that cannot easily be decoded or narrativized, and that does not necessarily have to do with sexuality. See *Sentimental Bodies*.

91. Patricia Williams, *The Alchemy of Race and Rights*, pp. 148–64.

92. Peggy C. Davis, "Neglected Stories and the Lawfulness of Roe v. Wade," p. 309.

Chapter 4

1. Ware, *Home Life*, 15–17; Auden, "The Cave of Making," in *About the House*, p. 8.

2. Hawthorne, "The Custom House," p. 149.

3. Hawthorne, *The House of the Seven Gables*, p. 351. All subsequent references are given in parentheses in the text.

4. Michaels, *The Gold Standard*, Thomas, *Cross-examinations of Law and Literature*, pp. 45–90; Gillian Brown, *Domestic Individualism*, pp. 63–95, and idem, "Hawthorne, Inheritance, and Women's Property."

5. Thomas, *Cross-examinations of Law and Literature*, pp. 47–50; Horwitz, *The Transformation of American Law, 1780–1860*; Friedman, pp. 230–45; Wood, *The Radicalism of the American Revolution*, pp. 269–70.

6. Michaels, p. 92.

7. Thomas, "The Construction of Privacy in and Around *The Bostonians*." A contrasting view of the relationship between the right of property and the right to privacy is offered by Michaels in "The Contracted Heart" (pp. 501–2), where he argues that in the beginning the right to privacy constituted, in effect, an amplification of property rights rather than a departure from them. But Michaels himself concedes in a footnote that "at least one branch of privacy law . . . has developed virtually without reference to property rights" (p. 526 n.13) and hence that privacy and property are not fully imbricated.

8. In Barthes's characterization; see *Mythologies*, p. 138.

9. D. A. Miller, *The Novel and the Police*; Brodhead, "Sparing the Rod."

10. In Glendon, *Rights Talk*, p. 56.

11. Glendon, p. 60; and see pp. 47–75. For a description of the development of the legal right to privacy in the twentieth century, see Tribe's detailed chapter entitled "Rights to Privacy and Personhood," in *American Constitutional Law*, pp. 886–990; and Richards, "The Jurisprudence of Privacy as a Constitutional Right."

12. Tribe, p. 889.

13. For a summary of these discussions, see Rule et al., *The Politics of Privacy*; Schoeman's introduction to *Philosophical Dimensions of Privacy*; and Young's introductory essay in *Privacy*.

14. Murphy, "Social Distance and the Veil," esp. p. 51.

15. Habermas, p. 11.

16. Flaherty, p. 14.

17. Quoted in Wood, *The Radicalism of the American Revolution*, p. 59. See also Flaherty, chaps. 2, 5, and 6. Flaherty claims that Puritans in fact enjoyed more privacy than is commonly assumed. He concedes, though, that their conception of the meaning of privacy and their opportunities for privacy were necessarily different from ours. Compare with Demos. A combination of factors in the Puritan household, Demos argues, leads one to ask whether privacy is a meaningful term in that society (p. 47).

18. Hawthorne, "The Minister's Black Veil," p. 378. Subsequent page numbers are given in parentheses in the text.

19. I borrow the term "hermeneutic desire" from J. Hillis Miller, "Theory—Example—Reading—History," p. 46. This essay and its accompanying response, "The Minister's Black Veil," provided the platform for a controversy between J. Hillis Miller and D. A. Miller and between the two schools of criticism that they represented. At issue were the contents of the space appropriated by the eponymous minister through the act of donning a veil, the contents of the psychic space he chose to shield from intrusion. J. Hillis Miller uses "The Minister's Black Veil" to explicate a relationship between language and history: since the veil as a sign refuses to be determined, he argues, language and history can never be happily reconciled; since all a reader could ever encounter behind the sign of the veil is another sign, every attempt to fill in the historical contents of the story is, at best, falsified. To this deconstructionist argument D. A. Miller responded with a new historicist one. On the contrary, he claims, "The Minister's Black Veil" fully resonates with historical meaning. As we have learned from Foucault and others "how seamlessly our culture conjoins subjectivity, secrecy and sexuality," the veil cannot but be read in primary reference to the historically specific categories of patriarchal sexual repression and oppression. Each regarded the other as dangerously ontologizing the story, reducing it to a preformed, ahistorical theory.

What I would like to ask, however, is what kind of historical meaning we might read in fiction if we change the question we pose from an ontological to a spatial-epistemological one. My interest is in historicizing the borders that writers inscribe to define the spaces of individual privacy, rather than in attempting to decipher the elusive contents of these spaces. In that sense, it is the history of space itself that I argue is important to a historical reading of fiction.

20. Flaherty, pp. 35, 51–58. See also Foley, *The American House*, for detailed plans of houses in sixteenth to twentieth-century America; and Clark, "Domestic Architecture as an Index to Social History."

21. Blackstone, 4 Commentaries on the Laws of England *223.

22. Otis and Adams are quoted in Long, *The Intruders*, p. 24.

23. See Justice Douglas's famous delivery of the opinion of the Court in *Griswold v. Connecticut*, 381 U.S. 479 (1965).

24. Glendon, p. 48.

25. Habermas, pp. 10–11.

26. Flaherty, pp. 219–32.

27. Foucault, *Power/Knowledge*, p. 153.

28. The growth of the census is a good example of that. Seipp, in *The Right of Privacy in American History*, shows in detail how the census, in the course of the nineteenth century, developed from a means of providing data for congressional apportionment to a multipurpose tool for providing data for federal

government use and for business interests. Other historians show that, despite the census's becoming confidential in 1840, the anxiety over its intrusiveness did not lessen. James A. Garfield stated in 1870, for instance, that "the citizen is not adequately protected from the danger, or rather the apprehension, that his private affairs, the secrets of his family and his business, will be disclosed to his neighbors ... [or be] made the quarry of bookmaker and pamphleteers" (quoted in "The Right to Privacy in Nineteenth Century America," p. 1905).

29. These examples are drawn from Welsh, *George Eliot and Blackmail*, esp. chap. 3 and pp. 52–72. Habermas bases the definition of what he calls the "critical" civil sphere precisely on this tension between the growth of a secluded private sphere and the growing interest in invading it: "Because, on the one hand, the society now confronting the state clearly separated a private domain from public authority and because, on the other hand, it turned the reproduction of life into something transcending the confines of private domestic authority and becoming a subject of public interest, that zone of continuous administrative contact became 'critical' also in the sense that it provoked the critical judgement of a public making use of its reason" (p. 24).

30. Spacks, *Gossip*, pp. 28, 145.

31. Bloustein, "Privacy as an Aspect of Human Dignity," pp. 172–73.

32. Glendon, p. 49. The anxiety over the potential aggressiveness of this new technology was not limited to the United States. In 1899 in Germany, photographers burst into Bismarck's death chamber to obtain pictures of his corpse, to the great distress of his family. This led to one of the first discussions of the right to privacy (Glendon, p. 50). This real-life incident provides an interesting analogy to the fictitious scene in Hawthorne's *The House of the Seven Gables* in which the daguerreotypist finds the judge's corpse, an important scene for our later discussion.

33. White, *Tort Law in America.*

34. *State v. Armfield*, 9 N.C. (2 Hawks) 246, 247 (1822); *Wien v. Simpson*, 2 Phila. 158, 158–59 (Pa. Dist. Ct. 1857); *Hobbs v. Geis*, 13 Serg. & Rawl. 417, 418–19 (Pa. 1826); *Ilsley v. Nichols*, 29 Mass. (12 Pick.) 270, 277 (1832); *Oystead v. Shed*, 13 Mass. 520 (1816).

35. See, for example, Zimmerman, "Requiem for a Heavyweight." For an early case in American law that established that truth is no justification for libel, see, for example, *Commonwealth v. Blanding*, 20 Mass. (3 Pick.) 304, 312 (1826). The court ruled that "no state of society would be more deplorable than that which would admit an indiscriminate right in every citizen to arraign the conduct of every other, before the public, in newspapers, handbills or other mode of publication, not only for crimes, but for faults, foibles, deformities of mind or person, even admitting all such allegations to be true."

36. For example, *State v. Brunham*, 9 N.H. 34, 42 (1837); *Smith v. State*, 32 Tex. 594, 597–98 (1870); *State v. Bienvenu*, 36 La. Ann. 378, 382 (1884). Additional cases are cited in "The Right to Privacy in Nineteenth Century America," pp. 1908–9. The growing awareness of the role of court proceedings in violations of privacy resulted also in a new justification for excluding spousal testimony, to preserve "the sacred privacy of domestic life." (*Johnson v. State*, 63 Nuss, 313, 317 [1885], for example).

37. *McCuen v. Ludlum*, 17 N.J.L. 12 (1839). See also *Sharpe v. Stephenson*, 34 N.C. (12 Ired.) 348, 350 (1851), which adds that specific time and place are material in slander accusations, and that when the words charged are "general" they cannot be slanderous.

38. *Hoyt v. MacKenzie and Others*, 49 Am. Dec.178 (1848). This and the following court case are described in detail in Ernst and Schwartz, *Privacy*, pp. 24–43.

39. Ernst and Schwartz, p. 26.

40. *James Woolsey v. Owen B. Judd*, 4 Duer 379 (1855).

41. Tribe, p. 893.

42. Prosser, "Privacy [a Legal Analysis]," p. 104.

43. Warren and Brandeis, p. 76. All subsequent quotations from this article are given parenthetically in the text.

44. For other examples of the use of architectural terminology to describe the characters in the novel, see Chandler, *Dwelling in the Text*, p. 75; and Dahl, "The Architecture of Society and the Architecture of the Soul."

45. Gray discusses this anthropomorphism in more detail in "Hawthorne."

46. Hutner, *Secrets and Sympathy*, p. 6.

47. Pfister, p. 151.

48. Herbert, p. xvi.

49. Pfister, pp. 144–61; Herbert, pp. 93–97; Leverenz, *Manhood in the American Renaisssance.*

50. Spacks, p. 10.

51. Arac, *Commissioned Spirits.* The connection between Dickens and Hawthorne's "Sight from a Steeple" is on pp. 111–13. Dickens is quoted on p. 111, and Hawthorne on p. 112.

52. One of Holgrave's conversations with Phoebe, the angelic protector of the domestic sphere, is especially telling. In response to his inquisitive remarks about Clifford, Phoebe replies, "I cannot see his thoughts!—How should I? . . . I feel it to be not quite right to look closely into his moods. . . . I venture to peep in, just as far the light reaches, but no farther. It is holy ground where the shadow falls!" Holgrave, in turn, admits to her, "Had I your opportunities, no scruples would prevent me from fathoming Clifford to the full depth of my plummet-line!" (p. 505).

53. Quoted in Gray, p. 95.

54. See, for example, Caserio, "Supreme Court Discourse vs. Homosexual Fiction."

55. Quoted in Glendon, p. 55.

Chapter 5

1. Cooper, *Notions of the Americans*, p. 143; Emerson's quotation is from his journals, quoted by Neufeldt, *The House of Emerson*, p. 141.

2. Greeley's editorial is included in Harding, *The Days of Henry Thoreau*, p. 239.

3. Harding, *The Days of Henry Thoreau*, p. 241.

4. Harding, *The Days of Henry Thoreau*, p. 240.

5. This *Boston Atlas* review is quoted in Harding, *The Days of Henry Thoreau*, p. 335.

6. Alcott, "Thoreau," in *Concord Days*, included in Harding, ed., *Thoreau as Seen by His Contemporaries*, p. 42.

7. Arendt, *The Human Condition*, p. 39; Habermas, pp. 160, 162; Sennett, *The Fall of Public Man*, chap. 1.

8. Schudson shows the limited scope of the "authentic public sphere" in the context of the United States in "Was There Ever a Public Sphere?"

9. Emerson, "Self Reliance," p. 132.

10. Kimmel, *Manhood in America*, pp. 52, 58.

11. Mumford, *The City in History*, pp. 496–97.

12. See Baym's famous formulation in "Melodramas of Beset Manhood."

13. The summary that follows is based primarily on Buell, "Henry Thoreau Enters the American Canon," and Baym, "Early Histories of American Literature."

14. Quoted in Wortham, "Bryant and the Fireside Poets," p. 288.

15. Quoted in Wortham, p. 288.

16. Quoted in Baym, "Early Histories of American Literature," pp. 470–71.

17. Buell, pp. 26–27.

18. See Marsh's analysis of the solidification of the figure of the suburban, domesticated middle-class man in "Suburban Men and Masculine Domesticity, 1870–1915," esp. pp. 112–13.

19. Quoted in Emerson's obituary of Thoreau, "Thoreau," p. 240.

20. See esp. Abelove, from whom I borrow the phrase "grand narrative of connubiality" ("From Thoreau to Queer Politics").

21. Emerson, "Thoreau," p. 243.

22. Frank, *Our America*, p. 152.

23. Lukács, *The Theory of the Novel*.

24. Matthiessen, *American Renaissance*, pp. 626–56; Lewis, *The American Adam*, pp. 20–27; Porte, *Emerson and Thoreau*, pp. 184–90. Alongside these "escape" narratives, a parallel critical stance has been developed by such critics as Sherman Paul, Frederick Garber, and, more recently, H. Daniel Peck. These critics recognize the centrality of "home-making" in Thoreau's writing but attribute it less to the rise of the middle-class private sphere and more to a symbolic structure removed from social history. Thus, for Paul (pp. 318–23), Thoreau's building of the cabin is part of a greater "fable of renewal," the shedding in nature of the burdens of society. Garber (*Thoreau's Redemptive Imagination*, esp. pp. 1–65) reads Thoreau's desire for an enclosed private sphere as pertaining to the grand European romantic traditions of Rousseau and Hölderlin. The close relationship that he detects between the self and the home in Thoreau's thought is purely metaphorical, an expression of a desire to locate one's place in the world and thus "redeem" one's consciousness. Similarly, Daniel Peck (*Thoreau's Morning Work*, esp. pp. 117–58) reads Thoreau's interest in homemaking as part of his larger activity of "worlding," of philosophically familiarizing the world through the metaphor of dwelling. Garber and Peck, especially, help us realize how important the domestic metaphor was not only to Thoreau but also to the romantic tradition of which he is part; but their projects do not include an interest in how this metaphorical structure relates to social transformations particular to Thoreau's milieu: the rise of the middle class; the reconfiguration of gender definitions; and the proliferation of meanings with which the concept of the home was increasingly burdened.

25. Fisher, "Democratic Social Space."

26. Thoreau, *Walden*, pp. 575, 416. Subsequent references are given parenthetically in the text.

27. Fetterley, *The Resisting Reader*, p. viii; Goldman, "Feminism, Deconstruction and the Universal." For an example of the "feminization" of Thoreau, see Anderson, *The House Undivided*, p. 79. Anderson describes Thoreau, for example, as a "midwife" and as a "Diana."

28. Quoted and discussed in Bercovitch, *The Rites of Assent*, p. 311.

29. Sedgwick, *Between Men*, pp. 14–15.

30. Arendt, p. 30.

31. Nelson, "Thoreau, Manhood, and Race."

32. See, for example, Chodorow, "Being and Doing"; Keller, *From a Broken Web*; Butler, "Melancholy Gender/Refused Identification."

33. Benhabib, "The Generalized and the Concrete Other," p. 84.

34. My connection between Thoreau's spatial designs and the rise of the American suburb is inspired by Fisher, "Democratic Social Space." He traces the genealogy of the modern American landscape, beginning with Jefferson's map for the Western Territories, to argue that a particular spatial layout is constitutive of American identity. This layout—characterized by atomism, modularity, intelligibility (in the sense of conformity or transparency), and unity (in the sense that nothing exists outside of, or in opposition to, its grid)—is exemplified by *Walden* as well as by the modern suburb. I hope to supplement Fisher's discussion by pointing out, first, that Thoreau's writing indeed coextended with the early appearance of the middle-class suburb and, second, and more important, by highlighting the set of disavowals that combine to form this spatial grid.

35. For a discussion of the popularization of behavior manuals, see Halttunen, *Confidence Men and Painted Women*, pp. 1–55; and Kasson, *Rudeness and Civility*.

36. For a discussion of the pattern-book phenomenon, see, for example, Handlin, esp. pp. 3–88; and Wright, *Building the Dream*, pp. 73–113.

37. Matthiessen, pp. 133–75; Theodore Brown, "Thoreau's Prophetic Architectural Program"; Masteller and Carwile, "Rural Architecture in Andrew Jackson Downing and Henry David Thoreau," p. 508 (this last article stresses more Thoreau's disagreements with writers like Downing, but it still provides numerous connections between Thoreau's thinking and the domestic architectural discourse of his time); Tichi, "Domesticity on Walden Pond." While I agree with Tichi's underlying thesis that Thoreau should be read in relation to middle-class discourses of home economy, I wish to highlight in this chapter the difference between his texts and the texts of domestic writers like Beecher.

38. Quoted in Harding, *Thoreau as Seen by His Contemporaries*, p. 64.

39. Revising an early misconception that placed the rise of the suburbs in the post–Civil War era, two historical studies provide the basis for much of my discussion of the suburbs: Binford, *The First Suburbs*; and Jackson, *Crabgrass Frontier.*

40. Willis, "The Highland Terrace above West Point," p. 105.

41. Quoted in Jackson, p. 64.

42. Quoted in Jackson, p. 38.

43. Leo Marx, *The Machine in the Garden*, pp. 113–14.

44. Quoted in Jackson, p. 38.

45. A biographical anecdote shows how aware Thoreau was of the transformation of distances, which allowed the suburbs to flourish. In the fall of 1849, he wanted to use the library at Harvard College but, to his dismay, was told that library privileges were granted only to persons who lived within ten miles of the college. Thoreau immediately answered that the railroad had destroyed older calculations of distances and that Concord was now more accessible to Harvard than parts of Cambridge had been a few years before. He gained library privileges soon after (see Harding, *The Days of Henry Thoreau*, p. 267).

46. Gross, "Culture and Cultivation," p. 525.

47. Both quoted in Ryan, p. 147, emphasis added.

48. All three are quoted in Jackson, pp. 50, 62.

49. Clark, *The American Family Home*, pp. vi-xvi.

50. Ryan, pp. 179–85.

51. Downing, *The Architecture of Country Houses*, p. vi.

52. Mills, *White Collar*, p. 32.

53. Raymond Williams, p. 242.

54. Cabot, p. 431.

55. Paul, p. 12.

56. Quotation in Fowler, p. iii. See also Cleaveland, Backus, and Backus, *Village and Farm Cottages*.

57. Ranlett, intro.

58. See discussion on Cleaveland in Wright, *Building the Dream*, p. 84.

59. Willis, p. 110.

60. Jackson, p. 76.

61. Willis, p. 107.

62. Quoted in Hayden, *The Grand Domestic Revolution*, p. 36.

63. Lefebvre, pp. 274–75.

64. Quoted in Hayden, p. 36.

65. Quoted in Harding, *The Days of Henry Thoreau*, p. 125.

66. Ranlett, 37 (emphasis added).

67. Fowler, p. 8.

68. "Domestic Architecture," p. 60.

69. Alcott's immensely popular book was reprinted in many editions from the 1830s to the 1870s. This quotation is from the first edition: *The House I Live In: For the Use of Families and Schools*, pp. 23–24, 33.

70. Quoted in Adams, p. 265.

71. Downing, *The Architecture of Country Houses*, pp. 19, 378.

72. Anderson, pp. 76–78.

73. Downing, *The Architecture of Country Houses*, p. 19.

74. "Domestic Architecture," p. 58.

75. Karl Marx, "Alienated Labor," pp. 292–93.

76. Hayden; Marsh, "From Separation to Togetherness."

77. See, for example, Harding, "Thoreau's Homosexuality."

78. In this context, it is interesting that Thoreau's friend and follower Daniel Ricketson imitated Thoreau's experiment by building a shanty, filling it with books, and decorating its walls with his favorite quotations. As a second step, he built a house nearby for his wife and four children. Similarly, Emerson attempted to build a cabin near his house for his private intellectual pursuits (Harding, *The Days of Henry Thoreau*, p. 343).

79. Ryan, p. 179.

80. Jay, *America the Scrivener*, pp. 18–19.

81. Cavell, "Being Odd, Getting Even," p. 304.

82. Thoreau, "A Plea for John Brown," p. 144. Further references are given parenthetically in the text.

Chapter 6

1. Thoreau, *A Week on the Concord and Merrimack Rivers*, p. 220 (subsequent references are given parenthetically in the text); Auden, p. 4.

2. Fried, "Privacy [A Moral Analysis]," p. 211. See also Rachels, "Why Privacy Is Important," pp. 290–99. Another good example of this rhetoric is provided by Thomas Krattenmaker, who sees intimacy as "mutual reciprocal relinquishments of the self." "Without a reserve of privacy," he writes, "we would have nothing to share and, hence, nothing to build upon in our human relationships" (quoted in Silver, " 'Two Different Sorts of Commerce,' " p. 43).

3. Sennett, pp. 9–10, and passim. The liberal view of the self as constituted first in privacy, I suggest, is problematized by antebellum romantic writers, first, because the act of staking private territory is shown to involve the shunning of

an intimacy that precedes it (mostly intimacy with women), and, second, because, as I hope to show, the bounded, private self is nonetheless imagined to include within it a space for merger and intimacy with the other.

4. For a discussion of True Womanhood and intimacy, see, for example, Cott, *The Bonds of Womanhood*; Smith-Rosenberg, *Disorderly Conduct*; and Hansen, "Rediscovering the Social." Hansen complicates the equating of womanhood with privacy by describing the intricate social networks in which antebellum women were active.

5. Leverenz, p. 34; Hawthorne, *The Marble Faun*, p. 1089. Studies of the construction of unaffective manhood in antebellum America include, besides Leverenz, Herbert and Kimmel, *Manhood in America*. Lystra (*Searching the Heart*) describes heterosexual rituals of courtship as the only space for masculine expressivity.

6. Rotundo, *American Manhood*, pp. 75–91, and passim. See also Kimmel, "Masculinity as Homophobia."

7. Newfield, *The Emerson Effect*, pp. 91–109.

8. Emerson, "Self Reliance," p. 133.

9. See Baym, "Melodramas of Beset Manhood." American romanticism includes, of course, not only melodramas of boundedness but also romances of male bonding, typically between a white man and his racial other. As Wiegman proposes in "Fiedler and Sons," the romances of male bonding serve a specific purpose in American culture, that of casting both the racial other and the homosexual in the presymbolic, imaginary realm, thus serving the power structure of heterosexual white supremacy. I am here concerned with intimacy between white men of the same class, and hence with male bonding within, and despite, the laws of the symbolic.

10. Both the "feminized" and the "queer" Thoreau were born in the 1990s, the first, for example, in Anderson, p. 79; the second, most successfully in Abelove, from whom the phrase "grand narrative of connubiality" is borrowed, and Morris Kaplan, *Democratic Citizenship and the Politics of Desire*, pp. 177-205. Both readings are, in my opinion, somewhat overdetermined, eager to place Thoreau either fully within or fully outside heterosexual domesticity and antebellum bourgeois culture. Kaplan's otherwise fascinating reading of Thoreau, for instance, continuously insists on his "adversary stance toward prevalent systems of belief and personal position outside dominant social institutions" (p. 195). My problem with such a reading is that it fails to acknowledge the degree to which Thoreau still remains squarely within the normative-gender regime (most clearly, in his homophobia) even as he revises it in radical ways. In that sense, Warner's reading in "*Walden*'s Erotic Economy" is more satisfying (and more consistent with queering as a critical act) in that it refuses to "normalize [Thoreau's position] in order to validate it as 'critique,' still less as redemption" (p. 169).

11. Vogler, "Sex and Talk," p. 329. I borrow "depersonalizing intimacy" from Vogler, although what she means by it—an intimacy based on self-forgetfulness and erasure of boundaries—is, in many ways, different from the logic of intimacy I trace in American romanticism. In both cases, though, "depersonalizing intimacy" is imagined in opposition to the normative confessional intimacy in middle-class, heterosexual culture.

12. Thoreau, "The Landlord" (1843), p. 187. Subsequent references are given parenthetically in the text.

13. Benhabib, "The Generalized and the Concrete Other," pp. 83–86, and Hawthorne, "The Old Manse," p. 1147.

14. Benhabib, "The Generalized and the Concrete Other," p. 89.

15. Definition of "intimate" taken from the *Oxford English Dictionary*. On the connection between intimacy and an economy of signs, see Berlant, "Intimacy," p. 281.

16. Thoreau, *Journals*, 4: 176–77. Subsequent references are given parenthetically in the text.

17. Yacovone, "Abolitionists and the 'Language of Fraternal Love,' " pp. 87–88.

18. Warner, "*Walden*'s Erotic-Economy," pp. 171–72. Interestingly, while this passage sheds light on Thoreau's horror of being consumed by the intimate male other, his imagery soon reverses itself: instead of being swallowed by the reformer, he imagines the latter as intending to "dive into Henry's inmost depths." This reciprocity, where the reformer both swallows and penetrates "Henry," is the monstrous double of the idea of equal commerce in male intimacy that Thoreau constructs elsewhere.

19. Harding, *The Days of Henry Thoreau*, pp. 77–79.

20. Silver points out that older meanings of "commerce" include conversation, communication, and association, as well as trade.

21. Crain, *American Sympathy*, p. 179.

22. Quoted in Crain, p. 202.

23. Nelson, *National Manhood*, pp. ix–x.

24. On this point I depart from the work of Newfield, Ellison, and Nelson, whose keen analyses of intimacy between men in antebellum romanticism have been immensely useful. All three insist on the rigidly and profoundly hierarchical nature of white male bonding, a hierarchy that hides behind the façade of the democratic rhetoric of equality. I find that for Thoreau equality, far from a façade, is a necessary condition for male intimacy. As Morris Kaplan, too, proposes, for Thoreau "the self is not only expressive; it seeks to meet others on a higher ground than the daily grind of politics, to find them as neighbors and as friends, in ideals of mutuality and reciprocity. Thoreau calls for the founding of a new order in which equals meet and interact without sacrificing the integrity of their personal quests" (p. 194).

25. Ellison, "The Gender of Transparency," p. 585.

26. Quoted in Hixon, 59.

27. Crain, p. 152.

28. Cavell, *The Senses of Walden*, pp. 49–50, 54.

29. Winnicott, "The Capacity to Be Alone," pp. 31, 34.

30. On reification and de-essentialization in and by the capitalist marketplace in *Walden*, see Gilmore, *American Romanticism and the Marketplace*, pp. 35–51.

31. Johnson, *A World of Difference*, pp. 49–56.

32. Melville, "Hawthorne and His Mosses," p. 1156. Subsequent references are given parenthetically in the text.

Afterword

1. Gurstein, *The Repeal of Reticence*, pp. 3–4.

2. Quoted in Kay, "Privacy and the Ethics of Literature," p. 48.

3. Rosen, *The Unwanted Gaze*, p. 197; Post quoted in Kay, p. 48.

4. Habermas, p. 49.

5. Butler, *The Psychic Life of Power*, p. 29.

6. Quoted in Salecl, p. 7.

Bibliography

Abelove, Henry. "From Thoreau to Queer Politics." *Yale Journal of Criticism* 6.2 (1993): 17–27.

Adams, Timothy Dow. "Architectural Imagery in Melville's Short Fiction." *American Transcendental Quarterly* 44 (1979): 265–77.

Alcott, William. *The House I Live In: For the Use of Families and Schools.* Boston: Lilly, Wait, Coman and Holden, 1834.

Allen, Anita L. *Uneasy Access: Privacy for Women in a Free Society.* Totowa, N.J.: Rowman and Littlefield, 1988.

Anderson, Douglas. *The House Undivided: Domesticity and Community in American Literature.* Cambridge: Cambridge University Press, 1990.

Andrews, William L. "The Novelization of Voice in Early African American Narrative." *PMLA* 105.1 (1990): 23–34.

Arac, Jonathan. *Commissioned Spirits: The Shaping of Social Motion in Dickens, Carlyle, Melville and Hawthorne.* New Brunswick, N.J.: Rutgers University Press, 1979.

"Architecture in the United States." *North American Review* 58 (1844): 436–73.

Ardener, Shirley. *Women and Space: Ground Rules and Social Maps.* Oxford: Berg, 1993.

Arendt, Hannah. *The Human Condition.* Chicago: University of Chicago Press, 1958.

Aries, Philippe. *Centuries of Childhood: A Social History of Family.* Translated by Robert Buldok. New York: Knopf, 1962.

Arnot, David Henry. *Gothic Architecture Applied to Modern Residences.* New York: Appleton, 1849.

Arvin, Newton. *Herman Melville.* New York: William Sloane Associates, 1950.

Auden, W. H. *About the House.* New York: Random House, 1965.

Bachelard, Gaston. *The Poetics of Space.* Translated by Maria Jolas. Boston: Beacon, 1969.

Baker, Houston A., Jr. *The Journey Back: Issues in Black Literature and Criticism.* Chicago: University of Chicago Press, 1980.

Barker, Francis. *The Tremulous Private Body: Essays on Subjection.* London: Methuen, 1984.

Barthes, Roland. *Mythologies.* Translated by Annette Lavers. New York: Hill and Wang, 1972.

Baym, Nina. "Early Histories of American Literature: A Chapter in the Institution of New England." *American Literary History* 1 (1989): 459–88.

————. "Melodramas of Beset Manhood: How Theories of American Fiction Exclude Women Authors." In *The New Feminist Criticism: Essays on Women, Literature and Theory*, edited by Elaine Showalter, pp. 63–80. New York: Pantheon, 1985.

Beecher, Catharine. *Treatise on Domestic Economy*. Boston: T. H. Webb, 1842.

————, and Harriet Beecher Stowe. *American Woman's Home*. Hartford, Conn.: Stowe-Day Foundation, 1987.

Benhabib, Seyla. "The Generalized and the Concrete Other: The Kohlberg-Gilligan Controversy and Feminist Theory." In *Feminism as Critique*, edited by Seyla Benhabib and Drucilla Cornell, pp. 77–95. Minneapolis: University of Minnesota Press, 1987.

————. "Models of Public Space: Hannah Arendt, the Liberal Tradition, and Jurgen Habermas." In *Feminism, the Public, and the Private*, edited by Joan Landes, pp. 65–99. Oxford: Oxford University Press, 1998.

Benjamin, Walter. "Paris, Capital of the Nineteenth Century." In *Reflections*, edited by Peter Demetz, pp. 146–62. New York: Schocken, 1978.

Bercovitch, Sacvan. *The Rites of Assent: Transformations in the Symbolic Construction of America*. New York: Routledge, 1993.

Berlant, Lauren. "The Female Woman: Fanny Fern and the Form of Sentiment." In *The Culture of Sentiment: Race, Gender, and Sentimentality in Nineteenth-century America*, edited by Shirley Samuels, pp. 265–82. New York: Oxford University Press, 1992.

————. "Intimacy: A Special Issue." *Critical Inquiry* 24.2 (1998): 281–88.

————. "Live Sex Acts (Parental Advisory: Explicit Material)." In *Feminism, the Public, and the Private*, edited by Joan Landes, pp. 277–301. Oxford: Oxford University Press, 1998.

————. "National Brands/National Body: Imitation of Life." In *The Phantom Public Sphere*, edited by Bruce Robbins, pp. 173–208. Minneapolis: University of Minnesota Press, 1993.

————. "The Subject of True Feeling: Pain, Privacy, and Politics." In *Cultural Pluralism, Identity Politics, and the Law*, edited by Austin Sarat and Thomas R. Kearns, pp. 49–84. Ann Arbor: University of Michigan Press, 1999.

Bernauer, James, and Michael Mahon. "The Ethics of Michel Foucault." In *The Cambridge Companion to Foucault*, edited by Gary Gutting, pp. 141–58. Cambridge: Cambridge University Press, 1994.

Bertolini, Vincent J. "Fireside Chastity: The Erotics of Sentimental Bachelorhood in the 1850s." *American Literature* 68.4 (1996): 707–38.

Bhabha, Homi K. *The Location of Culture*. New York: Routledge, 1994.

Binford, Henry. *The First Suburbs: Residential Communities on the Boston Periphery, 1815–1860*. Chicago: University of Chicago Press, 1984.

Blackmar, Frank W. *Kansas: A Cyclopedia of State History, Embracing Events, Institutions, Industries, Counties, Cities, Towns, Prominent Persons, etc.* Chicago: Standard Pub. Co., 1912.

Blackstone, Sir William. *Commentaries on the Laws of England*. Oxford: Printed at the Clarendon Press, 1765–69.

Bloustein, Edward J. "Privacy as an Aspect of Human Dignity." In *Philosophical Dimensions of Privacy*, edited by Ferdinand Schoeman, pp. 156–202. Cambridge: Cambridge University Press, 1984.

Blumin, Stuart. *The Emergence of the Middle Class: Social Experience in the American City, 1760–1900*. New York: Cambridge University Press, 1989.

Borges, Jorge Luis. *Other Inquisitions, 1937–1952*. Translated by Ruth L. C. Simms. Austin: University of Texas Press, 1964.

Brodhead, Richard. *The School of Hawthorne*. New York: Oxford University Press, 1986.

———. "Sparing the Rod: Discipline and Fiction in Antebellum America." *Representations* 21 (1988): 67–98.

Brooks, Van Wyck. *The World of Washington Irving*. New York: E. P. Dutton, 1944.

Brow, Milton W. *American Art to 1900: Painting, Sculpture, Architecture*. New York: Harry N. Abrams, 1977.

Brown, Gillian. *Domestic Individualism: Imagining Self in Nineteenth-century America*. Berkeley & Los Angeles: University of California Press, 1990.

———. "Hawthorne, Inheritance, and Women's Property." *Studies in the Novel* 23 (1991): 107–18.

Brown, Theodore M. "Thoreau's Prophetic Architectural Program." *New England Quarterly* 38 (1965): 3–20.

Brown, Wendy. "Wounded Attachments." In *The Identity in Question*, edited by John Rajchman, pp. 199–227. New York: Routledge, 1995.

Browne, Ray Broadus. *Melville's Drive to Humanism*. West Lafayette, Ind.: Purdue University Press, 1971.

Brueckner, Martin. "Bachelor Hall: Bachelor City." *Theory@buffalo.edu* 1.1 (1995): 169–86.

Buell, Laurence. "Henry Thoreau Enters the American Canon." In *New Essays on Walden*, edited by Robert F. Sayre, pp. 23–52. Cambridge: Cambridge University Press, 1992.

Burgett, Bruce. *Sentimental Bodies: Sex, Gender, and Citizenship in the Early Republic*. Princeton, N.J.: Princeton University Press, 1998.

Bushman, Richard L. *The Refinement of America: Persons, Houses, Cities*. New York: Vintage, 1993.

Butler, Judith. "Melancholy Gender/Refused Identification." In *Constructing Masculinity*, edited by Maurice Berger, Brian Wallis, and Simon Watson, pp. 21–36. New York: Routledge, 1995.

———. *The Psychic Life of Power: Theories in Subjection*. Stanford, Calif.: Stanford University Press, 1997.

Cabot, Elliot J. "House Building." *Atlantic Magazine* 10 (1862): 423–32.

Calhoun, Craig, ed. *Habermas and the Public Sphere*. Cambridge, Mass.: MIT Press, 1993.

Caserio, Robert. "Supreme Court Discourse vs. Homosexual Fiction." *South Atlantic Quarterly* 88.1 (1989): 267–99.

Cavell, Stanley. "Being Odd, Getting Even: Threats to Individuality." In *Reconstructing Individualism: Autonomy, Individuality, and the Self in Western Thought*, edited by Thomas C. Heller et al., pp. 278–312. Stanford, Calif.: Stanford University Press, 1986.

———. *The Senses of Walden*. San Francisco: North Point Press, 1981.

Certeau, Michel de. *The Practice of Everyday Life*. Translated by Steven Rendall. Berkeley & Los Angeles: University of California Press, 1984.

Chandler, Marilyn R. *Dwelling in the Text*. Berkeley & Los Angeles: University of California Press, 1991.

Charvat, William. *The Profession of Authorship in America, 1800–1870*. New York: Columbia University Press, 1968.

Chase, Karen, and Michael Levenson. *The Spectacle of Intimacy*. Princeton, N.J.: Princeton University Press, 2000.

Chatfield, E. Hale. "Levels of Meaning in Melville's 'I and My Chimney.' " *American Imago* 19 (1962): 166–67.

Chesnut, Mary Boykin Miller. *A Diary from Dixie*. New York: Appleton, 1905.

Chodorow, Nancy J. "Being and Doing: A Cross-cultural Examination of the Socialization of Males and Females." In *Feminism and Psychoanalytic Theory*, pp. 23–44. New Haven, Conn.: Yale University Press, 1989.

Clark, Clifford Edward. *The American Family Home*. Chapel Hill: University of North Carolina Press, 1986.

———. "Domestic Architecture as an Index to Social History: The Romantic Revival and the Cult of Domesticity in America, 1840–1870." *Journal of Interdisciplinary History* 7 (1976): 33–56.

Cleaveland, Henry William; William Backus; and Samuel D. Backus. *Village and Farm Cottages*. New York: D. Appleton, 1856.

Cooper, Clare. "The House as Symbol of the Self." In *Designing for Human Behavior*, edited by Jon Lang et al., pp. 130–46. Stroudsburg, Pa.: Dowden, Hutchinson, and Ross, 1974.

Cooper, James Fenimore. *Notions of the Americans: Picked Up by a Travelling Bachelor*. 1828. Reprint. New York: Ungar, 1963.

Cott, Nancy. *The Bonds of Womanhood: "Woman's Sphere" in New England, 1780–1835*. New Haven, Conn.: Yale University Press, 1977.

Crain, Caleb. *American Sympathy: Men, Friendship, and Literature in the New Nation*. New Haven, Conn.: Yale University Press, 2001.

Crevecoeur, J. Hector St. John. *Letters from an American Farmer*. 1782. Reprint. New York: Penguin, 1981.

Dahl, Curtis. "The Architecture of Society and the Architecture of the Soul: Hawthorne's *The House of the Seven Gables* and Melville's *Pierre*." *University of Mississippi Studies in English* 5 (1984–87): 1–22.

———. "Arrowhead and the Razeed Roof: An Architectural Speculation." *Melville Society Extracts* 53 (1983): 6.

Davidson, Cathy N., ed. *No More Separate Spheres: A Next Wave American Studies Reader*. Durham, N.C.: Duke University Press, 2002.

Davis, Alexander Jackson. *Rural Residences: Consisting of Designs, Original and Selected, for Cottages, Farm-Houses, Villas, and Village Churches, etc.* New York, 1837.

Davis, Merrell, and William Gilman, eds. *The Letters of Herman Melville*. New Haven, Conn.: Yale University Press, 1960.

Davis, Peggy Cooper. "Neglected Stories and the Lawfulness of Roe v. Wade." *Harvard Civil Rights–Civil Liberties Law Review* 28 (1993): 299–394.

Dean, Tim. "Hart Crane's Poetics of Privacy." *American Literary History* 8.1 (1996): 83–109.

Degler, Carl N. *At Odds: Women and the Family in America from the Revolution to the Present*. New York: Oxford University Press, 1980.

Demos, John. *The Little Commonwealth*. New York: Oxford University Press, 1970.

Dimock, Wai-chee. "Criminal Law, Female Virtue, and the Rise of Liberalism." *Yale Journal of Law & the Humanities* 4 (1992): 209–47.

———. *Empire for Liberty: Melville and the Poetics of Individualism*. Princeton, N.J.: Princeton University Press, 1989.

"Domestic Architecture." *New Englander* 9.33 (1851): 57–70.

Douglas, Ann. *The Feminization of American Culture*. New York: Knopf, 1977.

Douglass, Frederick. "Fighting the Rebels with One Hand: An Address Delivered in Philadelphia, Pennsylvania, on 14 January 1862." In *The Frederick Douglass Papers, Series One: Speeches, Debates, and Interviews*, edited by John W. Blassingame, vol. 3, pp. 473–88. New Haven, Conn.: Yale University Press, 1985.

———. "The Heroic Slave." In *Autographs for Freedom*, edited by Julia Griffiths, pp. 174–239. Cleveland, Ohio: John P. Jewett, 1853.

Downing, Andrew Jackson. *The Architecture of Country Houses.* New York: Appleton, 1850.

———. *Cottage Residences.* New York: John Wiley, 1842.

———. *A Treatise on the Theory and Practice of Landscape Gardening.* New York: Wiley and Putnam, 1841.

"The Education of Girls." *Ladies' Repository* 2.2 (1868): 139–41.

Elliot, Emory, et al., eds. *The Columbia Literary History of the United States.* New York: Columbia University Press, 1988.

Ellison, Julie. "The Gender of Transparency: Masculinity and the Conduct of Life." *American Literary History* 4.4 (1992): 584–606.

Emerson, Ralph Waldo. "Self Reliance." In *Essays: First Series.* 1841. Reprinted in *Selected Writings of Emerson,* edited by Donald McQuade, pp. 129–53. New York: Modern Library, 1981.

———. "Thoreau." *Atlantic Monthly* 10 (August 1862): 239–49.

Emery, Allan Moore. "The Political Significance of Melville's Chimney." *New England Quarterly* 55.2 (1982): 201–28.

"The End of Prudence." *The Lady's Book* 22 (May 1841): 216.

Ernst, Morris L., and Alan U. Schwartz. *Privacy: The Right to Be Let Alone.* New York: Macmillan, 1962.

Fehrenbacher, Don E. *Prelude to Greatness: Lincoln in the 1850s.* Stanford, Calif.: Stanford University Press, 1962.

Fern, Fanny. *Ruth Hall.* 1854. Reprint. In *Ruth Hall and Other Writings,* edited by Joyce W. Warren, pp. 1–211. New Brunswick, N.J.: Rutgers University Press, 1986.

Fetterley, Judith. *The Resisting Reader: A Feminist Approach to American Fiction.* Bloomington: Indiana University Press, 1978.

Field, M. *City Architecture; or, Designs for Dwelling Houses, Stores, Hotels, etc.* New York: Appleton, 1854.

Fisher, Philip. "Appearing and Disappearing in Public: Social Space in Late-Nineteenth-century Literature and Culture." In *Reconstructing American Literary History,* edited by Sacvan Bercovitch, pp. 155–88. Cambridge, Mass.: Harvard University Press, 1986.

———. "Democratic Social Space: Whitman, Melville, and the Promise of American Transparency." *Representations* 24 (1988): 50–101.

———. *Hard Facts: Setting and Form in the American Novel.* New York: Oxford University Press, 1987.

Flaherty, David H. *Privacy in Colonial New England.* Charlottesville: University Press of Virginia, 1972.

Foley, Mary Mix. *The American House.* New York: Harper and Row, 1980.

Forgie, George B. *Patricide in the House Divided: A Psychological Interpretation of Lincoln and His Age.* New York: Norton, 1979.

Foucault, Michel. *The History of Sexuality,* Vol. 1: *An Introduction.* Translated by Robert Hurley. New York: Vintage Books, 1980.

———. "Interview with Stephen Riggins." In *Ethics, Subjectivity and Truth,* edited by Paul Rabinow, pp. 121–34. New York: New Press, 1998.

———. *Power/Knowledge: Selected Interviews and Other Writings, 1972–1977.* Edited by Colin Gordon. New York: Pantheon, 1980.

Fowler, Orson. *A Home for All.* New York: Fowler and Wells, 1848.

Frank, Waldo. *Our America.* New York: Boni and Liveright, 1919.

Franklin, Jill. *The Gentleman's Country House and Its Plan, 1835–1914.* London: Routledge and Kegan Paul, 1981.

Franzen, Jonathan. *How to Be Alone*. New York: Farrar, Straus and Giroux, 2002.

Fraser, Nancy. "Rethinking the Public Sphere: A Contribution to the Critique of Actually Existing Democracy." In *Habermas and the Public Sphere*, edited by Craig Calhoun, pp. 109–42. Cambridge, Mass.: MIT Press, 1993.

Freud, Sigmund. "Resistance and Repression." In *Introductory Lectures, the Standard Edition of the Complete Psychological Works*, translated and edited by James Strachey, vol. 16, pp. 286–302. London: Hogarth Press, 1957.

———. "Symbolism in Dreams." In *The Standard Edition of the Complete Psychological Works*, translated and edited by James Strachey, vol. 15, pp. 149–69.

———. "The 'Uncanny.' " In *The Standard Edition of the Complete Psychological Works*, translated and edited by James Strachey, vol. 17, pp. 219–52.

———. "The Unconscious." In *The Standard Edition of the Complete Psychological Works*, translated and edited by James Strachey, vol. 14, pp. 166–204.

Fried, Charles. "Privacy [a Moral Analysis]." In *Philosophical Dimensions of Privacy: An Anthology*, edited by Ferdinand David Schoeman, pp. 203–22. Cambridge: Cambridge University Press, 1984.

Friedman, Lawrence M. *A History of American Law*. New York: Simon and Schuster, 1985.

Fryer, Judith. *Felicitous Space: The Imaginative Structures of Edith Wharton and Willa Cather*. Chapel Hill: University of North Carolina Press, 1986.

Garber, Frederick. *Thoreau's Redemptive Imagination*. New York: New York University Press, 1977.

Garrison, William Lloyd. "The American Union." *The Liberator* 15.2 (January 10, 1845): 5.

Gates, Henry Louis. *Figures in Black: Words, Signs, and the "Racial" Self*. New York: Oxford University Press, 1987.

Gatta, John. " 'Busy and Selfish London': The Urban Figure in Hawthorne's 'Wakefield.' " *ESQ* 23.3 (1977): 164–72.

Gilmore, Michael T. *American Romanticism and the Marketplace*. Chicago: University of Chicago Press, 1985.

Girouard, Mark. *The Victorian Country House*. New Haven, Conn.: Yale University Press, 1979.

Glendon, Mary Ann. *Rights Talk: The Impoverishment of Political Discourse*. New York: Free Press, 1991.

Goffman, Erving. *The Presentation of Self in Everyday Life*. Garden City, N.Y.: Doubleday, 1959.

Goldman, Irene C. "Feminism, Deconstruction and the Universal: A Case Study on *Walden*." In *Conversations: Contemporary Critical Theory and the Teaching of Literature*, edited by Charles Moran and Elizabeth F. Penfield, pp. 120–31. Urbana, Ill.: National Council of Teachers of English, 1990.

Goldsby, Jacqueline. " 'I Disguised My Hand': Writing Versions of the Truth in Harriet Jacobs's *Incidents in the Life of a Slave Girl* and John Jacobs's 'A True Tale of Slavery.' " In *Harriet Jacobs and Incidents in the Life of a Slave Girl: New Critical Essays*, edited by Deborah M. Garfield and Rafia Zafar, pp. 11–43. Cambridge: Cambridge University Press, 1996.

Goodell, William. *The American Slave Code in Theory and Practice: Its Distinctive Features Shown by Its Statutes, Judicial Decisions, and Illustrative Facts*. London: Clarke, Beeton, 1853.

Gowans, Alan. *Images of American Living: Four Centuries of Architecture and Furniture as Cultural Expression*. Philadelphia: Lippincott, 1964.

Gray, Richard. "Hawthorne: A Problem." In *Nathaniel Hawthorne: New Critical Essays*, edited by A. Robert Lee, pp. 88–109. London: Vision, 1982.

Gross, Robert A. "Culture and Cultivation: Agriculture and Society in Thoreau's Concord." In *Material Life in America, 1600–1860,* edited by Robert Blair St. George, pp. 519–34. Boston: Northeastern University Press, 1988.

Gurstein, Rochelle. *The Repeal of Reticence: America's Cultural and Legal Struggles over Free Speech, Obscenity, Sexual Liberation, and Modern Art.* New York: Hill and Wang, 1996.

Habermas, Jürgen. *The Structural Transformation of the Public Sphere: An Inquiry into a Category of Bourgeois Society.* Translated by Thomas Burger. Cambridge, Mass.: MIT Press, 1992.

Hale, Sarah J. *Boarding Out: A Tale of Domestic Life.* New York: Harper, 1846.

Hall, Edward T. *The Hidden Dimension.* New York: Anchor, 1969.

Halttunen, Karen. *Confidence Men and Painted Women: A Study of Middle-class Culture in America, 1830–1870.* New Haven, Conn.: Yale University Press, 1982.

———. "Gothic Imagination and Social Reform." In *New Essays on Uncle Tom's Cabin,* edited by Eric J. Sundquist, pp. 107–34. New York: Cambridge University Press, 1986.

Handlin, David. *The American Home: Architecture and Society, 1815–1915.* Boston: Little, Brown, 1979.

Hansen, Karen V. "Rediscovering the Social: Visiting Practices in Antebellum New England and the Limits of the Public/Private Dichotomy." In *Public and Private in Thought and Practice,* edited by Jeff Weintraub and Krishan Kumar, pp. 268–302. Chicago: University of Chicago Press, 1997.

Harbison, Robert. *Eccentric Spaces.* New York: Knopf, 1977.

Hardesty, Nancy A. *Women Called to Witness: Evangelical Feminism in the 19th Century.* Nashville, Tenn.: Parthenon Press, 1984.

Harding, Walter. *The Days of Henry Thoreau.* New York: Dover, 1962.

———, ed. *Thoreau as Seen by His Contemporaries.* New York: Dover, 1989.

———. "Thoreau's Homosexuality." *Journal of Homosexuality* 21.3 (1991): 23–45.

Harper, Phillip Brian. *Private Affairs: Critical Ventures in the Culture of Social Relations.* New York: New York University Press, 1999.

Haven, Alice B. "Mrs. Bowen's Parlor and Spare Bed–Room." *Godey's Lady's Book* 60 (February 1860): 136–51.

Hawthorne, Nathaniel. "The Custom House." 1850. Reprint. In *Nathaniel Hawthorne: Collected Novels,* edited by Millicent Bell, pp. 115–57. New York: Library of America, 1983.

———. "Fire-Worship." 1843. Reprint. In *Nathaniel Hawthorne: Tales and Sketches,* edited by Roy Harvey Pearce, pp. 841–48. New York: Library of America, 1982.

———. *The House of the Seven Gables.* 1851. Reprint. In *Nathaniel Hawthorne: Collected Novels,* edited by Millicent Bell, pp. 347–628. New York: Library of America, 1983.

———. *The Marble Faun.* 1860. Reprint. In *Nathaniel Hawthorne: Collected Novels,* edited by Millicent Bell, pp. 849–1242. New York: Library of America, 1983.

———. "The Minister's Black Veil." 1836. Reprint. In *Nathaniel Hawthorne: Tales and Sketches,* edited by Roy Harvey Pearce, pp. 371–84. New York: Library of America, 1982.

———. "The Old Manse: The Author Makes the Reader Acquainted with His Abode." 1846. Reprint. In *Nathaniel Hawthorne: Tales and Sketches,* edited by Roy Harvey Pearce, pp. 1123–49. New York: Library of America, 1982.

———. "Peter Goldthwaite's Treasure." 1838. Reprint. In *Nathaniel Hawthorne: Tales and Sketches,* edited by Roy Harvey Pearce, pp. 522–41. New York: Library of America, 1982.

————. "Wakefield." 1835. Reprint. In *Nathaniel Hawthorne: Tales and Sketches*, edited by Roy Harvey Pearce, pp. 290–98. New York: Library of America, 1982.

Hayden, Dolores. *The Grand Domestic Revolution: A History of Feminist Designs for American Homes, Neighborhoods and Cities.* Cambridge, Mass.: MIT Press, 1981.

Hedrick, Joan D. *Harriet Beecher Stowe: A Life.* Oxford: Oxford University Press, 1994.

Henry, Katherine. "Angelina Grimké's Rhetoric of Exposure." *American Quarterly* 49.2 (1997): 328–55.

Herbert, T. Walter. *Dearest Beloved: The Hawthornes and the Making of the Middle-class Family.* Berkeley & Los Angeles: University of California Press, 1993.

Hewitt, Martin. "District Visiting and the Constitution of Domestic Space in the Mid-Nineteenth Century." In *Domestic Space: Reading the Nineteenth-century Interior,* edited by Inga Bryden and Janet Floyd, pp. 121–41. Manchester: Manchester University Press, 1999.

Hillier, Bill, and Julienne Hanson. *The Social Logic of Space.* Cambridge: Cambridge University Press, 1984.

Hixon, Richard F. *Privacy in a Public Society: Human Rights in Conflict.* New York: Oxford University Press, 1987.

Holbrook, J. *Ten Years among the Mail Bags; or, Notes from the Diary of a Special Agent of the Post Office Department.* Philadelphia: H. Cowperthwait, 1855.

Honig, Bonnie. "Toward an Agonistic Feminism: Hannah Arendt and the Politics of Identity." In *Feminism, the Public, and the Private,* edited by Joan Landes, pp. 100–134. Oxford: Oxford University Press, 1998.

Hoover, Merle M. *Park Benjamin: Poet and Editor.* New York: Columbia University Press, 1948.

Horwitz, Morton J. *The Transformation of American Law, 1780–1860.* Cambridge, Mass.: Harvard University Press, 1977.

"Household Skeletons." *Putnam's Monthly* 4 (1855): 384–91.

Hutner, Gordon. *Secrets and Sympathy: Forms of Disclosure in Hawthorne's Novels.* Athens: University of Georgia Press, 1988.

Jackson, Kenneth T. *Crabgrass Frontier: The Suburbanization of the United States.* New York: Oxford University Press, 1985.

Jay, Gregory S. *America the Scrivener: Deconstruction and the Subject of Literary History.* Ithaca, N. Y.: Cornell University Press, 1990.

Johnson, Barbara. *A World of Difference.* Baltimore, Md.: Johns Hopkins University Press, 1987.

Jung, C. G. *Memories, Dreams, Reflections.* Edited by Aniela Jaffé. Translated by Richard Winston and Clara Winston. New York: Pantheon Books, 1963.

Kaplan, Amy. "Manifest Domesticity." *American Literature* 70.3 (1998): 581–606.

Kaplan, Morris B. *Democratic Citizenship and the Politics of Desire.* New York: Routledge, 1997.

Kasson, John F. *Rudeness and Civility: Manners in Nineteenth-century America.* New York: Hill and Wang, 1990.

Kay, Guy Gavriel. "Privacy and the Ethics of Literature." *Queen's Quarterly* 108.1 (2001): 46–55.

Keller, Catherine. *From a Broken Web: Separation, Sexism and Self.* Boston: Beacon Press, 1986.

Kennedy, J. Gerald. *Poe, Death, and the Life of Writing.* New Haven Conn.: Yale University Press, 1987.

Khan, Masud. *Hidden Selves: Between Theory and Practice in Psychoanalysis.* London: Hogarth Press, 1983.

Kimmel, Michael. *Manhood in America: A Cultural History.* New York: Free Press, 1996.

———. "Masculinity as Homophobia: Fear, Shame, and Silence in the Construction of Gender Identity." In *Theorizing Masculinities,* edited by Harry Brod and Michael Kaufman, pp. 285–99. Thousand Oaks, Calif.: Sage, 1994.

Laffrado, Laura. " 'Far and Momentary Glimpse': Hawthorne's Treatment of Mrs. Wakefield." In *New Interpretations of American Literature,* edited by Richard Fleming and Michael Payne, pp. 34–44. Cranbury, N.J.: Associated University Press, 1988.

Laing, R. D. *The Divided Self: An Existential Study in Sanity and Madness.* New York: Penguin, 1969.

Landes, Joan, ed. *Feminism, the Public, and the Private.* Oxford: Oxford University Press, 1998.

Lane, Christopher. The *Burdens of Intimacy: Psychoanalysis and Victorian Masculinity.* Chicago: University of Chicago Press, 1999.

Laslett, Barbara. "The Family as a Public and Private Institution: An Historical Perspective." *Journal of Marriage and the Family* 35 (1973): 480–91.

Leach, William. *True Love and Perfect Union: The Feminist Reform of Sex and Society.* New York: Basic Books, 1980.

Lefebvre, Henri. *The Production of Space.* Translated by Donald Nicholson–Smith. Oxford: Blackwell, 1991.

Leslie, Eliza. *Miss Leslie's Behaviour Book: A Guide and Manual for Ladies.* Philadelphia: T. A. Peterson and Brothers, 1859.

———. *Mr. and Mrs. Woodbridge, with Other Tales Representing Life as It Is: And Intended to Show What It Should Be.* Providence, R.I.: Isaac H. Cady, 1841.

Leverenz, David. *Manhood in the American Renaissance.* Ithaca, N.Y.: Cornell University Press, 1989.

Lewis, R. W. B. *The American Adam: Innocence, Tragedy and Tradition in the Nineteenth Century.* Chicago: University of Chicago Press, 1955.

Lincoln, Abraham. *The Collected Works of Abraham Lincoln.* Edited by Roy P. Basler. New Brunswick, N.J.: Rutgers University Press, 1955.

Litman, Vicki Halper. "The Cottage and the Temple: Melville's Symbolic Use of Architecture." *American Quarterly* 21 (1969): 630–38.

Long, Edward V. *The Intruders: The Invasion of Privacy by Government and Industry.* New York: Frederick A. Praeger, 1967.

Lukács, Georg. *The Theory of the Novel: A Historico-philosophical Essay on the Forms of Great Epic Literature.* Translated by Anna Bostock. Cambridge, Mass.: MIT Press, 1971.

Lukacs, John. "The Bourgeois Interior." *American Scholar* 39.4 (1970): 620–30.

Luria, Sarah. "The Architecture of Manners: Henry James, Edith Wharton, and the Mount," *American Quarterly* 49.2 (1997): 298–327.

Lynes, Russell. *The Art-Makers: An Informal History of Painting, Sculpture and Architecture in Nineteenth-century America.* New York: Dover, 1970.

———. *The Domesticated Americans.* New York: Harper and Row, 1957.

Lystra, Karen. *Searching the Heart: Women, Men and Romantic Love in Nineteenth-century America.* Oxford: Oxford University Press, 1992.

MacFarlane, Lisa Watt. "The New England Kitchen Goes Uptown: Domestic Displacements in Harriet Beecher Stowe's New York." *New England Quarterly* 64.2 (1991): 272–91.

MacKinnon, Catharine A. *Feminism Unmodified: Discourses on Life and Law.* Cambridge, Mass.: Harvard University Press, 1987.

Macpherson, C. B. *The Political Theory of Possessive Individualism.* New York: Oxford University Press, 1962.

Marsh, Margaret. "From Separation to Togetherness: The Social Construction of Domestic Space in American Suburbia, 1840–1915." *Journal of American History* 76 (1989): 506–27.

———. "Suburban Men and Masculine Domesticity, 1870–1915." In *Meanings for Manhood: Constructions of Masculinity in Victorian America,* edited by Mark C. Carnes and Clyde Griffen, pp. 111–28. Chicago: University of Chicago Press, 1990.

Marx, Karl. "Alienated Labor." In *Writings of the Young Marx on Philosophy and Society,* edited and translated by Loyd D. Easton and Krut H. Guddat, pp. 287–300. Garden City, N.Y.: Anchor, 1967.

Marx, Leo. *The Machine in the Garden: Technology and the Pastoral Ideal in America.* New York: Oxford University Press, 1964.

Masteller, Richard, and Jean Carwile. "Rural Architecture in Andrew Jackson Downing and Henry David Thoreau: Pattern Book Parody in *Walden.*" *New England Quarterly* 57 (1984): 483–510.

Matthiessen, F. O. *American Renaissance: Art and Expression in the Age of Emerson and Whitman.* New York: Oxford University Press, 1941.

Melville, Herman. "Bartleby, the Scrivener." 1843. Reprint. In *Herman Melville: Pierre, Israel Potter, etc.,* edited by Harrison Hayford, pp. 635–72. New York: Library of America, 1984.

———. "Hawthorne and His Mosses." 1850. Reprint. In *Herman Melville: Pierre, Israel Potter, etc.,* edited by Harrison Hayford, pp. 1154–71. New York: Library of America, 1984.

———. "I and My Chimney." 1856. Reprint. In *Herman Melville: Pierre, Israel Potter, etc.,* edited by Harrison Hayford, pp. 1298–1327. New York: Library of America, 1984.

Merish, Lori. *Sentimental Materialism: Gender, Commodity Culture, and Nineteenth-century American Literature.* Durham, N.C.: Duke University Press, 2000.

Michaels, Walter Benn. "The Contracted Heart." *New Literary History* 21.3 (1990): 495–532.

———. *The Gold Standard and the Logic of Naturalism.* Berkeley & Los Angeles: University of California Press, 1987.

Mill, John Stuart. *On Liberty.* London: Longman, Roberts & Green, 1869.

Miller, D. A. "The Administrator's Black Veil: A Response to J. Hillis Miller." *ADE Bulletin* 88 (1987): 49–53.

———. *The Novel and the Police.* Berkeley & Los Angeles: University of California Press, 1988.

Miller, Edwin Haviland. *Salem Is My Dwelling Place: A Life of Nathaniel Hawthorne.* Iowa City: University of Iowa Press, 1991.

Miller, J. Hillis. "Theory—Example—Reading—History." *ADE Bulletin* 88 (1987): 42–48.

Mills, C. Wright. *White Collar.* New York: Oxford University Press, 1951.

Morris, Debra. "Privacy in Public: 'Acting Up' as a Politics and Erotics of Resistance." Unpublished manuscript.

———. "Privacy, Privation, Perversity: Toward New Representations of the Personal." *Signs* 25.2 (2000): 329–51.

Mumford, Lewis. *The City in History: Its Origins, Its Transformations, and Its Prospects.* New York: Hartcourt, Brace and World, 1961.

Murphy, Robert F. "Social Distance and the Veil." In *Philosophical Dimensions of Privacy*, edited by Ferdinand Schoeman, pp. 34–55. Cambridge: Cambridge University Press, 1984.

Nedelsky, Jennifer. "Law, Boundaries, and the Bounded Self." *Representations* 30 (1990): 162–89.

Nelson, Dana D. *National Manhood: Capitalist Citizenship and the Imagined Fraternity of White Men*. Durham, N.C.: Duke University Press, 1998.

———. "Thoreau, Manhood, and Race: Quiet Desperation versus Representative Isolation." In *A Historical Guide to Henry David Thoreau*, edited by William E. Cain, pp. 61–94. New York: Oxford University Press, 2000.

Neufeldt, Leonard. *The House of Emerson*. Lincoln: University of Nebraska Press, 1982.

Newfield, Christopher. *The Emerson Effect: Individualism and Submission in America*. Chicago: University of Chicago Press, 1996.

Newman, Lea Bertani Vozara. *A Reader's Guide to the Short Stories of Herman Melville*. Boston: C. K. Hall, 1986.

"New York Daguerreotyped: Private Residences." *Putnam's Monthly* 3 (1854): 233–48.

Pateman, Carole. *The Disorder of Women: Democracy, Feminism, and Political Theory*. Stanford, Calif.: Stanford University Press, 1990.

Patterson, Orlando. *Slavery and Social Death: A Comparative Study*. Cambridge, Mass.: Harvard University Press, 1982.

Paul, Sherman. *The Shores of America: Thoreau's Inward Exploration*. Urbana: University of Illinois Press, 1958.

Pearce, Sandra Manoogian. "Secret Closets and Ashes: Melville's 'I and My Chimney.'" In *Creative and Critical Approaches to the Short Story*, edited by Noel Harold Kaylor Jr., pp. 81–95. Lewiston, N.Y.: Mellen, 1997.

Peck, Amelia. *Alexander Jackson Davis: American Architect, 1803–1892*. New York: Rizzoli, 1992.

Peck, H. Daniel. *Thoreau's Morning Work: Memory and Perception in* A Week on the Concord and Merrimack Rivers, *the* Journal, *and* Walden. New Haven, Conn.: Yale University Press, 1990.

Pfister, Joel. *The Production of Personal Life: Class, Gender and the Psychological in Hawthorne's Fiction*. Stanford, Calif.: Stanford University Press, 1991.

Phelan, Shane. *Identity Politics: Lesbian Feminism and the Limits of Community*. Philadelphia: Temple University Press, 1991.

Phillips, Adam. *On Kissing, Tickling, and Being Bored*. Cambridge, Mass.: Harvard University Press, 1993.

Pleck, Elizabeth. *Domestic Tyranny: The Making of Social Policy against Family Violence*. New York: Oxford University Press, 1987.

Poe, Edgar Allan. "The Masque of the Red Death." 1842. Reprint. In *Poe: Poetry and Tales*, pp. 485–90. New York: Library of America, 1984.

Polk, Noel. "Welty, Hawthorne, and Poe: Men of the Crowd and the Landscape of Alienation." *Mississippi Quarterly* 50.4 (1997): 553–65.

Porte, Joel. *Emerson and Thoreau: Transcendentalists in Conflict*. Middletown, Conn.: Wesleyan University Press, 1965.

Prosser, William L. "Privacy [a Legal Analysis]." In *Philosophical Dimensions of Privacy*, edited by Ferdinand Schoeman, pp. 104–55. Cambridge: Cambridge University Press, 1984.

Rachels, James. "Why Privacy Is Important." In *Philosophical Dimensions of Privacy: An Anthology*, edited by Ferdinand David Schoeman, pp. 290–99. Cambridge: Cambridge University Press, 1984.

Ranlett, William H. *The Architect: A Series of Original Designs, for Domestic and Orna-mental Cottages and Villas.* 1849. Reprint. New York: Dewitt and Davenport, 1976.

Rebora, Carrie. "Alexander Jackson Davis and the Arts of Design." In *Alexander Jackson Davis: American Architect, 1803–1892,* edited by Amelia Peck, pp. 22–39. New York: Rizzoli, 1992.

Renza, Louis A. *Edgar Allan Poe, Wallace Stevens, and the Poetics of American Privacy.* Baton Rouge: Louisiana State University Press, 2002.

———. "Poe's Secret Autobiography." In *The American Renaissance Reconsidered, Selected Papers from the English Institute, 1982–3,* edited by Walter Benn Michaels and Donald E. Pease, pp. 58–89. Baltimore, Md.: Johns Hopkins University Press, 1985.

Reynolds, David S. *Beneath the American Renaissance: The Subversive Imagination in the Age of Emerson and Melville.* Cambridge, Mass.: Harvard University Press, 1988.

Richards, David A. J. "The Jurisprudence of Privacy as a Constitutional Right." In *Privacy: A Vanishing Value?* edited by William Bier, pp. 135–51. New York: Fordham University Press, 1980.

"The Right to Privacy in Nineteenth Century America." *Harvard Law Review* 94 (June 1981): 1892–1910.

Robertson-Lorant, Laurie. *Melville: A Biography.* New York: Clarkson Potter, 1996.

Rogin, Michael. *Subversive Genealogy: The Politics and Art of Herman Melville.* Berkeley & Los Angeles: University of California Press, 1979.

Romero, Lora. *Home Fronts: Domesticity and Its Critics in the Antebellum United States.* Durham, N.C.: Duke University Press, 1997.

Rosen, Jeffrey. *The Unwanted Gaze: The Destruction of Privacy in America.* New York: Random House, 2000.

Rosenberry, Edward Hoffman. *Melville and the Comic Spirit.* Cambridge, Mass.: Harvard University Press, 1955.

Rotundo, E. Anthony. *American Manhood: Transformations in Masculinity from the Revolution to the Modern Era.* New York: Basic Books, 1993.

Rule, James, et al. *The Politics of Privacy.* New York: New American Library, 1980.

Ryan, Mary P. *The Cradle of the Middle Class: The Family in Oneida County, New York, 1790–1865.* Cambridge: Cambridge University Press, 1981.

Rybczynski, Witold. *Home: A Short History of an Idea.* New York: Viking, 1986.

Sale, Maggie. "To Make the Past Useful: Frederick Douglass' Politics of Solidarity." *Arizona Quarterly* 52.3 (1995): 25–60.

Salecl, Renata. "The Exposure of Privacy in Today's Culture." In *Privacy in Post-communist Europe,* edited by Arien Mack and Andras Sajo. A special issue of *Social Research* 69.1 (2002): 1–8.

Samuels, Shirley, ed. *The Culture of Sentiment: Race, Gender, and Sentimentality in Nineteenth-century America.* New York: Oxford University Press, 1992.

Sanborn, Geoffrey. "Keeping Her Distance: Cisneros, Dickinson, and the Politics of Private Enjoyment." *PMLA* 116.5 (2001): 1334–48.

Sargent, Charles E. *Our Home, or the Key to a Nobler Life.* Springfield, Mass.: W. C. King, 1885.

Schafer, Roy. "Narration in the Psychoanalytic Dialogue." *Critical Inquiry* 7.1 (1980): 27–53.

Schoeman, Ferdinand, ed. *Philosophical Dimensions of Privacy: An Anthology.* Cambridge: Cambridge University Press, 1984.

Schudson, Michael. "Was There Ever a Public Sphere? If So, When? Reflections on the American Case." In *Habermas and the Public Sphere,* edited by Craig Calhoun, pp. 143–63. Cambridge, Mass.: MIT Press, 1993.

Scott, Joan Wallach. "Gender: A Useful Category of Historical Analysis." In *Gender and the Politics of History*, pp. 28–52. New York: Columbia University Press, 1988.

Sealts, Merton M., Jr. *Pursuing Melville, 1940–1980: Chapters and Essays.* Madison: University of Wisconsin Press, 1982.

Sedgwick, Eve Kosofsky. *Between Men: English Literature and Male Homosocial Desire.* New York: Columbia University Press, 1985.

———. *Epistemology of the Closet.* Berkeley & Los Angeles: University of California Press, 1990.

Seipp, David J. *The Right of Privacy in American History.* Cambridge, Mass.: Harvard University Program on Information Resources Policy, Publication 78–4, July 1978.

Sennett, Richard. *The Fall of Public Man.* New York: W. W. Norton, 1974.

Showalter, Elaine. "Family Secrets and Domestic Subversion: Rebellion in the Novels of the Eighteen Sixties." In *The Victorian Family: Structure and Stresses*, edited by Anthony S. Wohl, pp. 101–16. New York: St. Martin's Press, 1978.

Silver, Allan. " 'Two Different Sorts of Commerce': Friendship and Strangership in Civil Society." In *Public and Private in Thought and Practice*, edited by Jeff Weintraub and Krishan Kumar, pp. 43–74. Chicago: University of Chicago Press, 1997.

Sklar, Kathryn Kish. *Catherine Beecher: A Study in American Domesticity.* New Haven, Conn.: Yale University Press, 1973.

Slater, Judith. "The Domestic Adventurer in Melville's Tales." *American Literature* 37.3 (1965): 267–79.

Smeins, Linda E. *Building an American Identity: Pattern Book Homes and Communities, 1870–1900.* Walnut Creek, Calif.: AltaMira, 1999.

Smith-Rosenberg, Carroll. *Disorderly Conduct: Vision of Gender in Victorian America.* New York: Oxford University Press, 1985.

Sowder, William J. "Melville's 'I and My Chimney': A Southern Exposure." *Mississippi Quarterly* (1963): 128–45.

Spacks, Patricia Meyer. *Gossip.* New York: Knopf, 1985.

Spain, Daphne. *Gendered Spaces.* Chapel Hill: University of North Carolina Press, 1992.

Stepto, Robert B. "Sharing the Thunder: The Literary Exchanges of Harriet Beecher Stowe, Henry Bibb, and Frederick Douglass." In *New Essays on Uncle Tom's Cabin*, edited by Eric J. Sundquist, pp. 135–52. Cambridge: Cambridge University Press, 1986.

———. "Storytelling in Early Afro-American Fiction: Frederick Douglass' 'The Heroic Slave.' " *Georgia Review* 36.2 (1982): 355–56.

Stowe, Harriet Beecher. *House and Home Papers.* Boston: Fields, Osgood, 1869.

———. *A Key to Uncle Tom's Cabin.* Boston: John P. Jewett, 1853.

———. *Lady Byron Vindicated.* Boston: Fields, Osgood, 1870.

———. *Sunny Memories of Foreign Lands.* Boston: Phillips, Sampson, 1854.

———. *Uncle Tom's Cabin; or, Life among the Lowly.* 1852. Reprint. New York: Library of America, 1982.

Thomas, Brook. "The Construction of Privacy in and Around *The Bostonians*." *American Literature* 64 (1992): 719–47.

———. *Cross-examinations of Law and Literature.* Cambridge: Cambridge University Press, 1987.

Thoreau, Henry David. *Journals.* Princeton, N.J.: Princeton University Press, 1981.

———. "The Landlord." In *Excursions*, pp. 187–98. Boston: Houghton Mifflin, 1863.

———. "A Plea for John Brown." 1859. Reprint. In *Thoreau: Political Writings*, edited by Nancy L. Rosenblum, pp. 137–58. Cambridge: Cambridge University Press, 1996.

———. *Walden*. 1854. Reprint. In *Henry David Thoreau: A Week, Walden, etc.*, pp. 321–588. New York: Library of America, 1985.

———. *A Week on the Concord and Merrimack Rivers*. 1849. Reprint. In *Henry David Thoreau: A Week, Walden, etc.*, pp. 1–320. New York: Library of America, 1985.

Tichi, Cecelia. "Domesticity on Walden Pond." In *A Historical Guide to Henry David Thoreau*, edited by William E. Cain, pp. 95–122. New York: Oxford University Press, 2000.

Tocqueville, Alexis de. *Democracy in America*. Edited by Richard D. Heffner. New York: Penguin, 1984.

Tomes, Robert. "Houses We Live In." *Harper's New Monthly Magazine* 30.180 (1865): 735–41.

Tompkins, Jane. *Sensational Designs: The Cultural Work of American Fiction, 1790–1860*. New York: Oxford University Press, 1985.

Tribe, Laurence. *American Constitutional Law*. Mineola, N.Y.: Foundation Press, 1978.

"The Value of the Union." *Harper's New Monthly Magazine* 4 (December 1851–May 1852): 415–17.

Vaux, Calvert. "Parisian Buildings for City Residents." *Harper's Weekly* 1 (December 19, 1857): 809–10.

———. *Villas and Cottages*. New York: Harper and Brothers, 1857.

Vidler, Anthony. *The Architectural Uncanny: Essays in the Modern Unhomely*. Cambridge, Mass.: MIT Press, 1992.

Vogler, Candace. "Sex and Talk." *Critical Inquiry* 24.2 (1998): 328–65.

Wald, Priscilla. *Constituting Americans: Cultural Anxiety and Narrative Form*. Durham, N.C.: Duke University Press, 1995.

Ware, John F. W. *Home Life: What It Is, and What It Needs*. Boston: Wm. V. Spencer, 1864.

Warner, Michael. *The Letters of the Republic: Publication and the Public Sphere in Eighteenth Century America*. Cambridge, Mass.: Harvard University Press, 1992.

———. "The Mass Public and the Mass Subject." In *The Phantom Public Sphere*, edited by Bruce Robbins, pp. 234–56. Minneapolis: University of Minnesota Press, 1993.

———. "*Walden*'s Erotic Economy." In *Comparative American Identities: Race, Sex, and Nationality in the Modern Text*, edited by Hortense J. Spiller, pp. 157–74. London: Routledge, 1991.

Warren, Joyce W. "Introduction." *Ruth Hall and Other Writings*. New Brunswick, N.J.: Rutgers University Press, 1986.

Warren, Samuel, and Louis Brandeis. "The Right to Privacy [The Implicit Made Explicit]." In *Philosophical Dimensions of Privacy*, edited by Ferdinand Schoeman, pp. 74–103. Cambridge: Cambridge University Press, 1984.

"The Wayside: Home of Authors." Available from *http://www.nps.gov/mima/wayside/Histfrm1.htm*. Accessed May 3, 2005.

Weintraub, Jeff. "The Theory and Politics of the Public/Private Distinction." In *Public and Private in Thought and Practice*, edited by Jeff Weintraub and Krishan Kumar, pp. 1–42. Chicago: University of Chicago Press, 1997.

Weldon, Roberta F. "Wakefield's Second Journey." *Studies in Short Fiction* 14.1 (1977): 69–74.

Welsh, Alexander. *George Eliot and Blackmail*. Cambridge, Mass.: Harvard University Press, 1985.

Welter, Barbara. "The Cult of True Womanhood." *American Quarterly* 18 (1966): 151–74.

Wheeler, Gervase. *Homes for the People in Suburb and Country.* New York: Charles Scribner, 1855.

———. *Rural Homes; or Sketches of Houses Suited to American Country Life.* Rochester, N.Y.: Auburn, Alden, Beadsley, 1853.

White, G. Edward. *Tort Law in America: An Intellectual History.* New York: Oxford University Press, 1980.

Wiegman, Robyn. "Fiedler and Sons." In *Race and the Subject of Masculinities,* edited by Harry Stecopoulos and Michael Uebel, pp. 45–68. Durham, N.C.: Duke University Press, 1997.

Wigley, Mark. "Untitled: The Housing of Gender." In *Sexuality and Space,* edited by Beatriz Colomina, pp. 327–89. New York: Princeton Architectural Press, 1992.

Williams, Patricia. *The Alchemy of Race and Rights.* Cambridge, Mass.: Harvard University Press, 1992.

———. "Meditations on Masculinity." In *Constructing Masculinity,* edited by Maurice Berger, Brian Wallis, and Simon Watson, pp. 238–49. New York: Routledge, 1995.

Williams, Raymond. *Keywords: A Vocabulary of Culture and Society.* New York: Oxford University Press, 1985.

Willis, Nathaniel Parker. "The Highland Terrace above West Point." In *Home Authors and Home Artists, on American Scenery, Art, and Literature,* pp. 105–12. New York: Leavitt and Allen, 1852.

Winnicott, D. W. "The Capacity to Be Alone." In *The Maturational Process and the Facilitating Environment: Studies in the Theory of Emotional Development,* pp. 29–36. New York: International Universities Press, 1965.

———. "Communicating and Not Communicating Leading to a Study of Certain Opposites." In *The Maturational Process and the Facilitating Environment: Studies in the Theory of Emotional Development,* pp. 179–92. New York: International Universities Press, 1965.

———. *Playing and Reality.* New York: Basic Books, 1971.

Wood, Gordon S. *The Creation of the American Republic, 1776–1787.* New York: Norton, 1969.

———. *The Radicalism of the American Revolution.* New York: Random House, 1993.

Woodruff, Stuart C. "Melville and His Chimney." *PMLA* 75 (1960): 283–92.

Woods, Mary. "The First American Architectural Journals: The Profession's Voice." *Journal of the Society of Architectural Historians* 48 (1989): 117–38.

"A Word for Man's Rights." *Putnam's Monthly* 5 (1856): 208–13.

Wortham, Thomas. "Bryant and the Fireside Poets." In *The Columbia Literary History of the United States,* edited by Emory Elliot et al., pp. 278–88. New York: Columbia University Press, 1988.

Wright, Gwendolyn. *Building the Dream: A Social History of Housing in America.* Cambridge, Mass.: MIT Press, 1981.

———. *Moralism and the Model Home.* Chicago: University of Chicago Press, 1980.

Yacovone, Donald. "Abolitionists and the 'Language of Fraternal Love.'" In *Meaning for Manhood: Constructions of Masculinity in Victorian America,* edited by Mark C. Carnes and Clyde Griffen, pp. 85–95. Chicago: University of Chicago Press, 1990.

Yarborough, Richard. "Race, Violence, and Manhood: The Masculine Ideal in Frederick Douglass's 'The Heroic Slave.'" In *Frederick Douglass: New Literary and Historical Essays,* edited by Eric J. Sundquist, pp. 166–87. Cambridge: Cambridge University Press, 1991.

Yeatman, Anna. "A Feminist Theory of Social Differentiation." In *Feminism/ Postmodernism*, edited by Linda J. Nicholson, pp. 281–99. New York: Routledge, 1990.

Young, John B., ed. *Privacy*. Chichester, U.K.: John Wiley, 1978.

Zaretsky, Eli. *Capitalism, the Family, and Personal Life*. New York: Harper and Row, 1973.

Zimmerman, Diane L. "Requiem for a Heavyweight: A Farewell to Warren and Brandeis's Privacy Tort." *Cornell Law Review* 68 (1983): 292–368.

Index

Acknowledgments

In this book I argue for the need for privacy and solitude, but through writing it I learned much about the need for collaboration, exchange, and intimacy. I have many people to thank for that lesson and for their crucial interventions at various stages of this project.

My oldest debts are to Wai-Chee Dimock, Philip Fisher, and, especially, Michael Gilmore, who read an earlier version of the manuscript. I thank them for their guidance and no less for showing me what it means to be an engaged reader, writer, and teacher.

I am grateful for the remarkable warmth and generosity of my colleagues at Tel Aviv University, many of whom are also former teachers. Conversations with Elana Gomel, Bob Griffin, Karen Alkalay Gut, the late Talma Yizraeli, and Shirley Sharon Zisser helped shape my ideas at several crucial junctures. As chair of the English Department, Hedda Ben Bassat offered just the right combination of support and pressure to see me through the book's completion. Zephyra Porat read the entire manuscript, and her keen insights improved my understanding of my own argument—and of its limitations. Special thanks to Hana Wirth Nesher, who, from my earliest forays into American literature, has always provided inspiration, support, and friendship.

A 1999 summer humanities institute, "The Question of Privacy," at Dartmouth College provided an ideal setting for developing my ideas. I thank all the participants for their input, especially Don Pease and Jeff Weintraub, for their cogent critique of several of my arguments. The work of two participants in this seminar had a direct impact on mine. I remain indebted to Debra Morris for her formulation of privacy as a form of reprieve from power and to Lou Renza for his analysis of the crucial link between privacy and American literature. Lou, the seminar's comoderator, turned out to be my ideal interlocutor, and I thank him for his intellectual generosity and personal warmth.

Other friends, colleagues, and teachers provided inspiration and support along the way. I am grateful to Einat Avrahami, Barbara Hochman, Walter Benn Michaels, Timothy Powell, Marilyn Reizbaum, Grantland Rice, Nancy Schnog, Jennifer Travis, and Priscilla Wald. At the University of Pennsylvania Press, my thanks go to Jerry Singerman, Ted Mann, Erica Ginsburg, and Kathryn R. Bork for their advice, creativity, and patience. Special thanks to the two readers for the press, Dana Nelson and Joel Pfister, for their incisive feedback.

Portions of this book have been previously published. Parts of Chapters 1 and 2 appeared as "Divided Plots: Interior Space and Gender Difference in Domestic Fiction," in *Genre* 29.4 (1996): 429–72, copyright © 1997 The University of Oklahoma. Chapter 4 appeared as "Hawthorne's Romance and the Right to Privacy," in *American Quarterly* 49.4 (1997): 746–79, copyright © 1997 The Johns Hopkins University Press. Chapter 6 is from *Boys Don't Cry? Rethinking Narratives of Masculinity and Emotion in the US*, edited by Milette Shamir and Jennifer Travis, copyright © 2002 Columbia University Press. I thank the publishers for permission to reprint.

I feel unusually blessed by the love and faith of my parents, Daniela and Shimon Shamir, who contributed to this book in more ways than I could possibly list here. Sharon Shamir, Roy Shamir, and their families provided sibling solidarity and moral support. I thank Orna Bird for her incredible talent for giving, and Leah Levin for putting everything in the right perspective. Most of all, I am grateful to Avi Marchewka, whose love kept me going. With his intelligence, understanding, and generosity of spirit, he made this book happen.